What If?

Strategic Alternatives of WWII

edited by

HAROLD C. DEUTSCH
AND DENNIS E. SHOWALTER

THE EMPEROR'S PRESS
Chicago, Illinois

Printed and Bound in the United States of America

Cartography by David L. McElhannon
The maps in chapters 4, 5, and 11 were based on originals created by David M. Glantz

ISBN 0-883476-07-0

The Authors

Thomas M. Barker
Carlo D'Este
Harold C. Deutsch
Walter S. Drea
Walter S. Dunn
David M. Glantz
Robert M. Love
Peter Hoffmann
D. Clayton James
John K. Munholland
Bernard C. Nalty
Samuel J. Newland
Richard J. Overy
Frederick D. Parker
Paul Schratz
Dennis E. Showalter
Gerhard L. Weinberg
Anne Wells
Herman S. Wolk

What if?

Introduction

Harold C. Deutsch

Alternative history, counter-factual history—there are a number of ways by which we can designate historical suppositions when, here or there, on one human pathway or another, consideration is given to factors other than those which ultimately proved to determine the course of events. No discipline is more congenial than history to speculation on what might have occurred if, at some forking of the road, affairs had moved in a different direction. There will, of course, always be differences of view on how far the historian may digress from the beaten path in such speculation. He will prove more venturesome if he remains mindful of the fact that all life is shaped by potentialities. Awareness that the more challenging of these should not be ignored professionally is evidenced by the common practice of dwelling on the concluding phases of historical studies on how, at critical junctures, affairs could well have moved in a different direction. In fact, the historian may well discover that the examination of such possibilities can assure a more thorough understanding of what ultimately did occur.

Looking for answers to queries on the "what ifs" of history compels more searching examination of factors which, though not finally determining, still formed a vital part of the fundamental picture. Evaluating and interpreting these factors leads to new avenues of investigation that invite or even compel intensive scrutiny. Response to this challenge is calculated to provide a more comprehensive form of historical analysis. It does not convey a license for descent into flights of fancy. The pages that follow are not the intellectual meanderings of idle hours, but the fruit of intensive analysis. Above all, each of these essays has sought the stamp of plausibility.

Plausibility, as the necessary brake and control element, has been our most essential guide. It is the most vital rule of historical interpretation generally. It is the more essential in view of the inexactitude of so much historical evidence. In his stimulating and provocative presidential address before the December 1986 meeting of the American Historical Association, William H. McNeill stressed "the elastic and inexact" element of history and characterized much of what has been produced as "myth," largely made-to-order in response to bias, prejudice, and ideological or national interests. McNeill held this to be especially true when dealing with human conduct. He had little faith of its gaining in exactitude through the strivings of iconoclastic revisionists. There seems here a strong argument that only in the light of competing alternatives can one approach objective reality. In its truest sense, history needs to observe that flexibility which is aware at every significant juncture of alternatives and their limitations.

If history, even that which strives most sincerely to approximate the Ranckean ideal of "wie es eigentlich gewesen," tends to take the form most satisfactory to those who write it, how much less will many expect of its alternative form which lacks the discipline of a factual framework? If, as McNeill argues, the historian is subject to a constant inclination to write what best suits him, how much greater may be the temptation to do so in the relatively unfettered area of alternative history? Awareness of this, especially of taking the "if only" approach, has perhaps led us as often as not to depict a course of events involving even greater hazards or disastrous consequences than those of the road actually thought to have been taken. It has helped to minimize for us the "multiple commitments" that sway us in the study of the past. We can only submit ourselves here to the judgment of our readers.

By attending to the most demanding "what ifs" of history, we can anticipate significant progress in relation to such fundamental and endlessly debated problems of historical interpretation as determinism and the role of accident and of the individual. An impressive number of historians of renown have maintained that "objective historical forces" basically decide the course of human affairs and that little or nothing beyond them can turn them aside. An equally eloquent and probably growing number would hold with Isaiah Berlin that the difficulty with determinism is that one can do nothing with it. If contingency, diversity, personality and chance are to be eliminated from history, he holds, one would find oneself in an area without signposts or dimension. Yet the lives of nations, like those of individuals, are beset by potentialities. Nowhere does this appear more true than in dealing with eras of protracted world conflict when every human resource and social, economic, ethnic and political factor somehow comes into play. In short, except in terms of broadest and most fundamental superiority of resources, the idea of an inevitable outcome is highly questionable.

It is easy to argue persuasively the truism that the lessons of history are best derived from what actually happened, rather than from what nearly happened. It should be added, however, that what happened becomes more fully comprehensible in the light of the contending forces that existed at moments of decision. Understanding of the total historical setting is bound to contribute to a clearer view of the actual course of affairs. Unless we can reconstruct the realities of the historical conjunction, no lesson we can draw from it can achieve completion. Events must be appraised in terms of the competing alternatives if history is to claim subjective reality. As much was stressed by Hugh Trevor-Roper in a provocative essay a half decade ago.[1] We should perceive here, he argued, the opportunity for deriving lessons from the past which history as a mere record of decisions will frequently ignore.

In dealing with a protracted conflict period such as that of World War II beginning with numerous European and African theaters and developing into a true world conflict by extension into the Pacific, the number of problems lending themselves to consideration of alternative courses is infinite. Every imaginable area of national and international activity was continually in play. Problems of domestic politics, national policy, diplomacy, coalition affairs, economic mobilization, and social impacts — all were present. And none were more hospitable than those concerned with military affairs to the weighing of alternatives. In both the Atlantic and Pacific areas the clash of armies, navies, and air forces shared in and competed for the limelight. Most fundamentally our selection of "what ifs" for consideration has been guided by the desire to deal with the more significant junctures of the conflict, notably such as have been subjected to widespread controversy. No doubt we have also been mindful of the particular expertise and insights of our contributors.

Inevitably consideration of each "what if" has required a certain amount of background in the form of some review of the actual course of events. In view of the high expertise of the various contributors in the areas with which they deal, early drafts tended to lack focus on the suggested alternative course of affairs. We hope that the end result in each case has been an appropriate balance.

Readers of these pages will here and there discover varying and occasionally clashing viewpoints where topics cross lines or are in some way related. Though in some instances this has been brought to the attention of the concerned contributors, there has been no concerted effort to bring contrasting views into line. Any student of history knows or should know that one frequently gains the most insight from confrontation with opposing interpretations that oblige one to review ones own opinions and to check their logic. It is our conviction, also, that the presentation of varying interpretations can convey better understanding of the complexity of the concerned issues and how much can be gained from looking at problems from varying perspectives.

A number of these essays are the fruit of collaboration. Where this is the case, the order of the names given is entirely alphabetical and in no sense measures relative contributions.

Though most of the discussions in the volume are presented in essay form, in a number of instances contributors have chosen to give freer reign to their imaginations and have developed detailed scenarios. We feel that this diversity of treatment will be welcomed by our readers.

Words fail me in seeking to express my appreciation of the assistance I have received from Edward M. Coffman. "Mac" did not feel sufficiently at home in the World War II era to undertake one of the "what if" assignments, but generously offered to assist in the editorial process to whatever extent we might desire. He has proved a tower of strength in every way we have called upon him; has read pre-final drafts, and made innumerable useful suggestions. We owe him a great debt of gratitude.

Dennis Showalter initially agreed to act as back-up editor in the event it should prove difficult for me to continue. Aside from collaborating with me on a number of essays, he has read and critiqued my personal contributions and has ever been at hand with valuable advice and suggestions. We are particularly grateful for his important assistance in reviewing our practice of footnoting and achieving something like a common pattern.

To our great distress, Captain (Ret.) Paul Schratz died in the very week in which he completed and submitted the final draft of his important chapter on the conclusion of the war with Japan. Paul was the author of a number of important books and served in various significant submarine commands. It grieves us greatly that he can not share in the satisfactions associated with the completion of our project.

---

[1]   Hugh Trevor-Roper. "The Last Decade in History", in New York Review of Books, Vl5/Nll6. October 27, 1988

Chapter 1

Dress Rehearsal Crisis 1938

Harold C. Deutsch

A. What if in September 1938, the western powers had foresworn appeasement or lagged in it sufficiently to permit German military conspirators to strike at Hitler?

Among the innumerable might-have-beens that mark crucial phases of the history of the Hitler regime, some of the more significant arise in relation to the Munich crisis of September 1938. Of these none is more central than that concerning the consequences if the western powers had set more severe limits to the concessions they were prepared to make to German pressures on Czechoslovakia. Most commonly it is assumed that greater firmness on their part would have led to the launching of a second World War. Such speculation, however, loses much of its meaning if the result had been the overthrow of the regime or still, if that should fail, dramatic changes in the complexion of German, European and world affairs.

Many students of the period are convinced that the attempt to remove Hitler would have been launched. Arguments concern mainly the prospects of success and the probable consequences of success or failure. Space is lacking for analysis of the relations between the dictator and the *Generalitaet* (general officer corps) after his accession to power in 1933. It must suffice to note that, by the summer of 1938, successive purges of the military leadership had severely reduced the ranks of those hostile or lukewarm toward the regime or who had ventured to take issue with aspects of Hitler's forced-draft armament program.[1] The climax had been reached only a few months previous to the September crisis. As a sequel to the removal of Minister of War, Werner von Blomberg, and army commander, Werner von Fritsch, no fewer than fourteen generals had been summarily retired and forty others shifted to unfamiliar surroundings and command relationships.

Fritsch at the time of his removal by one of the filthiest intrigues of the Nazi period was Germany's most prestigious soldier. In his place Hitler chose the weak and highly vulnerable Walther von Brauchitsch, whom he placed under heavy obligation by financial favors that enabled him to get rid of a wife who stood in the way of marriage with a lady of questionable background.[2] Even more fateful was the forced resignation in late August of Chief of the General Staff Ludwig Beck.

Beck had climaxed a series of protests against Hitler's intention to take military action against Czechoslovakia in late September by reading to the army group and army commanders on 4 August a memorandum condemning the dictator's policy. He had hoped that Brauchitsch, who agreed with him in principle, would join him in seeking what amounted to a general strike of the generals. But Brauschitsch would not read the speech Beck had prepared for him. Though the commanders with two exceptions (Walther von Reichenau and Ernst Busch) supported Beck's position and asked Brauchitsch to convey this to Hitler, he took the steam out of the procedure by sending the memorandum to the Fuehrer through the dismayed army adjutant rather than presenting it personally. Hitler's response was to rail against Beck as the "saboteur" of his armament and foreign policies. The chief of staff had no alternative but to resign, leaving office on 28 August.

To all appearances, Hitler's mastery of the military seemed complete. What he failed to appreciate was that by slamming the door on protest and discussion, those who felt that he was leading Germany to disaster had only the choice of conspiracy. By eliminating Fritsch and Beck, seen by many as their final recourse in the struggle against tyranny, there remained only the choice of purging the state by toppling the regime itself.

The first conspiratorial dress rehearsal had grown out of the crisis over the removal of Beck. In the high command of the army itself, the spark had come largely from Franz Halder, deputy chief of staff and vociferous critic of the regime. He had been the moving spirit in Beck's entourage in urging drastic action on behalf of Fritsch.

Halder in the summer of 1938 is judged too often in terms of the drained, eroding spirit of the early war period when, at critical junctures, his loss of nerve was decisive in the failure of resistance plans to bear fruit. In September 1938, in any event, he did not show the reluctance to assume responsibility that he demonstrated later in 1939 and early 1940.

A critical feature in Halder's more positive demeanor during the Munich crisis may well have been greater confidence in the thoroughness of the preparations for a coup as compared to those of later years. Never again, not in the fall and winter of 1939-1940, at a number of stages in 1943, least of all in July 1944, did plans and dispositions approximate in proficiency and completeness those of the weeks before Munich.

A feature that does much to explain this was that, after 1938, one could never be certain of the presence in Berlin of the key figures of the conspiratorial group. Their various duties had scattered most of them over the numerous fronts and occupied territories. In particular, only then was it possible to count on the full drive of the vital motor center represented by the Abwehr, the armed forces intelligence service directed by Admiral Wilhelm Canaris.

No major personality of the Third Reich is subject to more contradictory estimates than this enigmatic personage. Controversies concerning his aims and motivations will no doubt persist. For us it must suffice that, after welcoming the Third Reich, he was so utterly disillusioned as to assemble in the Abwehr directorate a cluster of rabid anti-Nazis down to the secretaries. He had been a moving spirit for action during the Fritsch crisis and, to the spring of 1940, played a vital role in resistance projects. Thereafter, frustrated and the victim of a pronounced fatalistic streak, he confined himself essentially to a supportive role.

Canaris was apprised of all plans and preparations but left an essentially free hand to the prime movers in his entourage. Of these chief of staff and Central Division head Hans Oster was most noteworthy. He was direct where Canaris was deliberate and at times devious, impulsive where the Admiral was wary, and of a heroic mold no one has ascribed to his chief.

A brief outline must suffice to sketch the more vital aspects of the plans and preparations for a coup d'etat in the late summer of 1938. A major resistance center existed in the Foreign Office among whom the principal figure was Baron Ernst von Weizsaecker, the deputy foreign minister. It was he who early in September dispatched to London a final appeal to stand up to Hitler on his military threat to Czechoslovakia. The message was transmitted by Theo Kordt, then chargé d'affaires of the German embassy, to Foreign Minister Lord Halifax in a late night meeting of 7 September at No. 10 Downing Street. Kordt was only the last of a string of emissaries who made the pilgrimage to London that summer. He told Halifax that the army leaders were prepared to overthrow the regime if Hitler persisted with military action.

Virtually all studies have assumed that, in view of the notorious insecurity of Paris, no similar pleas were directed toward France. Actually Carl Goerdeler had carried an early version to Prime Minister Daladier in May and General Beck personally met a French emissary in a hotel in Basel about a week after Kordt's meeting with Halifax.[3] At least as startling is the hitherto unknown fact that, relying on President Roosevelt's opposition to Hitler's expansionism and hoping that he would stiffen backs in London and Paris, a similar message was dispatched to Washington. Probably due to the skepticism of Truman Smith, the American military attaché in Berlin, who could not conceive of German generals playing such a role, the message does not seem to have reached the President.

Civilians also formed the tentacles by which the Oster circle reached out to the Ministry of Justice, the Ministry of Economics, the Berlin Police Presidium, and Himmler's immediate entourage. The principal go-betweens were two further controversial figures, Hjalmar Schacht and Hans Bernd Gisevius. Schacht had been involved with opposition conventicles since 1936. His greatest service now was to help enlist the later Field Marshal Erwin von Witzleben, then commander of the Berlin military district *(Wehrkreis)*. Once committed, Witzleben could be relied upon to be the most staunch of the staunch. And as commander of all troops in the Berlin area his participation was crucial.

Gisevius was the link with Count Helldorff, the Berlin police president, whose deputy, Count Fritz Dietlof von der Schulenburg, had ties with resistance groups all over Berlin, and Arthur Nebe, head of the Criminal Department of Himmler's national police organization. Gisevius was also established in Witzleben's office to supervise planning for taking over the capital.

Illustrative of the role of other civilian volunteers is that of Theodor and Elisabeth Struenck, who had moved to Berlin from their native Dusseldorf largely to take part in the overthrow of the regime. Elisabeth served in innumerable ways as clearinghouse, letterdrop, messenger, hostess and chauffeur. Driving around the city with Witzleben and Count Brockdorff-Ahlefeld, commander of the Potsdam division, she clocked over 2,000 kilometers as they surveyed points to be occupied and estimated the forces required to take them over.[4]

Mention is rarely made of the significant help provided by Fritz Wiedemann, Hitler's company commander in the First World War and now his personal adjutant. For the seizure of the Reich Chancellory the information he fed Oster concerning affairs in Hitler's entourage and the routines of the building would be invaluable.[5]

The decisive payoff would be of course the seizure of the Chancellory and the person of the dictator. On its success would depend all further progress in toppling the regime and taking over the machinery of government. Nothing more dramatically illustrates the amateur side of the conspiracy than the intentions of the principals concerning Hitler. Most of them were ardent Christians who took seriously the commandment against killing. Some persisted in this attitude down to July 1944 and several quit the conspiracy when its plans came to center on assassination. In 1938 the intention was to take the dictator captive and either have him declared insane by a commission headed by the eminent psychiatrist Karl Bonhoeffer or subject him to an elaborate show trial revealing the crimes of his regime.

The hazards of either course appear obvious. Small wonder that such realists as Oster, though pretending to go along, were determined to eliminate Hitler for once and all. The seizure of the Chancellory was entrusted to two commando-type troops of about sixty young men commanded by Abwehr Major Friedrich Wilhelm Heinz. He had been a *Stahlhelm* (conservative veterans organization) leader and a good number of his men came from its former ranks. Others came from the Brandenburg sabotage regiment of the Abwehr. To stress the broad character of the anti-Nazi front, a number of students and union workers were included.

Heinz and his intimates among the participants were convinced that the only realistic procedure was to kill the dictator immediately and this was further concerted with Oster. Taking a leaf from the Nazi gangster book, the Fuehrer was to be shot while "resisting arrest" or "trying to escape."[6]

Our knowledge of detail is much limited by the fact that though much (far too much) was set on paper, including the provisions for the takeover of the Chancellory, ministerial buildings, major government agencies, post and telegraph offices, airports, radio stations and party offices, all was burned at a meeting of principals in Witzleben's Grunewald villa a few days after Munich. We thus must rely most largely on the memories of the small group who survived the post-July 1944 liquidations (Halder, Gisevius, General Thomas, Schacht, the Kordt brothers, and Elisabeth Struenck).

How close did it come to launching the coup prepared for September 1938? Twice that month the course of affairs led within an inch of Halder pressing the button that would be the signal for action. The first occasion arrived shortly after the conclusion of the Nazi Party annual meeting at Nuremberg of 12 September, when Hitler had made a particularly bellicose declaration with respect to Czechoslovakia. At that time, as Halder was being urged to give the required signal, the British announcement of Chamberlain's coming to see Hitler at Berchtesgaden on the fifteenth had ended such a possibility for the time being.

A more critical state of affairs was reached by 27 September, when Hitler and the western powers appeared to have reached an impasse and war looked to be around the corner. Hoping to whip up manifestations of public support, the dictator that afternoon staged a military parade through the heart of Berlin by tank formations of the 2nd motorized division from Stettin. The march was conducted in a fashion to imply that the troops were on their way to the Bohemian border. But the crowd of spectators were sunk in gloom and, when the Fuehrer appeared on his balcony to invite applause, he was for the first time since achieving power in 1933 met by glacial silence.

Did Halder that day make his climactic assault on Brauchitsch who, he had persistently assured his associates, was basically at one with him on avoiding a European war and would at the critical juncture prove cooperative? Some of the principal conspirators had never gained complete faith in Beck's successor and had concerted among themselves to have Witzleben give the decisive signal if Halder should procrastinate.

That Halder was ready to move and had finally managed to sweep Brauchitsch into the conspiratorial camp was attested by him to his associates at the time as well as in post-war testimony. It may also be hinted at by the invitation the latter extended to Fritsch to meet him that afternoon in his quarters in the Hotel Continental. While Fritsch's aide, the later Colonel Otto Heinz Grosskreuz, paced the corridor, the two generals conferred for some time.[7] Just what they discussed and possibly agreed will probably never be known. On the whole it appears most likely that Brauchitsch would not have called in Fritsch except to concert with him some positive steps.[8]

September 28 dawned with every portent that Hitler's order to march would be issued that day. Brauchitsch departed for the Chancellory from army headquarters to establish whether the Fuehrer was persisting in his course. If that should prove the case, Halder later claimed, his return to headquarters would have meant the immediate pressing of the fatal button. Instead Brauchistch brought the news that Chamberlain had enlisted Mussolini to propose to Hitler a meeting of the big four at Munich and that, short of permitting military action against Czechoslovakia, it appeared the Fuehrer's demands would be essentially met.

Events thereupon took their course as history has recorded them. However, if the Chamberlain government had pursued a different path or even had delayed matters for a day or two, the course of affairs could have been a far different one. This is to assume, of course, that Halder would have lived up to his promises or, failing that, that Witzleben had stepped in to force his hand by himself releasing the gathered forces. In view of the undoubted contrast between the two in character and determination, some students of the period incline more to the latter supposition. On the other hand, Halder, whose worst days of indecision still lay a year ahead, would have discovered it excruciatingly painful to draw back at the critical minute. In this instance, going along with his commitments meant yielding to the greater pressures. His confederates had done almost all the work of planning, preparation, and managing the foreign contacts whereas he had reserved to himself only the final go-ahead. He knew much, perhaps, virtually all, about the assurance delivered to London, Paris, and Washington. To call off the entire project at the critical stage would have earned him the disdain of all with whom he had concerted. He would have had to reckon, also, that the tracks left by him and his friends all over Berlin were likely to be discovered by the vengeful dictator.

The most critical imperative in the operation assuredly concerned a successful assault on the Reich Chancellory, presumably in the early morning hours of the 29th. Peter Hoffmann has devoted a book to relate in vivid detail the elaborate measures worked out to guard the dictator. These were no doubt formidable but not yet remotely what they became later and Hoffmann lists a string of deficiencies that would have made the building vulnerable to sixty determined men. The organization in two troops implies that two points of entry were targeted. In any event, in view of the information supplied by Wiedemann and the personal acquaintance of many conspirators with movements inside the Chancellory, the prospect of successfully eliminating Hitler would seem to have been favorable.

However, let it be assumed for the moment that the Fuehrer escaped from the building. Where could he have gone if he could actually have gotten out of Berlin? The most likely resort was his 10,000 man *Leibstandarte Adolf Hitler* which was deployed not far from the Czech border at Grafenwoehr. If he could have reached there, something like a civil war was an undoubted possibility. As his personal popularity had taken rather a nose dive during the previous days due to near panic about the prospect of a European war, the public would have been much divided. In any event, all thought of such a war would have vanished for the time being.

A more intriguing line of speculation derives from the assumption that the Fuehrer had vanished from the stage. Merely removing him from the picture would not yet by itself determine the fate of the National Socialist regime. Much, as in July 1944, would depend on dealing effectively also with his principal paladins, notably Goering. He had not yet publicly been declared Hitler's successor, though a secret disposition of 29 April of that year had named him as first in line with Rudolf Hess in second place. Vitally important was that Goering alone among the Nazi leaders had something of a national standing. Aside from popularity with broad sections of the population, he enjoyed considerable kudos in business circles, could still count on devotion in his Luftwaffe, and was known both in Germany and informed quarters abroad as a moderating influence in foreign policy. Even among the conspirators there were always some who, largely blind to his more vicious qualities, were at least inclined to consider him, hoping thereby to avoid both civil war and European conflict. They urged that his ideological drive was not genuine, being put on mainly to conform with that of Hitler. In some quarter something like the following is still said: "If Goering had taken over, Germany might well have become one of the most corrupt countries in the world but there would have been no Second World War." His laziness and sybaritic disposition seemed to promise this.

The question of a Goering government was probably less likely to arise in September 1938 than would have been the case if Hitler had been killed in July 1944. In the latter instance, the half-baked and largely improvised preparations did not provide for immediate elimination of Goering. Because of the wholesale destruction of opposition documents in October 1938 we do not know what had been planned to deal with Goering during the previous month. We know in a general way that there were dispositions to take care of Hitler's more dangerous lieutenants and as none of them were too well guarded, these are likely to have proved effective.

Halder, after much hesitation and one rather feeble attempt to sound out General von Rundstedt, had refrained from systematically contacting military commanders outside of Berlin. Of almost all of them, however, the conspirators could be fairly sure once the dictator was out of the way and there was no longer the impediment of the solemn oath the *Generalitaet* had been virtually tricked into swearing in August 1934 after the death of President von Hindenburg. It will be recalled that, with only two exceptions, all the commanders had declared their agreement with Beck's analysis of the consequences of an attack on Czechoslovakia. This was far from tantamount to following him in open revolt if Hitler had only been taken captive, one of the pressing reasons for choosing the road to assassination. With Hitler dead, especially too if Goering was out of the way, the generals would have rallied to a man to a provisional government that included the revered Beck and a figure so widely respected as Carl Goerdeler.

A government in which Beck and Goerdeler played key roles would have immediately repudiated Hitler's irresponsible expansionist policies and assumed in armament the fundamentally defensive posture Fritsch and Beck had favored. Beck saw Germany's position in Europe much as Bismarck had done after the war with France, when he said that the new Empire was just big enough to still be tolerable to its neighbors; further expansion would compel them to combine against it. As for Goerdeler, his journeys abroad and innumerable conversations with foreign statesmen and dignitaries had convinced him that Germany's position was no longer that of the twenties, that one could now count on making headway on legitimate claims without endangering the peace of Europe.[9]

One may assume, of course, that a Beck-Goerdeler government would have pursued what might be called the normal or traditional revisionist aims with respect to recovering the more painfully felt territorial losses of 1919, such as the Polish Corridor area, Upper Silesia, and African colonies. It would have been easy to see Germany restored to the position of a world power. But it would have pursued its aims without Hitler's threats or resort to war. In particular, it would have avoided like the plague anything smacking of Hitler's racial fantasies or indiscriminate eastern expansion.

Those who plotted to overthrow the Hitler regime in 1938 assuredly represented mostly the conservative forces of Germany but such as had been severely chastened by the harsh experience with totalitarian dictatorship. Most of them were monarchists of one stamp or another., For the sake of badly needed stability and as the result of even more severe chastening, democratic and social democratic elements were in many instances prepared to accept a moderate monarchy. There was some argument among the plotters between those who favored the elder son of the former Crown Prince, Wilhelm, and those who preferred the younger brother, Louis Ferdinand. The moderate views, modesty and general reasonableness and attractiveness of Wilhelm tended, despite his marriage to a commoner, to weigh the scales in his favor.[10]

One can assume that any type of successor government would have striven for revision of the more onerous provisions of the Versailles Treaty and restoring Germany as a European power. There could be no guarantee that in time, expansive urges would not again revive. But no leader of the future was likely to attempt again the role and more extravagant aims of Adolf Hitler.

B. What if war had come in September 1938 instead of a year later?

Dealing with this problem is in effect to contradict the major assumption to which the previous discussion had led: that there was less danger of war during the September 1938 crisis than has usually been supposed. If the western powers, as was the case, obliged by their far-reaching concessions a frustrated dictator to refrain from proceeding militarily against Czechoslovakia, a European war was avoided for the time being. The pronounced anti-war sentiment of the German public and the expressed opposition of virtually the entire *Generalitaet* gave him no choice but to set temporary limits to his bellicosity. Small wonder that in his fury he later proclaimed that if again a foreign envoy came to him with "offers" difficult to refuse, he would throw the fellow down the steps of the Reich Chancellory.

On the other hand, if Britain and France had set more severe limits to their appeasement, or perhaps delayed just enough to give the impression that they would do so, the launching of a coup by the military opposition would almost certainly have resulted. The likely consequence was the death of Hitler and the probable elimination of the National Socialist regime.

Be that as it may, in September 1938 the issue peace or war was real to all parties concerned, whether directly involved in the crisis or being concerned bystanders. British and French leaders were bound in their calculations to give weight to the military posture and establishments of potential allies or opponents as well as to other power factors (political, economic or naval) that might enter the picture if war came.

The prospective lineup of states that, at one time or another, might become involved in a conflict that resulted from a German attack on Czechoslovakia is riddled with question marks. The Czechs could only fight with any hope of success if backed by France and Britain. If driven to desperation, they might also risk war in the hope that, once engaged, the western powers would be compelled by shame and public sentiment to come to their aid. Thus, though the French government had on 1 July notified Prague that it should not look for help if war came as the result of its obduracy on the Sudetenland question, the French were known to be much divided on their course if Hitler should drive things to extremes. Six members of the Paris cabinet had personally informed the Czech ambassador, Stefan Osusky, that they would resign in public protest if France violated its treaty obligations.[11]

If France went to war, it would be difficult or impossible for Britain to hold off. London was virtually on record to act if, despite all warnings, Hitler persisted with military action. States which, like France, were committed to the Czechs by formal treaty were the Soviet Union and the remaining countries of the Little Entente, Romania and Yugoslavia. The Soviets were also allied with France but this tie had been greatly loosened by the world wide horror and disgust with the barbarous purges that had been going on since 1936. At least equally or more significant was the undermining of confidence in Soviet military capacities as a result of the slaughter of over half of the officer corps of the rank of major and above, commencing in June 1937.

15

So greatly was Soviet military power discounted in France that the French high command administered a string of snubs to the Soviet leadership. Moscow was not even invited to send observers to the 1937 autumn maneuvers. In April 1938 General Gamelin suggested to civilian authorities that if war came with Germany it might be just as well to have the Soviets remain neutral. They might be less of a help than a burden.

In pronouncements of Foreign Minister Molotov, the Kremlin did declare its resolve to live up to alliance obligations. But, even assuming what everyone now questioned, that Moscow could make an important military contribution, there was doubt about how it could bring power to bear. Germany could only be reached directly via Poland or, more round about, via Romania and Hungary. The Poles had made very clear their refusal to permit any passage. It is usually assumed that Bucharest did the same but its archives now show that it was less negative than has been supposed and that it was the Soviets who backed off.[12] To all intents and purposes, the Soviets were written off as a military factor of any importance in Paris and London (as well as in Berlin!).

In the case of Romania and Yugoslavia much would depend on the course adopted by the Hungarians. The pressures on Czechoslovakia had put Budapest into a revisionist fervor with respect to the Treaty of Trianon and Hitler counted heavily on Hungarian cooperation. But, though the Hungarians would have been ready enough to attack the Czechs in the rear, they had no taste for a European war. With Hungary standing aside for the time being, the Yugoslavs and Romanians were also inclined to await events.

As in 1939, Germany in the previous September could not count on the alliance of a single European state. Italy had abounded in assurances and Mussolini, in speeches during the second half of September, had publicly aligned himself with Germany. Assuredly, it would not be easy to retreat from this. A year later, however, a solemnly proclaimed Pact of Steel proved malleable enough for this purpose. For the sake of our discussion, we shall assume that the Italian dictator, fearful too about an army the British fleet would most probably cut off in Spain, would decide to take no chances for the time being.

Thus Germany could not expect military support from a single European state. Its best hope, in fact, lay in one of the least likely quarters imaginable — Warsaw. The prospect of a disintegrating or mutilated Czechoslovakia had raised annexationist fever there regarding the district of Teschen. The wisest heads in the Polish capital saw the folly of collaborating in a German aggression which all too likely might next turn eastward. There was also the sacrifice of the alliance with France, indispensable in any later showdown with Berlin. But the acquisitive urge was strong and for a time it seemed to predominate. Tragically the threatening posture was sufficient to induce the Prague government not to risk refusal to accept the Munich pact. President Benes was later to maintain that the likelihood of Poland joining in a German attack was decisive in a hairline resolve to accept the decree of Munich.[12]

Lack of certainty about Poland's course also had some part in weakening French determination in the Sudeten crisis. In calculating western resources in a showdown with Germany, Gamelin felt compelled to write off the Poles as active military collaborators and to give thought instead to the conceivability of their joining in the rape of Czechoslovakia.

In assessing the probably course of the war between Germany and the states which in 1938 would have been arrayed against her, it does not suffice simply to total up then available military resources.[13] Psychological factors, for one, played an extraordinary role. A principal feature involved western estimates of German capacities which varied between the exaggerated and the absurd. Hitler here may have won the greatest propaganda victory of our century.

16

Until in the spring of 1935 he denounced the military restrictions of Versailles, he did what he could to belittle the progress of armament in Germany. He could not afford an intervention that he lacked the means to oppose. Once he had admitted and blown up the facts, he went to the opposite tack to make out that the expanding Wehrmacht had actually reached a state where foreign interference would be hazardous. Most intimidating was the picture drawn of the burgeoning Luftwaffe. The everyday targets were the military members of the French and British embassies. The best illustration is probably the handling of the French assistant air attaché, the future General Stehlin. Clever use here was made of Goering's sister, Olga Riegele, of whom he was a cordial social acquaintance.[14] F. W. Winterbotham of British air intelligence was similarly fed highly colored information about the whole rearmament process. A real coup was achieved in dealing with Charles Lindbergh, whose worldwide fame in aviation assured him eager audiences in west European quarters. Lindbergh was suitably impressed and carried westward the message intended by Hitler and Goering.

Joseph Vuillemin, who commanded the French air force, had already progressed so far in self-deception that he scarcely required the elaborate performances staged for his benefit when he visited Germany in late August 1938. Reports from military representatives in Berlin and intelligence sources had already earlier in the year given him a magnified picture of the growing German air strength. In March he had told War Minister Daladier that, if war came with Germany and Italy as a result of a French intervention in Spain, his own planes would be shot out of the skies within two weeks. He now repeated the same gloomy verdict.

What has been said should not minimize the strong reasons for a real French and British concern about the growth of German air power. The French were far behind in their own program of build-up and modernization. The now nationalized aircraft factories were in a chaotic state, most of the fighters in service were obsolete, and none could fly as fast as German bombers. The British in the autumn of 1938 had but a single squadron of Hurricanes and another of Spitfires. Oxygen masks were so deficient that none could fly higher than 15,000 feet. Construction of the radar chain, such a lifesaver in 1940, had barely begun.

The state of British air defense actually had little to do with the realities of the military confrontation in September 1938 unless one thinks of a war pattern in 1938-1939 similar to the actual one of 1939-1940, in other words in the event of total allied defeat on the continent followed by German air attacks from French bases. German bluff had succeeded in giving government and people a nightmarish picture of immediately devastated cities (illustration: digging trenches in Hyde Park during the Munich crisis!). In actuality no German air armada could possibly strike London from Germany itself.

It has occasionally been alleged that the only real air threat against Germany in 1938 could have been exercised by Soviet planes flying from Czech bases. To the writer this appears fanciful. The Soviet air force in this period was in a state bordering on chaos. The military liquidations (they can be called no less) had struck, among other targets, at its leadership and the principal designers. It was filled with obsolete planes that were no match for Messerschmitt 109s or 110s. When one reckons in the time required to prepare bases and facilities, assemble necessary supplies, move planes and pilots, and work out a suitable offensive program, any chance of an effective air intervention on the part of the Soviets goes aglimmering. Most probably help would have arrived piecemeal and been destroyed in the same fashion.

Though we know less about it, we may assume that a program of deception parallel to that employed on the Luftwaffe was designed to confuse French and British military and government quarters with respect to German ground forces. But again, self-deception, a perverted wishful thinking that thrived on bad news, played a role. Almost from the start of the Hitler regime, French estimates on the German army were grossly out of line. At the time of the German repudiation of the Versailles restriction (spring 1935), its strength was assumed in Paris to be about 700,000 men (actual figure: 350,000). The often pot-bellied S.A. (brown-shirted storm troopers) were described as the equivalent of 60 reserve divisions — this one year after the morally devastating 1934 blood purge!

After the spring 1936 Rhineland occupation it was assumed that 295,000 men were stationed there (actual figure: 30,000 which included 15,000 *Landespolizei* or border police). In the spring of 1938 the West Wall (western parlance: Siegfried Line) which was scarcely begun was assumed to be complete.

It is a real problem to determine the degree to which such assumptions derived from false data played into French hands by German intelligence or other sources as against pure self-deception. French military and some civilian leaders sold on appeasement seem to have welcomed every scrap of evidence that supported a defensive posture even in the event of a conflict to do, in other words, as came naturally. The memories of the generations decimated in 1914-1918 were still overwhelming.

British estimates on ground forces were also out of line though less absurd than those of the French. At the time of the occupation of Austria, British intelligence reported Germany prepared to put 100 infantry divisions into the field as well as four to six tank divisions, roughly twice the front line strength at that period. British military planning still was dominated by assumed needs in the event of a conflict with Italy in the Middle East. In February 1938 the official program called for a field force of four infantry divisions and one mobile division to be assembled in an eastern theater.

German assumptions about the French potential were also dominated by pessimism that derived in part from eagerness to restrain the Fuehrer. The data with respect to numbers were essentially accurate though chief of staff Beck made the tactical mistake of trying to impress Hitler by beefing up estimates with the inclusion of questionable additions such as the Garde Mobile. This only served to infuriate the dictator.[15] The real overestimates had to do with quality. German military leaders, recalling French performance in World War I, were inclined to share world opinion that the French army was the best anywhere. The high estimate even extended to the staggering arms industry which an official German report labelled "in scope and production the strongest in Europe." In some measure such judgments no doubt were somewhat colored by military and economic specialists who hoped to discourage adventurism.

In mental and physical preparedness for the kind of war actually to be fought in 1940, the German ground forces were much superior in 1938 to their potential opponents. From the standpoint of mobile warfare (we will eschew the term "Blitzkrieg" with which the Freiburg research center is currently quarreling) Hitler's forces had the tactical advantage of having gone far to marry the two forms of highly mobile artillery represented by the tank and the dive bomber.[16] The combination performed devastating in the later German victories in Poland, France, Yugoslavia, Greece and, during the first eighteen months, in Russia. Except in the advance into Czechoslovakia, the air-tank team, insofar as it was ready, was not likely to find employment in the last months of 1938 or before the spring of 1939.

The French and British certainly did underestimate the dangers of mobile warfare as it was then being prepared in Germany. They were wedded to the idea of the superiority of the defense in most complete contrast to French doctrine on the eve of World War I or the ideas of J.F.C. Fuller propagated in Britain. In this addiction to defensive warfare it was not merely a question of adhering to a thesis that could be abandoned as new considerations demanded review. The French were largely frozen in by the enormous financial and psychological investment anchored in the Maginot Line. They were not even flexible within the defensive posture itself. The concentration of industrial and mineral resources in northwestern France made this prohibitive. The British, even if their World War I memories had not inclined them also to a defensive doctrine, had no choice but to follow the French lead.[17]

Though Gamelin proclaimed confidence that he would repel any German offensive, he did not even after such a repulse expect to launch an offensive of his own. In the spring of 1938 he told Daladier that, if war came with Germany and Italy over Spain, France could no more than pin down German divisions at the frontier. In the May weekend crisis a few weeks later he did speak of an offensive if the Germans attacked Czechoslovakia. But from an order he issued on 8 June it is clear that he had in mind only a reconnaissance in force in the Saarland. The almost instinctive inclination to marshal negative factors was shown in a sudden nose-dive of French appraisals of Czech powers of resistance.[18]

From what has been noted about the military/psychological disposition of the western powers, it appears evident that they would have fought no more offensively in 1938 than they did a year later. This is the more likely because of their far less pronounced sense of outrage in 1938. By the summer of 1939, Hitler's bad faith in seizing the remainder of Czechoslovakia brought conviction that concessions to him did not assure peace but gave him stepping stones to even more extreme demands. This comprehension may well have done most to reverse attitudes in the British Dominions and to make a profound impression in the United States. Both in the Dominions and in America, as well as in broad sections of the British public itself, the issue in 1938 had seemed centered in one of self-determination for the German-speaking regions of Bohemia. This illusion had been largely erased a year later.

On the German side, Hitler's seeming infallibility and an intensive propaganda campaign against the Poles had made their impact. There was also more basic hostility against Poland, which had annexed territories that had been part of the old Reich and not, as in the case of the Czechs, regions that happened to be German-speaking but had not belonged to the Hohenzollern Empire. In 1938 a sullen and apathetic nation and a disgruntled *Generalitaet,* whose top leadership had gone the road of conspiracy, would have been a heavy burden on the war effort. Assuming that hostilities had been launched, the Czechs would almost certainly have been overwhelmed, the more certain if the Poles had joined in. In analyzing Czech chances, it is often forgotten that the army, however high in reputation for training, weaponry, superb fortifications and industrial backing, was in considerable part composed of disaffected or lukewarm minorities. Close to three-fourths of the German-speaking conscripts failed to report on mobilization. Hungarians and Ukrainians were varyingly disaffected. Even the Slovaks were far less committed to the national cause than were the Czechs.

Assuming the conquest of Czechoslovakia, the accretion of German power would have approximated nothing close to the actual gains when the country was taken over without resistance. The highly modern equipment of the Czech forces, one of the leading arms industries of Europe, and a massive gold reserve fell undiminished into German hands. Both the fighting and staying power of the Reich were substantially increased for the war that came in 1939. It may further be assumed that the damage to the German forces would have been far greater than in the later war against Poland.

From what has been reviewed thus far it appears safe to assume that in 1938 the western powers would have stood by and marked time as they were to do during the agony of Poland. The situation, however, would have been considerably less favorable for Hitler than a year later. The German forces were far less formidable for offensive war against opponents of some strength. Substantial bodies of troops would have had to be diverted to guard their rear against possible Polish attack, particularly in East Prussia and Silesia. Thus an immediate offensive in the west after the Czechs were finished, ignoring weather and terrain as Hitler was to do a year later, would seem unthinkable. The generals, who in November 1939 came within a hair's breadth of acting, would almost certainly have revolted.

On the other hand, the staying power of the Reich in 1938 was abysmal The Romanians had threatened to cut off oil and grain shipments. The very substantial Soviet economic help, assured in 1939, especially in strategic materials, would not have been available. All in all, it appears highly likely that Hitler would have been prepared to negotiate on the basis of the fait accompli so far as the Sudetenland was concerned while agreeing to the restoration of remaining Czechoslovakia.

On their part, the western allies, with populations far less committed to seeing things through than they were later and with the Dominions and the United States standing apart, would seem to have been ready to accept a settlement on this basis. Saving face, they could say that, after all, this was what they had gone to war about in the first instance.

The end of this imagined phony war would hardly have assured "peace in our time." Hitler's control of Germany might have been somewhat impaired but Goebbels' propaganda machine could have repaired much of the damage. It is difficult to believe that the dictator would have reconciled himself to abandoning his extravagant goals for eastern expansion. Sooner or later, if at all possible, he was bound to resume his march.

C. What if one of the foreign military attaché plots to assassinate Adolf Hitler in the early spring of 1939 had been carried out successfully?

The foreign military attachés in Berlin during the Nazi period included a number of extraordinary personalities. Being comparatively young and enterprising, they had limited respect for their seniors, and for the more rigid rules of the diplomatic game. They were at times likely to pursue their own devices in ways that, if revealed, would have shocked their superiors. Those from the west and north of Europe were likely to have a particular detestation of the regime to which they were accredited. Their limited regard for official decorum opened them to ideas of direct action. Some of the attachés were also worked on systematically by younger and more ardent officers of the conspiratorial group about Admiral Canaris, head of armed forced intelligence (*Amt Ausland Abwehr*) In particular, Colonel (later General) Hans Oster, who developed real intimacy with several attachés, and probably had extensive relations with others of which little has thus far come to light.

The British military attaché, Colonel Frank Noel Mason-MacFarlane, was a particularly daring spirit, not at all averse to personal risks and somewhat reckless of disposition even when missteps could lead to national embarrassment. His dislike of the National Socialist regime and of Adolf Hitler personally is amply documented. When Hitler to all intents and purpose repudiated the Munich Agreement in March 1939 by marching into rump Czechoslovakia and making it a German dependency, Mason-MacFarlane shared the conviction in many British quarters that war had become inevitable if the German dictator remained in power. An opportunity to rid the world of Hitler for once and all promised to present itself on the occasion of the military parade on his birthday (20 April), when he would be exposed to public gaze on the reviewing stand. Mason-MacFarlane's flat was nearby and from its bathroom window he proposed to shoot the dictator, having secured a high-powered rifle with telescopic sights. The distance is said to have been 110 yards. But when the colonel went to London for authority to proceed with his scheme, he is said to have been turned down for what was labelled an act of "poor sportsmanship." The details of the affair are recorded in the Imperial War Museum of London.

There was, however another plan in formation that was independent of foreign government authorization. Under the leadership of the American polar explorer, Admiral Richard Byrd, something like an international consortium for the elimination of Hitler was formed. Among those privy to its plans was the deputy air attaché of France the later General Paul Stehlin, whose testimony is our principal source of information.[19]

Stehlin's importance in the Berlin scheme of things well exceeded his relatively minor official position in the hierarchy of the French legation. The German Luftwaffe had selected him as a major channel of misinformation to France on the supposed strength and development of German air power.

For the sake of the following scenario let us assume that one or the other of these plots had succeeded in killing Hitler in April, 1939. The German and European situations at that time unfortunately differed profoundly from what they had been seven months before during the September 1938 crisis. At that time, the odds would have favored a political takeover by opposition elements. As noted earlier in this chapter, plans and preparations for such a contingency exceeded by far in compass and efficiency those of later phases of the military conspiracy. Because of predominant anti-war sentiment, Hitler's hold on popular support and public imagination was then at its lowest ebb. The army leadership was close to united in opposition to the risk of a European war By April 1939, however, some of the leading conspiratorial figures were no longer in Berlin. Others had been transferred to different posts. Their detailed plans for takeover had been scrapped, most of them burned in General Witzleben's Grunewald fireplace. Munich had confirmed Hitler's prestige as a diplomatic wonder worker, even to many of his critics. The Fuehrer's assassination, instead of seeming to save the country from a disastrous war, would now have made of him a national martyr. The complete repudiation of the National Socialist regime at this stage would have been for practical purposes unthinkable.

Although Hermann Goering was not formally designated Hitler's successor until April 29, 1939, and the formal announcement was made early in September, it can be assumed that his succession would have been all but automatic. With the conspiratorial elements temporarily paralyzed, there could be no effective opposition for the time being. Even in 1938 some of the conspirators, lacking faith in the success of a complete turnover, had at times played with the thought of a halfway solution involving a government under Goering.

The same idea had been put forth from time to time by those who favored a monarchical restoration, a solution undoubtedly favored by the still largely aristocratic general officer corps. There had been talk about this in the final phase of the Bruening chancellorship. It would have had much of the support of the Catholic Center Party, and even of significant elements of the desperate Social Democrats, who regarded it as infinitely preferable to a Nazi-dominated government. There was the highly attractive figure of the elder son of the former Crown Prince, Prince Wilhelm.

The writer cherishes the memory of an entire night passed in a Koenigsberg apartment in July 1938 with Prince Wilhelm and two fellow officers of his reserve regiment. There could be no doubt about the Prince's solidly anti-Nazi sentiments and fundamental democratic sympathies. There is every reason to believe that he would have made a superb constitutional monarch. His death in the French campaign in 1940 was a real loss for Germany.

It does not appear entirely inconceivable that at some point Goering would be open to the idea of a monarchical restoration. Much as he loved power, he was even more addicted to showmanship. The offer of a princedom in a restored Hohenzollern Empire in which he could pose as "the second Bismarck" would not have been without attraction.

Undoubtedly the influence of the army in a Goering regime would generally have been a moderating one. Almost uniquely in the history of military establishments, most notably perhaps in Germany, Hitler's drive to unlimited rearmament had gone too fast for the army itself. Unrestrained expansion in the number of recruits threatened dilution in quality and training. Fritsch and Beck had basically favored a defensive posture. Senior staff officers and commanders were widely disposed to give heed to the warning voice of Hjalmar Schacht and other political economists that unrestrained military expenditures threatened ultimate economic collapse. Goering himself had not been entirely deaf to such warnings. He might rant about the need of "cannon before butter." But no one was more addicted to what "butter" stood for than Goering himself, and the need for more cannon certainly did not for a moment limit his personal extravagances. Now that the pressure from Hitler's obsessions was off, he might have gone back to some of Schacht's ideas on fiscal restraint. That would scarcely mean a personal rehabilitation of Schacht, whom Goering had been so personally instrumental in thrusting aside. It could be argued, however, that Hitler's extravagant armament program sooner or later threatened national bankruptcy. His departure, and with it the abandonment or at least the easing of the single-minded obsession with wholesale eastern expansion, might have cleared the way to something like rational economic policy.

Among the most interesting and significant consequences of Hitler's demise would be those associated with developments within the Nazi Party. The first reaction was almost certain to be something like a closing of ranks. Hitler's policy had been to encourage rivalries by duplicating responsibilities to the point where there were innumerable animosities, and scarcely a single close friendship, among his chief lieutenants. But it would now be a matter of hanging together if one did not wish to hang separately. This would probably evoke a tendency for a time to rally behind Goering, but that did not mean that everyone could now feel secure in his own particular political niche. Goering himself, for example, had much resented the way Himmler had been able to edge him out of the control and development of the political police. Not many months would pass before the pulling and hauling of the various inter-party rivalries could be expected to resume with new force. And there was little love lost between Goering and Goebbels. The latter was in many ways the most fanatical among the Nazi political leaders. Goering, on the other hand, was much the least ideological among them. His public poses might appear to give the lie to this, but they were assumed by those in the know to fall into line with the Fuehrer rather than representing strong political commitment. Goering, in short, can perhaps be labelled the most opportunistic of Hitler's paladins, ready to switch in any direction that promised to enhance his power.

Generally speaking, Party solidarity at lower levels without Hitler in the picture would leave a good deal to be wished for. The slaughter of so many Brown Shirt leaders in the June 1934 Blood Purge had left deep scars, so much so that as late as the 1938 Blomberg-Fritsch crisis, S.A. chief Victor Lutze had actually offered to cooperate with the Army against the S.S. While it would be too much to maintain that Nazism without

Hitler was bound to fade in Germany, there was small prospect of maintaining the élan and solidarity for which he had been the inspiration.

What of the Third Reich's anti-Semitic programs? Had it not been for the events of the previous half year one might have hoped for a substantial reversal of these policies. But the bitter memories of the November 1938 "crystal night" and the subsequent systematic plundering of the Jewish community cast an indelible shadow on any such prospects. Too many individuals and Party agencies were now too committed to extreme courses. Goering's own anti-Semitism sat lightly upon him. We need remind ourselves only of his famed "I will decide who is a Jew in the Air Ministry." What one could expect is that the Nazis' fanatical anti-Semitic drive would be somewhat allayed.

The area where Germany without Hitler was likely to see the greatest changes was in foreign relations. If his departure had taken place only a few weeks earlier, i.e. before his march into rump Czechoslovakia, the difference would have been far greater. It is highly doubtful whether Goering would have taken that step on his own. But now to repudiate that policy in which Goering had indeed taken a principal part would have gone against the normal rules governing national prestige. The most that could have been expected, at least for the time being, was some relaxation of the severities of German control over Bohemia-Moravia, perhaps with the grant of considerable autonomy. In any event we may be sure that Goering would not have installed a man of the stamp of Reinhard Heydrich as successor to Baron von Neurath as Reich Protector.

The primary issue for the policies of a post-Hitler regime would of course have been, a war with Poland in 1939? Hitler got away with the attack on Poland because the reputation he had gained via Munich as a diplomat had lent credibility among the generals to his claim that Britain and France would again prove quiescent. Goering, who had had a long-term assignment to butter up Polish leaders in the role of jovial host and hunting companion, would have found it psychologically easier to call off the dogs of war and pretend that no bellicose intentions had existed. He would almost certainly have gotten rid of the universally detested Ribbentrop and quite probably would have called back to the foreign ministry Baron von Neurath, who was generally respected in the western capitals. Goering had cooperated with him closely in September 1938 to prepare the way for the Munich compromise. In short, war with Poland in 1939 was unlikely in a Germany ruled by Hermann Goering.

Whether such a conflict could be put off indefinitely is another matter. The frontiers with Poland were the one foreign relations issue on which there was something like a national consensus in Germany. The post-1919 settlement in Upper Silesia was considered grossly unfair, and the Corridor a political and geographic impossibility. It was that issue, incidentally, on which Germany enjoyed a good deal of sympathy in Britain. If Hitler had *started* with Poland instead of imposing his pressures as the climax of a string of aggressive moves elsewhere, the British guarantee of that country would have been unthinkable. What does appear certain, however, is that no post-Hitler government of Germany would have seriously considered a war on Poland at the risk of a European and world conflict. At worst the continent could have expected a series of localized initiatives — perhaps culminating in a second Munich, this one honored by all the contracting parties.

In London and Paris the removal of Hitler would have evoked a vast sigh of relief. Though Goering was looked upon as a bombastic clown, enough was known about his lethargic and sybaritic disposition to assume that with his accession much of the aggressive drive would depart from Germany. Yet though anxieties about further expansive moves from Berlin would have been much allayed, the objective power of the expanded Reich offered reason enough for continued concern. One is reminded of Bismarck's dictum that the Reich as he had created it was already a satiated state, that the addition of further territory such as the possible annexation of the German-speaking parts of Austria would only pressure the neighboring states to unite against her. In short, the sheer strength of the post-1938 German Reich was enough to assure that France and Britain would draw closer together to restore a disturbed balance of power.

For the same reason, despite Stalin's resentment of western appeasement policies, the big currents of European affairs were such that, despite frequent setbacks, a growing Moscow-London-Paris entente could be predicted with some certainty. For the time being, relations between Moscow and Berlin would be much eased by Hitler's departure. Stalin had already in early March made a pronouncement to the effect that the contrasting ideologies of two countries should not impede cordial relations. Though this was to be taken with more than a grain of salt, it began the smoothing of the road between the two capitals that culminated in the Hitler-Stalin pacts of August and September. Though anti-Bolshevism remained strong in Germany, it would now lack the bite of Hitler's single-minded obsession with wholesale eastern expansion.

In the Far East the assassination of Hitler could well have meant the return to a policy leaning toward China. The switch to a pro-Japanese policy had been entirely his own and had come in 1935 with startling suddenness at the very time the future Field Marshal von Reichenau was in China with a gift for Chiang-Kai-Shek. He had been suddenly recalled. World War I memories had until then dictated predominant German sympathies for China. With Hitler out of the way and the elimination or at least weakening of plans for wholesale eastern expansion, Berlin's heavy banking on Japanese partnership against the Soviet Union would be much weakened. With the fading of the prospect of close relations with Berlin, there was likely to be some corresponding weakening of the influence of the militaristic expansionist trends in Japanese policy. The combination of the lessening of the prospect of German cooperation against the Soviet Union and the military setbacks suffered in 1938 and 1939 in border clashes with the Soviets would give pause to thoughts of northern expansion.

Curbing of Japanese ambitions in turn would be reassuring to the United States, and, combined with lowered anxiety about German expansion, could have some dampening effect on the accelerating naval program. Any amelioration of the more extreme Nazi policies, notably in the area of anti-Semitism, would also be reassuring and decrease anxieties about curbing German expansionism in Europe. In short, a Germany without Hitler would have significantly increased isolationist sentiments in the U.S. — perhaps, ironically, making Roosevelt's third-term victory over internationalist Wendell Wilkie a good deal easier.

[1] A brief survey of the course of relations between army and regime before the summer of 1938 may be found in Harold C. Deutsch, "German Soldiers in the 1938 Munich Crisis," in Francis R. Nicosia and Lawrence D. Stokes, eds., *Non-Conformity, Opposition and Resistance in the Third Reich* (London: Berg Publishers, 1990), 305-321

[2] See Harold C. Deutsch, *Hitler and His Generals: The Hidden Crisis of January to June, 1938* (Minneapolis: University of Minnesota Press, 1974), 220-227

[3] The full story of the Goerdeler and Beck missions as well as that of the opposition message to Washington may be found in Deutsch, "German Soldiers in the 1938 Munich Crises."

[4] Interview with Elisabeth Gaertner-Struenck, 18 April 1970

5. Wiedemann interview, 11 July 1970. The basic facts do not depend alone on his testimony.

6. Interview with Friedrich Wilhelm Heinz, 24 August 1958, and his 203 page manuscript, "Von Wilhelm Canaris zum NKVD."

7. Grosskreuz interview, 15 January, 1970.

8. One must at least reckon with the possibility that Halder's claim that he had converted Brauchitsch does not hold water. In that event, the commander-in-chief could have approached Fritsch to consult with him about a possible employment during the coming war, indicating that Brauchitsch was prepared to go ahead with it. Against this some weight may be given to the thesis that, as Brauchitsch seems to have had no thought of employing Fritsch in September 1939, he was not likely to have considered it a year earlier.

9. The list of those Goerdeler spoke to in the United States alone reads like a roll of figures who counted in foreign relations: Herbert Hoover, Cordell Hull, Henry Wallace, Henry Stimson, Henry Morgenthau, Jr., Owen D. Young, Sumner Welles, G. C. Messersmith. Only Franklin D. Roosevelt is absent.

10. As related to the writer by Ambassador Osusky.

11. Jiri Hochman, *The Soviet Union and the Failure of Collective Security*, 1934-1938 (Ithaca, NY: Cornell University Press, 1984), 194-201.

12. As related by him to his nephew, Vaclav Benes, who in turn recounted it to the writer.

13. Basic aspects of the military confrontation in 1938 between Germany and her prospective foes are searchingly analyzed by Williamson Murray in *The Change in the European Balance of Power, 1938-1939* (Princeton, NJ: Princeton University Press, 1984), 2177-263.

14. The essential story is in Paul Stehlin, *Temoinage pour l'histoire* (Paris: R. Lafond, 1964). Additional information was provided by General Stehlin in an interview of February 1970.

15. Interview with General Gerhard Engel, who had been Hitler's army adjutant, 24 June 1970.

16. The marriage was not officially consummated until the winter of 1938-1939.

17. The authoritative voice and pen of B.H. Liddell Hart preached that the advance of motorization actually strengthened the defense by conferring greater mobility in the use of machine and anti-tank guns. History, he argued, taught that the loser would be "the army which was the first to commit itself to the attack."

18. The French military attaché in Prague, General Fourchet, was so outraged that he later renounced his citizenship.

19. Interview with General Paul Stehlin, Paris, 12 February, 1975

Chapter 2

August-September 1939

John Kim Munholland

This chapter examines the last moments of peace in Europe and the situation that emerged after war erupted between Germany and Poland, sustained by Great Britain and France. Its approach will be that of creating an intelligence assessment by making an evaluation of alternative scenarios and then pursue the likely outcomes or options, in terms that are familiar to intelligence analysts as being possible, probably or likely. In examining alternatives to the events of this crucial period, we might consider first whether war might have been avoided entirely, and then to speculate upon other alternatives to the way in which the war became an enervating phony war in the absence of decisive action by the western allies. In short, the underlying issue is whether or not Hitler might have been prevented from having his war in 1939, or assuring that if the war came he might have been more effectively challenged, if not halted. The main concern is the question of deterrence, blocking Hitler, either by actions that would cause him to stop short of war or actions that might produce a change in regime and the elimination of Hitler. Could Hitler have been stopped, contained or frustrated in his ambitions, including his determination to have his war in Poland as a prelude to his destruction of the French army as a threat to his ultimate goal of *Lebensraum* in Eastern Europe?

A. What if Stalin had signed with the west?

In retrospect it appears that the Nazi-Soviet pact of 1939, an event that precipitated the outbreak of war in Europe and that struck observers at the time and since as a "thunderclap," was less surprising than the alternative of a political and military agreement with the western powers. The ideological war of words between the Soviets and Nazi Germany had obscured the hard reality that the western allies could offer Stalin less than could Hitler, who was prepared to concede temporarily a vast Soviet sphere of influence in the Baltic — a particularly important concern for Stalin — and Eastern Europe, notably a recovery of territory that had been "lost" to Poland as a result of the 1921 Treaty of Riga and a repossession of Bessarabia from Rumania. At least this was Stalin's assumption, tied to his conviction that the west needed his alliance more than he needed western support. The western allies wished to preserve the status quo in Europe and asked, belatedly, for Soviet willingness to risk war with Germany for non-existent gains. Stalin was determined that Russia would not bleed for the benefit of the British Empire and have nothing to show for his sacrifice. On the other hand, diplomatic exchanges with Germany that began after Stalin's speech to the Eighteenth Party Congress in March, 1939 hinted at regaining an impressive sphere of influence in Eastern Europe through an arrangement with Germany. The Soviets raised their demands, and from July 1939 there was little doubt that Hitler and Ribbentrop were prepared to meet them — at least temporarily.

The British and French guarantees to Poland ironically gave Stalin the ability to engage in a bidding war for his favor. When Chamberlain and Daladier offered their guarantees to Poland, they should have made such support meaningful with a previous or simultaneous agreement with the USSR in the spring rather than in August of 1939.

Without that assurance, the western guarantee to Poland gave Stalin an unexpected bargaining chip in dealing with Hitler. In turn, the failure to come to terms with Stalin deprived the west, as Hitler noted, of its trump suit. Thus, as of May 1939 any assessment of the prospects for a western agreement with the Soviets, rather than an arrangement with Germany, should have been rated as unlikely. Nevertheless, for the purposes of this argument, we assume that Stalin concluded in the summer of 1939 that Hitler remained a more serious threat to the USSR than did the capitalist west in both the long and the short term, and he chose to continue a path of containment by reaching agreement with the western delegation in August.

We know the conditions that Stalin would have insisted upon for any western alliance. Access of Soviet troops into Poland and Rumania and guarantees of Soviet security demands in the Baltic states would have been part of any arrangement with the west if the Soviets were to have an impact in deterring Hitler from an aggression in Eastern Europe. In short, Great Britain and France would have had to accept a Soviet sphere of domination in Eastern Europe from the Baltic to the western shore of the Black Sea. These were the conditions presented to the allied delegation when it arrived in Moscow on August 11 to begin conversations on a possible military convention. This was a substantial price. Nevertheless, "what if" these conditions had been met? Stalin had signed with the west, and Hitler had to contemplate a full scale war against three major powers if he insisted upon his invasion and military campaign in Poland in the late summer of 1939. Stalin also had need of the western alliance, and confronting Hitler in 1939 would have been less catastrophic for the USSR than in 1941. Would Hitler have pulled back from a full-scale European war that might have escalated into a world conflict in the event of a Soviet-western pact, or would he have plunged ahead with his determination to destroy Poland before embarking upon his campaign in the west?

While it is risky to guess what Hitler's reaction might have been, given his mood swings, it is clear that he was both determined to have his military conquest of Poland and anxious about the reaction of Great Britain. All accounts suggest Hitler's high degree of nervousness during the jockeying for position that summer; his edginess reflected his anxiety about keeping Great Britain out of his Polish war, even after the conclusion of the Nazi-Soviet pact and Ribbentrop's fatuous assurances that the British would never honor their pledge to Poland. Hitler cancelled orders for an attack literally at the last minute on August 25. This suggests a high degree of anxiety.

A major reason for this anxiety and the last minute cancellation was Hitler's realization that Mussolini would remain neutral in the event of a war with Poland. Just a few days earlier on August 22 in his speech to his military commanders at the Berghof, Hitler had boasted of Mussolini's loyalty as one of three major advantages that Germany had in the event of a war to crush Poland. In the early afternoon of the 25th this assurance was swept away when the Italian ambassador in Berlin, Bernardo Attolico, delivered Mussolini's telegram, informing Hitler that Italy would remain neutral in event of war with Poland. Hitler was visibly shaken by this news and immediately called General Keitel to cancel plans for the imminent attack. One of Mussolini's arguments, beside his army's lack of preparation, was his conviction that Britain would intervene, leaving Italy's coast exposed to the Royal Navy. Three days later Hitler had recovered his nerve and ordered an attack upon Poland, arguing that Italian neutrality best served Germany's interests. Thus, Hitler went ahead, and his hesitation of the 25th, while dramatic, was not a permanent renunciation.

Despite his determination to "resolve" the Polish question before the onset of the fall rains, Hitler might have been forced to at least a short-term postponement rather than confront a stiffened Great Britain, a hostile rather than a friendly and neutral USSR, and a still-feared French army on the western frontier. An Anglo-French-Soviet alliance *might* have deterred Hitler's aggression, at least in 1939. Without an isolated Poland, even a gambling risk-taker might have hesitated to precipitate a drawn-out two front war, something that Hitler claimed he would never do and something that the whole concept of blitzkrieg was designed to avoid. The historical judgment on whether or not a triple alliance of France, Great Britain and the Soviet Union, reviving the 1914 coalition, would have sufficed to postpone war in September 1939 is at best a conditional one; it *might* have worked. One scenario, then, is that the Soviet-western pact might have forced Hitler to abandon his plan for a Polish campaign in the later summer of 1939. Hitler's postponement would have been a disappointment, accompanied by the usual tirades, but it would have been no more than a temporary set-back to his determination to reorder the map of Eastern Europe and pursue his fundamental objective of expansion there. What the western-Soviet agreement would have caused may be seen as an alteration of Hitler's tactics, not his objectives.

A likely outcome of this postponement, then, would have been a further shuffling and period of maneuver in the alliance systems of Eastern Europe. Given Hitler's opportunism, Nazi foreign policy might have engaged in several ways of creating confusion among Hitler's likely opponents in Eastern Europe and might have spurred him to foster distrust and undermine the western-Soviet pact as well. With Hitler's predilection for pressing initiatives in several directions to see what might work to his advantage, one could imagine his beginning a campaign to promote German interests in Eastern Europe by trying to soften up Poland, even to the point of granting concessions that might undermine Poland's need for guarantees from the western powers. He could have worked upon the fears and antagonisms among the often quarreling states of Eastern Europe by embarking upon a series of bilateral deals. He could also have tried to undermine any western accord with the Soviet Union, perhaps by raising the stakes toward the Soviets, or by offering some olive branch to the west that might have left him free to turn eastward, assured that the French army would be neutral. Alternatively, his maneuvers in Eastern Europe might have assured neutrality, with the smaller states of the east serving as a buffer between Germany and the USSR. enabling him to concentrate upon an attack and, presumably, rapid victory against France and Great Britain. With a western agreement with the Soviet Union, his most likely first gambit would have been to find a way to neutralize the situation on his eastern frontier.

All of the states of Eastern Europe found themselves shaken by the events of Munich. Hitler might have seen an opportunity to embark upon a diplomatic offensive in which he would portray Nazi Germany as the guarantor of security in Eastern Europe against the dangers of Soviet intervention with western approval. The immediate goal would have been obtaining the neutrality of Eastern Europe through diplomatic means, including a systematic wooing of Poland. Hitler had pursued an option of this sort in his various proposals keeping the Poles quiescent as he turned his attention westward. This would have deprived the west of an issue — the protection of Poland's territorial integrity — that was at the heart of its guarantees.

Whatever Polish Foreign Minister Beck's reaction would have been, German efforts to strengthen ties with Poland and, for that matter, with the other smaller states of Eastern Europe would have represented a return to German diplomatic efforts during the winter of 1938-39 when, up to 25 March and the final dismemberment of Czechoslovakia, Hitler's intention was to neutralize these states. His tactic had been to get them to join the Anti-Comintern Pact, thereby assuring their passivity as he turned his attention toward the western allies and prepared for war in that direction. A signing of an Anglo-French-Soviet pact might easily have produced a renewed offensive in this sense whereby Poland, Hungary and Rumania, despite the serious ethnic quarrel between the latter two, would be urged to join this pact. This, of course, would have vitiated the British-French guarantee to Poland, and it would have required the burying of deep seated nationalistic conflicts in the region. Alternatively, as Hitler would do during his diplomatic offensives in the winter of 1940-41, he might well have negotiated a series of bilateral agreements in a "divide and conquer" diplomatic initiative. Hitler's preference for bilateral arrangements is well known. Given the remarkable fluidity of the diplomatic situation in Eastern Europe that followed Munich, however, another reversal in Hitler's plan of action was at least possible as a consequence of a western agreement with the Soviets.

A variation on this 1938-9 gambit might have been to split the USSR from the western allies by proposing some sort of vast Eastern European security pact with a German guarantee. Such an effort would have been undertaken as the necessary prelude to secure Hitler's eastern frontier while concentrating his forces against the western powers. One can assume that German diplomacy, orchestrated by Hitler, would have sent up several trial balloons in the winter of 1938-39, reflecting not only Hitler's tendency to gamble, but also his opportunism. An implication of Stalin's agreement with France and Great Britain would have been another shift in Nazi diplomacy, no longer to isolate Poland but to prepare for a war in the west. This preparation would undoubtedly have revived and strengthened the military leadership's opposition to a policy that would have led to a generalized European conflict. While war with Poland, if isolated, might have been acceptable to the High Command, a war against a British-French coalition, perhaps backed by a Soviet intervention into Poland, Rumania and the Baltic states, would have been regarded with alarm as a foolish plunge into a protracted conflict Germany could not win. A western-Soviet accord, followed by Hitler's return to his original notion of a western offensive to eliminate the threat of the French army prior to embarking upon his fundamental goal of *Lebensraum* in the east, might have galvanized the military opposition into renewed plotting after the Munich crisis had thrown them into confusion. We know that the opposition embarked upon a further round of conspiracies against Hitler, culminating in the events of November 5, 1939 when Brauchitsch quailed before an infuriated Fuhrer and backed away from pressing on with efforts to remove him. Without this victory and with only a possible Polish guarantee of neutrality, or even a Soviet/Eastern European non-aggression pact, the prospects of a successful campaign in the West would have looked even less promising than they actually appeared in November 1939. A revived opposition in the aftermath of an agreement between the western powers and the USSR, followed by a possible agreement between Nazi Germany and Poland, may be considered possible.

We know that the generals and the anti-Hitler conspirators were strongly opposed to any western adventure and most likely would have been just as determined to block a western campaign even with the reassurance of a neutralized eastern frontier. The German military leadership continued to regard the French army as a potentially dangerous adversary, and memories of the western front stalemate of 1914-18 were constantly in the minds of German commanders. A correspondingly reasonable assumption is that the opposition would have seen the plunge into war in the west as a dangerous folly that would have justified intervention to bring down the regime. To precipitate this drastic action, the military would have required firm evidence that a war in the west was coming and that their attempt would be generally supported both within the ranks of the army and by a civilian population equally fearful that a war with the west might become protracted, devastating and lead to defeat.

Might the existence of an agreement with the USSR have further stiffened the French and British opposition to Hitler, or have led them to engage seriously the internal German opposition? A delay of the outbreak of war in the east and renewed efforts of the opposition to prevent a conflict might have enabled further contacts between the conspirators and the western leadership. That such contacts took place, and would occur again during the phony war, is well known. Less certain is the response that might have been produced. Neither the British nor the French seemed persuaded that the resistance could end the regime with encouragement from western statesmen. More likely is the scenario in which the resistance would have had to rely upon its own resources for the coup, and clearly the military conspiracy would have required sound evidence that war with the west was inevitable and likely to lead to disaster for Germany. Whatever the attitude of the west, a successful coup would have ended the Nazi regime.

Another possible scenario is that Hitler might have pursued his war against Poland even with a western military agreement with the Soviet Union. Hitler appeared determined to have his war in Poland as early as May, before there was much more than rumor of a rapprochement between Berlin and Moscow. If the agreement between the west and Moscow allowed Soviet forces to enter Poland, and if the allies were committed to take forceful action against Germany's western border, Hitler might have hesitated to engage the Soviets in Poland. However, Hitler had an even greater contempt for the Soviet military, following the purges, than did the western allies. We now know, not only as seen in the Winter War with Finland but as a result of recent Soviet revelations, that Stalin's impact upon the Soviet army was even more devastating than anyone in either the west or Germany imagined at the time. Given Hitler's convictions that Soviet communism was rotten to the core and the Slavs were an inferior race, he might well have pressed on with his war in Poland, convinced that it would be over before the Soviets could get moving or the west could lift a hand to aid either their Polish or Soviet allies. When General Keitel expressed some of the military fear that an attack on Poland meant expansion into a general European conflict that might ultimately bring in the United States, Hitler assured Keitel that the Soviet deal was his insurance policy against such an eventuality. Hitler may well have gone ahead with his war against Poland with or without the Nazi-Soviet pact. What is certain is that he seems determined, after a brief crisis of nerves on August 25, to have had his war whatever the risks once the agreement was signed.

B. What if Hitler had recognized that the western powers would fight, and that a long war was in prospect?

The answer to this question takes us again back to the western guarantees to Poland that came in the Spring of 1939. Hitler could only assume that the Nazi-Soviet pact had checked allied assurances to Poland by depriving the western powers of any ability to bring meaningful aid in time. The preponderance of evidence suggests that Hitler was determined to eliminate Poland as a threat on his eastern border before turning west. Hitler's demands on Poland were calculated to be rejected, showing his determination to launch the military operation, whatever the risk. Hitler struck under circumstances in which he knew that the western powers would honor their obligations to Poland. He may have held a faint hope that the appeasers would again flinch, but it appears that in ordering his attack on Poland, he had decided to take the fatal plunge by eliminating the threat of a Polish "stab in the back" before dealing with the French army. In short, the preponderance of evidence suggests that Hitler had decided to have "his" war in

September, even if it meant a conflict with the west, and perhaps even because it meant dealing with the west sooner rather than later. Evidence for this view can be adduced indirectly from Hitler's seemingly diffident response to the news that Great Britain and France had declared war on Germany.

This apparent decision meant that Hitler accepted the risk not only of a local, but a general war in September 1939, despite the reservations of his military leadership, and despite Germany's lack of preparation for a long and drawn out war. We know that the Germany that went to war in September 1939 was not ready for a "total" war effort. Even into the attack on the USSR two years later, Germany had not mobilized for a full wartime economy. Hitler always claimed that the quick strikes of the lightning war obviated any need for long-term planning and preparation. At some point, of course, a huge war effort would be necessary. Nevertheless, given the lack of preparation in the west, his dismissal of the Soviet army as an effective fighting force, and his conviction that bluff and determination would prevail over the timorous democratic leaders, Hitler did not, as A. J. P. Taylor argues, blunder into a general war in 1939. To be sure, that war proved quite different from what he hoped to have: a quick victory, followed by some breathing space. For Hitler timing was all important. Having once accomplished his strategic objective of a neutralized eastern frontier, he could not hesitate too long before dealing with the threat in the west. That became apparent with the orders that Hitler gave almost immediately upon conclusion of the Polish campaign.

A corollary of this question is whether or not the certainty of a long war would have been a sufficient deterrent for Hitler. Here the temptation is to see Hitler holding back, sharing his generals' conviction that a long war would be fatal for Germany. This question is difficult to answer, even tentatively, since Hitler often acted on impulse to take advantage of a momentary opportunity. He held the conviction that a long war had been fatal for Germany in 1914-18, and his diplomatic-military strategies were predicated on avoiding that danger, primarily in avoiding a two-front war. The most reasonable speculation is that Hitler, particularly after the Nazi-Soviet Pact, became convinced that he had not only isolated Poland but avoided the trap of a two-front war. Had Hitler expected a longer war in 1939, then a quite different set of plans and preparations would at least have been initiated. We know that there was little of that; instead, Hitler cancelled plans for aircraft carrier development and for two proposed additional battleships that were to have been laid down. Hitler's war planning, like his diplomatic initiatives, had an improvised quality that belies any sense of urgency about preparations for a lengthy war effort.

It might be mentioned that Hitler did not see the war expanding beyond Europe. He was convinced that the United States would remain isolationist. If necessary, Japan might be useful in keeping the Americans isolated and in providing a baton to wave at the British Empire in Asia. It should be noted, however, that Hitler apparently set little stock in the Japanese alliance. His signing of the Nazi-Soviet pact had greatly alarmed Japanese leaders, who ultimately sought their own version of a non-aggression pact with the Soviet Union in April 1941 and decided to turn south in their pursuit of resources that would enable them to bring the war with China to a conclusion, despite the risk of war with the British Empire and the United States. Hitler showed little concern for these long-term or global implications of his decision to go to war in Europe, despite the grandiose nature of his speeches about world conquest and a thousand year Reich. Indeed, Hitler tended to disregard the global perspective in favor of a war for European domination.

It may be questioned whether or not Hitler would have been dissuaded from the war that began in Poland even if he had realized that it would last three years, since he tended to underestimate the long-term consequences of any event. This issue was crucial, however, to the arguments of the anti-war opposition, who correctly foresaw that in a longer conflict that would marshal the resources of the United States behind an anti-German, western alliance, the Germans would be at a disadvantage, even with the prospects of securing resources from the USSR as a result of the continuance of the Nazi-Soviet agreement. Had Hitler been committed to a long war of attrition against the British Empire, then his planning would have been quite different. Instead he remained supremely confident right up to the attack upon the Soviet Union in 1941 that he could eliminate his opponents one by one.

Hitler was confident that the war could be contained during his planning for the western campaign, and even up to the eve of his attack upon the Soviet Union in 1941. His refusal to listen to the cautions of his military leaders on the eve of the western offensive provides evidence of his determination to go ahead in the face of the reservations of his military professionals. Hitler had to defeat the French army: its elimination was a basic condition for one of his obsessions: an eastward expansion. In looking at Hitler's improvised tactics, historians sometimes overlook his permanent fixations. The principle that had decisive significance for his military planning was the securing of *Lebensraum* in the east. To accomplish this, the destruction of the French threat was essential, and it was important in 1938-1940 to move quickly while he held the advantage of a neutralized eastern frontier. He contemptuously dismissed his generals' reservations, most dramatically in the attempt by Brauchitsch and Halder to obtain postponement of the western operation on November 5, 1939. Once the French army no longer threatened, the gate to the eastern lands could be thrown open. Unlike his generals, who feared a reenactment of the World War I stalemate on the Western Front, Hitler saw an opportunity for a quick victory that might not occur again, but, if successful, would assure him of mastery on the continent, whatever Great Britain might do once France had fallen. He still did not believe that his war in Europe, fought in blitzkrieg fashion, meant a world war. Had Hitler shared his generals' concern about a general European or World War, he might have acted differently. But he would also have acted out of character.

C. What if the French had launched an all-out attack to help the Poles?

This question raises the issue of "the unfought battle" on the Franco-German front in September, 1939. The reasons why this battle was never undertaken have been extensively discussed. Explanations range from faulty intelligence, Gamelin's hesitation, a military leadership that took refuge in the strategy of a lengthy war of attrition, lack of political or moral will, obsession with the defensive strategy embodied in the Maginot line, memories of the bloodletting of 1914-1918 resulting in the "unborn generation" of military age [18-22 year olds] that was not available for military service during the mid and late 1930s, and even treasonous behavior or at least cowardice on the part of appeasers. We know that the French military leadership did not have plans for an offensive strike into Germany as an option available in September 1939. [The French army's operational plan was a counterpunch that involved a thrust into Belgium and the southern tip of the Netherlands as soon as a German offensive was launched in the west.] Gamelin's directive of May 31, 1939 called for an offensive of 35-38 divisions to be mounted by the fifteenth day of mobilization, but this proved to be no more than a "reconnaissance in force" as the Poles would discover to their dismay in September.

The French High Command neither revised its strategy nor seriously contemplated a major offensive that would most likely have involved violation of Belgian and Dutch neutrality. Despite the reputation of certain French leaders' record of appeasement, there is evidence that a stronger political will had developed in France following the Munich conference, seen in Daladier's break with the Popular Front, his decrees designed to strengthen defense industries, and a public consensus in favor of a much stiffer opposition toward Germany in the winter of 1938-1939. On the other hand, the dithering of the French political and military leadership during the time of the phony war, and the army's previous and disastrous experiences with "offensive" plans in 1914 and 1917, suggest that the chances of a rapid and radical change of French strategic doctrine was not likely to occur between the commitment to defend Poland in March 1939 and the attack upon France in May 1940. Recent scholarship suggests that French military leadership, despite its strong preference for a defensive strategy, was not unsympathetic to ideas of mobile, mechanized warfare. The difficulty is that this approach remained cast in a defensive context. The mobility into the low countries, which contributed to the disaster of 1940, remained largely part of a response to a German attack. The possibility of using Belgium for offensive operations against Germany may be seen in Gamelin's argument to Daladier that the right to use Belgian territory would permit the establishment of advanced air bases and offer a better terrain for an attack into the Ruhr than the narrow opening between the Rhine and the Moselle, which could be easily defended. This notion, however, remained no more than a hypothesis. The French government had no intention of violating its promise to respect Belgian neutrality.

These long-standing debates cannot be revisited here. Instead, as part of the "what if" of this question, the assumptions are that the French army had the option of an offensive operation prepared and available, and that the political leaders insisted that France fulfill the letter of its obligation to the Polish government to begin offensive operations against Germany in the west no later than two weeks after mobilization. In order for this "what if" to be developed, we must assume that French military and political leaders had the plans, the means, and the will to launch an offensive into Germany. Could this have been done in time to alter the outcome of the conflict? What would have been the most likely results both militarily and in terms of the future of the Nazi regime? And what might have been the outlines of a peace agreement, assuming the outcome of the French offensive was a victorious one?

Had the French launched an attack, it probably would have been successful. German defense in the west rested upon the incomplete fortifications of the West Wall and on a military force that was totally inadequate to meet a major attack. The postwar testimonies and memoirs of the German generals all express astonishment at French inaction. The German forces at the outbreak of hostilities consisted of twenty-five reserve and second line replacement and militia divisions that had little training for combat situations, backed by eleven first line divisions. (25 is the standard number: Goutard has his own reasons for exaggerating the figure). In his postwar testimony, General Jodl claimed that the reserves were poorly trained and their mobilization was extremely slow and disorganized. He declared that the German victory in Poland occurred only because there was no battle on the Western Front. General Westphal has left a similarly pessimistic assessment of German military strength in the west, noting that there was not enough ammunition for more than three days fighting. Morale for the German troops in the west was also considered less than desirable, no better than for French troops in 1940. One of the ablest of the German generals, Colonel General Kurt von Hammerstein, regarded his northern sector's defense as inadequate and even contemplated luring Hitler to Cologne as a way of eliminating the Fuehrer, reflecting both his hatred for the regime and his conviction that a war would be disastrous for Germany.

On the other hand, by 10 September the French army had mobilized one hundred ten first line divisions, of which eighty-five were available to Gamelin, making allowances for protecting the Italian frontier and providing for colonial defenses. All of the French tanks, some 3,200, could be used while almost the entire German armor was engaged in Poland. French artillery was available in large numbers and high quality, capable, according to Gamelin, of penetrating the German defensive works. British and French forces together had nearly one thousand fighter planes at this point, while most of the German aircraft had been concentrated in the east. In equipment the French had major advantages, although their tanks were not designed for rapid mobility, in manpower they held a nearly three to one superiority. Gamelin himself claims that as early as 4 September he had forty divisions mobilized in the central sector of the front between the Rhine and the Moselle, while the Germans were still assembling their troops in the west.

Senior German generals in the region maintained that the French forces would have reached Mainz, trapped the best German divisions in the Saar "sack," and taken the Ruhr within two weeks. With western Germany open much of the country's industrial strength would have been vulnerable. Beyond this, again according to Westphal, French forces could easily have crossed the Rhine and, as he noted at the Nuremberg Trial, "the whole face of Europe would have been changed." Decisive French action in the west would have in particular encouraged the German generals to turn against Hitler, confirming their fears that he was leading the country to disaster. Although alarmed at the consequences of a protracted war with the western powers, Halder doubted the willingness of the population or the army to support a coup unless some dramatic event, such as allied bombing of German industrial regions or a military defeat on the western front, occurred to convince German opinion that Hitler had embarked upon a fatal course. Without some dramatic demonstration that a war against the western powers might prove fatal or result in a protracted and debilitating war, the military resistance hesitated to act, although convinced that such a war would lead eventually to Germany's defeat. Had the western powers bombed German industrial targets in the west and/or invaded and occupied the western industrial regions of Germany, then Hitler might have suffered a decisive blow to his prestige in the eyes of the German people, who would have accepted a move to remove him. The military conspiracy revived after the triumph in Poland when it became apparent that Hitler was determined to move quickly toward an offensive against the western allies, producing the famous crisis of October and November, 1939. Was this crisis imminent in September, particularly as a reaction to a [presumably] successful French attack in the west?

The opposition continued to look at the western powers as their "natural allies." Would this alliance have been so natural in time of war, in the middle of a military campaign in Poland that promised victory and was generally supported by the military leadership? The basis for opposition to Hitler's military plans rested upon fears of a protracted western campaign, not upon concern for Polish military prowess. The danger of the Polish situation was that it would bring a response from the west that would threaten German security, and the French attack might have confirmed military concerns over the prospects of a long war, particularly one in which the French controlled crucial industrial resources. There was a strong and significant opposition to a war in the west after the Polish defeat, but opposing this war in the midst of a military campaign would have been difficult to mount.

While there appears to have been some revival of the opposition to Hitler in the Foreign Office, just before and after the outbreak of war, there were two gestures toward the western powers by the opposition during the actual course of the Polish campaign. One of these came through the efforts made by the former deputy mayor of Berlin, Fritz Elsas, to urge that the western powers attack in order to relieve the pressure on Poland. The outcome of this effort is significant and revealing. His contact, a member of the opposition in exile in Denmark, Dr. Hans Robinson, discouraged any action that might make it more difficult to end the war. The other attempt came from the military side when General Hammerstein made his "last play" to lure Hitler to Cologne on the pretext that this would deceive the allies on German strength in that sector. Once he had Hitler in Cologne, Hammerstein intended to kill him. The British were informed of this plot through their consul in Wiesbaden, but the assassination failed to occur when Hitler rejected the idea of going to Cologne at that time.

With Germany in danger, threatened by enemies to east and west, one can well imagine Hitler denouncing the treachery of it all and Dr. Goebbels creating a noisy propaganda campaign to whip up German feelings against the traditional enemy, France, [backed by Great Britain], which was playing a dangerous game of exposing both Germany and all of Europe to the spread of Communism. One can, then, imagine Hitler employing all means to generate mass support behind him, a man beleaguered for simply asserting Germany's rightful claims. Such an appeal to nationalism in a time when the state was in danger, would have made the actions of the opposition in toppling Hitler more than a little complicated. The opposition argued that Hitler was leading the nation to catastrophe, as indeed he was, but this might not have been the perception of the ordinary German citizen, however reserved popular opinion might have been about the news of war in Poland on September 1. Thus a French attack in the west, even if a military success, might have had the effect of rallying opinion behind the leader at a time when the country was in mortal peril.

A possibility, then, would have been a kind of call to arms from Hitler, Goebbels and the Nazi faithful. There is an alternative scenario in which the French invasion from the west provoked the military opposition to take matters into their own hands, overthrow Hitler and establish a regime that would seek terms from the invading powers. Hitler's call to arms might have had little success in stopping the advance of western forces, and could very well have produced not so much a rally of the Germans against the allied invasion as a response from the military in leading a coup against Hitler and a war policy that had brought military disaster upon the homeland. At the very least, the defeat in the west would have had to convince the German population, which was still hoping to avoid an expansion and continuation of the war, that Hitler's policies were dangerous and disastrous for Germany's interests to be successful. A French military success in the west would have created formidable problems, which the German generals recognized in their postwar assessments. The western allies would have been in control of the industrial resources that Germany needed to sustain a major war effort. We know, too, that Hitler feared the possibility that the allies might have pressured the Belgians and the Dutch into allowing allied use of forward bases for a bombing attack against Germany.

The psychological impact is another important consideration: mention already has been made of Halder's belief that a successful air and land offensive in the west might have pushed German opinion to recognize the disastrous consequences of Hitler's policies. Whether such a military defeat would have been enough to topple Hitler's regime remains at least open to question. Still, dictators most often do not survive military defeat, and on paper the prospect of an allied victory with an attack in the west was a good one. We know from the testimonies of the German commanders that the western defenses were not in good condition, and these forces lacked ammunition, perhaps no more than three days' supply was at hand, to continue a meaningful resistance.

Furthermore, with the bulk of the German army still entangled in Poland, there was little prospect of a rapid shift from east to west in time, or in sufficient force to halt the French led offensive. By September 5, Halder described Poland as practically defeated, and two days later plans were being drawn for the transfer of troops to the western front. This assessment gives the impression that the German army could have responded rapidly to a western attack. This is somewhat misleading, given the confusion that existed in the east, including clogged roads, breakdowns, and equipment that required replacement or refitting. The military campaign in Poland might be considered won by the end of the first week of fighting. It nevertheless still required the rest of the month for mopping up operations, and so not all of the German forces could be available for an improvised defence on the western front. Even the internal lines of communication which had helped Frederick the Great achieve his "miracle" and had enabled the Germans to stave off the Russians in 1914 would have been of less advantage in 1939, assuming that the French were quickly off the mark in the west. The extraction of a significant part of the German army from the east would have proven difficult and complicated by the inevitable confusion that follows in the wake of a rapid and successful campaign. When the victory in Poland was assured and Hitler asked his generals on September 27 to begin planning for a western offensive, the earliest date that they could provide for deployment was November 5. Thus, the quick victory in the east in 1939 created conditions that left Germany exposed and vulnerable in the west, certainly through the months of September and October, had the French army been equipped and prepared to seize the initiative.

Whether or not the circumstances of a French military success in the west in September 1939 would have been more likely to bring an action on the part of the German generals to remove Hitler than if the British and French had stood up to Hitler at Munich is difficult to judge. The Munich crisis was perhaps the better moment from the point of view of the opposition to Hitler, but 1939 was the point when the allies decided to stand firm. Certainly all of the leading generals, including Brauchitsch, Halder, Leeb, Bock, Rundstedt—virtually the entire Generalitat—had been approached. Many had shown a willingness to support a coup to remove Hitler under the right conditions. Perhaps the conditions in September 1939 were not as auspicious or as likely to lead to a coup as they had been the year before at the time of Munich, but certainly the leading German generals were as alarmed as ever at the prospect of a western campaign, seen in the conspiracies that developed in the aftermath of the Polish campaign. Thus, it is likely that the generals might have initiated a coup when confronted with the prospect of a serious military defeat in the west brought on by Hitler's reckless plunge into war.

Confidence in this option is tempered by the knowledge that even the bloodletting of the First World War did not produce an upheaval sufficiently powerful and organized to topple a government until the Russian revolution in 1917. Presuming that military defeat discredited Hitler, the opposition conspiracy would have required popular support. This might have come in the form of the dissident trade union leadership, which was prepared to engage in a general strike to halt the plunge toward war. Against this prospect is the loyal support that Hitler commanded from Nazi fanatics to whom he could appeal in 1939, just as he would in the summer of 1944. The assessment of a successful opposition coup against Hitler in the midst of the Polish campaign and a

French invasion must be tempered insofar as it would have required significant planning to remove not only Hitler, but much of the party leadership that could be blamed for bringing war and defeat upon Germany. The task of the opposition remained to convince that German people, or a least convince a significant element of the elites, that a long war was not winnable and was ruinous to Germany's status as a great power.

The need was to demonstrate, as surely a French victory in the west would do, that a war policy was disastrous not only in the long run, but in the short run as well. That task could not have been accomplished easily in September, 1939 without a decisive French military offensive deep into German territory that would have deprived Germany of its industrial base and left the country open to an extensive French occupation. Yet a successful French thrust and ensuing defeat might have been the catalyst for a military move against the man who was responsible for this state of affairs. That the attack and presumed victory in the west did not come was the result of the French command's commitment to a defensive strategy, and its expectation of eventual success in a long war of attrition.

Assuming the French had launched an attack, and Hitler did not survive this disgrace but was replaced by a German equivalent of Marshal Petain or a military-civilian directory, what might have been the shape of Europe? More to the point, what might have been the basis for a negotiated peace in September under these circumstances? We have some idea of what might have been the basis of a 'compromise peace' in the negotiations that occurred between the British and the anti-Hitler opposition through the intermediary of the Vatican during the winter of 1939-1940. Had these terms been accepted as the basis of a Germany without Hitler and, presumably, reorganized on conservative/authoritarian lines, the new German government would have been allowed to retain Austria, the Sudetenland and, presumably, a militarized Rhineland. The situation in September under the "what if" scenario would, of course, have been quite different and left the leaders of the coup in a difficult bargaining position.

Hitler's replacements may have had no choice, if the French attack were fully successful, but to accept the terms that the allies, and particularly the French government, would have dictated, just as Marshal Petain had no choice but to accept the terms imposed by Hitler in June 1940. It is hard to imagine that a victorious Daladier government would have been open to a peace settlement that would have been less draconian than the Treaty of Versailles. If the French army had penetrated no farther than the Rhine, it is hard to imagine that they would have quietly retreated from this position to allow a military-backed government, even one purged of Hitler and ostensibly committed to peace, to militarize the Rhineland and maintain possession of Austria. On the latter issue, the French had opposed the union of Germany and Austria in both 1919 and 1931. There was little they could do about the Anschluss in 1938. But a victorious French army on the Rhine in September 1939 would have been a different matter, since it would have stiffened French nationalism and raised again the long-standing fear of Germany. It is hard to imagine any French statesman not seeking absolute guarantees against renewed German aggression under these circumstances. In political terms, the French might well have insisted that the Germans give up all of Hitler's gains, beginning with the 1936 Rhineland action. In economic matters, one may well imagine the French insisting upon annexation of the Saar, and if they reached the Ruhr, asking for at least an internationalization of that industrial region to deprive Germany of its industrial base and warmaking capacity.

A peace that would have followed a successful coup against Hitler in September 1939 might have been a compromise peace that would have left Germany in possession of Austria and, possibly, the Sudetenland, only if the British had been the decisive voice at the peace table, arguing against the French nationalists that a harsh peace would only once again sow the seeds of a German revenge policy. Perhaps the western allies would have accepted a compromise, or even a generous settlement with Germany as the price of "peace in our time," which meant the Europe that Hitler had recast up to the time of Munich. It is just as likely that the allies, and particularly the French, would have balked at giving any of Hitler's winnings to Hitler's successors if the French army were on the Rhine, or in possession of Germany's key industrial resources in the west.

An "enlightened peace" settlement between the victorious allies and the new government in Germany might have been possible in September-October 1939, but is highly unlikely. Had the war ended in September 1939 with a French triumph in the west, with Hitler's overthrow and the installation of a military backed government in Berlin, one can safely predict that this would have ended the European phase of the Second World War for the moment. It would not have resolved the underlying territorial, ethnic, and national conflicts that Hitler had exploited in coming to power in the first place. The world would have been spared enormous suffering and grief; such horrors as the Holocaust would never have occurred had events transpired to overthrow Hitler and end the war in September 1939, but it is hard to see that the basis for a stable Europe would necessarily have emerged from the scenario described above. Such an outcome would have depended upon the enlightened self-interest of the French leadership and the restraint of the new people in power in Germany in reaching a peace settlement that would be reasonable, just and lasting, but this seems less likely than a punitive peace imposed by the victorious powers. If the French had attacked and defeated Germany in the west, Hitler might not have survived. It is, however, questionable whether a "peace of conciliation" would necessarily result from negotiations between the allies and his successors.

Chapter 3

Phony and Hot War 1939-40

Dennis Showalter

The spring and summer of 1940 were high-water marks of the Blitzkrieg, but German margins of triumph were narrower by far than they seemed to participants. The campaign of 1940 offers corresponding prospects for the consideration of alternative lines of development. The "what ifs" presented in this chapter focus on the campaign itself. They eschew broader questions. Had France possessed a different kind of army; had Britain begun rearming earlier; had political relationships among the western powers been closer—these and similar possibilities postulate essential differences in the warring societies and their military systems. Developing them requires exploring issues outside the scope of this volume, much less this chapter; and the result would be an alternate history of the twentieth century rather than the Second World War. The following discussion avoids contrary-to-fact assumptions at the operational level as well: a second Napoleon in command of France; a Wehrmacht equipped with different models of tanks and aircraft; or a British Expeditionary Force deployed along the Meuse River instead of in central Belgium. It highlights instead behaviors possible in the context of circumstances, behaviors requiring concrete decisions other than those actually made.

Within these guidelines, among the alternatives unpursued in the first six months of 1940 five stand out as offering significant opportunities for changing the path of history. The first involved a clear choice:

A. What if the Germans had not invaded Scandinavia?

On April 8, 1940, German forces invaded Denmark and Norway in a combined-arms *tour de force* whose strategic results were at best questionable. To heavy naval losses were added the long-term burden of garrisoning a vulnerable coastline and a hostile population. During and after the war, Germany's leaders claimed they acted in part to forestall an allied initiative in Scandinavia. What if Germany had accepted the risk of sustaining Scandinavian neutrality, relying on diplomatic and economic means to secure the Reich's position in that region?

A Scandinavian operation was extremely tempting to French and British governments that initially sought large returns for small investments. Almost from the war's beginning Winston Churchill had proposed to block shipments of iron ore to Germany from Sweden through the north Norwegian port of Narvik by mining Norwegian territorial waters. On February 16, 1940, the British destroyer *Cossack* boarded a German tanker in Norwegian waters to rescue seamen captured by the *Graf Spee*. And the allies did finally lay mines in Norwegian waters on the night of April 7/8, independently of German movements and expecting a German response. The presumed German action against Norway would then inspire Norwegian acceptance of allied forces in Narvik and the southern ports.

Had Germany eschewed the invasion option it would have been highly imprudent for the allies to land troops in a Norway that stubbornly asserted its neutral rights. Had they done so, a German counterattack, with results paralleling the historical scenario, would certainly have followed.

A more promising, though perhaps less likely, alternative involved supporting the mine campaign with submarines and surface ships. German responses to this maritime campaign would have depended heavily on the strategic visions of Hitler and Raeder. The German admiral's concept of the navy's role suggest that his preferred reaction would have been to employ Germany's entire surface fleet to secure passage for the ore ships. Hitler might have agreed at least initially. But fleet and squadron actions under the conditions prevailing in the Arctic Ocean during April and May heavily favored the British. In these circumstances, particularly given the Luftwaffe's short-ranged aircraft and lack of interest in maritime operations, the *Kriegsmarine* may well have lost as

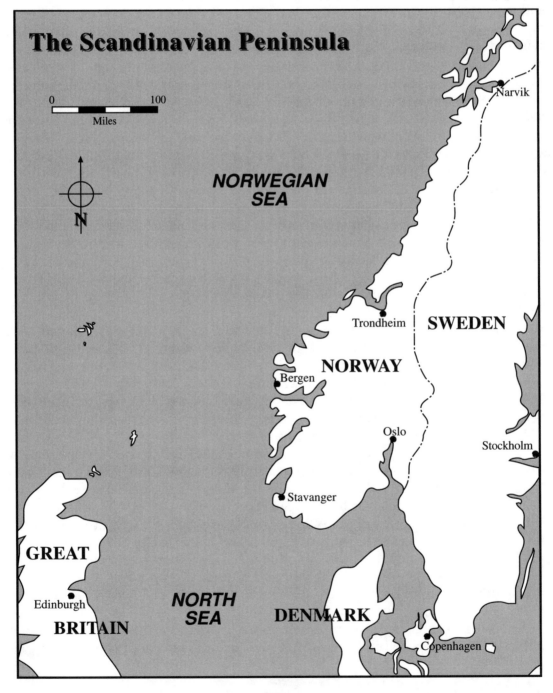

The Scandinavian Peninsula

heavily in this alternate scenario as in the historical sequence of events. The allies might have gained an advantage without the losses and humiliations they sustained in Norway during the spring of 1940.

Materially at least, the invasion of Norway was an unmitigated disaster for the *Kriegsmarine.* After World War I German naval strategists had touted the advantages of Scandinavian bases for Germany's surface fleet. When the fighting was over, too few warships were left for the new bases to matter: three cruisers, and only nine destroyers. But the losses off Norway had a more immediate consequence. Might the presence of the three cruisers, the ten destroyers, and the smaller vessels lost in Norwegian waters have altered the German navy's approach to an invasion of the British Isles?

The question involves strategic as well as operational perspectives. The German navy under Raeder had developed as a force with blue-water pretensions. It possessed neither the plans, the staffs, nor the material for a major amphibious operation. Improvising the necessary organization, and impressing the necessary shipping from a civilian economy already overstrained by war or disrupted by conquest, were formidable tasks in themselves. No "genius for war" the Germans might possess was likely to be carried over to the motley assemblage of barges, tugboats, and fishing smacks with civilian crews and civilian skippers, that would make up the German invasion fleet under the most favorable circumstances.

The prospects for an invasion seemed even more desperate in the absence of anything remotely resembling an effective naval screen for the proposed operation. Moreover the very ships the *Kriegsmarine* most lacked after Norway — cruisers and destroyers — were the ones most vital for the kind of close quarter fighting, much of it at night, that was certain to accompany a landing attempt. Whatever Goering's promises, no sailor would trust the security of such an operation entirely to the Luftwaffe, particularly given the bitterness of inter-service rivalries in Hitler's Germany. The presence of the ships lost in the north would most likely have acted as a security blanket for the navy. Their operational role would be less important than their positive effect on the *Kriegsmarine's* overall confidence in the prospects of an invasion. Ultimately, however, the mounting of Sea Lion would have still depended on air superiority. The German navy of 1940 had a good deal more self-confidence than its Imperial predecessor — but that confidence did not extend to accepting an unsupported death-grapple in the English Channel with a British fleet defending its homeland.

A continued supply of iron ore from Sweden was perceived as an absolute requirement for the economy of the resource-poor Reich. As early as April, 1939, the Wehrmacht High Command stressed the necessity of sustaining both Sweden's willingness to make deliveries and the transport routes themselves. In fact Sweden remained for most of the war a reliable commercial partner. Did the invasion of her neighbors convince Sweden that discretion was the better part of neutrality? Would ore have continued to flow so freely into Germany without the example set in Norway and Denmark?

The weight of evidence suggests that Sweden's German policy was only marginally influenced by events elsewhere in Scandinavia. Though public opinion was markedly anti-Nazi, the government saw no merit before or after Operation Weser in provoking what was clearly a hopeless fight. Swedes entertained no significant delusions about Hitler. But neither did they perceive any feasible alternative to supping with the devil and using the longest possible spoon. Germany was too close; the Baltic was too small; potential allies were too far away to facilitate heroic defiance. The Transit Agreement of July, 1940, making Swedish railways available for German troop movements, was a direct product of Norway's collapse, but there are no grounds for believing Sweden would have resisted such a demand even without the invasion. Particularly after the fall of France, Britain could have offered Sweden no more than token land and air forces, routed through Narvik—a move certain to provoke a German response. Compliance with Germany's less outrageous demands, combined with judicious reminders about the vulnerability of iron mines to sabotage, would have been Sweden's most probable first lines of defense even had Hitler honored Norwegian and Danish neutrality.

On 10 May 1940, Neville Chamberlain resigned as Britain's premier. While his conduct of the war had been the subject of consistent criticism both from the opposition benches and within his own party, it was the botched Norwegian campaign that produced the vote of confidence that reduced the government's margin to the point where Chamberlain could no longer govern. What if the Germans had not invaded Scandinavia in April? Would Chamberlain have remained in office for another month during the crucial early days of the Battle of France?

Almost certainly the government would have fallen within a week of the German attack. Chamberlain's credibility was unlikely to survive Guderian's breakthrough at Sedan and French General Gamelin's one-word reply to the question of where were the French reserves: *aucune*. That week might, however, have proved decisive. Winston Churchill would have had just that much less time to find his feet, to establish himself as a presence around which Britain could rally. Churchill, moreover, would have assumed office in the middle of a debacle rather than at its beginning. His grasp of events in historical fact was by no means as secure as his memoirs assert. In this alternative scenario, Churchill's energy and determination might well have generated a "Galloping Gertie" effect, adding to the confusion while attempting to overcome it. In this context, perhaps the most important consequence of the German invasion of Scandinavia was the role it played in bringing Churchill in touch with his destiny just a few vital days earlier.

B. What if the Germans had launched their main attack through Belgium instead of the Ardennes?

A second significant turning point in 1940 came when the Germans decided to make the focal point of their attack the Ardennes instead of the more obvious and traditional route through Belgium. The high command was reluctant to mount a western offensive under any circumstances. Initial plans for "Case Yellow" proposed sending seventy-five divisions, including most of the army's armored and motorized divisions, across the low countries to engage the enemy in what was expected to be an encounter battle in central Belgium. Even before Hitler became involved in the planning process, the army's high command was growing increasingly dissatisfied with this unpromisingly conventional proposal. The concept was modified, then abandoned. Instead the *Schwerpunkt* of the German offensive was fixed in the Ardennes—and the rest is history. But what might have happened had the general staff remained committed to the original notion? What if Hitler's solipsistic instincts had led him to reject the recommendations of Erich von Manstein, and instead insist on a drive through Belgium — which was, after all, the plan of campaign he had repeatedly and emphatically ordered implemented between October and January?

Despite its significant resemblance to the German operations plan of 1914, the original version of "Case Yellow" owed more to Ludendorff than to Schlieffen. As in 1918, the army high command proposed to punch a hole and see what developed. It expected the western allies to move to Belgium's support, and anticipated a hard enough fight from the Belgians on the frontier to render further decisions heavily dependent on contingencies. Apart from this, the original German concept incorporated no proposals for destroying the enemy armed forces. This reflected to a significant degree the tactical/operational orientation of a German military whose concern for winning battles and campaigns led to an increasing neglect of strategic and grand-strategic issues. On the other hand wars are decided at their sharp ends, and the German General Staff knew its professional business.

The most likely final version of a sweep through Belgium and Holland, projected from the modifications made to "Case Yellow" between October and January, would have involved parallel thrusts on either side of Liège. Army Group B, the northern wing would have two panzer corps; Army Group A, one. The *Schwerpunkt* could be adjusted according to the pace of events. The aim of the campaign would be "to engage in a battle forces as large as possible... and to defeat them, creating thereby favorable conditions for carrying on the war..."

An attack made under these conditions would have reflected the continued reluctance of its planners to mount an offensive in the west at all. It would also have played into a French war plan that emphasized the necessity of advancing as rapidly as possible into a Belgium that still refused a military alliance, then, presumably supported by the British, establishing a defensive position that could halt the German advance. French generals and French staff officers were students and creatures of a doctrine emphasizing the importance of firepower as opposed to maneuver. They had no intention of becoming engaged in an encounter battle that would highlight the weak points of their system and the strengths of the Wehrmacht. "Case Yellow 1" would have been a corresponding test of strengths. What factors might have governed the initial encounter?

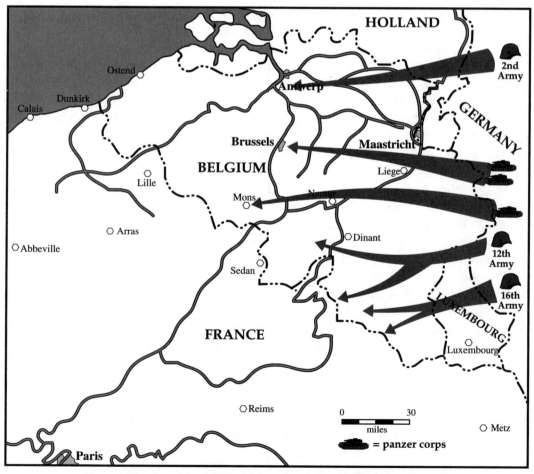

German Plan for a drive into Belgium rather than through the Ardennes.

43

The first was surprise. "Case Yellow 1," like its historical version, depended heavily on the Germans' getting the jump on their adversaries. There appear to be no significant reasons why a Belgian variant should have been any more obvious to its intended victims than the Ardennes alternative actually proved. Neither allied intelligence nor allied reconnaissance was more obviously capable of discovering concentrations across the Meuse than in the Eifel.

The second crucial consideration was speed: breaking through the Belgian frontier fortifications and the Belgian army as quickly as possible. Here again the Germans would have been at no significant disadvantage compared to historical events. The sophisticated surprise attack on Eben Emael, using glider troops and hollow charges, was a tactical operation, not dependent on the overall strategic focus of the campaign. The Belgian army put up a harder fight than is generally recognized, but common sense indicates it was unlikely to improve its performance against German forces that would have been considerably stronger in numbers and armor. A third consideration involved Holland — specifically the "Breda variant" that allotted a half dozen of France's best divisions to drive north and support the Dutch. French commander Maurice Gamelin had planned this move in November, 1939, independently of any sense or knowledge of specific German intentions. There is no reason to assume he would have abandoned it in this alternative scenario, and instead sent the Breda divisions into central Belgium or held them in reserve.

With the underbrush trimmed away, the progress of "Case Yellow 1" would have depended heavily on air superiority. The Luftwaffe's excellent communications and highly-developed ground organization gave it a high degree of operational mobility. That mobility, however, would have been at a significant discount in a battle for air superiority over Belgium that, perhaps even more than on the ground, would have been a head-on encounter depending heavily on the respective fighter arms. Recent accounts have shown that the French air force gave an excellent account of itself in 1940 despite being taken badly off balance. The Hurricanes of the BEF's Air Component also proved successful against the Messerschmitts. As much to the point, the Luftwaffe's Stukas and medium bombers would have had to focus their efforts in a limited operational area, becoming correspondingly vulnerable to enemy fighters. And — though this is more speculative — allied attack aircraft might not have been sacrificed in hopeless interdiction strikes against German bridges, as they were along the Meuse. In the final analysis numbers, quality and organization favored the Germans enough to give them victory in this alternative scenario. The victory, however, was likely to have been far less spectacular than was the historical case.

A similar point can be made for the ground fighting. The key to the blitz campaign of 1940 was mobility — getting inside the enemy's loop of initiative and forcing him off balance. How well might that concept have been implemented in Belgium? It is first of all questionable whether the panzer divisions would have been used in a breakthrough role, as opposed to exploitation. Once turned loose they would have found far less scope, geographic and military, for maneuver than was the actual case in 1940. The set object of the campaign involved *engaging* and *defeating* the enemy. German tanks, unlike their successors of 1944-45, were not designed for stand-up fighting. When the light mechanized divisions of the French Cavalry Corps met XVI Panzer Corps in the Gembloux Gap on 12-13 May, tactical honors were about even. Would the presence of more Mark II's, with their thin armor and 20 mm guns, have done more than offer the Somuas additional targets? The German advance in "Case Yellow 1" would have been unprecedentedly swift — but not probably quick enough to prevent the French and British forces from concentrating as planned, along the Dyle River.

Once in position the allies put up a hard fight even as their flank and rear disintegrated. What might they have achieved in this alternate scenario? Certainly both flanks would have been vulnerable to German mobile forces, and their rear areas subjected to even heavier attacks than they actually received from a Luftwaffe most probably able by now to concentrate its forces. On balance the test would have been of doctrines and fighting power. The French army's methods emphasized defense at the tactical level; British troops demonstrated their traditional stubbornness time and again during the actual fighting. While antitank warfare was still in its infancy, BEF two-pounders and French 25- and 47-millimeter guns might well have taken a heavy toll even of boldly-handled panzer formations. The Germans, on the other hand, with their emphasis on initiative, decentralization, and infiltration, were almost certain to erode enemy positions somewhere. And once that erosion was accomplished the panzers, or what remained of them, could have been turned loose a second time.

But to what end? In the most logical development of this scenario the channel ports would fall into German hands, cutting off escape for a BEF in any case likely to be too closely engaged on its front to make a Dunkirk feasible. The military destinies of France and Britain would have been correspondingly linked, even should Belgium — as seems likely—have concluded a separate peace before being completely overrun. That link, however, was not necessarily a step to joint catastrophe. While "Case Yellow 1" might have generated a French collapse, the more likely outcome would appear to be a tactical/operational victory in Belgium and northeastern France, but one leaving Germany's mobile forces, ground and air, too weakened to exploit decisively.

A feasible sequel might have involved an operational pause before proceeding deeper into France — particularly in the context mentioned above, of the army high command's doubts about the entire project. And the results? Perhaps a negotiated peace as France and Britain counted their losses and thanked their stars for nothing worse. Perhaps the overthrow of Hitler by an officer corps disaffected by incomplete success. In any case the Fuehrer's stock would have stood by no means as high at the end of this hypothetical campaign as it did in the historical scenario. Nor would the Wehrmacht have been as likely to cultivate the insouciant overconfidence that paved its road to Stalingrad. What if?

C. What if the Germans had pushed the attack on Dunkirk?

On 24 May the later Field Marshal Gerd von Rundstedt, commanding Army Group A, ordered his armored divisions to close up to the "Canal Line" of Lens-Gravelines, and halt there. Hitler endorsed the order the next day. Not until the 27th did the tanks roll again, and by that time the British had the way to Dunkirk barred. There seems to be no question that the German mobile forces could have continued advancing. Their surprise and indignation at being stopped is clear even in those relatively sober documents, the formation war diaries. With an unbroken string of successes behind them, officers and men were confident they could end the fighting in the north in a matter of days. Instead 338,000 French and British escaped through Dunkirk between 27 May and 4 June.

German failure to halt the evacuation is generally and appropriately recognized as a major long-range turning point in the Second World War. It has been variously explained as a desire to spare the panzers for later operations, as a sop to Goering's pride in his Luftwaffe, and as a reflection of Hitler's vague hopes for a peace with Britain. Not only Hitler, but many of the army's senior officers, had served in Flanders during World War I. They retained vivid memories of the region's all-devouring mud, and feared getting their tanks hopelessly bogged. But what if these concerns had not inhibited action? After the war Heinz Guderian, commanding XIX Panzer Corps, said that Field Marshal Walther von Brauchitsch later told him that the army high command hoped Guderian would disobey the order, as he had others during the campaign. What if the Wehrmacht had followed its own aphorism of *"klotzen nicht kleckern,"* and concentrated is full efforts on capturing Dunkirk or reducing the Dunkirk perimeter before the allies could remove their forces?

On 24 May Guderian's lead elements were thirty miles closer to Dunkirk than the bulk of the BEF. No significant combat forces barred their way. Any ad hoc opposition scraped up in Britain and thrown ashore was no more likely to engage the panzer divisions in a debilitating street fight than had the garrisons of Boulogne and Calais. Possibilities for a British counterattack against Dunkirk were even more limited. The BEF was already heavily engaged, and in this scenario likely to be even more heavily pressed along its front by the Germans of Army Group B. Apart from that fact, neither doctrine, training, nor command had prepared British forces for this kind of improvised operation. As late as 1945 the British army performed best in set pieces.

The most obvious positive allied response to the loss of Dunkirk involved a reprise of the abortive counterattack at Arras of 21 May. This operation would have presumably involved stronger forces, and the British high command would not have been looking over its collective shoulder towards the Channel ports as frequently as some accounts say was the historical case. On the other hand, the ad hoc nature of the attack would have been even greater than was the actual case, and the available tanks far fewer in number. Lord Gort and his subordinates, moreover, were by 24 May psychologically detached from the Battle of Flanders, mentally committed to an evacuation in ways difficult to reverse overnight. The most likely outcome of a German thrust to Dunkirk, in short, would not have been exactly the collapse of the BEF, but its paralysis — ending in a *Kesselschlacht*, somewhere between Lille and Ypres, engulfing all nine of the BEF's regular and first-line territorial divisions. The remaining labor and service troops could have been rounded up at the Germans' leisure. They would have had nowhere to go.

A second alternative scenario involving Dunkirk begins with the German armor held back and the British and French establishing a defensive perimeter, as in the historical version. But what if the Germans had mounted a concentrated, all-out effort to prevent the evacuation by increasing the force of their attacks against the allied positions, perhaps using armored forces extensively for support and short-range exploitation? What if, after the Belgian surrender, Fedor von Bock had driven — or been ordered to drive — the infantry of his Army Group B harder? What if the Germans had made more use of their medium and heavy artillery against the Dunkirk perimeter?

Here the outcome would have been decided at the tactical level. In the historical scenario, French and British rear-guards bought enough time for most of the fighting formations to be evacuated. Their sacrifices and successes, however, were in good part reflections of a "last man syndrome" on the German side. If the generals were looking forward to the coming Battle of France, the lieutenants, sergeants, and privates had no desire to be the last one killed in Belgium. Overcoming this inertia — itself a reflection of the hard fighting of the previous two weeks — would have challenged the higher commands, but not necessarily daunted them.

Whether greater efforts in this context inevitably prefigured a decisive German breakthrough to the beachheads is open to question. With nowhere to run, the fighting elements of the BEF and the French 1st Army can reasonably be expected to have stood their ground. Far fewer of them, however, would have been likely to disengage successfully — two or three divisions' worth of British, half that many French, seem optimistic estimates. The troops evacuated from Dunkirk would have included a much higher proportion of rear echelon formations, service elements, and stragglers. Staffs and senior officers could have been selectively withdrawn to serve as the nucleus of a reconstituted army. The probable negative effect on the morale in the armed forces and the nation at large might well have prevented even this move. One thing is certain. After this scenario the cutting edge of any subsequent British war effort would have had a correspondingly different structure. In the context of actual events in the desert, the Mediterranean, and northwest Europe, that might not have been entirely disadvantageous!

A third alternate possibility moves into the air. What if the Luftwaffe had mounted a more concentrated effort over Dunkirk? Unfavorable weather conditions hindered the German air crews by day. The absence of any effective night-fighting capacities gave the evacuation between six and eight undisturbed hours in twenty-four. But suppose, instead of attacking the aircraft factories of Paris or the roads and railroads of the Rhône Valley, the Luftwaffe had focussed on the port and the beaches of Dunkirk?

The most promising targets, left relatively undisturbed in the historical scenario, were the British Channel ports. Heavy medium-bomber raids on Dover and the smaller harbors were well within the Luftwaffe's capacity. Launching them, however, would have done little more than inaugurate the Battle of Britain on terms highly unfavorable to a Luftwaffe still without a network of forward bases for its short-ranged fighters. Presuming a German refusal to be drawn into such a struggle, Dunkirk itself would have been the focus of a major air battle. For most of Operation Dynamo the harbor, not the open beaches, was the major evacuation route, and it was there the Heinkels and Dorniers were likely to do the most damage. They might also have confronted the RAF with a vital decision.

From the beginning of the German Offensive, Fighter Command's Air Chief Marshal Sir Hugh Dowding had insisted — steadfastly or rigidly, depending on one's viewpoint — that his Spitfires and Hurricanes must be held back for the defense of Britain itself. Even over Dunkirk, British aircraft were committed sparingly. What might have been the pressure on Dowding with Dunkirk's port facilities ablaze, with beaches even more heavily crowded than was the historical reality? Might Fighter Command have been drawn into, or committed itself to, an air-superiority battle on the far side of the Channel? As late as 1942, the RAF's offensive fighter sweeps over France were characterized by significant weaknesses of command and control. Would 1940 have witnessed a better performance? And how many of the men who bailed out over England four months later, then returned to fight as squadron or wing commanders, might instead have finished the war as German prisoners?

Had the RAF done no more than it did in reality, the limitations of air power have been sufficiently highlighted by later events to suggest strongly that the Luftwaffe of 1940 could not by itself have halted the evacuation as long as the British were willing to send in their ships. What it could have done was to increase evacuation's material and moral costs. The bulk of the British troops came home with a sense that at least part of the system worked. The army had been ruinously beaten. The "brylcreem boys" of the RAF had been conspicuously absent over the beaches. But everyone could "thank God for the Navy!" Had the evacuation been disrupted, had it been brought nearer to the level of *sauve qui peut* as would be the case at Singapore, the effect on both British morale and British politics might well have been significant.

The Luftwaffe lost something else over Dunkirk: its reputation for infallibility. This was no small sacrifice in the Byzantine world of German military politics, and might well have been averted had the British been driven off the Dunkirk beaches instead of being pushed off. Would a command structure without something to prove have fought the Battle of Britain in quite the same way? We will never know.

A final alternative scenario for Dunkirk involves the possibility of a German "hot pursuit." Operation Sealion proved abortive. But in the aftermath of the evacuation, what might have happened if the Germans had sent what remained of their airborne troops across the Channel, supporting them with a relatively small ground force, packed into anything that would float and launched against a narrow front?

The prospects for such an operation seem limited. The Luftwaffe would have faced significant problems gaining even temporary air superiority of the kind necessary for an air assault, given the lack of suitable bases and a developed administrative structure in the forward operational area. A large-scale airborne operation is an extremely complex process, and in 1940 lacked any precedents. Planning for such a contingency was legitimately at the very lowest priority of a Luftwaffe with far bigger and more dangerous fish to fry. Nor had the German paratroopers and air landing forces recovered from their mauling in Holland, where Dutch forces held in light regard had inflicted heavy losses in men and decimated the vital transport wings. The shock of an invasion in the aftermath of Dunkirk might — just might — have taken Britain out of the war. But Germany did not possess, and could not reasonably have created, an airborne force strong enough to deliver that kind of initial punch.

And could the paratroopers have been reinforced? Especially in the context of the *Kriegsmarine's* continued preoccupation with Norway, could it have collected and organized enough shipping in the immediate aftermath of Dunkirk to transport and land even two or three divisions in the face of a Royal Navy committed to a fight to a finish? The complexity and the vulnerability of subsequent amphibious operations for Tarawa to Salerno suggests that an improvised German attempt to land in England during the summer of 1940 would have more closely resembled Dieppe than Normandy. There was no guarantee that German assault troops could either have fought their way ashore or been effectively supported in a beachhead. Once inland and reinforced by a panzer division or two, the Germans would have given Britain its most formidable external military challenge since 1066. Getting there, however, was the rub in summer 1940, as it proved to be in the fall.

The evacuation of Dunkirk brought almost a quarter-million men of the BEF home in organized formations. What might have been the consequences of a disaster on the beaches, or a surrender further inland? If only fragments of her first-line forces had returned, might Britain have been more receptive to peace terms? Or might Operation Sealion, the projected large-scale German invasion, have appeared more attractive to Hitler and the Wehrmacht in the absence of the Dunkirk veterans?

That the loss of the BEF would by itself have brought Britain to the conference table is questionable. Operation Dynamo brought back men, not equipment — and experience from Norway to Flanders showed that rifles and bayonets made only marginal contributions to the kind of war the Germans had introduced. Certainly Britain's defenses were stronger with the BEF than without it. But there were enough trained and partially-trained formations to man Britain's beaches and furnish an operational reserve, even if most of Lord Gort's men had vanished into German POW camps. What was lacking in the summer and fall of 1940 were not men in uniform, but tanks, antitank guns, artillery pieces. These shortages did not encourage surrender in 1940, and would have been no greater had the BEF itself failed to return. Certainly its loss would have been a major blow to national morale, but the army was no more than Britain's third line of defense. Especially given Churchill's determination to continue the fight, the Royal

Navy and the RAF would have to have been broken to make negotiations a probable aftermath to a surrender at Dunkirk.

It is similarly difficult to perceive Operation Sealion as being facilitated by the BEF's capture. The German army was confident in its capacity to defeat with relative ease any land forces the British could pit against an invasion, even one of the strength projected in Sealion's later, limited version. Whether this confidence was misplaced may be open to debate, but nothing in the German records indicates the kind of respect for the British army's fighting power that might have encouraged greater optimism in the absence of that army's first line. Operation Sealion was doomed by the Luftwaffe's failure to establish air superiority and the *Kriegsmarine's* inability to mount the landing—not the presence of the Dunkirk divisions in Britain's order of battle.

One final, more remote speculation might be offered in this context. Had the BEF been destroyed, would Britain have committed the resources it did in fact to building up a heavy bomber force? Would the national focus have changed, by necessity, to forming and equipping ground divisions? Or would Britain, perceiving no other alternative, have committed herself even more fully to Trenchardian concepts of air power and its potential? Important though the bomber offensive was as the only means of striking directly at Germany until 1943, it seems most likely that Churchill's government would in fact have taken the more cautious path and rebuilt an army strong enough to project Britain's power overseas, as well as to defend the homeland. But how long would that process have required? Many of the British formations that fought in Tunisia 1942-43 had been evacuated from Dunkirk, yet they showed to limited advantage against an improvised German resistance. What might have been the fate of entirely new divisions? It is one more question that tantalizes by having no answer.

D. What if France had continued the war?

The final battle for France began on 5 June. Twelve days later the French government asked for an armistice. The necessity of France's capitulation remains a subject for debate. But what if instead France had continued the fight, either voluntarily or because Hitler refused to negotiate? The latter point is by no means improbable. A total victory over France might not have been in Hitler's interest, but the Nazi dictator was a man of whim as well as will. Besides, what better way to show Britain the hopelessness of her situation than by laying France completely prostrate?

What might have been the consequences for Germany had a Vichy government never existed, had Hitler instead forced a choice between surrender and exile? The most logical outcome would have been an enhancing of Germany's westward and Mediterranean orientations. While *resistance* might have been no greater in a totally-occupied France than a partitioned one, *opposition* would probably be enhanced by the absence of a "middle way." Consolidating German rule would in itself have absorbed significant attention from a Nazi order that produced conquerors rather than proconsuls. It is unlikely that a German occupation of France in 1940 would have completely distracted Hitler from his ideologically-based concern with Russia. But such a scenario offered significant opportunities for attracting Hitler the opportunist. Diplomatically, German relations with Spain and Italy would have become more comprehensive and complex. Militarily, with German troops all along the Pyrenees Operation Felix, the projected strike against Gibraltar through Franco's Spain, might have seemed a more practical option. Choking off the Mediterranean might have appeared far less of a strategic diversion than was the actual case in 1941. What might Erwin Rommel have done with a battle-hardened panzer group in lieu of his improvised Afrika Korps?

A second alternative consequence of France remaining in the war as a government in exile would have been the continued presence of the French navy on the allied side. This factor must not be exaggerated. Britain's great need between 1940 and 1943 was for escort ships; the French navy was a surface-action force. The decisive naval operation of those years took place in the Atlantic; French warships were best adapted to the Mediterranean. Friction between the allies would doubtless have been enhanced while the navy remained France's principal military contribution and negotiating counter. But aside from the advantages gained by Britain's avoiding the tragedy of Mers-el-Kebir and the fiasco of Dakar, French naval forces would have provided a useful margin of security, if not superiority, in the Mediterranean. French destroyers might have freed their more adaptable British counterparts from fleet work for escort duties. And French crews, with large cadres of experienced seamen, could have manned enough escort vessels to deserve their own chapter in an alternative history of the Battle of the Atlantic.

A third scenario with significant possible consequences involves French withdrawal to North Africa. This was far more likely than a simple flight to London. The local commander-in-chief, General Noguès, enthusiastically urged the prospect. Premier Paul Reynaud seriously considered it. His successor, Philippe Petain, went so far as to order part of the government to relocate. What prospects existed for carrying on France's war from her colonies?

While North Africa's military resources had been drained for the *metropole*, they were far from exhausted. The North Africans had done some of the best and hardest fighting in France and Belgium. As many as fifteen divisions could easily have been raised from formations held back as garrisons, supplemented by troops from sub-Saharan Africa and recruits drawn from the still-plentiful manpower of Algeria, Morocco, and Tunisia. The colonial formations actually engaged in Italy and France in the war incorporated large numbers of Frenchmen. In this scenario, while not many organized formations would have escaped the collapse, enough individuals and small units were likely to make their way across the Mediterranean, or be transshipped from Britain, to provide cadres and specialists for the new divisions.

Equipment would have posed a far greater problem than manpower. North Africa had no armament industry. Britain had no resources to spare. U.S. lend-lease (itself a speculation in this presumed context) was most likely to be sent to the British Isles, the point of greatest ostensible danger. The French "Army of North Africa" would have emerged as a throwback to the early 1930's: infantry armed with rifles and machine guns, supported by horse-drawn artillery and screened by cavalry employing a mix of horses, trucks, and motorcycles, with a few battalions of modern tanks giving the whole scene cachet.

The French, however, could have counted on a relatively strong air force. Many of the *Armée de l'Air's* surviving first-line fighters and bombers were capable of making a one-way flight across the Mediterranean. Those that were not, the Morane-Saulnier 406's and Bloch 152's, were no great loss. Even during the fighting these obsolescent models had been giving way to Dewoitine 520's and Curtiss Hawks. France, moreover, had placed orders for modern aircraft in the U.S. — orders that could be delivered to Casablanca as well as Marseilles, and that would have provided useful mounts for the relatively large numbers of planeless pilots that were likely to hitch rides south rather than accept German captivity.

The Hawks and Havocs from the U.S. were not an equal match for the Luftwaffe's first line. But the prospects of a German pursuit across the Mediterranean under the conditions of 1940 were negligible. Not only was Britain the more threatening enemy; it offered a far easier target. The English Channel was narrower than the Mediterranean

Sea. A Wehrmacht unable to cope with the former would hardly have been likely to tackle the latter except under administrative, as opposed to operational, conditions.

That point suggests that a hypothetical "Army of North Africa" might have done its first fighting against the Italian colony of Libya. Its existence alone would probably have deterred the disastrous Italian invasion of Egypt. And while prewar French plans vis-à-vis Libya were essentially defensive, as indicated by the existence of the Mareth Line, a British attack with anything like the success of Sir Richard O'Connor's actual offensive would probably have evoked a French response. The probable outcome would have been the occupation of Tripoli three years earlier.

As for Axis reinforcements, a French fleet that in this scenario would almost certainly have been concentrated in the Mediterranean was in a good position to challenge successfully Italian convoys — not least because that was the kind of mission on which the French navy had concentrated its prewar training. French naval forces added to a British Mediterranean fleet handled by an admiral of Cunningham's capacities would have thrown the material deficiencies and command shortcomings of the Regia Marina into even bolder relief than did the actual course of events — and might have made the African campaign no more than an occupation of hopelessly-isolated Italian outposts.

One final scenario based on French continuance of the war deserves consideration. While metropolitan France would have been spared the worst of the Vichy/Gaullist hostility, the evidence of Belgium and Holland suggests that tension between those were left and those who stayed would still have infused postwar French politics to a significant degree. A more promising alternative involves the relationships that might have developed between a French government based in Algiers, and the governments and peoples of North Africa. Even before the war there was talk of the French Empire becoming a French Commonwealth. It is unnecessary to hypothesize gratitude on the part of an administration in exile to suggest that a hard-line attitude of the kind France manifested after 1945 might have been more difficult to sustain in a situation where the power to act independently, as opposed to being a British or U.S. puppet, depended heavily on North African participation. The client governments of Tunisia and Morocco, and the budding Algerian nationalist movement, would have been in the position of interacting on an everyday basis with a government whose members were likely to be drawn from a Left and Center already inured to compromise. *On s'arranger* has been a motto of French politics at least since 1870. Might French-North African relationships have been differently "arranged" had Renaud decided to continue the fight for French independence from the French Empire?

E. What if Britain had sued for peace in 1940?

To generations nurtured on Winston Churchill's rhetoric of Britain's finest hour, the question may seem a particular absurdity. But Churchill's accession to his country's highest office was by no means inevitable. Chamberlain's failure to form a national coalition after the Commons vote on May 8, 1940, initially brought to the fore not Churchill, but Foreign Secretary Viscount Edward Halifax. Unlike Churchill, Halifax enjoyed the confidence of the Crown, the prime minister, and his own party. He would have been supported by the Liberal and Labour parties. His peerage was not an insurmountable barrier to the effective exercise of office, however much Halifax might have thought so. And while in actual history it was 1963 before peers were allowed to disclaim their titles, a national emergency of the kind Britain faced in 1940 would certainly have facilitated an earlier version of the Peerage Act, or some equivalent

51

enabling Halifax to enter the Commons as premier — if he had wanted the job. At the crunch, however, Halifax lacked confidence in himself and stood down in favor of Churchill. What if Halifax had accepted the opportunity?

Edward Halifax had for years been closely identified with Chamberlain's policy of appeasement, from both principle and pragmatism. As Viceroy of India he had negotiated successfully if temporarily, with Mohandas Gandhi, and possessed corresponding faith in the power of negotiations to control ideologies. His support for war had been a reluctant acceptance of a choice between two great evils. His reaction to events in France blended shock and despair. Like everyone else in the cabinet, Halifax was stunned by the French army's collapse. In December 1939, he had expressed a belief that should France make peace, England could not carry on alone. In the War Cabinet meetings of 26-28 May, with the BEF apparently on the edge of destruction around Dunkirk, Halifax urged using Mussolini as a mediator to ascertain Hitler's peace terms. Even if these included surrendering part of the empire, Halifax believed that might be preferable to further destruction or a hopeless last stand.

Halifax was as determined as Churchill to secure Britain's integrity and independence. But in the contest of his actual behavior it seems quite likely, that as prime minister he would have at least sought to open negotiations for peace. Mussolini would almost certainly have seized the opportunity to establish himself — in his own mind, at least — as Europe's new power broker. The Battle of France had left the Italian dictator eating the dust of his one-time emulator. A British initiative of the kind favored by Halifax was just the thing to pique Mussolini's vanity.

The outcome of the negotiations would have depended heavily on Adolf Hitler. Insofar as the Nazi dictator had policies, as opposed to goals, he seems during the summer of 1940 to have been interested sincerely in at least testing England's interest in what Andreas Hillgruber calls a "global grand solution" involving a compromise with England. Such a peace would discourage U.S. intervention, clear the way for an ideologically-based war with Russia, and — not least — divide Britain's counsel, making her correspondingly vulnerable to what later generations would call "Finlandization." He believed "one more demonstration of our power" was necessary to bring about the negotiations he sought. Had Halifax in fact made the overtures, they would almost certainly have been accepted.

The outcome of these hypothetical peace talks moves into the realm of pure speculation. Much would have depended on the skill of the participants. Certainly Halifax by this time entertained no delusions about Hitler. The British premier would have balked at anything remotely resembling the terms imposed at Compiègne. The Royal Navy and the Royal Air Force would have been non-negotiable issues. Hitler for his part was almost certain to demand colonial concessions — which Halifax might have granted for the sake of a cease-fire. Assuming the parties were able to reach terms, an armistice, rather than a peace, seems a logical outcome for this alternative scenario. Both sides could see obvious short-and long-term benefits. The *Kriegsmarine* would have the opportunity to continue with its Z-Plan to build an ocean-going battle fleet. Hitler and his generals would be free to concentrate on a form of war they understood, waged against an enemy they were certain of defeating. Britain for her part would have bought time — time to restore her shattered armed forces, to develop an American connection, to mobilize a Commonwealth whose participation in the war to date had been much less enthusiastic than in 1914. The Halifax-Hitler armistice would have meant little more than a pause between rounds.

A second scenario involving a British peace initiative depends on Winston Churchill being freed of his belief in the prospect of rapid, large-scale American help for his beleaguered island. As early as June 15 he urged Roosevelt to declare war, if only for its psychological effect. His chiefs of staff insisted that without full economic and financial support from the U.S. prospects for success were grim.

Churchill's hopes for immediate U.S. participation in the war was the product of wishful thinking reinforced by Franklin Delano Roosevelt's mastery of obfuscation. The American president never discouraged Churchill's optimism. But suppose Roosevelt had been less sanguine about Britain's prospects. Suppose that, under pressure from Republicans, America-Firsters, and peace advocates, he had informed the British Premier, bluntly and unmistakably, that Britain indeed stood alone?

Winston Churchill in 1940 was a man without a party, a man whose political behavior over the past thirty years had generated mistrust and hostility on both Left and Right. He was also both less and more than the single-minded paladin of his own legend. He was plagued by objective doubts, as well as his more familiar "black dog." However inspiring he might be in public, he spoke in private on several occasions in 1940 of the prospects of a negotiated peace. The question, he argued, was whether Britain could get acceptable terms. But his definition of "acceptable" might well have been altered by an unambiguous American declaration of non-intervention. His decision to fight on was by no means absolute. The historical Churchill was almost as prepared as Halifax to trade territory for peace — "Malta, Gibraltar, and some African colonies" are mentioned in Neville Chamberlain's diary. Further concessions might have been at least thinkable in a context of complete isolation.

Whether Churchill would himself have initiated the negotiations is more debatable. Certainly his critics in and out of Parliament would have attacked him — accurately — as the British politician least likely to bring peace talks undertaken from weakness to a successful conclusion. Under pressure, Churchill might have resigned. More likely he would have either been ousted or like Chamberlain in May, retained in office with a margin too small to be effective in the situation. And his probable successor? Almost certainly Halifax would have overcome his self-deprecation to serve his country in its hour of need — with results along the lines discussed above.

A third possibility for a British peace initiative lay at the grass roots. Recent research in the social history of wartime Britain indicates that national morale was by no means dominated by the grim determination to endure and prevail that has been enshrined in national mythology. The war itself came as a shock to a people dominated by the memories of 1914-18 and the illusions of the 1930's. The disaster in France and the helter-skelter retreat from Dunkirk generated a widespread apathy by no means the most promising matrix of national resistance. Britain in 1940, moreover, was still a class society, "a nation of hats and caps," deeply scarred by depression and unemployment. Even Churchill was by no means confident in public morale at the outbreak of war. What if, in the aftermath of Dunkirk, the British public had demanded a new version of "peace with honor"? Censorship had not entirely muzzled the press; wartime controls were by no means as rigid as they later became; Parliament was a locus of free speech. Could popular agitation, popular reluctance to continue a struggle whose outcome even the country's leaders questioned, have brought about a change in Britain's German policies? Could Britain's social revolution have begun in 1940 instead of 1945?

The answer would have depended first of all on the intensity of the protests, and on their capacity to generate leadership from outside the existing political establishment. The British Communist Party, obsessed with internal concerns, was an unlikely source. "Red Ellen" Wilkinson had the necessary charisma, but her gender was against her. Sir Oswald Moseley comes to mind from the right, but would almost certainly have been too controversial. The leaders of a "peace now" movement were most likely to be unknown — back-benchers at the most, acting from a mix of opportunism, enthusiasm, and conviction. The level of support would have depended heavily on a bandwagon effect that generated a sense of purpose in a time when no one knew what would happen next.

And the outcome? Most probably a new government — arguably a national coalition with Clement Attlee as premier and Halifax playing a major role. Such a government was unlikely to seek a war on two fronts; almost certainly it would have sought negotiations. And that process in turn might well have generated a paradox. The temptation in such a scenario would have been very strong for Hitler to overplay his hand by demanding concessions unacceptable even to determined advocates of peace. It is not impossible to imagine Halifax returning from a final meeting brandishing a paper and saying "we sought peace with honor; Hitler offers only war to the knife!" The rest must remain pure speculation, in the context of a Britain whose future development would have differed in essence from the Britain of history.

Peace between Britain and Germany would have had wider implications as well. Even before Hitler announced on July 31, 1940, his intention to "destroy" Russia, the army high command had regarded a Soviet war as only a matter of time. And that war was not merely a means to the greater end of convincing Britain to surrender by eliminating her last potential continental ally. It is virtually certain that even in the aftermath of peace in the west, preparations for Operation Barbarossa would have continued. Nazi Germany's next set of goals, ideological and geopolitical, lay in the Slavic East. It was Russia that offered the resources, the living space, and not least the slave labor demanded by Hitler's predatory system both as ends in themselves and as means to the further enhancement of Nazi power.

Strategically, Germany would have likely benefited from an enhanced bandwagon effect both in her occupied territories and in east-central Europe. With Britain removed from the equation, accommodation would have been the only reasonable choice from Norway to Vichy France. Neither Yugoslavia nor Greece could have entertained hopes for a British-supported "third way" between Nazi Germany and Communist Russia. The extent of the actual delay imposed on Barbarossa by the Balkan campaign of 1941 remains a subject of debate. But without a British military presence in the eastern Mediterranean, it is virtually certain that the Balkan states would have made the best terms they could with Europe's new hegemonic power and its Italian ally.

What would have been the operational results of an Anglo-German peace on a Russo-German war? It seems highly unlikely that the invasion would have been launched earlier than the spring of 1941. Even when he hoped for Britain's capitulation, Hitler set May 1941 as his target month. There were no real prospects of an immediate shift of forces to occupied Poland and a lightning strike against an unprepared enemy. It would have been impossible to transfer the bulk of the German army eastwards after the fall of France and still have enough time left to mount a decisive campaign before winter changed the equation. Even if contingency plans for such an operation had existed, the risks of alarming the Soviet Union were too great to be accepted in the context of an alternative. Britain's surrender in the summer of 1940 would have offered the chance to strengthen Germany's diplomatic position with Russia's neighbors while integrating the resources of Europe into an irresistible mass attack on Nazism's principal enemy — and all without the distraction of an air and sea campaign in the west, or of sideshows in the Mediterranean. For Hitler and his generals, the decision would have been obvious: lull Russia into a sense of temporary security, then strike when the *rasputitsa*, the spring thaw, was over: attack, that is, in later April or early May, 1941.

Chapter 4

Hitler's Attack on Russia

David M. Glantz & Samuel J. Newland

Hitler's decision to attack the Soviet Union in June 1941 has generated considerable historical controversy. Among the most controversial "What ifs" concerns the timing of the German attack.

A. What if the Germans had delayed Barbarossa until after dealing with Great Britain (in 1942 or 1943)?
David M. Glantz

A German delay of up to two years in launching Operation Barbarossa could have had a significant effect on immediate conditions surrounding the attack and on the initial course of operations. It is not likely, however, that such a delay would have altered the outcome of the war. German postponement of Operation Barbarossa until 1942 or 1943 presumes that Germany would have been able to defeat or neutralize Great Britain. Although direct German invasion of the British Isles was thwarted in 1940 and would probably have been unlikely in 1941, a broad German thrust through the Balkans into the Middle East (an expanded Mediterranean strategy) in time could have brought Britain to its knees. Such an outcome would have cleared Germany's southern flank and rear and permitted German military planners to adhere to their schedule for an invasion of the Soviet Union in May of 1942 or 1943, thus avoiding the delay which they experienced in 1941.

On the other hand, one must recognize that expanded German military operations in the Middle East and Mediterranean basin could conceivably have tied down large German forces, or done damage to German units, which would have required repair by the time Barbarossa actually began: recall German casualties in the Crete operation.

Assuming the Germans succeeded in clearing their southern flank, neutralizing Britain, and assembling an imposing military host to conduct Barbarossa, the delay of one or two years would have posed other problems for the Germans. First, it is unlikely that the Germans could have achieved in 1942 or 1943 the degree of surprise they achieved in 1941, in particular since they would not have benefited from the deceptive effect which the Balkan operation had on the Soviet government in spring 1941.

Second and even more important, by 1942 the Soviet military reorganization and re-equipment program, which had begun in 1940, would have been close to completion, if not fully complete. The Soviet armored force of 29 mechanized corps, so woefully deficient in requisite tanks in June 1941 and so poorly trained and equipped with the 1,443 model T-34 and KV tanks in 1941, surprised the Germans and locally slowed the German attack. By 1942 most of the ten Soviet mechanized corps in the border military districts, and the six which ultimately reinforced them, would have possessed a sizeable complement of the new tanks, enough to disrupt seriously German operations.

The restructuring and re-equipment program began in 1940 after the end of the Soviet-Finnish War, during which the Soviets did so poorly. It involved the streamlining of rifle forces (divisions), creation of mechanized corps, airborne corps, and anti-tank brigades, fielding of new model tanks (T-34, KV-1 and 2) and artillery, and a host of other measures. Soviet analysis of German operations in Western Europe spurred the efforts on. According to Soviet sources the program was to be completed by the summer of 1942.

By June 1941, T-34 and KV-1 and 2 strength was just short of 1,500, most in the border military districts. By summer 1942, this figure should have risen to over 16,000. Realistically, the figure should not have exceeded 5,000, but that number would have had a sizeable impact on operations. Regarding surprise, 6th Panzer Division's harrowing experiences with several battalions of Russian T-34 and KV-1 tanks was indicative of what an ever larger and better prepared Russian force would have achieved.

Had German intelligence detected the existence of the new models, and had Hitler sought to delay the attack until comparable German tanks were available, further delay would have ensued. The record of wartime armor production clearly demonstrates it was a technological race the Germans could not have won.

Given greater Soviet military capabilities, it is also more likely that Stalin would have considered some sort of preemptive action against Germany. If preemption did not occur, Soviet forces would have been better prepared than they were in 1941 to meet and defeat the actual German invasion.

B. What if Stalin had heeded clear warnings of the impending German attack and launched a preemptive attack as proposed by Zhukov?
David M. Glantz

One of the most intriguing "what ifs" has for years been rumored in western circles and has only recently been surfaced by the Soviets themselves. It involves a Soviet response, in the form of preemptive action, to the obviously maturing German threat in May and June 1941.

Throughout the spring of 1941, tensions grew between Germany and the Soviet Union. The Germans intensified their intelligence collection against the Soviet Union and began mobilization measures associated with secret plan Barbarossa. Soviet intelligence kept track of the German troop build-up in eastern Europe and received a significant amount of intelligence from diplomatic and military sources concerning the impending attack. Soviet concern over increasing German offensive preparedness was sufficient for Stalin and the General Staff to order preliminary mobilization measures of 13 May involving the mobilization and western deployment of five armies. The record of this and other measures, as well as the extensive Soviet intelligence files, have only recently been openly published.[1]

Among the newly published materials is an interesting proposal supposedly made in mid-May 1941 by Chief of the General Staff Zhukov to Stalin proposing a Soviet preemptive strike be conducted against mobilizing German forces. Zhukov's proposal, although probably only one of many made during 1941, and a rejected one at that, fits comfortably within the context of previous Soviet strategic planning and, in particular, the experiences of the January war games.

Entitled "Report on the Plan of Strategic Deployment of Armed Forces of the Soviet Union to the Chairman of the Council of People's Commissars of 15 May 1941" and co-signed by Timoshenko, Zhukov's report began with the words:

> Considering that Germany, at this time, is mobilizing its forces and rear services, it has the capability of forestalling [pre-empting] our deployment and delivering a surprise blow. In order to avert such a situation, I consider it necessary to on no account give the initiative of action to the German command, to pre-empt the enemy deployment and to

The Zhukov Proposal
15 May 1941
Concentration of Forces
(Variant)

BALTIC SEA

ESTONIA

Leningrad

Tallinn

Luga

LATVIA

Riga

27th
Army
6 div.

Velikiye Luki

★ Moscow

28th
Army
Vyazma
10
divisions

Subsequent
Strategic Objective

LITHUANIA
8th Army
8 div.

22nd
Army
6 div.

Smolensk

Vilna

E. PRUSSIA

3rd Army 6 div.

Western Front

Minsk

24th
Army
9 divisions

11th Army 14 div.

13th
Army
10 div.

10th Army
13 divisions

Bryansk

10th Army 14 div.

Warsaw

4th Army 6 div.

Gomel

Kursk

Pocket 100
German
divisions

5th
Army
8 div.

21st Army
14 divisions

Belograd

Southwestern
Front

Kharkov

6th Army
14 div.

16th
Army
14 div.

First Strategic
Objective

26th Army 14 div.

19th Army
13 divisions

12th Army
8 div.

4 div.

Baita

9th Army
15 div.

Kherson

Areas seized by USSR
after September 1, 1939

BLACK

Sevastopol

SEA

FIGURE 1: ZHUKOV'S PROPOSED PLAN, 15 MAY 1941

57

attack the German Army at that moment when it is in the process of deployment and has not yet succeeded in organizing the front and cooperation of its forces.[2]

The report then set out strategic objectives for the proposed operation designed to defeat and destroy the estimated 100 German divisions already assembling in eastern Poland. The first [initial] strategic objective was to destroy German forces assembled south of Brest and Demblin and, within thirty days, to advance to a line running from north of Ostrolenka, south along the Narew River, through Lowicz, Lodz, Kreuzberg, and Oppeln to Olomouc (see figure 1). Subsequently, Soviet forces were to attack north or northwest from the Katowice region to destroy German forces in the center and northwest wing of the front and seize the remainder of former Poland and East Prussia.

The immediate mission of Soviet forces during the first phase of the strategic operation was to break up German forces east of the Vistula River and around Krakow, advance to the Narew and Vistula Rivers, and secure Katowice. Specific missions to carry out this task were:

a) Strike the main blow by Southwestern Front forces toward Krakow and Katowice to cut Germany off from her southern allies.

b) Deliver the secondary blow by the left wing of the Western Front toward Warsaw and Demblin to fix the Warsaw grouping and secure Warsaw, and also to cooperate with the Southwestern Front in destroying the Lublin group.

c) Conduct active defense against Finland, East Prussia, Hungary, and Rumania and be prepared to strike a blow against Rumania if favorable conditions arise.[3]

Zhukov calculated the Soviet attacking force of 152 divisions would be faced by roughly 100 German divisions.

Zhukov's report suggests the following conclusions: first, as of 5 May 1941, Soviet intelligence estimated German strength opposite their borders in excess of 107 divisions. This included 23 to 24 in East Prussia, 29 facing the Western Special Military District, 31 to 34 opposite the Kiev Military District, 6 located near Danzig and Poznan, 4 in the Carpatho-Ukraine, and 10 to 11 in Moldavia and Norther Dobrudja. Eighteen more divisions were then rumored to be enroute. While Zhukov's estimate of German strength on 15 May was close to accurate, it certainly would not have been when the Soviet had been able to mount their preemptive assault.

Second, Soviet deployments of 15 May were insufficient for the mounting of such an offensive. Between them, the Western and Southwestern Fronts counted about 102 divisions (see figure 2). Strategic second echelon and reserve forces were just then beginning their deployment forward and would arrive in stages between early June and mid-July. Thus, to establish requisite force strength for the offensive, Zhukov's plan could not have been implemented until mid-June (30 days) at the earliest, and by then German force strength would have also risen. For Zhukov to have reached his desired correlation of forces, the attack would have had to occur after 60 days of preparation (in mid-July). That, of course, would have been too late to have preempted the Germans and denied them surprise.

Third, in addition to correlation of forces problems, the dismal performance of Soviet forces in Poland and Finland, the sorry state of training and force readiness, the major equipment and logistical shortfalls in the Red Army, and the half-completed force reorganization would have made any offensive action by the Red Army simply folly. In light of these realities, Stalin's decision to ignore Zhukov's proposal seems to have been prudent. Thus, speculation concerning what might have occurred within the context of the major Soviet "what ifs" has no basis in fact.

FIGURE 2: THE ZHUKOV PROPOSAL FORCE AVAILABILITY

C. What if Stalin had adopted the supposed Shaposhnikov proposal for concentrating defenses along the Stalin line (pre-1939 borders)?
David M. Glantz

For years historians have speculated about what would have occurred if the Soviets had met the German onslaught with a defense based on the "Stalin line" rather than one anchored on the post-September 1939 Polish border. Such speculation proceeds from two premises: first, that such a defense would have had greater success, since German forces would have had to cross over up to 300 kilometers of lightly defended terrain before reaching the main Soviet defensive positions (with concurrent loss of surprise); and, second, that Red Army Chief of Staff, B.M. Shaposhnikov had proposed such a defense only to have the proposal rejected by Stalin.

Neither claim is substantiated by either fact or existing conditions. The supposed Shaposhnikov plan required the positioning of main Soviet border military district forces along the pre-September 1939 Polish-Soviet borders in the heavily fortified positions of the Stalin line. Covering forces would operate in the wide sector between the new border and the Stalin line with the mission of preventing surprise attack, delaying the German advance, and protecting the full mobilization of Soviet main forces (see figure 3). Essentially, the plan required mobile mechanized and armored forces, unsupported by infantry and aviation, to conduct a mobile defense across an expanse of 300 kilometers from the Baltic Sea to the Carpathian Mountains and from the Western Bug River to the 27th meridian.

The "Shaposhnikov Plan" is suspect in two basic respects. First, the Soviets reject its very existence, writing:

> There is no doubt whatsoever, that the essence of the investigated plan resembles strategic nonsense. Such a proposal could not have emanated from B.M. Shaposhnikov, who deeply understood the nature of contemporary war, who possessed vast knowledge in the realm of military history, who had great military-historical understanding and who was the author of a series of original strategic deployment plans of the Soviet armed forces in a variety of international conditions, which were affirmed after careful discussion by the Central Committee and Soviet government.[4]

Second, the plan itself would have been unrealistic and unsound. The Soviets themselves cite precedents which underscore the folly of such a defense. During the Napoleonic Wars, Russian attempts to use Barclay de Tolly's army in a similar covering force role, as a foil for a subsequent successful defense and counteroffensive by Bagration led to French occupation (albeit brief) of Moscow. German use of similar covering forces along the Marne in 1918, instead of producing successful German defense, led to a steady and disastrous German withdrawal.

In June 1941, a "maneuver defense" would have accorded the Germans an almost unobstructed advance of 300 kilometers and probably produced disastrous losses in the most powerful and mobile of Soviet forces before decisive battle resulted along the Stalin line. Deprived of mobile reserves, in short order Soviet main forces in the Stalin line defenses would have been rendered as irrelevant as French forces massed in their Maginot fortresses.

FIGURE 3: THE SHAPOSHNIKOV PLAN

D. What if Hitler had striven to make allies of the Soviet people?
Samuel J. Newland

Among many surprises that greeted Allied troops as they invaded Hitler's Fortress Europe was the staggering number of non-Germans who served loyally with or in Hitler's *Wehrmacht*. During the Normandy landings, Turkestanis and Cossacks in German uniform opposed Allied forces. Allied soldiers, noting that most of the former Soviets were led by Germans, were certain that these non-Germans were virtually herded into battle at gunpoint as cannon fodder. Why else would anyone from an occupied country fight for the Germans? In particular, why would someone from the Soviet Union fight for a system whose record of cruelty against Slavic people in World War II is well documented?

Four factors contributed to large numbers of Soviet peoples serving with the Wehrmacht. The first was bitter hatred of the oppressive Communist regime. While acknowledging the atrocities of the Germans in the occupied Soviet Union, the reader should remember that the Germans only occupied Soviet territory for some 2-3 years. This short period of time naturally limited the number and scope of atrocities, even if official German policy did not. But by the time the Germans arrived, the people of the Soviet Union had already endured over 20 years of barbarism at the hands of their own government(s). Once Lenin and his Bolsheviks had won, for years after the Revolution those who opposed them were either exterminated or incarcerated in the camps which became an integral part of Soviet culture. This, together with the immense loss of life during the Revolution, made opposition to the Soviet system a high risk proposition But those who survived, and/or their families, held a bitter hatred for the Marxist/ Leninists/Stalinists. It was a hatred which quickly reemerged when the Germans drove the Soviet government out of European Russia in 1941-42.

Secondly, closely akin to those who simply hated the Bolsheviks and their system were those who specifically hated Stalin. In the interwar years many families in Soviet Russia had suffered from the oppression of the Stalin era. Once Josef Stalin solidified his control over the Party apparatus in the late 1920's, he established a regime based on terror and oppression. The first consequences of his system were the brutal collectivization movement (1928-30) and the subsequent famine when some 5-10 million people died. This was followed by a purge of the party leadership which eliminated most of the early Politburo membership other than Stalin himself. The political purge was followed by the witch hunt of the Soviet military — the Tukhachevski affair — which decimated the high ranking Soviet military leadership. In addition to these campaigns against selected groups, Stalin and his henchmen systematically oppressed Soviet citizens from all walks of life. As an end result, even many Russians who believed in the Marxist system hated Stalinist oppression, and were more than willing to assist in seeing Stalinism destroyed.

Thirdly, it should be held in mind that the Soviet Union was not a nation — in the traditional sense. Instead it included some 120 nationalities, many of which were forcibly integrated into Imperial Russia (or the Soviet Union) within 100 years prior to World War II. Many of these nationalities had not been fully integrated into the culture or language of the Great Russians, or of the new Marxist Soviet Union, when the German attack occurred. Most significant were the people of the Baltic States forcibly annexed in 1940, the Ukrainians, and the people of the southern tier of Soviet republics who had more in common with the Turks, Iraqis, and Iranians than the people of European Russia. Given their respective desires to retain their unique identities and cultures, and the pressures and persecution they were subject to by Stalin's regime, it is not surprising that many of these people would regard the Germans, who gave them national legions, regiments, and even divisions, as their potential liberators.

For a final and most obvious reason why some Soviets worked with the Germans, in the first six months of Barbarossa, one spectacular German victory succeeded another. By November 1941 some 2,053,000 Soviet soldiers had become prisoners of war, and the figure continued to climb. March 1942 found Alfred Rosenberg's Ostministerium stating that 3,600,000 Soviet soldiers were German prisoners. The staggering prisoner bags from the first two years of the war extended German logistical capabilities beyond limits that in any case were set to provide standards far below those accepted for "western" prisoners. By accident and design the vast POW enclosures established by the Germans became hell holes of disease, starvation and death from exposure. Many Soviet soldiers were more than willing to do anything to escape from these places of almost certain death.

The potential for mobilizing became evident to the German officers who interviewed Stalin's son after his capture. According to their findings, Stalin did not worry so much about the foreign enemy, the enemy from outside. His major concern was the enemy within, and the possibility that someone could spark a war of national liberation that would cause the Soviet people to rise up and cast off his system.[5] What types of appeals could have been successful in causing such a national war of liberation?

A direct anti-Stalinist campaign would have likely been the most effective. Since Stalinist oppression had affected virtually every element of Soviet society, to include loyal and dedicated party members, such an appeal would have approached universality. The Germans could call for the Soviet people to rise up and throw off the oppressive yoke of Stalin and establish a new and more humane state. Or the appeal could have centered on throwing off Stalin's rule, which had in fact corrupted many of the basic tenets of Marx and Lenin, so that a bona fide Marxist state could develop.

If such an approach was thought inappropriate by Nazi ideologues, the Germans could have appealed to the agrarian workers on the vast Soviet collectives and state farms, promising them land and prosperity by returning the land to private ownership. Many peasants had thought that the Russian Revolution would bring them land and the freedom to work it. Instead, the collectivization drive initiated by Stalin placed Soviet farmers on either state farms or collectives, dashing their hopes for their own plots of land and the ability to market their own produce. The widespread bitterness over the collectivization of agriculture and the brutality associated with the implementation of this program made it a logical appeal for German propagandists.

A third approach that would have promoted widespread interest, could have been an appeal to the scores of Nationalities that composed so much of the population of the Soviet Union. The citizens of the three Baltic states, Ukrainians, Armenians, Georgians, and the Crimean Tatars, to name only a few, all had a history of seeking independence from Russian/Soviet rule. Even the Tsar's traditional praetorian force, the Cossacks, sought self-rule. Promises of independence or autonomy could have been a highly effective tool for defeating the Soviets. That such a strategy could and did work can be illustrated through the case of Bronislav Kaminsky. In the Autumn of 1941, General Rudolf Schmidt, commander of the 2nd German Panzer Army, placed Kaminsky, a former Soviet official, in charge of pacifying part of the Bryansk forest, an area infested by partisans. Kaminsky organized local anti-partisan units, and soon the area was under his control and partisans were no longer a serious threat. The Germans were so pleased that they eventually allowed the development of a self-governing region, with executive authority in Kaminsky's hands. Kaminsky became both the civilian and military administrator of the Lokoty Self-Governing District. He was allowed to organize a small army called the Russian People's Army of Liberation (RONA), a force that would ultimately be large enough to have its own artillery section and a complement of T-34 tanks. His Liberation Army was never larger than a German division but Kaminski's success and the adaptability shown by his German sponsors were a hint of what could have been if the Germans had been willing to use other than military means to defeat the Soviet Union.

The Kaminsky model, solely a military initiative, was replicated on several other occasions. When German units entered the Caucasus area, they again planned for self-governing regions. They had the highest hopes in a Cossack self-governing region. This experiment allowed the Cossacks to establish their own local government, based on established traditions and form ministries for agriculture, education and health services. In addition, the Cossack Ataman had the authority to raise and command military forces for the liberation of their homeland from Bolshevism. So successful was the Cossack region that once the Germans were driven from the Caucasus, the self-governing region and some of the population moved westward with them; by the war's end, the Cossacks were located in northern Italy!

Could extending and systematizing such appeals have actually caused the Soviet army to disintegrate and/or the Soviet peoples to rise up against their government? Evidence seems to indicate that they had an extremely good chance for success if coupled with fair and reasonable treatment of both the people in the occupied areas and the large numbers of POWs. That such a concept was a reality was shown by the fact that in 1941, as the Germans advanced through the western Soviet Union, they were greeted in many areas as liberators rather than conquerors.

Above and beyond the friendly crowds and the refreshments provided to weary soldiers, Soviet citizens offered more tangible assistance to the advancing Wehrmacht. In the Ukraine, many German units were pressed for manpower to fight a war and simultaneously garrison territories. The 49th German Mountain Corps solved this problem by asking, through local city leaders, for indigenous volunteers to provide security forces to guard their own communities. Everywhere on the entire Eastern Front, German units, weakened by heavy fighting, informally recruited former Soviet soldiers to drive trucks, work with supply units, handle rear area security and, before 1941 was over, even fill vacancies in front-line combat units. Citizens and soldiers cooperated without the necessity for oppressive German oversight because so many of them felt few ties with the hated Stalinist regime.

A German call to the populace for liberation from the Stalinist system was unthinkable, in the context of Nazism's eastern program. The campaign planned and initiated by Hitler against the Soviet Union was intended to smash the Soviet army, destroy the Soviet state, eradicate once and for all from European life the scourge of "Jewish Bolshevism," annex selected sections of European Russia for German colonization or settlement, and sublimate the Slavs and all of their aspirations in all areas controlled by German political or military organizations.

So serious was Hitler about a campaign of destruction against the Soviet Union and its citizens that from the onset, he forbade the Wehrmacht to allow Slavs to bear arms and fight as allies with the Germans. It was only because the Armed Forces, desperate for men, began to recruit Slavs into the German army that a movement to use Soviet citizenry developed. But the fact that, from June 1941 until the end of the war, Soviet citizens chose to fight against Stalin and with the Germans *despite* the latter's increasing reverses, indicates a deep-seated dissatisfaction among large numbers of Soviet citizens and a unique opportunity for the Germans. It was an opportunity to conduct a campaign to liberate the people of the Soviet Union and appeal to them to rise up against

Stalinism, thus supplementing military means with political. To appeal to the Soviet people for an anti-Marxist campaign could have been counter productive because there were many in the Soviet Union who believed in the promises of Marx and thought that Marxism still offered hope for the future if the country could be rid of Stalinism. In all likelihood the best chance for such an appeal would have focused on destroying the Stalinist system and appealing to the nationalities. What if the Germans had posed as liberators? What could have been the possible outcome and conduct of the war?

A scenario in which the Germans were liberators might have proceeded as follows:

On 29 July 1940, with Operation Sea Lion looming on the horizon and the campaign to bring Britain to her knees seemingly coming to a successful conclusion, Hitler announced to the *Wehrmacht* high command that he intended to attack the Soviet Union. From late July 1940 until January 1941, *Wehrmacht* planners attempted to develop a campaign plan in keeping with Hitler's directions, only to conclude that the task as outlined by the Fuehrer was virtually impossible. According to General Alfred Jodl, who was totally supported by all of the principals on the *Oberkommando des Heeres* staff, a successful campaign with the goals Hitler had established, was virtually impossible. Conversely, Jodl reported, there was a excellent chance for a campaign to succeed if Hitler were willing to sublimate or set aside some of his goals so that the most important element of his campaign might be realized, i.e. the destruction of the Soviet Union with its presently constituted Marxist government.

Though clearly annoyed that his military commanders would question the parameters of a campaign which he personally had established, Hitler allowed his high command to continue. Drawing on plans devised by Admiral Wilhelm Canaris' *Abwehr* and the army's own *Fremde Heer Ost*, it was proposed that when German units attacked the Soviet Union, the entire front would be saturated by a propaganda campaign announcing that German forces were attacking the Soviet Union to free its peoples from the yoke of Stalinism and to prevent the rest of Europe from having to live under the specter of threats from Stalin. The appeal would call for the citizenry of the Soviet Union to rise up and destroy Stalinism. Specific appeals would be addressed to the peoples of the Baltic states, the Ukrainians, Georgians, Armenians, as well as other national groups, drawing on their special grievances and implying that with victory the nationalities might expect favorable treatment, even autonomy with the assistance of the Germans.

All elements of the Wehrmacht would be instructed to regard themselves as liberators. Despite years of linked anti-communist/anti-Slavic themes in official German publications, the German military must see its true mission as destroying communism. It was communism which had corrupted the Slavic people, and the Wehrmacht's goal was to liberate the Slavs from the Communist scourge so they could become productive members of European society. As the army advanced, prisoners were to be treated well.

As soon as possible after capture, Soviet soldiers would be invited to join a liberation army and play a role in destroying Stalin. Philosophical support and actual manpower would be solicited as well from the large Russian emigre communities in Belgrade, Paris, Berlin and Manchuria, calling for the old soldiers of the revolution and their descendents to assist in destroying Stalin.

Once the army had liberated areas from Soviet forces, self-governing regions would be organized. These areas would be based on nationalities, and would be responsible for security, raising taxes (in part to support the liberation effort) and all of the other functions expected of a legally recognized government. German advisers and liaison personnel would be assigned to each area. It would be their responsibility to ensure that German goals were always kept in the forefront. Thus the keystones for German victory would be the strength and skill of the German army, the substantial manpower available through using anti-Stalinist forces, and the ability to draw on the resources of the secure rear areas to provision the German army.

Within this hypothetical program could have been the seeds of a German victory against the Soviet Union. Consider how it might have worked. Germany mustered over three million men for the Barbarossa offensive against the Soviet Union. This, together with assistance provided by allied countries, provided a very respectable attacking force. Conversely, the German army suffered casualties of 150,000-160,000 monthly, this figure based on day-to-day fighting and excluding major battles. General Franz Halder's diary brought this into clearer perspective by noting that from June 22, 1941 to June 20, 1942, the German army suffered 1,299,784 casualties which amounted to 40.62 per cent of the attacking force.[5] Some of these casualties returned to the front following convalescence, nevertheless the German army was slowly bleeding to death on the Eastern front.

Would the hypothetical Jodl proposal have helped? In historical fact, there never was a concentrated or official attempt to recruit Russian prisoners into German service. Appeals addressed to serving or former Soviet soldiers were, by and large, designed for propaganda purposes, not to gain the badly needed manpower and equipment resources available in Soviet Russia. What were the prospects if the appeals had been sincere? Once the Battle of Smolensk was over and the city was in German hands, the new city leadership, pleased with the liberation from Stalin's tyranny and with encouragement from Field Marshal Fedor von Bock's Army Group Center, formed a "Russian Liberation Committee." They indicated to the Germans their willingness to spearhead a move to raise a Russian Liberation Army of one million men. Their proposal was forwarded to the Fuehrer Hauptquartier, where it languished and was never officially answered.[7]

Even more intriguing, on August 22, 1941, the 436th Soviet Regiment, commanded by Major Ivan Kononov defected to the Germans. Its commander had indicated as early as August 3, in the midst of a successful counterattack against the Germans, that his entire regiment was willing to serve as the nucleus of a Liberation Army. Though their defection was accepted and Kononov and his men would fight against Soviet troops for the remainder of the war, the Liberation Movement he sought to lead was never authorized.

These are only two of many similar opportunities that presented themselves to Germans during the first year of the war. It is significant to note that, even though Hitler's, and thus the German Army's, policy was against enlisting Slavs into German service, General Ernst Koestring estimated that some 500,000-600,000 Soviet citizens were serving in the German army in the period 1942-43.[8] They served in a number of capacities: as unarmed support personnel, front line soldiers in the Wehrmacht, local security forces in the occupied areas, and as pilots and air crew in their own volunteer air force. So great were their actual numbers, and so effectively did German commanders hide them from doctrinaire National Socialists, that their true strength and the extent of their service will probably never be know. After over 25 years of research, the writer is firmly convinced that altogether somewhere between 1-3 million served during the course of the war. If this many Soviet citizens could be recruited without an official campaign and in contradiction to official German policy, how many could have been enlisted with a determined and aggressive program to seek the help of the citizenry in a war of liberation and extend it as indicated in this scenario?

If Hitler had permitted the building of liberation armies, ensured the humane treatment of prisoners, and sanctioned the establishment of a reasonable occupation government, the consequences for the Eastern front would have been staggering. As

German armies reached dangerously close to Moscow in the first week of December 1941, what would have been the impact of having available several hundred thousand additional troops, a liberation Army dedicated to ousting Stalin from the seat of government. When the bitter winter of 1941 struck, what if a Russian Liberation Army was on line, equipped with Russian heavy equipment built to withstand the rigors of Russian winter. Tractors, trucks, and tanks had been left behind as junk by the advancing and victorious German army that planned to complete its campaign before winter set in.

Or what if the German army had possessed the luxury of having few worries about rear area security? To fight a war with a front line roughly 1,800 miles long and occupy an area of over one million square miles was indeed a Herculean task. What if the rear areas had been governed by their own people who ensured security through local militia groups, freeing the armed forces for the task of fighting the war? That it could and did work, where permitted by enlightened army leaders is a documented fact.

None of this was to be. In Hitler's new Europe, Slavs were to be subjugated, not entrusted with new, enlightened and popular governments. Hitler desired only to wage a war of conquest and destruction which was designed to destroy the Soviet state and Marxism and subjugate the Slavs. A strategy which would have included a combination of political appeals, accommodation with the people, and aggressive military action was simply not allowable.

To recognize fully the opportunity missed by the Germans, one only needs to contemplate that between one to three million Soviets served loyally with the Germans, many clear up to the war's end. Often they served without first class equipment. They fought loyally even though ridiculed by some Germans. They fought without any official hope or promises for a better future. What if Germany had actually offered to liberate them, to offer them a future for a new Europe? If the scenario included in this chapter had been implemented, Germany might have been virtually handed a world-shaping victory on a silver platter.

[1]   M. V. Zakharov, *General'nyi shtab y predvoennye gody* [The General Staff in the prewar years], Moscow, Voenizdat, 1989, 258-261.

[2]   V. Karpov, "Zhukov." Komunest voorushennykhsil [Communist of the armed forces}, No. 5 (March, 1990), 61.

[3]   Ibid., 68.

[4]   Zakharov, 225.

[5]   Wilfred Strik-Strikfeldt, *Against Stalin and Hitler: Memoir of the Russian Liberation Movement* (New York: The John Day Company, l973), pp. 32-33.

[6]   Franz Halder, *The Halder Diaries: The Private War Journals of Colonel General Franz Halder* (Boulder: Westview Press, 1976), p. 1468.

[7]   Strik-Strikfeldt, pp.45-47

[8]   General Ernst Koestring, Interrogation of General Ernst Kostring by the Historical Interrogation Commission, August 30-31, 1945, by Lieutenant Colonel O. J. Hale, pp. 8-9, U.S. National Archives.

Chapter 5

Germany versus the Soviet Union

David M. Glantz

German Intelligence and Soviet Realities

There has been no conflict more replete with disputes concerning "what might have been" than the war on the Eastern Front. For over forty years, former German generals and German historians have reviewed the first two years of war with a jeweler's eye to detect those decisions, which, from their perspective, adversely affected the course and outcome of the war. More often than not, their critiques have reflected Cold War attitudes and lamented German failure to vanquish the Bolshevik menace to Western civilization. Ironically, while glossing over the root causes of war, they have made Hitler the scapegoat for German military failure. By focusing on Hitler's whimsical decision making, they have attempted to vindicate the judgement of the army leadership as Hitler denied it its rightful victory.

One fundamental factor undergirds the outcomes of all "what ifs" pertaining to German military operations against the Soviet Union after 22 June 1941. It is the correlation of German and Soviet military strength after June and the mobilization capabilities of the Soviet state. In short, it is likely that German failure to detect or appreciate actual and potential Soviet military strength ultimately predetermined the outcome of Operation Barbarossa and the war as a whole and rendered quite superfluous virtually all subsequent operational "what ifs."

What then was the scale of that German intelligence failure? During the planning period for Operation Barbarossa, German intelligence underassessed the active strength of the Red Army and maintained a flawed picture of its composition, in particular vis a vis the Soviets' armored force. Curiously enough, this had not been the case when German planning commenced in summer 1940, but increasingly it became true as the Germans apparently failed to detect Soviet General Staff mobilization measures implemented throughout the ensuing year (or, as the Soviets referred to it, the "creeping up to war").

In August 1940 the Germans estimated Soviet military strength at 151 infantry divisions, 32 cavalry divisions, and 38 mechanized brigades, at a time when actual Soviet ground force strength was 152 rifle divisions, 26 cavalry divisions, and 9 newly forming mechanized corps (each composed of 2 tank divisions and 1 motorized rifle division).[1] Although German estimates of Soviet regular infantry and cavalry forces were close to accurate, the Germans began a long-lasting process of underestimating Soviet armored strength. Against this force the Germans postulated their own attack force of 147 divisions (24 panzer, 1 cavalry, 12 motorized infantry, and 110 infantry), a force which would remain stable throughout subsequent planning.[2]

The final German assessment of Soviet strength, prepared in early June 1941, estimated a force of 170 infantry divisions, 33½ cavalry divisions, and 46 motorized and armored brigades (equivalent to 15 divisions). At this time the Red Army active strength was 196 rifle divisions, 13 cavalry divisions, 61 tank divisions (58 with mechanized corps and 3 separate), and 31 motorized rifle divisions (29 with mechanized corps and 2 separate). Of this total the Germans assessed Soviet strength in the border military districts at 118 infantry divisions, 20 cavalry divisions, and 40 mobile brigades (a total of about 150 divisions) whereas actual Soviet strength was 171 divisions of all types. In the remainder of European Russia, German intelligence estimated there were about 32 Soviet divisions, when, in fact, about 100 existed.[3]

These figures underscore two major faults in German assessments of existing Soviet military strength. First, the German did not adequately keep track of the scale of Soviet readiness efforts. While this was true of military districts along the border, it was even more pronounced in the internal military districts where mobilization could be better concealed. Second, the Germans had an inadequate appreciation of Soviet force restructuring, in particular restructuring associated with the Soviet mechanization program. As late as 22 June, German intelligence continued to count older Soviet tank brigades and cavalry divisions without realizing that most of these had reformed into tank and mechanized divisions and mechanized corps. By 22 June the Germans had identified one mechanized corps each in the Baltic, Special Western and Special Kiev Military Districts out of the sixteen which were actually there (in various stages of formation). Nor did the Germans detect the large antitank brigades formed in the border districts designated to cooperate with the new mechanized corps.[4] It is true, however, that German operational and tactical proficiency largely compensated for this intelligence failure. Nevertheless, the failure established a pattern which would persist in the future with inevitable negative effects.

Far more serious than this problem was the German failure to appreciate the size and efficiency of the Soviet mobilization system. German estimates tended to look only at active Soviet forces, that is, those maintained in peacetime at various levels of combat readiness. They did not, however, detect or closely examine Soviet mobilization or spin-off divisions, which had seemingly insignificant cadre and equipment complements in peacetime. This was perhaps understandable in light of German estimates that the Barbarossa operation would be over in about four months, before the Soviets could generate significant new combat-ready forces. The German High Command reasoned that any new Soviet units could be dealt with in successive stages of the operation.

To appreciate the scale of this German failure, it is only necessary to review the actual Soviet mobilization record. Soviet armed forces strength on 22 June 1941 was 20 armies (14 along the western border and 6 in the Far East), 303 divisions (31 in the process of forming), and about 5.0 million men.[5] By 1 July 1941 the Soviets had called 5.3 million men into military service. Between 22 June and 1 December 1941, increased personnel call-ups permitted the Soviets to field 291 new divisions and 94 brigades. Of this total 70 were brought to strength and transferred westward from internal military districts and 27 were dispatched westward from the Far East, Central Asia, and Trans-Baikal Military Districts. The remaining 194 divisions and 94 brigades were formed anew from cadre in the mobilization base. Subsequently, in 1942 the Soviets formed 50 new divisions and reformed 67 divisions.[6]

By November 1942, the Soviet mobilization system had created a total of 367 rifle divisions, 193 rifle brigades, and 118 tank or mechanized brigades. This was followed by the creation of 42 divisions and 44 brigades between November 1942 and December 1943. While prewar German estimates had postulated an opposing force of up to 300 divisions, in fact, by December 1941 the Soviets had been able to mobilize and deploy a force of over 600 divisions. This permitted the Soviets to lose well over 100 divisions during the initial period of war and still survive.[7]

The Soviets mobilized and deployed these forces in waves of reserve armies throughout the first year of war. The wave effect put at the disposal of the *Stavka* (High

Soviet Dispositions on 31 July, 1941 and Reinforcements to 31 December, 1941

——— 31 July, 1941
- - - - August-December, 1941

Figure 1

Command) sizeable fresh strategic reserves after each operational disaster and provided staying power for the Red Army.

The first wave of Soviet reserve armies mobilized prior to the outbreak of war. Between 13 May and 22 June, to bolster existing forces in the border military districts, the Soviets deployed forward five armies from interior military districts (16th, 19th, 20th, 21st, 22nd), two of which closed into the forward area in June and the remainder in early July. After the German offensive swallowed up these armies, along with covering armies along the border, in July 1941 a new wave of eight Soviet reserve armies took up positions east of Smolensk, where they were joined August by a ninth reserve army (43rd) (plus three more on the northern and southern flanks).[8] The presence of these armies in July and August prompted the stiff Soviet resistance around Smolensk that slowed German progress and contributed to the German decision to strike at Kiev in order to clear their southern flank.

In early October 1941, after the Soviets had fielded three more armies, the Germans broke through Soviet positions near Viaz'ma and Briansk and, by mid-November, approached Moscow, certain that one final successful lunge would secure the Soviet capital. As Soviet resistance on the approaches to Moscow stiffened, Stalin again marshaled his strategic reserves, amassing in the Moscow region six reserve armies, which he ultimately employed to spearhead the Soviet December counteroffensive. Simultaneously, on the flanks the Soviet threw into combat four more reserve armies to stiffen defenses in the Leningrad and Rostov regions (see figure l).[9]

This mobilization and deployment process continued even after the German 1941 strategic drive had been blunted. In spring 1942, anticipating a new German strategic thrust, the Soviet High Command formed ten new reserve armies (number 1-10) and an experimental 3rd Tank Army (see figure 2). It deployed the mostly conscript reserve armies on a broad front from Vologda in the North to Saratov and the Volga River in the south. While German Operation "Blau" unfolded, propelling German forces across southern Russia into the Don River bend and on to Stalingrad and the Caucasus, the *Stavka* renumbered these armies and threw them into combat, primarily in the Voronesh and Stalingrad regions. At the same time the *Stavka* formed three additional tank armies (1st, 4th, and 5th), which participated in the summer and fall operations in southern Russia.

All the while, additional Soviet armies formed on the base of armies defeated or depleted in earlier operations (e.g. in April 1942, 53rd Army was created from 34th Army, in October 1942, 65th Army formed from badly damaged 4th Tank Army). The force generation process also drew NKVD forces into the regular force structure when, in October 1942, 70th Army formed in the Ural Military District on the base of NKVD troops from the Far Eastern, Trans-Baikal, and Central Asian Military District.[10]

After November 1942 the process of forming new reserves slowed, in part because of the already existing Soviet numerical superiority. From November 1942 to December 1943, the Soviets created 2 new combined-arms armies and 3 new tank armies and a total of 42 divisions and 44 brigades. From that time forth, most new conscripts were used to fill existing formations.[11]

The net result of this comprehensive mobilization program was Soviet creation between 13 May 1941 and December 1943 of over forty armies of various types and composition. The formation and almost constant maintenance of a sizeable strategic reserve enabled the Soviet High Command to survive crisis after crisis in the first eighteen months of war by fielding fresh troops after each operation had run its natural course, and at a time when German forces were most vulnerable. This, in large part, explained the extraordinary staying power of the Red Army and, as we shall see,

71

FIGURE 2

rendered virtually all disputes regarding German operational decision-making (the "what ifs") superfluous.

A. What if German Army Group Center had continued its advance on Moscow in August 1941 rather than participating in the Kiev operation?

Within the context of mobilization realities, one of the most controversial German "what ifs" was the decision by Hitler in July 1941, over OKW and OKH objections, to halt the drive on Moscow and, instead, deal with Soviet resistance in the Kiev region. After a month-long debate (and delay), on 25 August Guderian's Second Panzer Group and Second Army of Army Group Center turned south and joined with Army Group South forces to encircle and destroy over 600,000 Soviet troops in the Kiev region. The immense Kiev encirclement struck a devastating blow against Soviet forces in the south but delayed the resumption of German operations against Moscow for about thirty days (25 August—2 October).

The decision to strike at Soviet forces around Kiev was conditioned by three realities: heavy Soviet resistance at Smolensk, where the Red Army had committed four fresh reserve armies to combat (29th, 30th, 24th, 28th); prospects for continued heavy resistance on the road to Moscow (where, in actuality, five more armies—31st, 32nd, 33rd, 34th, and 43rd—were deploying, and two others—49th and 50th—were forming); and the lucrative target of Soviet forces in the Kiev-Gomel area, which, if not dealt with, could pose a threat to Army Group Center's right flank. In retrospect, the wisdom of the German drive southward hinges on the question of what could the Germans have accomplished in a late August thrust to Moscow. As it was, the ensuing Kiev operation, because of Stalin's refusal to permit the Southwestern Front to withdraw from the Kiev trap, cost the Soviets over 600,000 men and opened the southern Soviet Union for a subsequent broad-front German advance.[12]

Had the Germans commenced an advance on Moscow in late August, they would have had to contend with these facts. First, their estimates of Soviet military strength were still too low. German intelligence had detected some, but not all, of the Soviet reserve armies between Smolensk and Moscow, but they had no inkling of the fact that additional reserves were available for commitment in the fall of 1941. Most German commanders were simply too optimistic to develop a realistic view.[13] Second, German casualties by late August exceeded 650,000 men, or roughly 20 percent of their original 3.4 million man attack force. Panzer divisions were severely worn down (to roughly 50 percent strength), and casualties had reduced overall German strength to an equivalent of about 83 divisions.[14] These depleted forces would have to have contended with over 200 Soviet divisions (in the German estimate) and an actual figure closer to 300. Third, had the Germans marched directly on Moscow, they would have left a sizeable Soviet force on their right (southern) flank in the form of the Soviet Central Front. Experiences in the Rogachev area in July and in January 1942 west of Moscow demonstrated the seriousness of the flank threat.[15]

For the sake of argument, let us presume the Germans continued their offensive against Moscow in late summer 1941. It is certainly reasonable to assume a German August drive on Moscow would have accomplished at least as much as did the October thrust, this is, the encirclement of Soviet forces in the Viaz'ma region (see figure 3). Since the actual Briansk encirclement of October 1941 resulted largely from the southerly positioning of Guderian's Second Panzer Group and an August thrust would likely have had Second Panzer Group advancing further north, perhaps on Briansk itself, the

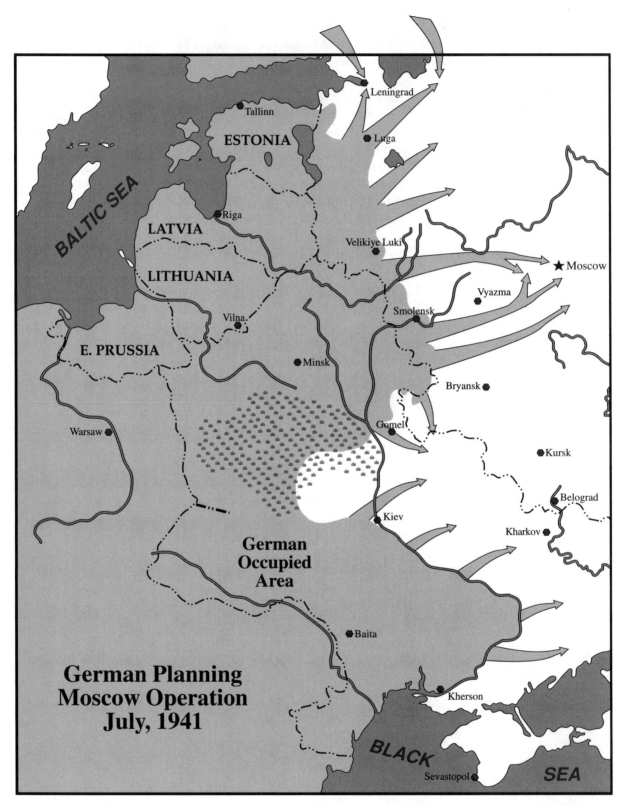

FIGURE 3

August attack would probably have completely encircled Soviet 19th, 16th, 20th, 24th, 32nd, and 43rd Armies, but not 50th, 3rd, and 13th Armies.[16]

The actual German October offensive brought its forces to the approaches to Moscow in late November, with some delays caused by deteriorating weather. The German advance finally expired in the first few days of December. Presuming an even more rapid advance in August, or even earlier, German forces could have approached Moscow in early to mid-October with an armored spearhead the Soviets could not have halted short of the capital. It is probable that Soviet forces could have held the flanks north of the Volga River and Volga reservoir and south of Elets and probably the Oka River line south of Kolomna. Deteriorating weather after 6 October would have rendered the Volga and Moscow Rivers as severe obstacles and would have hindered the German advance just as they reached the Moscow region. This period of rainy weather and mud finally ended during the second week of November. There is no doubt that, if the Soviets had decided to defend Moscow (in Stalingrad fashion), they could have held out in the city throughout October. There is some doubt as to whether the Germans could have effected a successful envelopment of the city in October to cut off supply routes to the defenders. Thus, in the best case, German forces could have reached Orekhovo-Zuevo, encircled the city, probably defended by Soviet 49th and 5th Armies, and had to contend with the problem of clearing Moscow of its defenders. In the worst case, the Germans would have been tied down in a struggle for the city itself.

In both circumstances by late November and December 1941, the Soviets would have been able to employ a new wave of reserve armies, including 10th, 26th, 1st Shock, 37th, 39th, 56th, 57th, 58th, 59th, 60th, and 61st Armies. They had also reconstituted 20th and 28th Armies by late November. Two of these armies (26th, 1st Shock) were available to reinforce Soviet forces in the Moscow region in October, and the remainder became available throughout November and December. Three of the armies (56th, 57th, 59th), which were actually committed elsewhere along the front, could have been rerouted to Moscow. Finally, it is also reasonable to assume that armies ultimately used to reinforce the Southwestern Front after the Kiev debacle, if that debacle had not occurred, could have been diverted northward toward Moscow (such as 37th Army activated in October 1941).

The key rail network from the south and east to Riazhsk and Riazan and from the north and east to Iaroslavl' would likely have been available for the Soviets to effect large concentrations north and south of Moscow. Given Soviet potential strength in late November, it is unlikely that German Army Group Center would have reached much beyond Moscow. Nor could Army Group South have achieved more than reducing Kiev, reaching the Dnepr River line, and seizing the approaches into the Crimea. Since the Soviets did not significantly reinforce their forces in the Leningrad region by late November, the situation there and south of Lake I'lmen would likely have developed as it actually did.

Based on the relative strength of Soviet and German forces after November 1941 and the manner in which the two High Commands conducted subsequent operations, one can reconstruct a reasonable postulation of the course of subsequent combat, at least through 1943. This reconstruction presumes subsequent Soviet force mobilization and deployment as they actually occurred.

Subsequent operations probably would have unfolded in the following strategic stages:
1. Soviet winter offensive against German forces around Moscow;
2. German summer offensive against Soviet forces in the southern USSR (figure 4);
3. Soviet winter offensive against German forces in the southern USSR;

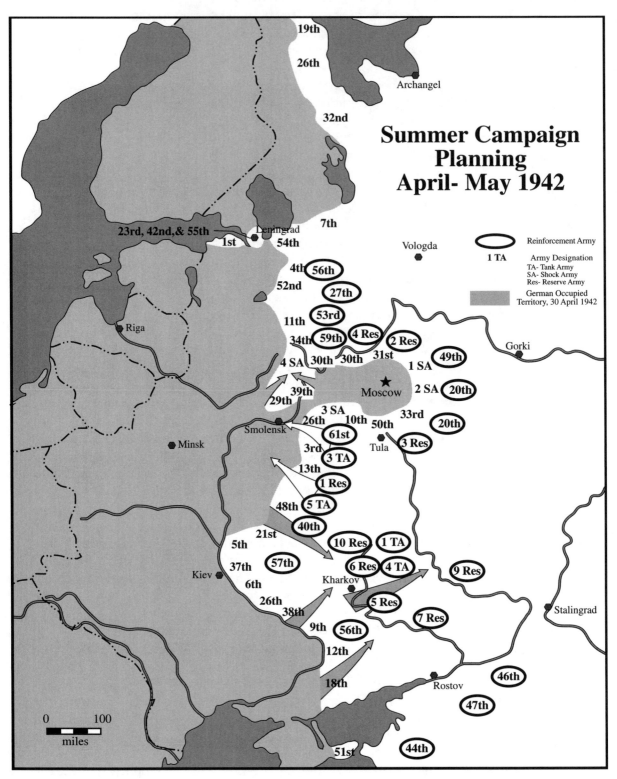

FIGURE 4

4. German winter counteroffensive in the southern USSR;

5. German summer offensive in 1943 and Soviet strategic counteroffensive.

If there is a remarkable resemblance between conditions as they actually existed along the Eastern Front in September 1943 and those which this scenario describes, it is because during war there are fundamental factors at work, which seem to overcome episodic and transitory events and govern the course and outcome of combat. In the case of the Eastern Front (and I suspect, to some extent, elsewhere), these fundamentals included the military correlation of forces, the will of a nation's population and political leadership, the style *(kultura)* of commanders and staffs (style of war), and psychology of a people, and the economic strength of the state. When these factors are weighted and permitted to operate, while the details of the scenario frequently change, the outcome does not. In this sense this scenario deals not only with the initial "what if"—concerning the fall of Moscow—but also subsequent operation "what ifs."

B. What if the German 1942 summer offensive had been focused on Moscow?

A German strategic offensive in the summer of 1942 against Soviet forces in the Moscow region would have been a difficult operation for the Germans and would probably have resulted in a replay of the results of the fictitious German seizure of Moscow in 1941.

Soviet strategic defenses in the spring of 1942 were concentrated on the Moscow axis. Soviet forces occupied multiple strong defensive positions echeloned in depth, the bulk of new Soviet reserve armies and the newly reorganized tank corps were positioned in the Moscow region, and the most competent field commander, Zhukov, commanded the defense. In a sense, Soviet defenses resembled a weaker version of the defense the Soviets established at Kursk in 1943.

Despite the strong defenses, a concentrated German thrust could have penetrated into operational depths, but at a high cost in men and material. Conceivably, German forces could have besieged or taken Moscow, but, thereafter, their situation would have been as precarious as it turned out to be at Stalingrad in November 1942. The probably Soviet counteroffensive could have destroyed elements of Army Group Center in the same manner as German Sixth Army was actually destroyed at Stalingrad. Again, the correlation of forces was the key ingredient in likely German failure.

What if the German 1942 summer offensive had concentrated on a single objective (e.g. Stalingrad)?

Had the German 1942 summer offensive concentrated on securing the single objective of Stalingrad, it is more likely the Germans could have taken the city and a more sizeable portion of the west bank of the Volga River north and south of the city. German forces would have suffered higher casualties while seizing the city, and it is doubtful whether they could have avoided employing allied (Rumanian, Italian, Hungarian) forces to secure their long flanks. The overall correlation of Soviet and German forces would have persisted, and Soviet reserve armies and newly formed tank forces would have launched a counteroffensive, although against a larger German salient, defended by a greater concentration of forces. The Germans could perhaps have avoided the catastrophic loss of Sixth Army but would nevertheless have been forced to withdraw westward into the Donbas region.

C. What if the Japanese had joined the German attack prior to December 1941?

Japanese war planning looked either east or northwest, but did not envision operations in both directions. In August 1939 at Khalkhin Gol in Manchuria, the Soviets had seriously blooded Japanese forces.[17] The memory of that defeat had lingered. The Japanese also well knew that Soviet fortifications covering the coastal regions were extensive and would require significant forces to overcome. Even after the commencement of Operation Barbarossa, between 32 and 59 Soviet divisions manned these defenses.[18] By that time, the Japanese government had signed a non-aggression treaty with the Soviet Union, and military authorities were planning for a strike eastward against the United States Pacific possessions in support of the Japanese strategic drive into southeast Asia and the southwest Pacific.

It is clear that debates continued within the Japanese High Command regarding strategic military priorities, and these debates included consideration of action against the Soviet Union. Throughout the summer and fall of 1941 the non-aggression pact, uncertainties regarding the outcome of Operation Barbarossa, and Japanese planning for its operations in the Pacific and Southeast Asia precluded consideration of an attack on the Soviet Far East. German defeat at the gates of Moscow reinforced the Japanese decision to honor the non-aggression pact with the Soviet Union Despite Japanese reluctance to become involved in a two-front war with the U.S. and the Soviet Union, Japanese Kwantung Army planning remained offensive in its orientation until mid-1944, although by that time any thoughts of offensive action against the Soviet Union would have been sheer folly.

Some have argued that Soviet Siberian divisions played an instrumental role in the Red Army's December 1941 victory at Moscow. While Far Eastern divisions indeed contributed to victory at Moscow, the reserves which the *Stavka* committed to combat in the Moscow region were drawn from all points of the compass. Many of those divisions which came from the Far Eastern and Trans-Baikal Military Districts would likely have marched westward regardless of Japanese intentions or actions. In fact, most began their westward movement well before December. Soviet High Command war planning consistently accorded highest priority to victory in the West. In the unlikely case the Japanese had conducted a limited attack against the Soviet Far East, the Stavka would have required the region to fend for itself and trade space for time until adequate reinforcements became available in 1942. There was, of course, the clear precedent of the Civil War years, when the Bolsheviks concentrated on prevailing in the key western theater before restoring its position in the far eastern theater. Soviet interwar years war planning confirmed that strategic position.[19]

Reflections.

The course of history reflects a certain momentum derived from what the Soviets often call "objective reality." While they tend to use the term subjectively to explain an ideological process of inevitable change with predetermined ends, there is some truth in this description. They themselves are today falling victim to the very same imperatives of objective reality, stripped of its ideological glitter.

There were such imperatives at work once the war on the Eastern Front was unleashed. It was an uncontrolled struggle for survival on the part of both Germany and the Soviet Union. As one perceptive German veteran noted:

"Fighting against the Russians was more than a sport, as it had been in North Africa — of course a sport with firing. But these ...people ...with oriental eyes and with smallpox marks, they made us shiver in our bones, and we felt all the time in Russia, from the first weeks on, that it was not just two armies against each other, but that it was a fundamental system on both sides struggling."[20]

In such a struggle, in the last analysis a single faulty decision paled against the vast scale and intensity of combat. The rapier's thrust had a telling effect in the chess-like war in North Africa. in Russia, a rapier's thrust granted temporary advantage, but, in a war waged with meat axes, that advantage was only fleeting. While there was still art in battle, in the end strength, will, instinct, and sheer power prevailed, rendering virtually all "what ifs" largely superfluous.

[1] For German estimates of Soviet strength, see "The German Campaign in Russia, Planning and Operations (l940-l941),: DA Pamphlet No. 20-261a, Washington, D.C.: Department of the Army, March 1955, 7; Soviet figures in V. A. Anfilov, *Proval blitskriga* [The failure of blitzkrieg], Moscow: "Nauka," 1974, 117-124, and numerous other sources.

[2] Ibid., 7.

[3] Ibid., 42. Soviet strength figures from V. Danilov, "Sovetskoe glavnoe komandovanie v predverii otechestvennoi voiny" [The Soviet high command on the threshold of the patriotic war], *Novaia i noveishaia istoriia* [New and newest history], No. 6 November-December 1988, 4.

[4] See *Lage der Roten Armee im europaischen Russland abgeschlossen am 20 VI. 41* Abteilung Fremde Herre Ost, H3/1346, NAM T-78, 677, which shows all assessed Soviet unit locations in the border military districts.

[5] Danilov, 4.

[6] V. Zemskov, "Nekotorye voprosy sozdaniia i ispol'zovaniia stratigicheskikh reservov" [Some question of the creation and use of strategic reserves], *Voenno-istoricheskii zhurnal.* [Military-historical journal] No. l0 October 1971, 14. Hereafter cited as VIZH; A. G. Khor'kov, "Nekotorye voprosy strategicheskogo i razvertyvaniia Sovetskikh Vooruzhennykh Sil v nachale Velikoi Otechestvennoi voiny" [Some questions of the strategic deployment of the Soviet armed forces at the beginning of the Great Patriotic War]. VIZH, No. 1 January 1986. 13.

[7] V. Golubovich, "Sozdanie strategicheskikh reservov" [The creation of strategic reserves], VIZh, No. 4 April 1977, 12-19. Soviet losses during 1941 are difficult to determine because many divisions listed by the Germans as destroyed were, in fact, reformed around surviving remnants of the former divisions. It is clear that the Soviets lost more than 100 division equivalents.

[8] M. V. Zakharov, *General'nyi shtab v predvoennye gody* [The General Staff in the prewar years], (Moscow: Voenizdat, 1989), 258-262, provides details of the April-July mobilization process. Subsequent mobilization described by Khor'kov, 11-13; and A. I. Evseev, "Manevr strategicheskimi rezervami v pervem periode Velikoi Otechestvennoi voiny" [The maneuver of strategic reserves in the first period of the Great Patriotic War], VIZh, No. 3 March 1986, 11-13

[9] Evseev, 12-14. See also Robert G. Poirier and Albert Z. Conner, *Red Army Order of Battle in the Great Patriotic War,* draft manuscript.

[10] Poirier and Conner; SVE.

[11] Evseev, 13-14. By 31 December 1943, the Soviets had created eleven guards armies from existing armies, as well as five tank armies and a fifth shock army.

[12] Stalin's decision to hold Kiev has also been at the center of historical controversy. Had the Germans mounted an attack on Moscow in July or August, they would not have been able to encircle the Soviet Kiev grouping. This would have left a sizeable Soviet force on Army Group Center's long right flank. Without the destruction of the 600,000 man force defending Kiev,

it is unlikely Army Group South could have made significant gains east of the Dnepr River in the fall of 1941.

[13] Most German assessments in early fall presumed the Soviets had expended virtually all their reserves. Illustrative of this fact are numerous entries in the diary of General F. Halder, German Army Chief of Staff.

[14] E. F. Ziemke and M. E., *Moscow to Stalingrad: Decision in the East*, Washington, D. C., Center of Military History, United States Army, 1987, 45

[15] During operations in July 1941, Soviet forces launched counterattacks near Rogachev and west of Bobruisk. During the latter, several Soviet cavalry corps gained the German rear, and the former evoked the following comment from Guderian:

"Since July 13th the Russians had been launching heavy counterattacks. Some twenty enemy divisions moved from the direction of Gomel against the right flank of my Panzer Group ... All these operations were controlled by Marshal Timoshenko, with the obvious objective of belatedly frustrating our successful crossing of the Dnieper." H. Guderian, *Panzer Leader*, New York, Ballentine Books, 1965, 144.

The twenty divisions Guderian described were three fresh divisions and remnants of about four others badly damaged in earlier operations. If this event could evoke such notice when the German flank extended less than 100 kilometers, how much greater the threat would have been against an even more weakly defended 350 kilometer flank extending from the Dnepr River to Moscow.

[16] German Army encirclements of Soviet forces were notoriously porous. In the actual Viaz'ma and Briansk encirclements, sufficient Soviet forces escaped to reconstitute many of the encircled divisions and armies. The larger postulated encirclement would have been no different. In fact, because of its larger size, it would have been more difficult to seal off totally.

[17] At Khalkhin-Gol a Soviet force of 57,000 men under future Marshal Zhukov annihilated two Japanese divisions, which two months earlier had made a small incursion into Mongolia.

[18] For a Japanese appreciation of Soviet far eastern defenses, see "Study of Strategical and Tactical Peculiarities of Far Eastern Russian and Soviet Far East Forces," *Japanese Special Studies on Manchuria, Vol XIII,* (Tokyo: Headquarters, Army Forces Far East, Military History Section 1955). In particular, it details Soviet use of fortified regions to compensate for the relative paucity of line divisions. During the war, the Far Eastern Front dispatched 23 divisions and 19 brigades to the European theater. Strength in the Far East averaged 1 million men in from 32 divisions (or division equivalents) in 1942 to 59 divisions in May 1945 (rifle brigades and fortified regions counted as ½ divisions).

[19] Zakharov, 124-138, provides details of Soviet war planning between 1938-1941.

[20] David M. Glantz, ed., *From the Don to the Dnepr: Soviet Offensive Operations December 1942 - April 1943, 1984 Art of War Symposium, A Transript of Proceedings,* (Carlisle, PA: U.S. Army War College, 1984), 432. Quoting a comment by General Lingenthal.

Chapter 6

Pearl Harbor

Edward J. Drea, Frederick D. Parker, Harold C. Deutsch & Dennis M. Showalter

A. What if the Japanese Navy had launched a second strike against Pearl Harbor on 7 December 1941?
Edward J. Drea

On the morning of December 7, 1941, Japan launched a surprise attack against United States military installations of Oahu, Hawaiian Islands. Three hundred and fifty planes launched from six Imperial Japanese Navy aircraft carriers struck the U.S. Pacific Fleet, then anchored at the naval base at Pearl Harbor, as well as airfields, barracks, and other military installations on the island. In less than two hours, Japanese airmen had left eight battleships, three light cruisers, three destroyers, and four auxiliary craft either sunk, capsized or damaged. Ninety-seven U.S. naval aircraft and seventy-seven U.S. Army Air Force planes were destroyed. Another eighty-eight Army planes had suffered various degrees of damage. Airfields and installations were heavily hit. The raid killed more than 2,400 Americans, 2,008 of whom were Navy personnel, and wounded another 1,178. Japanese losses were twenty-nine planes, one large submarine, and five midget submarines. Nevertheless, the Japanese attack was not a total success. Pearl Harbor's docks, cranes, and oil storage areas were untouched.

The Second Strike
Several months before the Pearl harbor attack, the Imperial Japanese Navy had organized the First Air Fleet by bringing together in one operational unit the First and Second Carrier divisions. The First Carrier Division's two fleet carriers *Akagi* and *Kaga* had been converted from a battle cruiser and battleship keel respectively. Each was more than 800 feet long and displaced over 40,000 tons. Together they held 82 Zero fighters and 53 Val dive bombers. The smaller *Hiryu* and *Soryu* of the Second Carrier Division carried 33 Zeros, 36 Vals, and 36 Kate level bombers, some of which were modified as torpedo bombers. The Fifth Carrier Division's two new, large 30,000 ton fleet carriers were nearly 800 feet long. *Zuikaku* and *Shokaku*, combined for another 11 Zeros, 54 Vals, and 51 Kates, 30 of the latter modified as torpedo bombers.

It was shortly after 10 A.M. on the *Akagi's* bridge when Nagumo spotted black specks far to the south. Soon afterwards the six carriers began welcoming home the jubilant flight crews. High seas, tricky winds, and worsening weather challenged deck crews and pilots, but the superbly nurtured flying skills of the navy's top-notch airmen were equal to the task. Flight officers who recovered on the *Akagi* reported to Air Officer Masuda who tabulated their claims on a large blackboard set up on the flight deck near the bridge. It soon became apparent that the raid had been a great success and subsequent pilot debriefings underlined the victory. The Japanese had sunk four battleships and crippled the American battle fleet. They had inflicted heavy damage on four other battleships, four cruisers, and three destroyers. They estimated that the raid had destroyed about 100 American aircraft (actually 65 of all types), most of them on the ground.

Fuchida reported the battle damage to a straight-faced Nagumo who listened quietly until Fuchida completed his account. Rear Admiral Kusaka Ryunosuke, Nagumo's chief of staff, then questioned Fuchida about which targets to attack next Without hesitation Fuchida said the dockyards and the fuel tanks. Nagumo then observed that of the 29 aircraft shot down, 20 were lost from the second wave or twelve per cent of its 168 planes. Seventy four other planes had been damaged.

Type	Lost	Damaged	Total	Launched	% Lost/Damaged
Zero	9	23	32	81	39%
Kate	5	10	15	104	14%
Val	15	41	55	169	32%

More to the point, his striking power was seriously diminished. On the positive side, his fighter force suffered the least damage in the strike and could be counted on to protect the carriers against an enemy aerial counterattack. Many of the damaged aircraft could be quickly repaired and made operational. Yet two imponderables had to be factored into any second strike. How many American aircraft remained at Pearl Harbor and where were the missing American carriers?

If Nagumo opted for a second strike against the installations and oil tanks around Pearl Harbor, he would have to commit his fleet to at least another twenty-four hours within striking distance of the target. The element of surprise, which all pilots agreed was decisive in the opening attack, would be sacrificed and losses would probably exceed those of the morning's second wave. Returning pilots, especially those from the second wave, talked about thick anti-aircraft fire and dozens of American fighters racing frantically around the Hawaiian skies. Cumulative losses might so weaken Nagumo's air arm that it would be unable to defend the task force against the American carriers. Moreover, after their return the warplanes had been re-configured for attacks against surface ships. Maintenance crews were also repairing dozens of lightly damaged aircraft and it would take them until nightfall to re-fit and re-arm the planes for another strike. At 2 P.M. as the carriers turned northward, Nagumo retreated to his cabin, and the assembled staff officers exchanged resigned glances that conceded that the operation was over.

Two hundred miles west of Hawaii, Task Force 8, commanded by Vice-Admiral William Halsey aboard the carrier *Enterprise*, learned of the attack on Pearl Harbor. *Enterprise* was on the return leg to Pearl Harbor after delivering twelve U.S. Marine aircraft to Wake Island on December 4. Halsey had launched eighteen aircraft on a routine flight from the carrier to Ford Island. They arrived in the midst of the Japanese attack and lost five aircraft. After they had re-fueled and re-armed at Ford Island, the surviving aircraft began searching for the Japanese fleet.

At 10:15 A.M. Halsey received a priority message from Admiral Kimmel that two Japanese carriers had been sighted about 30 miles southwest of Barbers Point which was only ten miles from Pearl Harbor. Hastily launched air crews flew to the area but could find no trace of the alleged enemy fleet, although they did spot the cruiser *Minneapolis* which was the source of the mistaken report. Then a radio direction finder intercepted a radio transmission from a Japanese carrier almost due north of Pearl Harbor. Direction-finders record simultaneously reciprocal bearings, and in this instance the interpreter reversed the direction from almost due north to almost due south. Around noon Halsey ordered his task force to turn on a south course towards the false bearing. Unknown to the admiral or the task force, a Japanese submarine I-74 had been shadowing his fleet since early Sunday morning.

Meanwhile Task Force 12, three heavy cruisers, *Chicago, Portland*, and *Astoria* and five destroyers organized around the carrier *Lexington*, commanded by Captain Frederick C. Sherman were about 400 miles southeast of Midway Island, where they were bound to deliver eighteen aircraft to that Marine garrison. Admiral Kimmel originally ordered Sherman to rendezvous with Halsey about 150 miles west of Pearl Harbor. When Halsey reported his southward course, Kimmel in turn directed Task Force 12 to proceed on a southerly heading to meet Task Force 8 in the waters northeast of Hawaii. Kimmel also requested that Lieutenant General Walter C. Short, the Army commander on Oahu, order his four surviving B-17s to patrol the waters in a fan shaped area due south of the islands. Short further directed the commanding general of Hawaiian Air Force, Major General Frederick L. Martin, to ready the seventy-five remaining operational fighter, reconnaissance, and pursuit aircraft for combat and to insure that ammunition was distributed immediately to the dozen or so Army anti-aircraft installations around Pearl Harbor.

Aboard the I-74 Lieutenant Commander Ikezawa Masao was about to make a fateful decision. After spotting the *Enterprise* task force in the false dawn of December 7th, he had shadowed the 20,000 ton carrier throughout the morning. Rough seas and swells could cover his attack, but when *Enterprise* swung southward at high speed the submarine, which could only make eight knots submerged, would soon be left in its wake. Instead of trailing the zig-zagging warships, Ikezawa opted to drop back from the task force, then surface and broadcast its position on an open radio frequency reserved for just such sighting reports. Shortly before 2:30 P.M., I-74 broke the rough ocean surface long enough for its radio operator to tap out in Morse Code an enciphered priority signal "ENEMY WARSHIPS SIGHTED; ENTERPRISE CLASS CARRIER; POSITION 21-40 NORTH 162-30 WEST; COURSE 170; SPEED 25 KNOTS." Three hundred miles northeast, *Akagi's* communications officer deciphered the message and ran to the carrier's bridge. One hundred and seventy miles nearly due east, U. S. Navy intercept operators used radio direction finding gear to fix the position of the submarine's radio transmitter. Hawaii dispatched an urgent message to Task Force 8 that identified the location of a suspected enemy submarine. Two of the nine destroyers screening *Enterprise* turned north and set off at full speed to search the suspected area. While they hunted I-74, another momentous decision had been made on the *Akagi*.

The six carriers were about 300 nautical miles northwest of Oahu when Nagumo, Kusaka, Fuchida, Genda, and a few other staff officers huddled in *Akagi's* wardroom. Why was *Enterprise* steaming south at high speed away from the strike force? Genda thought it might be headed to meet *Lexington* and combine forces, but Fuchida was less certain, suggesting it might head for Johnston Island. Certainly *Enterprise's* departure left Pearl Harbor uncovered, unless the Americans planned to swing east and return to the naval base. The screening force of eleven submarines of the Third Submarine Force deployed south of Oahu would intercept such a maneuver.

Nagumo then reviewed the earlier debate about the feasibility of a second strike on the tank farm and the dock and repair facilities at Pearl Harbor. The destruction of the American battleships left Nagumo's fleet immune to surface attack. If his ships reversed course and sailed at 20 knots, by 0600 on December 8 they could be about 200 nautical miles east-north-east of the American base. From there the carriers could launch an attack by Vals and Kates while the torpedo-configured Kates could be kept on *Zuikaku* and *Shokaku's* flight decks ready for action if the enemy carriers reappeared. He had enough Zeros to fly air patrols above the fleet and could dispatch his cruisers catapult launched float planes on long-range reconnaissance missions.

Several of the assembled staff officers suggested that a concentrated attack on Pearl Harbor by the entire carrier force was necessary to inflict the destruction of the docks, facilities, and oil tank farm. Nagumo quickly cut them short. He was unwilling to commit everything to a second strike. It was imperative, he insisted, to maintain a large reserve as long as the two American carriers were loose. His decision to withhold *Zuikaku* and *Shokaku's* planes from the attack coupled with the aircraft lost and damaged in the attacks left fewer than 150 aircraft available for the second strike.

Japanese staff officers aboard *Akagi* assumed that the Americans at Pearl Harbor would be on full alert, so they looked for ways to reduce losses. The best way was to minimize the time that their air crews would have to spend over the targets and be susceptible to enemy ground fire. The oil storage farms and dockyard works were on the east side of Pearl Harbor. If the raiders struck from that direction, they would drop their bomb loads before they encountered the heaviest shipboard anti-aircraft defenses. Then lightened by the loss of their bombs, the planes could fly faster and maneuver better to escape the enemy flak or pursuit aircraft. An attack out of the morning sun might also interfere with anti-aircraft optical range finding instruments and throw off the aim of enemy gunners. The advantage of a smaller, compact force was that it could be concentrated in tight echelons capable of executing a one-pass attack with minimum losses. Because fewer aircraft were participating in the second strike, the carriers could also recover them faster than the previous day so the fleet could retire quickly from Hawaiian waters. It was risky, yet the destruction of the logistics infrastructure at Pearl Harbor was a prize well worth the gamble. After reviewing the plan and confident that his large reserve could protect the carriers and his fleet, Nagumo ordered reverse course. The flagman on *Akagi's* bridge semaphored the command to the other warships. In complete radio silence the superbly trained sailors of the battle fleet turned their ships so methodically to follow the *Akagi's* wake that it reminded one sailor of the grand fleet annual maneuvers.

Far to the south, I-74 was maneuvering for its life. The two American destroyers had initially detected the submarine around 1600 and maintained a strong sonar contact with it for the next several hours. With each passing minute the *Enterprise* task force drew farther and farther from the hunted submarine. Ikezawa had no way of knowing that the American carrier had already reversed course to the northeast. He would never know because shortly afterwards the destroyers depth charged I-74 to the surface and finished off the submarine with gunfire. There were no Japanese survivors. Meanwhile Sherman's Task Force 12 was plowing through the seas at a steady 22 knots to make the pre-designated rendezvous with Halsey west of Oahu.

At dawn on December 8, Nagumo's six carriers were about one hundred and forty miles due north of Hilo, Hawaii and sailing into the wind. Shortly afterwards *Akagi* and *Kaga* launched 40 Zeros. The two light carriers *Soryu* and *Hiryu* sent a total of 40 Kates, and 40 Vals into the skies. After forming above the carriers, the pilots turned due east for Pearl Harbor 200 miles away. Twenty Zeros left the formation to form an air cover and patrol for the fleet. Aboard *Shokaku* 30 torpedo-configured Kates were ready on the deck for immediate launch if enemy carriers appeared. *Zuikaku's* flight deck was packed with Vals and Kates to fill out a powerful reserve to ward off any threat from enemy carriers. As soon as the strike force was airborne, Nagumo's task force turned to course of 313 degrees and headed northwest at 25 knots.

Nagumo's hurriedly drawn plan depended on precise timing. The two large oil tank storage areas at Pearl Harbor bracketed the docks, piers, and installations along the south side of the harbor opposite battleship row. Fuchida expected the Americans to be waiting for another attack, so he wanted the Val dive bombers to strike the harbor installations just before the Kates bombed the oil storage tanks. If the oil tanks were hit first, thick smoke might obscure the other nearby targets that lay between the tanks and the water. Ideally the last Val would pull off its target just as the first Kate dropped its bomb load.

The Army Air Force's Opana Mobile Radar Unit station at Kahuka Point, about thirty miles north of Pearl Harbor had detected the December 7 Japanese raid about fifty minutes and 130 miles before the first bombs fell on battleship row. At that time the enlisted radar operators were told not to worry because the blips on the oscilloscope were caused by a scheduled flight of four engine B-17 heavy bombers arriving in Hawaii. Now almost twenty-four hours later, the same radar screen showed a medium size green blip approaching Oahu from the east. This time officers grabbed the phone to alert the air bases. All operational Army Air Force planes — thirty-six P-40s, sixteen P-36s, and four P-26s—and a handful of available Marine and Navy fighters scrambled to intercept the attack.

Thirty minutes and 60 miles to the east later, American pilots sighted three tiers of aircraft off the north coast of Molokai Island. The forty Vals at 10,000 feet approaching Oahu at 200 miles per hour were trailed at a five mile interval by 40 Kates positioned 5,000 feet higher. Twenty Zeros hovered still higher over both formations Eight Army Air Force P-36s accelerated to their top speed of 310 miles per hour to close on the slower, bomb laden Vals while nine F4F-4s climbed at 300 miles an hour to challenge the Kates. Twenty of the faster P-40s also began climbing to place themselves between the interceptors and the Zeros. Half the Zero pilots dived into the attackers and the others engaged the P-40s. Although slightly faster, the P-40 was less maneuverable than the Zero whose pilots snap-rolled their planes to evade pursuers and line up victims. Against the slower P-36s and F-4Fs, the Zeros were deadly and drove off the attackers, shooting down four of them without a single loss. Outnumbered 2 to 1 by the P-40s, the Japanese pilots held their own, claiming two P-40s in exchange for two Zeros. One Val was smoking and losing altitude, and a Kate had disappeared from formation. The attack was over in less than five minutes but, more than the loss of four planes, the determined American pilots had thrown the tightly scheduled Japanese formations into disarray, particularly the lower flying Vals. Concerned about another fighter attack, flight leader Genda fired a green flare that told pilots to attack. Already twelve miles ahead of the Vals, the Kate bombers pressed on at full speed to Pearl Harbor.

Although the Japanese pilots expected to encounter a stiff defense, they were unprepared for the heavy flak thrown up by the Army anti-aircraft batteries. The inexperienced American gunners, however, were not leading the planes sufficiently to achieve the full effect of their firepower and many of their shells burst too low and behind the Japanese aircraft because the glare of the morning sun did throw off their aim. Still the big anti-aircraft guns did enough damage, especially when combined with the barrage from several warships scattered throughout the large harbor. Five more Kates and two Vals crashed to earth and further disrupted the delicate timing of the attack. The distance lengthened between the Kates which were nearing their targets and the Vals. With orders to make only one pass over the oil storage farms, the Kates had to make their bomb run before the Vals which reversed the order in the plan.

The first of four 'V' waves of nine Kates lost two aircraft before they released their bomb loads on the western oil tank farm below. Several bombs hit two of the tanks causing large secondary explosions. Billowing smoke obscured the target for the second wave which flew through intense anti-aircraft fire. Veteran pilots 'juked' their bombers to throw off the gunners' aim. It also threw off their aim and their bombs dropped just west of the vulnerable tanks. One minute and six Kates fewer the third echelon bore in on the eastern cluster of storage tanks. Bombs hit one big tank with a reverberating roar and rush of black oily smoke. In the last wave pilot officer Suzuki Toranosuke wondered how the American gunners could keep firing through the flames and smoke he saw through his windshield. Still flak bursts buffeted his plane and he had no idea whether or not his bombs hit the target. Instead of reversing direction, the Kates continued to fly almost due west skirting Ford Island before heading across Oahu for open water. A few American pilots were airborne and in deadly pursuit. Zero fighters tried to block the angle of attack but the Americans, regardless of losses it seemed to Suzuki, closed on the now ragged Kate formations. Several Japanese bombers were streaming oil or leaving smoke trails as they tried to keep formation.

The dive bombing Vals fared little better. They had to navigate through heavy flak and the dive lower into machine gun and 20 millimeter bursts of fire. Flying Sergeant Second Class pilot Takahashi Koji and his observer of the same rank Matsui Katsu had flown from *Zuikaku* on December 7 to bomb Hickam Field. This morning the two airmen found themselves in a seven plane 'V' formation that was supposed to strike the dry dock installations. The Americans were using smokescreens to mask the dock, and the thick black smoke from the burning oil tanks drifted over the harbor obscuring the shoreline. It was not only difficult to see their target, but it was also nearly impossible to judge their altitude in relation to the ground during a steep dive. Matsui called out at least three Vals that never reappeared after their attacks. Suddenly their plane shuddered and both knew they had been hit. Takahashi released his bombs about where the dock should be, but could not tell if they had any effect. How much different than yesterday. The crippled Val struggled west and made its northern turn uncontested. Other Japanese planes were not as lucky.

After ten minutes and about 60 miles north of Oahu, the American pursuit planes broke contact with the retreating Japanese. Fuchida circled the broken force counting planes. His quick assessment showed that 14 Kates, 9 Vals, and 4 Zeros were missing. At least six planes were too damaged to maintain formation and it appeared that they would have to ditch at sea at any moment. Another 33 planes lost, but this time they represented thirty-three per cent of the attacking force. The strikes on the oil tanks appeared successful because bright orange flames mixed with thick black columns of smoke could still be seen from fifty miles away. The attacks against the dock yard facilities seemed ineffective to Fuchida. It could not be helped. The airmen had to return to their carriers quickly in order to withdraw before the Americans discovered their whereabouts.

At Pearl Harbor soldiers, sailors, and oil company workers battled to control the damage and stop the spreading flames from igniting more oil storage tanks. About 30 per cent of the western oil tank farm had been destroyed, but remarkably the pumping facilities were unscratched. The eastern group of tanks fared better despite the spectacular explosion when two tanks on the perimeter of the field exploded. Superficial damage marked the dock installations where labor gangs were already restoring docks and cranes to working order. Exhausted anti-aircraft crews found themselves lugging ammunition to use against another attack. During their debriefings, American pilots reported shooting down fifty enemy planes, an exaggeration to be sure, but there was sufficient evidence in the form of wrecked Japanese aircraft to show that the second raid had cost the enemy dearly without inflicting the degree of destruction and mayhem of the December 7 raid.

One hundred and sixty miles east-north-east of Pearl Harbor *Akagi, Kaga, Hiryu,* and *Soryu* began receiving 65 returning planes (two Kates were last seen losing altitude after dropping from formation). Nagumo's only purpose was to get away before American carrier aircraft or long range reconnaissance planes discovered his fleet. Shortly after the morning air raid alert, three PBY Catalinas, the U.S. Navy's land-based patrol planes, and four B-17 heavy bombers had been launched to find the enemy carriers. The PBYs were all that remained of 36 planes, 33 of which Japanese flyers destroyed on 7 December at the sea plane base in Kaneohe Bay. Together with the B-17s the PBYs flew fan-shaped patterns in search areas that extended from 300 miles due north of Oahu to 300 miles due east. By this time Halsey and Sherman had joined forces about 200 miles west-north-west of Pearl Harbor and were heading on a west-north-west course. In other words about 400 miles separated the opposing carrier forces and the gap was closing quickly.

Nagumo ordered his cruisers to launch their float scout planes and his battleships added their reconnaissance aircraft to the patrols sweeping the waters north and west of Hawaii on the lookout for enemy ships. The fleet increased speed to 30 knots and anti-aircraft crews broke out ammunition. Zero fighters circled the task force looking for any intruding enemy aircraft. At 1330 a Zero pilot spotted an ungainly PBY and promptly shot it down. The communications center on the *Akagi*, however, intercepted a coded radio message from the doomed American plane.

Four hundred miles to the northwest, *Enterprise* picked up a radio transmission that stated, "ENEMY FLEET SIGHTED 21 - 15 NORTH 155-50 WEST; BEARING - - -" Halsey estimated that the enemy had to continue heading northwest because any other direction either brought the Japanese closer to American airpower or placed them farther away from their base. Several other PBYs had also overheard the radio transmission and were heading for the last reported location of the Japanese task force. Nagumo resigned himself to the appearance of more American reconnaissance planes and ordered ten more Zero fighters into the air to greet them. Deck crews prepared for combat while *Shokaku* and *Zuikaku's* mechanics and armorers readied more than 100 torpedo planes and dive bombers for action. *Hiryu* and *Soryu's* planes had, of course, to be re-fueled, re-armed, and re-configured for attacks against ships and this would take at least eight hours. Rather than risk all the carriers and use all the remaining daylight, Nagumo ordered his two light carriers to separate from the other four carriers and run northwest at 30 knots. Aboard *Akagi* Nagumo instructed his two battleship captains on the *Hiei* and *Kirishima* to ready their anti-aircraft defenses and close in to protect the remaining carriers. If the task force commander had slapped both officers the effect could not have been greater. Battleships were supposed to lead the battle line, not convoy aircraft carriers.

About thirty minutes after the carriers split formation, another PBY appeared on the horizon ducking in and out of cumulonimbus clouds. Zero pilots went racing for the plane, but it again vanished in the towering clouds. Certain that his latest position and bearing was now in American hands, Nagumo waited for word from his scout planes. Land-based planes no longer concerned him because the task force was beyond the range of all but the heaviest B-17 bombers. Yet there was no further intelligence about the American carriers since I-74's report the previous morning. It was 1435 when a float plane pilot from *Hiei* radioed in the clear of his sighting of an enemy carrier at 23-10 North 115-30 West bearing 065 degrees. Then the transmission broke into static. A quick plot located the fleet about 250 miles northwest of the Japanese task force and blocking its escape route. If the report was accurate, was the carrier *Lexington* or *Enterprise*? Was the other American carrier nearby or had the carriers joined forces? Any enemy attack by carrier planes was likely within the next ninety minutes. Nagumo hesitated. He was reluctant to launch all of *Shokaku* and *Zuikaku's* torpedo and dive bombers until he learned the location of the second American carrier. He ordered *Shokaku's* torpedo planes and dive bombers to attack the American carriers with ten Zeros from *Akagi* as escorts. Twenty other Zeros from *Kaga* would commence air patrol to defend the task force. *Zuikaku* would remain in general reserve and continue to ready its bombers for a possible strike.

By 1510 the torpedo-configured Kates were airborne and on their way toward the enemy carriers. Float planes from heavy cruisers *Chikuma* and *Tone* had preceded the flight and were attempting to pinpoint the exact location of the American carriers. One hour earlier *Lexington* and *Enterprise* had launched 110 aircraft. All 28 of *Lexington's* dive bombers and torpedo planes joined with 21 dive bombers and a like number of torpedo planes from *Enterprise* in an all-out strike against the Japanese fleet. Six fighters from *Lexington* and twenty one from *Enterprise* maintained an air umbrella over the American task force. *Enterprise* carried 15 more fighters on her deck, ready to launch if needed. The *Chikuma's* float plane sighted the massed formation of American warplanes and twenty minutes later at 1530 discovered the two carriers in the distance. The Kates altered course to adjust for the latest intelligence.

About this time the first navy torpedo planes were meeting Zero fighters with predictable results. One after another the slow, ponderous torpedo planes fell under murderous cannon and machine gun fire. Engaged by the anti-aircraft guns of two battleships, more torpedo planes fell into the sea. Still they pressed their attack, flying at low level over the battleship escorts and toward the two carriers. One group of three planes released its torpedoes at *Akagi*, but the Japanese skipper skillfully maneuvered the big carrier from the torpedoes' path. *Zuikaku* was less fortunate and took a torpedo hit in her rear starboard area. The force of the explosion also damaged the rudder and propeller, forcing the big carrier to slow to eight knots. To score this one hit, 29 American torpedo bombers and their three man crews had been lost. The six surviving aircraft headed to the west just as 35 dive bombers began their concentrated attacks on the stricken *Zuikaku*. Three bombs exploded in quick succession on the flight deck and the explosions ignited a fire that caused a chain reaction as Vals and Kates exploded one after another. *Zuikaku* was now dead in the water, a flaming wreck spewing smoke and steam into the sky.

The second flight of dive bombers went after *Akagi*. A final flight of seven dive bombers struck at *Akagi* and managed to score one hit that damaged the flight deck and elevators. Nagumo watched in near despair as the American pilots pressed home their attacks despite fearsome losses. Then the attack was over as suddenly as it began. *Akagi's* gun crews were cheering until someone pointed to a burning hulk about three miles off their port bow. Its fire raging out of control, *Zuikaku's* captain ordered his men to abandon ship. He remained aboard as the ship burned brightly through the night before sinking early on December 9.

While the Americans who had survived the battle were making their way home to their carriers, Japanese pilots were meeting American fighters which were screening the two ships. The Kates fared no better against fighter planes than their American counterparts, but the pilots shared a similar brand of courage. A Kate cartwheeled into the sea while the surviving flight of five conducted a textbook scissors attack. Three Kates wheeled in at low level on *Lexington's* starboard and two others on her port bow. Two of their five torpedoes intersected against *Lexington's* hull stopping the carrier which listed heavily to port. Then a burning Kate smashed into *Lexington's* superstructure killing most of the command group and setting off secondary explosions. The order was given to abandon ship. Of the 30 attacking Kates, only eight survived to return to *Shokaku*.

Both sides were spent. On December 8 alone, the Americans lost forty-seven aircraft, 117 pilots or air crew members, and the carrier *Lexington*. Nagumo had neither the stomach nor the airmen and planes for another battle. Besides the loss of *Zuikaku*, the Japanese had lost 90 planes and 211 elite air crew members in the two days of fighting. *Akagi* had suffered light damage and soon returned to operations. In return they had crippled the American battle fleet at anchor in Pearl Harbor, but had not seriously damaged the oil tank farms or repair facilities that were critical to the American war effort in the Pacific. They had sunk an old carrier, the *Lexington*, but had lost one of their newest carriers in the battle. It is true that the strike force returned to Japan unmolested, but it is also true that Admiral Yamamoto Isoroku accepted responsibility for Nagumo's actions and offered his resignation when he made his formal report on the battle to the Navy Ministry on 29 December, 1941. As we know, his request was denied and the diminutive admiral returned to his Pacific battlegrounds where he was later killed in action. Nagumo's command decisions on December 7 and 8 remain controversial.

Analysis

Fifty years after the Pearl Harbor attack, naval strategists and historians on both sides of the Pacific are unanimous in their criticism of Nagumo's conduct of the so-called Battle of Hawaii. The most vociferous critics point out that the Japanese squandered their carrier air superiority for the Hawaii operation. General Douglas MacArthur's air chief, General George C. Kenney, who fought the Japanese army and navy air forces in the Solomons and New Guinea, insisted that the Japanese never fully appreciated that air power had to be concentrated for massive strikes against objectives. As we have seen, Nagumo neither used all six carriers in the second strike on Pearl Harbor nor in the naval engagement off Hawaii. Instead of his piecemeal attacks, critics allege, an all-out second strike might have destroyed the naval installations.

Oddly enough the controversy over Nagumo's conservative tactics originated during the Pearl Harbor Hearings. Two American admirals testified that if Nagumo employed all his aircraft in a second strike, he would have been able to destroy the oil tank farms as well as dock facilities. American and Japanese naval experts also fault Nagumo's decision to launch a weak second strike against Pearl Harbor on December 8. They observed that the American defenders were on full alert and expecting a follow-up attack. In such circumstances, the pilots who flew the second mission had little prospect of success and indeed were able to accomplish the limited damage to tank farms and facilities that they did only because of their elite flying skills and raw courage. In effect Nagumo's indecision offset their bravery. Several authors have noted, however, that the second raid alone cost the Japanese another 33 planes and 71 precious pilots or air crew. When one adds those casualties to the aircraft and pilots lost when *Zuikaku* exploded, the second strike appears as a grave strategic error that left the Imperial Navy fatally weakened in subsequent operations. Numerous Japanese commentators have recalled Nagumo's cautious nature to argue that he hedged his bets on the second strike by withholding such a large reserve from the raid. The admiral, of course, was unavailable to explain his actions having perished on Saipan in July 1944.

Each side lost a carrier in the Battle of Hawaii, but the *Zuikaku* was a new ship, that had joined the fleet in 1941 and carried 58 aircraft, while *Lexington* had been converted in 1927 from a battle cruiser hull to a carrier. While the *Lexington* was a sentimental favorite because so many of the Navy's World War II carrier leaders had once trained on the old carrier, its loss could easily be made good. *Zuikaku's* loss was irreplaceable and the extra carrier was sorely missed at Midway seven months later. For that reason, the pre-eminent American naval historian declared the two-day Battle of Hawaii an American strategic victory. He reasoned that the losses of obsolete battleships, though painful, did not affect greatly the strategic course of the war in the Pacific. The loss of a first-line carrier by Japan, however, exerted significant material and psychological influence on the later Coral Sea (April 1942) and Midway (June 1942) operations.

Elaborating on this interpretation, a recent school of Japanese revisionist historians argue that the Battle of Hawaii colored Yamamoto's later decisions during the disastrous Battle of Midway in June 1942. They allege that Yamamoto was determined to avoid charges that he, like Nagumo at Hawaii, failed to commit his entire carrier air force and thus squandered the possibility of a great victory. Yamamoto, the theory runs, compensated at Midway by throwing all his carrier forces into the losing battle. Though provocative, such an interpretation relies on extensive interviews with Japanese participants and is based more on their subjective evaluations than on any documentary sources.

No discussion of the Battle of Hawaii would be complete without a mention of the alleged plot of American President, Franklin D. Roosevelt, to draw Japan into war. First enunciated by an American historian who maintained that the president's public and private views about America's entry into World War II were not only contradictory but also that Roosevelt was leading the nation to war, the interpretation has spawned a variety of conspiracy theories. Most "plot-advocates" turn to the massive amount of intercepted Japanese Foreign Ministry material "to prove" that Roosevelt and other high ranking leaders in Washington knew that a Japanese attack against Pearl Harbor was imminent. They allege that Roosevelt and other leaders kept this intelligence in order to force the Japanese "to fire the first shot" of the war. In fact the hysteria of December 7 in the United States was somewhat mitigated the following day by inflated Allied reports of the damage they inflicted on the Japanese task force during the Battle of Hawaii. Nevertheless conspiracy enthusiasts insist that the fact that American carrier aircraft intercepted Yamamoto's task force after the second attack shows that they could have done it before the attack. Such hypotheses usually depend on draping various tatters of evidence on the Pearl Harbor framework which enables them to give their theories the appearance of originality. Although careful examination of their sources reveals a haphazard patchwork whose seams split with disappointing regularity, these revisionists continue to enjoy some popularity.

Because the Pearl Harbor attack is still embroiled in controversy, can anything definitive be said about the event nearly a half-century later? Fifty years after the event the judgement of historians is that if the Japanese had used all six carriers in two mighty strikes against the U.S. Navy based at Pearl Harbor, its logistics infrastructure, and nearby airfields, they would have inflicted damage at least severe enough to impede U.S. naval operations in the Pacific Ocean for eighteen months. The consensus is that Nagumo was ill-suited temperamentally to command the task force. Neither side was satisfied with the results of the Battle of Hawaii and this may explain why the air and naval engagement continues to generate heated controversy after all these years.

B. What if the United States had been able to read the Japanese naval code JN-25 with its message of the coming attack?
Edward J. Drea & Frederick D. Parker

In late September 1940, American cryptanalysts solved the Japanese Foreign Ministry's most secret communications cipher. This joint effort took eighteen months and involved U.S. Army and Navy cryptanalysts as well as civilian code-breakers working for both services. From the fall of 1940 until the Japanese attack on Pearl Harbor in December 1941, American cryptanalysts deciphered hundreds of Foreign Ministry cables whose translations were made available to the president and other high-ranking civilian and military leaders in Washington, D.C. These deciphered Foreign Ministry cables clearly indicated that Japan was planning some kind of military action against southeast Asia in December 1941. Foreign Ministry officials, however, were not privy to Imperial Navy operational plans, so their messages spoke in broad terms of "things happening automatically," but not in specifics like military objectives. Without access to the Japanese navy's operational ciphers, American leaders were aware of Japan's warlike intentions but unaware that the naval, air, and military bases at Pearl Harbor were the targets of a Japanese carrier aircraft attack.

Breaking JN-25, the Imperial Japanese Navy's operational code.

On a humid mid-summer night in August 1941, a small fire broke out in the Japanese embassy in Washington, D.C. Fortunately a passerby noticed the smoke and quickly summoned the fire department. Despite the protests of the Japanese embassy guards, the fire chief insisted on evacuating the building because of the thick black smoke. Before leaving, code clerks placed all their cryptanalytic library in specially designed safes. They notified the chief of embassy security who, in turn, called the army and naval attachés to the embassy. That evening, however, the Japanese naval attaché was aboard a yacht sailing along the Potomac.

The smoky fire proved more persistent than it looked, but at midnight, after four hours of fighting what turned out to be an electrical fire, the firemen allowed everyone back into the embassy. Fortuitously the naval attaché returned at approximately the same time. A thorough investigation of the embassy communications' room and the code room where the safes were kept revealed no evidence that the firemen had tampered with them. An official report to the embassy regretted the need to evacuate the Japanese diplomatic personnel, and then went into numbing detail about the short-circuit that sparked the blaze. There was no mention in the report about four very special firemen—a locksmith, a professional safecracker, and two officers assigned to the Office of Naval Intelligence.

The fire was, as we know today, a sham that allowed naval intelligence operatives to enter the Japanese embassy. Picking locks was child's play, but the code room safes resisted unlocking for nearly two hours. In the time remaining, the two officers photographed as much of the JN-25 code as their surreptitious schedule permitted. While they could not copy all of the code book, they stole enough of it to allow a break into JN-25 the following month.

U.S. Navy cryptanalysts in the Philippines had been studying JN-25, but a major cryptographic change in December 1940 complicated their efforts. They understood the cryptographic system used by the Japanese, but were unable to recover sufficient code group meanings to make sense of any JN-25 messages. As relations between Japan and the United States deteriorated throughout 1941, the Office of Naval Intelligence proposed a break-in and burglary of the Japanese embassy in order to obtain the JN-25 code book. It is unclear whether or not President Franklin D. Roosevelt approved the theft, but a July 1940 memo exists from the Secretary for the Navy, Frank Knox, to the head of the Federal Bureau of Investigation, J. Edgar Hoover, requesting Hoover's cooperation in a "sensitive matter" involving a foreign embassy. Knox also refers to Captain Theodore S. Wilkinson's recommendation. Wilkinson was the head of ONI.

Although the exact provenance of the August break-in remains shrouded in secrecy, the results of the burglary are well known. The stolen code group meanings combined with the cryptanalysts' existing knowledge of the JN-25 encipherment system enabled U.S. Navy code breakers to read large portions of the hitherto sacrosanct Japanese navy's general purpose code. Between September and December 1941, more than

26,000 Japanese naval messages in various cryptographic systems were intercepted. Originally only eight of the 53 naval officers in Op-20-G, the navy's Communications Division in Washington, were assigned to study the Japanese fleet's general purpose code, JN-25. After cryptanalysts began reading JN-25 with regularity, more officers found themselves assigned to the general purpose code. Nevertheless, many messages went undeciphered. Only one in ten was considered significant enough to translate into English, and among these fewer than 200 pertained specifically to the proposed Pearl Harbor attack. As events proved, this handful of messages was enough.

A 5 September 1941 broken Japanese naval message warned that "a state of complete readiness for battle operations must be achieved by the first of November." Another message just four days later from the Chief of Staff, Combined Fleet, enjoined his subordinate commanders to be "fully prepared for commencing war operations by the first part of November." In early October specific details of Japanese plans for war began to appear in decrypted messages. Cables from the 1st Air Fleet told of aerial torpedo attack exercises involving four aircraft carriers in Kagoshima Bay on Japan's southernmost main island of Kyushu. Follow-up messages in late October talked about "near surface" (or shallow running) torpedoes and the need to complete adjustments to aerial torpedoes by November 5. Another radiogram from the Chief of Staff 1st Air Fleet revealed that three carrier divisions, a total of six aircraft carriers, were using these modified torpedoes. November messages from the Commander, Carrier Division 2, referred to torpedo firing exercises in Kagoshima Bay against anchored capital ships. Similar references to dive-bombing and strafing exercises by dozens of carrier aircraft were decrypted and made available to naval intelligence.

Intelligence analysts called attention to the similarity between the present Japanese carrier pilots' training and the British carrier raid against the Italian Fleet at anchor at Taranto in southern Italy the previous November. This surprise attack was still fresh in their memories because it had devastated the Italian navy, leaving half its battle fleet out of action for six months and shifted the balance of naval power in the Mediterranean. The purpose of the Japanese training, however, was unclear to American analysts. Were they experimenting because of the Taranto precedent in order to defend against similar surprise attacks or were they planning such an attack? The most likely target of such an attack, all agreed, was the British naval bastion at Singapore on the southern tip of the Malayan Peninsula. The British Prime Minister's recent dispatch of two capital ships to Singapore and an aircraft carrier soon to follow gave credence to this logic.

When combined with naval traffic analysis and deciphered Japanese diplomatic cables, the JN-25 decrypts clearly revealed a "Southern Operation." It was known that Japan's Third Fleet was building up in French Indochina for some type of operation; that an expanded naval air force communications network was operational in south China and Indochina; and that transfers of naval land-based aircraft from the Japanese home islands to the Japanese Mandated Islands in the Central Pacific, Taiwan, and Indochina had recently been completed.

Based on this evidence, Admiral Husband E. Kimmel, the Commander in Chief of the United States Fleet at Pearl Harbor, was in receipt of Admiral Harold A. Stark's, Chief of Naval Operations, first war warning. It was issued on 24 November and alerted the commander-in-chiefs of the Pacific and Asiatic fleets that a surprise Japanese attack from any direction, including an attack on the Philippines or Guam, could be expected. Stark's immediate concern was based on recently decrypted Japanese Foreign Ministry cables which revealed that "things are automatically going to happen."

Reports from the 14th Naval District Communication Intelligence Unit, available on 26 November, disclosed that Japan's Second and Third fleets had formed a strong task force. Possibly operating with carriers of the Second Carrier Division, the fleet might be readying themselves for operations in Southeast Asia while components of the task force operated from the Marshalls and the Palaus. The following day the 16th Naval District Communication Intelligence Unit countered that analysis by stating that it was impossible to confirm that carriers and submarines were in the Marshalls because the best sources indicated that the First and Fifth Fleet carriers were still in home waters near the Sasebo-Kure area. Intelligence analysts were less certain of the whereabouts of the Second Carrier Division. Radio calls did suggest that the Second Fleet was on the high seas, but the evidence was too slim to conclude that the Second Carrier Division was attached to the southern task force.

These latest reports did re-emphasize a continuing Japanese interest, evident since October, in an as yet unidentified southern operation. This military intelligence coupled with the MAGIC decryptions that disclosed the failing state of the peace negotiations compelled Stark to signal to his top lieutenants again to be vigilant against a Japanese attack likely to occur in the next few days. His November 27 message began bluntly, "This dispatch is to be considered a war warning," and proceeded to outline a likely Japanese amphibious attack against the Philippines or the Malayan Peninsula or possibly the Netherlands East Indies. Subsequent messages dispatched on November 29 warned that negotiations with Japan appeared terminated and that "hostile action possible at any moment." At no time was Pearl Harbor mentioned and American authorities thought that Guam, Wake, and the Philippines were the likely targets of Japan's southern sweep. A warning dispatched on 30 November fixed American attention on the Malayan Peninsula as the probably site for attack by an overseas expedition.

Last minute negotiations between Japan's emissaries in Washington and the Secretary of State, Cordell Hull droned along, but the evidence from decrypted Japanese Foreign Office cables implied that the Japanese were playing a double-game. So too did evidence from Japanese naval radio networks. Traffic analysis, that is the study of radio message networks, showed that preparations were underway for a southward advance against Malaya, the Dutch East Indies, and perhaps the Philippines. Patterns of radio broadcasts between Combined Fleet headquarters and flagships of the Combined Fleet suggested that the Second Carrier Division was moving south. Otherwise the First and Fifth Carrier divisions remained absent from radio communications and were presumed to be refitting in home waters from where they would soon join the southern task force.

Meantime, radio messages dispatched by the chief-of-staff, 1st Air Fleet revealed that the objective of the carrier fleets was far beyond their ordinary cruising range. Fleet oilers were to conduct re-fueling exercises with carriers, and the warships themselves would carry extra fuel in drums or tins on board. A 5 November message made plain that all four carriers of 1st Air Fleet—*Akagi*, *Kaga*, *Hiryu*, and *Soryu* were involved in loading and storing extra fuel drums. A key decrypt, dated December 1, explained that a fleet oiler was scheduled to depart the great naval base at Yokosuka, Japan, two days hence and proceed eastward to a point northeast of Wake and northwest of Midway by 8 December. Why was a fleet oiler planning to loiter in the central Pacific?

The fleet oiler mystery was linked to the movements of a Japanese officer from Tokyo to the headquarters of 1st Air Fleet which was temporarily located aboard the battleship *Hiei*. A related message transmitted on November 18 stated that the officer would be picked up in late November at Hitokappu Bay on Etorofu Island in the southern Kurile chain. A third message, sent 20 November by the staff of the Second Submarine Division reported that submarine I - 19's eastward movement crossed three communications' zones — Yokosuka, Ominato on the northeastern coast of Japan, and thence to 1st Air Fleet's zone in the Kuriles. Neither the schedule for the fleet oiler nor the presence of 1st Air Fleet Headquarters in the Kuriles lent credence to their participation in a southern strategy because these operational forces were moving away from southeast Asia and the Singapore base. Yet sufficient radio intelligence existed to indicate that Japan was prepared for offensive action somewhere in the so-called southern region. A 27 November message carried the former Chief of the Naval General Staff Admiral Prince Fushimi Hiroyasu's personal message to Commander-in-Chief of the striking force, Vice-Admiral Nagumo Chuichi, wishing him "long and lasting battle fortunes."

All of these decryptions accurately monitored the movements of the striking force. The first echelons of Nagumo's fleet had sailed from the Kure naval base on the Inland Sea in early November. Meanwhile pilots continued their low-level attack training by launching shallow-running torpedoes in Kagoshima Bay until the carriers had sortied in echelon from Kure between 10 November and the 18th. On 22 November, while Japanese and American diplomats negotiated in Washington, the Hawaii strike force assembled in Hitokappu Bay. Warships topped off their fuel tanks, strapped additional barrels of fuel oil on their decks, and, at eight A.M. 26 November, weighed anchor and steamed south to rendezvous with fleet oilers which would refuel them on their long voyage to Hawaii.

U.S. Naval intelligence was certain that the Japanese were about to strike, but unsure of the exact target. Naval communications analysts reported deciphering three messages between 10 November and 25 November that enjoined the fleet to maintain wartime radio silence on shortwave from 11 November. A later radiogram instructed the departing carriers to maintain radio silence when shifting aircraft. A final message of 25 November from the Commander-in-Chief, Combined Fleet, Admiral Yamamoto Isoroku, ordering all ships of the Combined Fleet to cease radio communications except in cases of "extreme emergency."

Naval communications analysts in Washington and in Hawaii recognized that radio silence was an indication of either impending operation action or total inactivity, for example when a warship or a fleet was in home port. They did not agree, however, on the purpose of Yamamoto's order. Washington argued that the 25 November description was part of an elaborate pattern of communications' deception designed to cover a strike against British Malaya and the Netherlands East Indies. Analysts reasoned that the messages related to a northern route were designed to divert attention from an attack on the British naval base at Singapore. Hawaii insisted that the imperial fleet had put to sea and was somewhere in the north Pacific. Its destination remained uncertain.

The location of the Japanese carriers was the key to the puzzle, but U.S. Naval intelligence was unable to locate them. If the carriers had indeed moved to the Kuriles, could the mysterious fleet oiler be waiting to rendezvous with them in the central Pacific? If so, did the Japanese intend to attack the American outposts at Guam, Wake, Midway, or perhaps the Philippines? Yet if these places were the Japanese targets, the exercises against anchored ships appeared excessive for the few warships that they might find in Manila Bay or the other scattered islands. The major anchorage was, of course, at Pearl Harbor, but its extreme distance from Japan left any attacking force exposed to American retaliation. These were the central issues in the highly secret debates that continued in Washington about the Japanese purpose.

Meanwhile, the three carrier divisions and their accompanying warships and support vessels were plowing through the grey seas of the north Pacific en route to Pearl Harbor. On 2 December, the entire strike force took on an added sense of urgency. From Tokyo Admiral Yamamoto broadcast a priority coded message to the Combined Fleet

"This dispatch is Top Secret. This order is effective at 1730 on 2 December. Climb Nitakayama 1208, repeat 1208." Nitakayama, a Formosan peak, was the highest point in the Japanese Empire and its symbolic value as the code word to execute the Pearl Harbor attack was clear to the Japanese recipients. In plain language, Yamamoto had ordered the attack on Pearl Harbor to commence on December 8, Tokyo time, or Sunday, 7 December 1941, in Hawaii. U.S. Navy intercept stations deciphered Yamamoto's coded message by December 3, but intelligence analysts argued over its exact meaning. They all agreed that Japan intended to open hostilities with the United States on December 8. The question was where the first battle would occur.

With Yamamoto's Nitakayama message in hand, Admiral Stark dispatched another war warning to Admiral Kimmel. Stark's December 4 cable read, "There are recent indications that Japan will open hostilities on December 8. Available intelligence suggests the presence of at least one Japanese carrier task force operating in northern Pacific waters. Although carrier location is tenuous, desire you institute air patrols immediately to cover the area north of the Hawaiian Islands to distance of 800 nautical miles. Inform of patrol routes and schedules."

Long-range aerial patrol was the Navy's responsibility and for the task Kimmel had a total of eighty-one PBY patrol aircraft in the Hawaii area, including twelve at Midway. Of these, fifty-four were the newest model which had only recently arrived in Hawaii and were still undergoing operation shakedown tests. There were not enough aircraft to cover a full 360 degree sweep of the islands, but the latest message gave priority to northern patrol routes. Kimmel ordered his PBYs at Midway to commence easterly patrols (he had not been informed about the possibility of a Japanese fleet oiler in the area). He allotted twelve PBYs to patrol Hawaii's northern sea frontier. To have four aircraft available to cover the northern approaches during daylight hours required two shifts of four PBYs each. The remaining four PBYs served as spare aircraft and a source of back-up crews to insure coverage during periods of routine maintenance on the aircraft.

The initial patrols on December 5 extended in a fan-shaped arc 800 nautical miles north of Hawaii and proved uneventful. At dawn on 6 December four PBYs of the second day's reconnaissance patrol departed the U.S. Navy seaplane base at Kaneohe Bay, Oahu. Climbing to seven thousand feet, the pilot set a course due north at a steady 160 miles per hour. The other seven crewmen passed the next five hours scanning an empty sea and following an ingrained routine broken only by occasional radio checks. The navigator had just opened a thermos of coffee when a enlisted observer reported an unidentified aircraft off the port wing. Two crew members quickly confirmed the sighting and then the navigator spotted the tell-tale wakes of at least two ships.

On his emergency frequency, the radio operator transmitted a brief coded signal, "Unidentified aircraft and ships 29-50N 157-00W; heading 180." The ensign piloting the ungainly PBY continued due north in search of the mother ship which had launched the fighter aircraft. Instead the forward observer shouted over the voice intercom that a task force of about two dozen warships was off the starboard wing at two o'clock. About the same time the two aircraft, now positively identified as Japanese Zeros, peeled off and made dry-run firing passes at the slow-moving PBY apparently hoping to scare it away. By this time the PBY radio operator was broadcasting emergency messages in the clear as fast as he could handle the operator's key. Aboard *Akagi*, Admiral Nagumo Chun'ichi saw the PBY a few minutes before a radio operator handed him an intercept of one of the plain-language broadcasts. Nagumo did not hesitate. His communications room ordered the fighter cover not to fire on the American plane. With radio silence broken, Nagumo then transmitted a coded message to the task force ordering it to reverse course. (This message was intercepted and later decrypted in Hawaii). The PBY circling over the fleet duly reported the change of course.

At Pearl Harbor Kimmel ordered an immediate alert. All ships in the harbor made steam and prepared to sortie to meet the Japanese task force. Naval aircraft either flew to other nearby fields or were placed in reveted areas. Army anti-aircraft crews broke open boxes of live ammunition and all Army fighter aircraft were dispersed across several airfields. The Oahu commercial radio station was ordered to announce that Army and U.S. Marine patrols would enforce an eight P.M. to dawn curfew and an island-wide blackout. All available PBYs were alerted to stand by for patrols north of Hawaii. At dusk eight PBYs started due north under orders to cover an area stretching 1,000 miles north of Pearl Harbor.

Word of the sighting of a Japanese fleet reached Washington shortly before 9 P.M. By 10:30 President Roosevelt was meeting with his senior military, naval, and diplomatic advisors who determined that the State Department would lodge an official protest to the government of Japan. On 7 December 1941, Secretary of State Cordell Hull called the Japanese Ambassador to the United States, Nomura Kichisaburo, to the State Department to deliver the protest personally.

By the time Nomura received the protest, Japanese attacks against Malaya and the Dutch East Indies had commenced. Because Nagumo's ask force had been unable to accomplish its mission against Pearl Harbor, however, Imperial Headquarters ordered the planned attack against the Philippines cancelled. Consequently the Japanese attacks on the British and Dutch colonies of 8 December (December 7th in the United States) found the U.S. Navy fully alerted for war with Japan but unable to aid the European belligerents.

When the facts surrounding Roosevelt's handling of this war-scare became known great controversy resulted. Roosevelt personally decided not to reveal to the Japanese that American codebreakers were reading their diplomatic and naval ciphers. Unable to make public the cryptographic evidence, the State and Navy departments had to accept the Japanese Navy's reply to Washington that the task force was merely conducting a fleet exercise in international waters. Indeed the deciphered JN-25 messages made plain that Japan had much more in mind, but Roosevelt's insistence on security considerations prevented the declassification and release of those messages for almost fifty years. When a young graduate student accidentally discovered the documents in a dusty Hollinger Box in the National Archives, the public uproar reopened the raw wounds that characterized American domestic politics in early 1942.

Because the Japanese did not attack American territory or possessions on 7 December 1941, Roosevelt could not persuade Congress to declare war against Japan. Isolationist sentiment against American boys dying to preserve European colonial empires was too strong for even a master politician to overcome. The United States stood by as Japan overran Malaya, the Netherlands East Indies, the Bismarck Archipelago, and moved onto New Guinea. In May 1942 Japanese warships intercepted an American convoy carrying lend-lease supplies to the Soviet port at Vladivostok. The U.S. Navy cruiser *U.S.S Honolulu* and five destroyers escorting the American merchantmen refused to heave to and obey Japanese instructions. To this day it remains uncertain who fired the first shot, but the result was two American and one Japanese destroyers sunk, one merchantman sunk, one captured, and two damaged. American casualties were 472 killed or wounded which included 52 merchant seamen. With *casus belli,* Congress did declare war against Japan — by a margin of a single vote!

Such muddled antecedents made the Pacific War of 1942-1945 an unpopular and divisive conflict lacking a common purpose to bind Americans together in a national effort. Many liberals objected to the notion of bailing out colonial empires while conservatives denounced the idea of spilling American blood to aid a communist regime. More thoughtful commentators lamented that Japan was the wrong enemy to fight while Adolph Hitler's Nazi Germany was gobbling up Europe and North Africa.

The American war against Japan was a naval effort fought to gain supremacy in the Pacific. Early U.S. Navy thrusts into the Japanese Mandates were beaten back after the first aircraft carrier battles in history. Meanwhile Japanese ground troops conquered the Philippines by December 1942, but even this loss did not galvanize public opinion in the United States. Instead the navy's botched Mandates Campaign and subsequent inability to relieve the besieged Philippine garrison became the subjects of congressional inquiry.

The Central Pacific became the focal point of the American strategy. After bloody island fighting American Navy-Marine task forces broke through Japanese defenses by mid-1945 and liberated the Philippines. By that time, however, Roosevelt had been defeated in his quest for a fourth term and the Republican president heeded the voices of the electorate and entered into peace negotiations with Japan. This so-called "sell-out" cost the Republicans the White House in 1948 as the Democrats denounced them for throwing away the opportunity for victory.

Meanwhile in Europe the German dictator Adolph Hitler and Joseph Stalin's Soviet Union fought four years to exhaustion before they too concluded a negotiated peace. On June 22, 1951, during a long harangue on the occasion of the tenth anniversary of the German invasion of the Soviet Union, Hitler revealed that his greatest fear at that time was that the United States would find some pretext to enter the European War and tip the balance in favor of the Soviet Union.

Great Britain, crippled by the loss of her Far Eastern bases and colonies of Burma and Malaya sued Japan for peace in 1943 in order to concentrate all her forces against Hitler. Many Americans regarded this as an act of treachery, but, as historical scholarship has shown, Britain was exhausted from four years of fighting Germany and two of fighting Japan.

In strategic terms, the results of the negotiated settlements of the Pacific and European wars resulted in the creation of four great power blocs. The United States controlled the eastern and southwest Pacific from Midway to the Philippines and thence to Papua, New Guinea. Japan held sway over the northern and western Pacific, holding an arc from the Kuriles through the Indochina Peninsula into the Netherlands East Indies. Burma became a neutral buffer zone between Japanese dominated Malaya and British controlled India. Hitler's Third Reich enslaved western Europe, except Great Britain, and the Mediterranean. The Soviet dictator held the USSR east of Kiev. By 1950 there were two superpowers emerging — the United States and Nazi Germany which by early 1952 had entered a state of cold war.

C. What if Hitler had not declared war on the United States after Pearl Harbor?
Harold C. Deutsch & Dennis E. Showalter

On 11 December 1941, four days after the Japanese struck at Pearl Harbor and its Pacific Fleet, the Nazi dictator declared war on the United States. His motivations for this fateful step count among the most mystifying of Hitler's twelve years of rule. The debates concerning this decision will no doubt continue for generations. So illogical did it seem even to his principal henchman and successor designate, Hermann Goering, that it slipped his memory. When questioned about it at Nuremberg, Goering exclaimed in disbelief: "We declare war on you? But didn't you first declare war on us?"

The proposition that no rational explanation is possible continues to have wide support. Some analysts (e.g., Sebastian Hafner) hold that in the aftermath of the military disaster at the gates of Moscow, Hitler gave up hope of victory. By adding the United States to the forces arrayed against him, he set the stage for a Wagnerian finale. This makes Hitler the victim of a compelling death wish. It may be argued that considerably more evidence for such a degree of irrationality must come to light in order to sustain such an abstract psychological interpretation. If Hitler was driven by suicidal urges, many of his survival and victory-oriented courses in the remaining years of war would have made small sense.

A second interpretation, supplied by a large body of direct evidence, is that Hitler's assessment of the American war-making potential was so abysmally inaccurate that he appraised the general impact of Japan's entry into the war far above that of the United States. In his mind the Americans were a mongrel people, not fitted to make effective use of their undoubtedly vast human and material resources. The morrow of Pearl Harbor witnessed a tumble of words and gestures giving voice to his obsessions. On hearing at Wolf's Lair of the Japanese assault, he acclaimed this a vital turning point and rushed out through the snow to apprise Keitel and Jodl. To Foreign Office representative Hewel he effervesced: "Now it is impossible for us to lose the war. We now have an ally who has not been vanquished for three thousand years."[1] That evening he summoned the officers of his staff to a lively champagne party and amazed all by violating his hitherto fixed rule against alcohol consumption by taking some sips himself.[2]

Returning to Berlin on 9 December, the Fuehrer assured Japanese ambassador Oshima that the United States would not prove a formidable foe: "How can you expect a nation to fight whose only god is the almighty dollar?" One might take such effusions as momentary exuberance if there were not impressive indications of their prevailing over the following months. When the Washington military attaché, General von Boetticher, was repatriated with the rest of the embassy staff via Teheran and was immediately summoned to the Fuehrer, he naturally assumed that he would be questioned at length on the American military and industrial potential. But his two briefcases of notes and documents were never opened. For an hour and a half Hitler orated about the "Jewification" of America with a President whose family name must obviously once have been Rosenfeld and whose wife, from her general physiognomy, could be judged to be of Negro origin.[3]

A third and logically kindred explanation that has been offered for Hitler's fatal step considers it an exercise in short-range *Realpolitik*, the necessary price of Japan's entry into the war and the accompanying division of American resources between two distant theaters. This would give assurance for Japan lasting the course while Germany finished with the Soviets in 1942. Subsequently the Americans would shrink from a war of attrition against the united resources of Europe under Nazi control.

If Hitler indeed pursued such a line of reasoning, it was most likely a rationalization to justify his response to the string of insults and unneutral injuries to which he had been subjected by the Roosevelt administration during the preceding year. Moreover, Hitler had no objective need to follow through what pledges and assurances he had made to Japan before 7 December.[4] Japan's decision to "jump off the roof" had been made independently. Hitler's determination to go to war with the United States may well have been largely emotional—the release of pent-up resentments that he at last felt free to indulge. It was as if a trussed-up Fuehrer had been subjected to blows in the face from a hitherto immune Uncle Sam and could at last hit back.

The actual course of affairs amply illustrates that a German defeat became certain once Hitler was at war with the United States. For the second time within less than six months, Hitler without compelling reasons made war on one of the superpowers of the post-war world. But what if he had acted as if nothing was changed by the American involvement with Japan? What if the Fuehrer had seen the advantage of leaving well enough alone, of allowing Japan to fight as best she could the war she had initiated? The ball would have been in the American court.

Would the United States have declared war on Germany at this time?

Opposition to American participation in the war was widespread to the very day of Pearl Harbor. Selective service had been extended by a single House vote. Polls showed support for aid to Britain but also stressed keeping this short of war. Roosevelt's program of rearmament was acceptable because of its emphasis on a defensive posture. There was much hostility to Nazi Germany but, even during the war that now came, this remained a far cry from the visceral loathing reserved for Japan.

Given these circumstances, it appears questionable whether the President would have ventured to urge declaring war on Germany after Pearl Harbor. The Japanese coup had given the nation a measure of unity hitherto undreamed of and, indeed, unique in American history. This union of hearts and of national purpose would have been compromised and conceivably shattered by a heated debate on extending the war to the European Axis. The frequent postwar charge that the President had maneuvered to bring America into the war with Germany via the Asian back door would have sprung to life then and there, with negative impacts even on fighting the war in the Pacific. The "Asia firsters" protestations even before 7 December that Roosevelt was sacrificing true national interests on behalf of Britain would have gained new force. They would have offered a rallying point for a broad spectrum of administration critics on domestic issues from the New Deal to the third term.

Many Americans no doubt went along with the President when, in his "fireside chat" of 9 December, he flailed the European Axis as having in effect sicked Japan onto us. It is noteworthy, however, that Roosevelt did not associate this denunciation with a recommendation to declare war on Germany and Italy. From Magic intercepts, he knew of course that the Axis was about to relieve him of this burden. But, even if he had not been able to anticipate this, it is highly questionable whether he would have urged such declarations at this juncture. And, had he done so, the response from Congress would have been highly questionable. At the very least, a politically devastating debate was in prospect. The weight of logic thus inclines one to the assumption that Roosevelt would not have maneuvered to extend the war at this time.

Few analysts would venture the opinion, much less a conviction, that the European and Pacific wars would have continued indefinitely without the United States becoming in some way entangled in the former. The impact upon the world scene, of course, would have depended essentially upon time and circumstance of American entry into the European conflict. The longer the postponement, for example, the greater became the chance of America becoming so committed to the Pacific that the "Europe first" formula of the Anglo-American pre-Pearl Harbor agreement would have become irrelevant.

It is usually thought that Roosevelt would have continued to seek opportunities to bring America closer to and, in time, into the European war. This is, of course, to assume that he himself would not have become so caught up in Pacific affairs as to begin thinking of Europe as a distraction. In any event, consummate politician that he was, Roosevelt might have chosen to bide his time, ignoring Germany temporarily while working behind the scenes to bring Congressional leaders to support a war on two fronts across two oceans. If this process had continued through 1942, and assuming affairs on the Eastern Front had gone much as they did by the end of that year, the decline of Hitler's fortunes would have reduced in some measure the pressures for American intervention. In any event, further discussion will be based on the thought of America not being involved as a full belligerent in the European war in 1942.

Probable Consequences for the War in Europe

If one commences with the proposition that there would have been no full American war with Germany in 1942, one is driven toward the conclusion that the fighting in Europe might well have resulted in a stalemate. American assistance was vital to Britain in the Battle of the Atlantic and for a clear-cut victory in the Middle East. It also played a significant, though still not fully admitted, role in the rejuvenation of the Soviet war effort.

In the Atlantic battle the assistance rendered in 1941 would probably have continued in much the same form during 1942. Any extension would have depended upon the probable Roosevelt policies as they developed after Pearl Harbor. If the President sought to escalate his support of Britain and the Soviet Union to the point of forcing a final break with the Axis, he would do what he could to increase protection of convoys as far eastward as possible, perhaps even to British ports, welcoming resulting frictions. He would have to proceed with caution if, as appears likely, the popular American mood was sensitive to whatever threatened to impede national absorption in the Pacific conflict. However, since Britain would now by the grace of Japan be our ally in the Far East, a corresponding feeling of greater solidarity with our British friends was likely to result. This could be manipulated to foster greater sympathy for Britain's fate in the old world. It thus appears likely that there would have been increasing popular support for the existing measures to assist British convoys and of lend-lease aid to Britain and the Soviet Union. Without direct American involvement, victory over Germany in the Battle of the Atlantic, given the escalating performance of Ultra, would still have been probable. It might, however, have been delayed and reduced in scope.

The war in the Middle East and the Mediterranean generally would have been much tougher for Britain. There would have been no Operation Torch or takeover of French and Italian North Africa. The possibility that Hitler at some point would have forced Franco's hand to associate Spain more closely with the Axis would have been greater. The five hundred Grant and Sherman tanks that arrived in time to play a critical role in the El Alamein victory would scarcely have been forthcoming. Rommel, however ill supported, might have remained on the frontier of Egypt and the Axis might have mounted an over-delayed invasion of Malta. In sum, there could have been little thought of sweeping Italy out of the war in the summer of 1943. Looking at a worst-case scenario, the Mediterranean might yet have become something like an Axis lake.

The Soviets, with only Britain's rapidly eroding forces available to create distractions for Germany in the west, could have entertained little hope of an early "second front." American military and economic aid would to some extent have remained forthcoming, but probably at a sharply reduced level. Absent direct involvement in the European war, it is difficult to perceive anything like the flood of American materiel that helped so much to stiffen Soviet forces in the last two years of the struggle. Though Lend-Lease in 1943 was not yet the vital factor in the Soviet war effort that it later became, the outlook with America continuing to stand aside was still discouraging. Stalin's repeated demands for a "second front now" are an indication of his evaluation of a future American impact on the course of the war. What if the Russo-German campaigns of 1942 had been fought with the uncomfortable knowledge that this time the Yanks were not coming? Most probably Stalin's still mysterious, rather half-hearted peace overtures to Germany in the summer of 1943 would have been pushed more seriously if the outlook for eventual military victory had been that much more bleak.[5]

Few students of the European war would argue that a reduced, and generally more grudging, American support of Britain and the Soviets would have brought victory to Hitler. Nevertheless, removing America from the equation suggests a drawn-out war between the great continental powers—a war perhaps periodically interrupted by truces, each in turn broken by a savage renewal of fighting. In that contest Germany would have had some opportunity to consolidate her position in the occupied lands of western and central Europe, though whether the Reich would have done so is another question. A compromise peace of mutual exhaustion nevertheless seems a reasonable assumption—perhaps accompanied by Hitler's overthrow or death from natural causes.

Britain for her part was by 1942 impregnable to German invasion but equally incapable of threatening the continent with her own resources. At most she might have undertaken something against the German forces of occupation in Norway. In the context of a German-Soviet stalemate, Churchill or his successor might well have sought rapprochement, formal or informal, in the effort to avert complete exclusion from Europe. And in that case — but here we leave the realm of alternative history and enter that of historical speculation.

To return to both greater realism and a less gloomy scenario, there are strong reasons to argue that, before a genuine European stalemate had been reached, America would have taken a more vigorous hand in the game. As war production skyrocketed and enlistments exceeded what could possibly have been utilized in the Pacific, the national mood, accentuated by the common cause made with Britain in the Far East, promised to become increasingly amenable to European involvement. Worsening relations with Germany, most probably associated with a steadily escalating support of Britain in the Battle of the Atlantic, could well have brought affairs to a critical stage by late 1942, when the U-boat war was reaching the height of its intensity.

Supposing the entry of the United States into the European conflict toward the turn of the year, a strategic pattern quite different from the one actually then reached would have prevailed. There would have been greater impatience in Washington with any diversion from the aim of striking as soon as possible at the heart of Hitler's empire. Except perhaps for a rescue expedition to succor a foundering British force in the eastern Mediterranean, appeals to concentrate upon the "soft underbelly" of the Axis would have elicited meager response. Concentration rather than peripheral nibblings would have been the watchword. An earlier D-Day in this context? Perhaps even in 1943? But here again we find ourselves in the realm of speculation.

Probable consequences for the war in the Pacific

Next to FDR personally, the element in the American leadership most leaning toward involvement in the war against Nazi Germany resided in the Pentagon. Amidst the outburst of national outrage at the Japanese "sneak attack," the first impulse was to throw all into the conflict in the Pacific. Somewhat astonishingly, this was quickly enough stifled so that, when Churchill arrived in Washington some three weeks later, he was gratified to note a continuing commitment to the "Europe first" strategy.[6] But what if there had been no war with Germany? One can only surmise how much, in the months that followed, attention, hopes, and planning would have focused on the Pacific within the Pentagon. The same might have been true in some measure with the President himself.

Even in the actual historical scenario, the shock of the Japanese attack drew a high percentage of America's immediately deployable resources westward. More National Guard units were to fight in the Pacific than in Europe. As late as 1943, American troop strength in the ETO was less than in the Pacific. And from Admiral King downward, the

Pacific remained the Navy's principal theater emotionally and psychologically throughout the war. In the absence of a shooting war with Germany, shelving all the Rainbow plans and reviving Plan Orange would hardly have called for major adjustments. The color and force of Douglas MacArthur would have focussed national attention to a degree that much exceeded the divided attentions that actually prevailed during this period.

On the other hand, it is questionable whether a "Pacific first" option could have absorbed enough military resources to influence significantly the conduct of a European war that, in our scenario, began near the turn of the year 1943. After Midway, America's war in the Pacific was handicapped less by shortages of men and materials than by difficulties in transporting and sustaining her forces in the theater. The presence of more divisions, or more aircraft of the types available in 1942 - 1945, would have had limited consequences. The balance of naval forces did not swing decisively in America's favor until 1943, as the new construction joined the fleet. In historical fact, King saw to it that landing craft were never in decisively short supply in either the central or southeast Pacific theaters. The absence of European requirements for these vessels would have facilitated MacArthur's and Nimitz's operations but hardly altered them essentially.

In a situation where Germany and the United States never went to war, or did so only in 1943, a likely outcome seems a major Japanese peace initiative no later than the last quarter of 1944. By that time the imbalance of forces would have been plain to the most determined militarists — though the striking power of the U.S. Navy might not have been much greater than it actually was in history. America's response might have been one of opening negotiations. It might also have taken advantage of the much larger ground and air forces available in the absence of a German war to launch a campaign on the Asian mainland. The urge to do more in Burma and China might have begun to play a role as early as 1942.

The latter possibility must not be exaggerated. Under many circumstances, the United States would have kept one eye on Germany and been correspondingly reluctant to become involved in unfamiliar terrain halfway around the world. Probably America would have continued the war roughly along the strategic lines actually pursued, with Japanese capitulation antedating the completion of the atomic bomb. What that could have implied in the cold and hot wars of post-war generations is anyone's guess.

[1]   David Irving, *Hitler's War* (New York: Viking, 1977), 352.

[2]   Interrogation of Jodl's deputy, General Walter Warlimont, by Harold C. Deutsch, September, 1945. Warlimont, whose year of study in the United States of the American economy had fitted him to judge realistically the American potential, was himself so downcast that he retired to his room and sat in the dark sunk in gloomy forebodings.

[3]   Interrogation of Friedrich von Boetticher by Harold C. Deutsch, September 1945.

[4]   Hitler at times expressed contempt for those who kept to agreements when they became unprofitable. The Japanese, though much encouraged by his assurances through Ribbentrop of 21 and 28 November 1941, no doubt would have gone to war without them.

[5]   The fuller story of these overtures counts among significant aspects of Stalin's policies on which there should be welcome clarification as the restrictions on Soviet archives are relaxed or lifted.

[6]   Virtually on the morrow of Pearl Harbor, the War Department convened a committee of eight to make a quick reassessment of the strategic situation. A preliminary straw vote found seven of the officers agreeing that the Pacific should now receive principal attention. Then, one by one, those favoring this view changed sides until in the end there was unanimity that the "Europe first" concept should be preserved. Conversations with General Haywood S. Hansell, Jr., October 1948. Hansell was a participant in the committee's deliberations.

Chapter 7

The Pacific War

D. Clayton James & Anne Sharp Wells

A. What if MacArthur had been left to surrender on Corregidor?

The Philippines were doomed whether or not General Douglas MacArthur stayed on Corregidor, as implied by the above question. A foremost authority on the Pacific war maintains, "The defense of the 7,100 islands in the Philippine archipelago, lying in an exposed position 7,000 miles from the west coast of the United States, was over thirty years the basic problem of Pacific strategy. From the start it was apparent that it would be impossible to defend all or even the major islands."[1]

United States war plans in effect at the time of the Pearl Harbor attack (Rainbow 5 and War Plan Orange 3) stated that the American and Filipino armed forces in the archipelago could hold out for only four to six months in the event of a Japanese invasion. The main forces on Luzon, considered the most strategically significant island of the Philippines, would withdraw to the Bataan peninsula and the four small island fortresses at and near Corregidor, from which they would protect Manila Bay. According to some Orange editions, American ships would try to reinforce the Philippine forces before the four to six months were up; unless they were somehow successful, the Japanese would definitely take the Philippines.

With the crippling of the United States Pacific Fleet at Pearl Harbor during the first strike of the war, any substantial reinforcement of the Philippines became impossible, making the islands' surrender to the Japanese inevitable. Even without the losses at Pearl Harbor, successful reinforcement by the United States would have been uncertain. Within several weeks of the first Japanese air attacks against Philippine targets on December 8, 1941, most remaining American naval and air forces in the Philippines had moved to the Netherlands East Indies. Although President Franklin D. Roosevelt and War Department officials, especially Army Chief of Staff George C. Marshall, tried to get aid to the American forces remaining in the Philippines, they held no real hope of success. Roosevelt wrote Secretary of War Henry L. Stimson on December 30, 1941, "I wish that War Plans [Division] would explore every possible means of relieving the Philippines. I realize great risks are involved but the objective is important."[2] On February 9, 1942, Roosevelt wrote to MacArthur about "the desperate situation to which you may shortly be reduced — I particularly request that you proceed rapidly to the organization of your forces and your defenses so as to make your resistance as effective as circumstances will permit and as prolonged as humanly possible."[3]

The President decided to order MacArthur out of the Philippines to prevent the Japanese from capturing him when the inevitable surrender came. The records do not indicate whether FDR gave any consideration to leaving him to surrender on Corregidor, but General Marshall and Secretary of War Stimson are known to have favored his rescue. On February 22, Roosevelt issued the orders for MacArthur to leave the islands, with the eventual destination of Australia. MacArthur requested that he be allowed to leave at the time he considered best. Actually, he and his wife and four-year-old son, along with seventeen members of his staff, did not depart until March 11 on the hazardous journey to Australia.

Lieutenant General Jonathan M. Wainwright, who succeeded MacArthur in the Philippine command, surrendered to the Japanese in early May. Bataan had fallen a month earlier. It is difficult to imagine that MacArthur's continued presence on Corregidor could have prevented the capitulation to the Japanese, although the surrender would perhaps have been executed with less confusion. There were problems associated with obtaining formal authorization from the United States government to surrender; with attempts by Wainwright to prevent the surrender of forces in the southern Philippines by telling them to report to MacArthur; and with Wainwright's subsequent orders to them to surrender on his authority because he feared a massacre of his forces on Corregidor, since they had already laid down their arms. Some of this would possibly have gone smoother with MacArthur still in command on Corregidor, but the fact that the Philippines were doomed would not have been affected.

If MacArthur had surrendered to the Japanese in the Philippines, what would have been the personal effect on him? As a high-ranking officer, his treatment as a prisoner of war would have been better than that of captured enlisted men. As was the case with the other senior American officers in the Philippines, as well as Dutch and British commanders and high colonial officials captured during the fall of Southeast Asia, MacArthur would probably have been moved with them to prison camps (segregated from lower-ranking prisoners) in Formosa and later in Manchuria for the duration of the war. His wife and young son would probably have been interned in Manila and returned to the States in an exchange of civilian internees arranged by the Japanese and American governments.

Assuming MacArthur survived the period of captivity, his professional career would have ended with the war or soon afterward. In 1945 he was sixty-five years old (and he had already retired once from the Army, in 1937). Had he been held captive throughout the war, he would definitely not have been named to head the postwar occupation in Japan, nor would he have been given command of the United Nations forces in the Korean War five years later. To carry the point to its logical extreme, without MacArthur, a well-known successful general, in charge in Tokyo when the Korean War started, President Harry S. Truman would have been more hesitant to send military forces to Korea, and MacArthur's military career would not have ended with a dismissal by that President. Indeed, during the worst moments of their collision in 1951, Truman probably wished that FDR had left MacArthur on Corregidor.

If he had not evacuated MacArthur, Roosevelt would have suffered some domestic political fall-out for permitting the Japanese to capture such a high-ranking general, and the American public would have been furious with the Japanese. But Americans were already so angry about Pearl Harbor that MacArthur's capture could not have added much more wrath.

If MacArthur had been left to surrender on Corregidor, what would have been the effect on the war against Japan? Though the Allies would have won, the actual conduct of the war would have been different. Some operations would have remained the same, such as the decision to take Guadalcanal because of the Japanese threat to the line of communications between the United States and Australia. The role of the United States in operations in Burma and China would not have grown because of the enormous logistical difficulties in deploying men and materiel to those areas, the steadfastly low priority of the China-Burma-India theater in the global planning of the Joint Chiefs of Staff, and the delegation of the strategic direction of the war in China to Generalissimo Chiang Kai-shek's headquarters, and in Burma to the British Chiefs of Staff Committee and the British-dominated Southeast Asia Command of Admiral Louis Mountbatten.

There would have been unity of command over American forces in the Pacific, with Admiral Chester W. Nimitz the likely head. He had been transferred to Pearl Harbor immediately after the Japanese attack and therefore was in the right spot. Also, in the dual theater command structure that included MacArthur, Nimitz was his counterpart, so Nimitz would have been the logical person to head the unified effort with MacArthur out of the picture. The close relationship of Admiral Ernest J. King, chief of naval operations and commander in chief, United States Fleet, with Nimitz and the frequency and detail of their communications, both in person and otherwise, would have given King and Nimitz a strong joint input in determining the United States course in the Pacific war. The American effort would have been predominantly naval (including Marines), as prewar plans had decreed.

The Pacific Ocean Areas theater of Admiral Nimitz would have received larger elements of the United States Army and Army Air Forces if MacArthur had not been the Southwest Pacific chief. Nevertheless, the leaders of those forces probably would not have been permitted much input into strategic planning at Nimitz's headquarters. The lack of a voice in such matters was a frequent complaint of Lieutenant General Robert C. Richardson, commander of Army ground and air forces in that theater, even when these were greatly increased for the Okinawa invasion in the spring of 1945. Perhaps some of the senior commanders who did serve in the Southwest Pacific under MacArthur, such as Generals Walter Krueger, Robert L. Eichelberger, and George C. Kenney and Admirals Thomas C. Kinkaid and Daniel E. Barbey, might have received commands in the later stages of the Pacific war, but the senior Army officers more likely would have gone to European assignments.

Although MacArthur had wanted the supreme Pacific command himself, he later observed regarding the need for unity of command in the Pacific struggle:

"Of all the faulty decisions of war perhaps the most unexplainable one was the failure to unify the command in the Pacific. The principle involved is the most fundamental one in the doctrine and tradition of command. In this instance it did not involve choosing one individual out of a number of Allied officers, although it was an accepted and entirely successful practice in the other great theaters. The failure to do so in the Pacific cannot be defended in logic, in theory, or in common sense…. It resulted in divided effort, the waste, diffusion, and duplication of force, and the consequent extension of the war, with added casualties and cost. The generally excellent co-operation between the two commands in the Pacific … was no substitute for the essential unity of direction of centralized authority. The handicaps and hazards unnecessarily resulting were numerous, and many a man lies in his grave today who could have been saved."[4]

Nearly all the senior commanders who served under Nimitz in the Pacific Ocean Areas theater and under MacArthur in the Southwest Pacific Area theater expressed similar sentiments after the war.

Would the war against Japan have ended any sooner with a different American command structure and different commanders? Of course, it is assumed that as far as commanders go, not only MacArthur but the officers who actually left the Philippines with him would not have participated in the war. If the end of the war could have been accomplished only by the atomic bomb, the changed command organization would not have shortened the war. If the different command arrangement and allocation of resources had proved to be more effective against Japan, leading to surrender without use of the atomic bomb (and the opportunistic Soviet entry into the war), then perhaps the answer is affirmative. However, the hostilities in Europe would have had to terminate much earlier.

It is unlikely that the war against Europe would have ended any sooner with a different American command structure and different commanders in the Pacific. There is no doubt that Anglo-American strategy would still have put the defeat of Germany first. Would Pacific operations have received fewer resources without MacArthur's strong and public pleas for more assistance to the war against Japan? Even though King did not like MacArthur or the very existence of his theater, MacArthur's constant requests and demands on behalf of the Pacific did bolster King's arguments for more emphasis on the war with Japan. Without having to send Army ground and air forces to MacArthur and the Southwest Pacific Area, Marshall would have devoted even more attention to the European war. There would have been more imbalance in American overseas deployments, with more of the Army and Army Air Forces units sent to the war in Europe and more of the Navy and Marine forces to the conflict in the Pacific.

MacArthur's absence would not have deterred Australia's growing alienation from the United Kingdom. Before the Southwest Pacific Area theater was formed and the United States began to send ground, sea, and air forces to Australia to build up a base of operations for a counteroffensive northward in 1942, Prime Minister John Curtin and his Labor government in Canberra already were angered over the British retention of Australian Army divisions in the North African desert war at a time when Australia considered its own defenses inadequate in the face of the advancing Japanese juggernaut through the Southwest Pacific. MacArthur did not lessen Australian frustration with the British, although for a while he did make the United States more popular in Australia, often teaming up with Curtin to demand from American and British leaders more resources for the war in the Southwest Pacific. Before the midway mark of the war, though, many Australians were alienated by MacArthur's arrogance and by the American soldiers' rowdiness and ethnocentrism.

Australia was too important as one of the last places in Southeast Asia and the West Pacific not dominated by Japan, as an important source of war materials and military manpower and as a future base of offensive operations, for the United States to totally ignore it. The first allied combined command, the American-British-Dutch-Australian Command (ABDACOM), had been formed in the Australian-East Indies area, so it would have been logical for the United States to participate in another combined command in the area. The new allied theater in March 1942 became the Southwest Pacific Area, and in the absence of MacArthur it is likely that the command, manpower, and material resources would have been provided largely by Australia. There would have been less contact with United States operations, which would have been concentrated in the Central Pacific.

An Australian, probably General Thomas Blamey, would have been named supreme commander of the Southwest Pacific theater. Australian ground forces, with support from American air and sea forces of moderate strength, would have conducted largely holding operations above Australia. Limited offensive operations to regain oil fields in Java, Borneo, and Sumatra might have been carried out by Blamey's army, particularly late in the war when Japanese forces in the Dutch East Indies had been drained by transfers to other combat zones.

By late 1943 Australians deeply resented the Anglo-American strategic leaders' disdain of Australia as an unequal alliance partner. By the time of the United Nations Conference at San Francisco in the spring of 1945, Australia had become a vociferous leader of the small nations against the major powers in world affairs. In the immediate postwar years she appeared at times more antagonistic toward the United Kingdom and the United States than toward even the now menacing Soviet Union.

If Australia had been given command of the Southwest Pacific theater, if she had been allowed to conquer and retain at least a portion of the East Indies, and if an Australian voice had been permitted in the highest strategic councils of the Western Allies, Australia's estrangement from Britain and America probably would not have occurred. On the other hand, the sensitivities of Australia were of no great concern to statesmen and high commanders in Washington and London as long as Australia's national security was dependent upon the Anglo-American alliance. Therefore it was unlikely during World War II that Australia would have been able to gain leverage by brief control of the Southwest Pacific theater that could have been translated into more satisfactory postwar relations with America and Britain or into large territorial spoils in the Pacific after the war.

B. What if MacArthur had been obliged to bypass the Philippines?

This eventuality almost took place, and in retrospect some members of the American high command believed it would have been the wiser course. Before the possibilities and limitations of other options are considered, the evolution of the actual decision on the reconquest of the Philippines will be traced briefly.

When General MacArthur escaped from Corregidor in March 1942 and made his way through Japanese lines to Australia, his train stopped for a short time at Adelaide while en route to Melbourne, where he was to establish his new allied theater headquarters. At the Adelaide railroad station he proclaimed to a group of correspondents and onlookers that President Roosevelt had ordered him to go to Australia "for the purpose, as I understand it, of organizing the American offensive against Japan, a primary object of which is the relief of the Philippines. I came through and I shall return."[5] All across the free world his words "I shall return" made headlines, although there was no provision at that time in the plans of the United States Joint Chiefs of Staff nor the Anglo-American Combined Chiefs of Staff for MacArthur to lead, as he assumed, a future counteroffensive to liberate the Philippines employing largely American Army ground and air units.

Indeed, since the early editions, in the 1920s, of War Plan Orange, the American contingency plan for a possible conflict with Japan would be primarily naval. They envisioned the decisive drive following a westward course from Pearl Harbor toward Tokyo, spearheaded by United States Navy and Marine forces operating east and north of the Philippines.

Because plans during World War II for the final defeat of Japan were not seriously considered by the Joint Chiefs and their subordinate planning committees until late 1943 when the offensive momentum and the superiority in men and materiel had definitely shifted to the allied side in the Pacific, MacArthur's pledge to return to the Philippines went unchallenged for quite a while in official strategic planning sessions in Washington. By the spring of 1944, however, allied offensives were penetrating deep within Japan's West Pacific defense perimeter, and a decision was obviously needed on the future axis of advance to Japan.

The Joint Staff Planners, the Joint Strategic Survey Committee, and the Joint War Plans Committee, each consisting of senior Army and Navy officers and reporting to the Joint Chiefs of Staff, had narrowed the choices to southern Formosa, Amoy and its vicinity on the coast of China, or Luzon in the northern Philippines as the most strategically important and logistically reasonable targets prior to direct operations against the main Japanese home islands. The Joint Chiefs of Staff approved directives that spring for the autumn advance of MacArthur's Southwest Pacific Area forces into

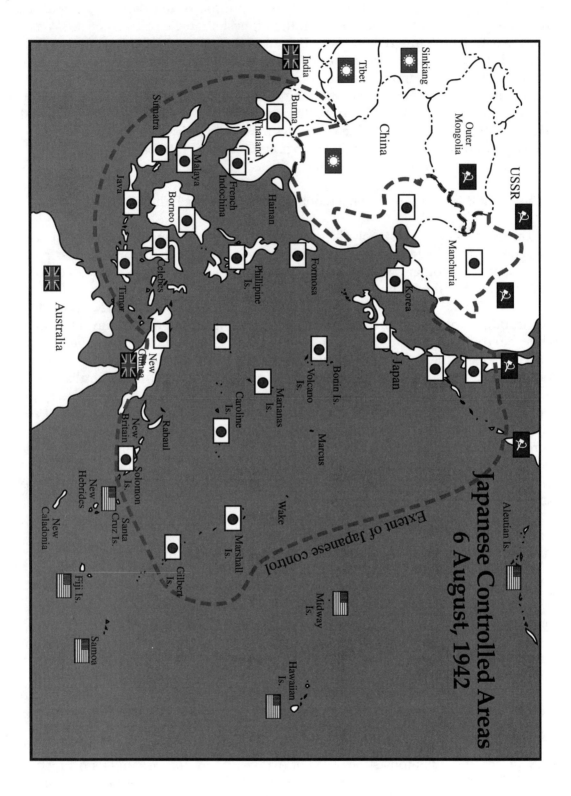

Japanese Controlled Areas
6 August, 1942

Extent of Japanese control

Australia

India
Burma
Thailand
Sumatra
Malaya
Java
Borneo
French Indochina
Hainan
Celebes
Timor
Philippine Is.
Formosa
New Guinea
New Britain
Rabaul
Solomon Is.
Santa Cruz Is.
New Hebrides
New Caladonia
Caroline Is.
Marianas Is.
Marcus
Volcano Is.
Bonin Is.
Wake
Marshall Is.
Gilbert Is.
Fiji Is.
Samoa
Midway Is.
Hawaiian Is.
Japan
Korea
Manchuria
China
Tibet
Sinkiang
Outer Mongolia
USSR
Aleutian Is.

the southern and central Philippines but held in abeyance any decision on where the principal pre-Japan amphibious assault would take place and whether it would be commanded by him or Admiral Nimitz, the head of the Pacific Ocean Areas theater. Admiral King, the chief of naval operations, had long opposed ground operations in the Philippines and warned of a potential bloodbath on Luzon. After disagreeing with King in the formative Joint Chiefs' sessions on Pacific plans and tentatively defending the idea of a MacArthur-led advance to Luzon, by May 1944 General Marshall, the Army Chief of Staff, and General Henry H. Arnold, the Commanding General of the Army Air Forces, began to yield somewhat in the months-long debate. They were increasingly inclined to think that the Formosa objective would be obtainable more rapidly and at less cost than Luzon, the most strongly fortified Philippine island.

At Pearl Harbor in late July 1944, Roosevelt, MacArthur, Nimitz, and Admiral William D. Leahy, who was the chairman of the Joint Chiefs and chief of staff to FDR, conferred on future Pacific strategy. MacArthur was persuasive in arguing that not only strategic but also humanitarian and political factors favored the Luzon target over Formosa. Nimitz thought both should be seized but Luzon first, though King, his superior who was in Washington, was known to oppose adamantly any move into the Philippines. Roosevelt and Leahy returned from the Oahu meeting apparently won over by MacArthur's argument for Luzon, but they did not pressure the Joint Chiefs to accept their views when they returned to the States.

The Joint Chiefs and their planners continued to debate the alternatives until early October when King and his strategic advisers finally concluded that an amphibious assault on Formosa would not be logistically feasible in the near future or even by March 1945, as King had earlier predicted. Thereupon the Joint Chiefs, with presidential approval, issued directives on October 3 to MacArthur authorizing his invasion of Luzon in December and to Nimitz approving his plans to assault Iwo Jima in January and Okinawa in March.

The Joint Chiefs never formally cancelled the Formosa plan, but it was not seriously considered again—nor was the plan to establish an Amoy beachhead revived. The Luzon, Iwo Jima, and Okinawa operations all had to be postponed considerably because of the logistical shortages and delay in securing Leyte in the central Philippines.

As King had predicted, the Luzon campaign, which lasted from January to August 1945 with a large Japanese force still battling by V-J Day, became the costliest operation of the Pacific war in terms of American ground forces killed in combat. In fact, two of the four bloodiest campaigns of the war with Japan in numbers of United States troops killed in ground action were in the Philippines: Luzon, 8,200; Okinawa, 7,400; Iwo Jima, 6,900; Leyte, 3,500.

If the Joint Chiefs could have foreseen that Luzon's liberation would be far longer and bloodier than the four-week campaign MacArthur promised, it is quite doubtful that they would have selected Luzon over Formosa (or Amoy). In fact, they probably would have terminated the northward advance in the Southwest Pacific theater with MacArthur's conquest of Netherlands New Guinea in July 1944.

A number of additional factors might have led them to decide to bypass that archipelago. First, if MacArthur had not been in a position to influence the President and the Joint Chiefs in decision-making in 1944, King surely would have gotten his way on enveloping the Philippines. The absence of MacArthur's input at this stage of the war would have come about either because he had been taken prisoner in the Philippines in early 1942, he had been killed during his long, perilous journey by PT-boat and B-17 from Corregidor to Australia that March, or he had been relieved as Southwest Pacific theater commander after suffering another defeat in his next campaign, which was the hard-fought six-month operations to recapture Papua, New Guinea.

Second, the transfer of the bulk of United States ground, air, and sea forces from the Southwest Pacific to the Central Pacific after the disappointing Papuan struggle, along with additional shipping and service forces for Nimitz's theater, may have made it possible by autumn of 1944, after the Marianas had been secured, to move directly on to Formosa without capturing Luzon first.

Third, an earlier end to the war in Europe, perhaps in the fall of 1944, would have permitted the redeployment of American forces from the European and Mediterranean theaters to buttress a Central Pacific forces' assault on Formosa. Such a massive shift of power might have made possible the bypassing of both Formosa and Luzon and, instead, an assault of Kyushu directly, as Marshall at one time suggested during the actual Joint Chiefs' discussions in 1944.

If there had been no allied invasion of the Philippine Islands, the consequences for the Southwest Pacific Area, the allied theater that MacArthur headed, would have been far-reaching during both the wartime period and the postwar era. As earlier suggested, there would undoubtedly have been no operations by Southwest Pacific forces above the equator. Most of the American units would have been transferred to the Central Pacific command. There would have been no conquest of Morotai in the Halmaheras by MacArthur's troops nor of the Palau Islands by Nimitz's forces, since both advances were planned solely in support of future Philippine assaults. Deleting the Palaus operations would have meant the battle for Peleliu, one of the costliest and strategically most needless operations of the Pacific war, would not have occurred.

It is likely that MacArthur would have been named in mid-1944 or earlier as commander of all Army forces in the war with Japan and Nimitz as head of all Navy and Marine elements in that conflict, which was accomplished in fact in the spring of 1945 by a Joint Chiefs' directive in preparation for the impending invasion of Japan. Australian General Thomas Blamey, who actually headed allied ground forces in the Southwest Pacific, probably would have been appointed to supreme command of that theater once its principal allied units were Australian. Under MacArthur they had been relegated to fighting mop-up actions and eliminating bypassed enemy garrisons south of the equator by 1944. Now, however, the Australians, who exhibited great interest in postwar territorial expansion in the Southwest Pacific areas that Japan and the Netherlands had formerly possessed, would have probably launched invasions of several Dutch East Indies islands west of New Guinea, especially Java and Borneo.

The postwar Indonesian nationalist movement would have been confronted with not only Dutch but also Australian resistance, possibly resulting in a complex three-cornered revolutionary war. Elements of the British-controlled Southeast Asia Command of Admiral Mountbatten, which actually first engaged the Indonesian rebels in armed clashes in the fall of 1945 before the Dutch returned, would have become entangled in even more fighting if the Australians were occupying some key East Indies islands, notably Java. Of course, there is the possibility that combined operations by the western forces might have suppressed the Indonesian revolution at least temporarily.

The impact on the Philippines would have been significant if that archipelago had been bypassed in 1944-1945, but it would not have been altogether as negative as MacArthur portrayed it gloomily at the Pearl Harbor Conference. When allied operations neared the islands, Japanese vessels carried many American prisoners of war from the Philippines to Formosa, Korea, Manchuria, and Japan. These "hell ships" got their nickname because many of them were sunk and thousands of Americans were killed when Pacific Fleet submarines and carrier-based aircraft attacked them at sea. The

Japanese butchery of American prisoners as well as Filipino civilians would have been less, since the atrocities usually were set off in waves of panic when the guards got news of an approaching allied invasion armada. One of the worst incidents was in December 1944 on Palawan Island in the southern Philippines where over 140 American veterans were ignited with gasoline or machine-gunned to death. During the savage battle for the city of Manila in February and March 1945, Japanese defenders of Intramuros, the old Spanish Walled City, panicked and slaughtered Filipino civilians caught in that area of central Manila, the final toll of atrocities approaching 60,000.

In Manila, as well as in countless towns and villages across the Philippine Islands, the devastation of battle was widespread as both sides locked in one fierce battle after another. American artillery fire and aerial bombing, including the first use of napalm, produced appalling casualties among civilians caught in the path of the fighting. It would be many years before the economic, social, and physical reconstruction and rehabilitation of the Philippines undid the ravages of war, which ranked among the worst suffered by any country in the Second World War. MacArthur's return and all the fighting it symbolized surely were mixed blessings to a land and people already poor and oppressed from nearly three years of Japanese occupation. The liberation of the Philippines, like the rescue of South Korea later, was attainable at a terrible price for those liberated.

As was true of other Asian peoples whose countries were occupied by the Japanese, the Filipinos at first appreciated the conquerors' slogan of "Asia for the Asiatics," Tokyo's talk of a Greater East Asia Co-prosperity Sphere, and the national independence that Japan promised. As the occupation wore on, however, the Filipinos became disillusioned with the proffered good intentions of the Japanese, finding them to be ruthless, tyrannical overlords bent on keeping the Filipinos in colonial bondage. If the Philippines had not been liberated by MacArthur's troops, the collaborationist regime that the Japanese established in the archipelago's national and provincial offices would have become more entrenched, but it also would have been increasingly challenged by a growing guerrilla movement.

The resistance movement in the Philippines actually became one of the largest and most effective in any Axis-occupied countries, reaching its peak as the invaluable right arm of MacArthur's regular units after they arrived in 1944-1945. Without such an invasion the allied shipments of arms and supplies to the rebel units operating on a considerable number of the 7,100 islands of the Philippines, as well as the important intelligence the guerrillas provided the allies about enemy forces' dispositions and plans, would have continued apace. Indeed, the allied logistical input to the resistance probably would have been far greater than actually occurred in order to keep Filipino morale high and imprisoned American soldiers and civilian internees hopeful.

At the end of World War II, possibly before any American officials returned, there would have probably been open fighting between the collaborationists and the guerrillas, culminating in a civil war that would have led to America's postponement of the independence (promised in the mid-1930s) to take place in July 1946. Whatever element might have emerged dominant in Philippine politics after the internal strife, most Filipinos would have experienced estrangement from the United States for a host of reasons, including the failure to defend the islands in 1941-1942, the bypassing of the islands in 1944-1945, and the part, whatever it might be, of America in the Philippines' postwar turmoil. In truth, whether MacArthur had returned or not, the United States would surely have been cast in the role of scapegoat for most of the woes the Filipinos suffered during and after the Second World War. Such was the almost universal fate of western imperial powers that attempted to return in whatever manner to their former

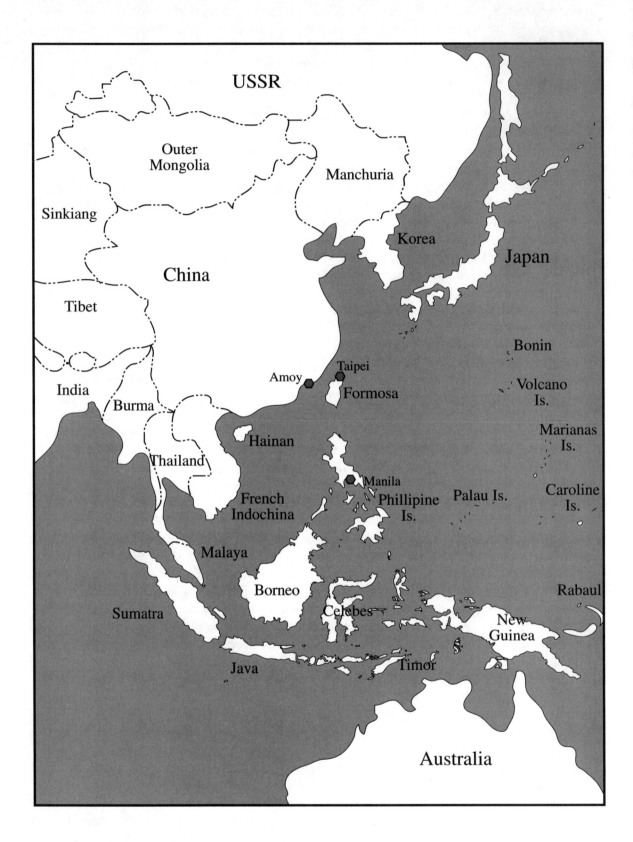

colonies, so powerful was the impetus of post-1945 nationalism in Africa, Asia, and the West Pacific.

On the positive side regarding the reconquest of the Philippines, it must be pointed out that the assets of not bypassing the archipelago proved to be significant. Over 438,000 Japanese troops were killed or became prisoners of war (wounded data are not known) during the Philippine campaign of 1944-1945, including the destruction of fifteen first-line army divisions. Japanese air strength had been reduced by thousands of planes and crews, while the battle for Leyte Gulf and lesser naval actions in Philippine waters had left the Japanese Combined Fleet virtually non-existent. In other words, much of the Japanese ground, air, and naval strength that otherwise might have been deployed against Nimitz's Central Pacific operations on Iwo Jima and Okinawa or against the projected invasion of Kyushu in November 1945, Operation Olympic, was wiped out in the Philippine operations.

By May 1945, American forces held nearly all the base areas that would be required to mount Olympic. By August, base development was well advanced all through the Philippines and the redeployment of American forces from the European theater to the islands was underway. American planes now had dozens of excellent air bases in the Philippines to interdict Japanese lines of communication in the South China Sea and further strangle Japan's economic support from Southeast Asia as well as cut off further enemy reinforcements to the East Indies. Finally, if thousands of Filipinos and Americans died during the liberation operations, at least by June 1945 millions of Filipinos and thousands of civilian internees had been freed, while law and order had been restored in most areas of the Philippines. The liabilities of retaking the Philippines were many and serious, but the assets were by no means inconsiderable. Liberating or bypassing the islands, however, meant dilemmas for the United States during World War II and long afterward.

C   What if the Allies had invaded the Amoy and South Formosa areas?

If there had been no reconquest of the Philippines, it is highly probable that the Joint Chiefs would have authorized Nimitz to launch assaults on southern Formosa and the Amoy area during the fall of 1944. As already mentioned, the decision to bypass the Philippines would have released many of the American ground, sea, and air units of the Southwest Pacific theater for such Central Pacific invasions. The Pacific command organization would have been revised to accommodate MacArthur as commander of Army forces. No unity of command had ever been attempted in the war against Japan primarily because of inter-service frictions and the Navy's deep-seated opposition to any control of large naval forces by MacArthur. How a reorganized command arrangement for the Formosa-Amoy operations might have functioned is hard to imagine, though problems in communication and coordination would have undoubtedly been monumental. General Joseph W. Stilwell, the China-Burma-India commander and chief of staff to Chiang Kai-shek since the spring of 1942, was relieved in the autumn of 1944 and later headed the United States Tenth Army in the final stage of the conquest of Okinawa. It boggles the imagination to picture a command structure for the Formosa-Amoy operations that might have had Nimitz as theater commander and Pacific Fleet chief, MacArthur as overall head of Army ground and air forces, and Stilwell as commander of one of the invading armies. The chaotic command arrangement in Burma might have appeared tranquil in comparison.

In early August 1944, MacArthur sent one of his strongest messages to the Joint Chiefs (through Marshall) protesting an invasion of Formosa. He maintained: "The

Formosa campaign itself can not be supported logistically without adequate bases in the Philippines. . . . An attempt to execute a great campaign in the far reaches of the Pacific without the establishment of adequate bases would be fraught with the gravest danger of disaster, which, if incurred, would greatly lengthen the war and multiply losses."[6] The Joint Chiefs were well acquainted with MacArthur's skill in using hyperbole to support his arguments, but this time the Southwest Pacific general demonstrated a foresight that came only much later to his superiors.

Even though Vice Admiral Marc A. Mitscher's Fast Carrier Task Force had the capability by the autumn of 1944 of launching over 900 planes for a single mission, the number of Japanese airfields within range of southern Formosa and Amoy was enormous. Thousands of land-based aircraft could have been dispatched against Mitscher and later against the invasion armadas. In previous campaigns in both Nimitz's and MacArthur's theaters, allied counteroffensives had enjoyed aerial supremacy, in part because of the long distances from major enemy airfields. Also, in the Southwest Pacific campaigns, allied ground operations had been supported by General Kenney's powerful land-based Fifth Air Force. In a Formosa-Amoy campaign, for the first time since early 1942, the airpower advantage might lie with the Japanese.

The proximity of the projected combat zone to other Japanese concentrations of military strength, such as in northern Formosa, southeastern China, the Ryukyus, Luzon, and even Kyushu, meant also that not only could Japanese air units be reinforced readily but also enemy ground and naval forces could be built up and resupplied more quickly than the allies could mount in the Formosa-Amoy operations. Even if lodgments were attained by the allied amphibious forces, the battle for Leyte Gulf, the greatest naval engagement of all time, would seem small in comparison to the great sea and air clashes that the Formosa-Amoy assaults would precipitate. The fighting probably would have culminated in the destruction of Japan's Combined Fleet and the backbone of her airpower reserved for defense of the homeland, but the sea and air losses on the allied side would have been horrendous and the allied victory narrow, depending heavily on the vast reserves of American ships and planes that could have eventually been thrown into the fray.

The ground actions would not have remained limited to southern Formosa and the Amoy region despite King's planners predicting otherwise. Instead they would have led to long and costly operations to take the rest of Formosa, which would be necessary to protect the B-29 bases to be built on the south end of the island and to prevent Japanese spoiling attacks and raids on the allied build-up and base construction for a future invasion of Japan. American Marines had secured the Empress Augusta Bay area of Bougainville in 1943, and they and Australian relief units had expanded the perimeter somewhat; the bulk of the island, however, had been left in Japanese control without serious menace to allied activities in the bay area. But Formosa was a quite different situation; the northern part, if it remained in enemy hands, could be easily reinforced from China or the nearby Ryukyus, in contrast to Bougainville, which was soon isolated.

The ground forces required for a campaign on Formosa would have been enormous, and very difficult to sustain logistically. The Okinawa operation affords some basis for projecting strength and loss data. Okinawa comprised 454 square miles and was defended by 135,000 Japanese troops. It took 176,000 United States Army and Marine personnel to secure the island. Japanese ground losses were 128,000 killed or captured, while the American troop casualties were 40,000 killed, wounded, or missing. Formosa consisted of 13,087 square miles, and, with reinforcements pouring in from the Japanese strongholds nearby, the defending force could have been quickly built up to at least 350,000, comparable to the strength of the Japanese army on Luzon. Surely two

American armies would have been necessary to seize Formosa. The forces necessary to secure the Amoy region, as well as the losses incurred, would have been even larger.

More crucial than the expanded fighting on Formosa, the allied forces at Amoy would have become enmeshed in operations on the Chinese mainland. There the Japanese maintained well over half of all the ground forces they had deployed outside the home islands. In the summer and fall of 1944 General Yasuji Okamura, one of Japan's best commanders, led an 820,000-man army in the offensive across south China that overran several B-29 bases and sealed off the Amoy coastal region from the main Chinese forces east of Chungking. The allied beachhead at Amoy could not have expected help from the Chinese armies inland, so it is likely more allied troops would have been poured into the Amoy region to expand the perimeter and make it usable for new B-29 airfields and base preparations for mounting an invasion of Japan. In short, the Formosa-Amoy venture would have entangled the Central Pacific forces in costly, tangential operations, and Nimitz, the theater commander, would have come to view the escalating ground commitment with the same frustration Brer Rabbit must have felt when he got all four hands and feet stuck in the tar baby.

While the Formosa-Amoy operations undoubtedly would have been the bloodiest of the Pacific war short of an invasion of Japan, assaults on those two areas would also have meant that there would have been no invasions of Iwo Jima and Okinawa, two of the costliest Pacific campaigns. Nimitz simply would not have had the manpower or materiel to spare for such ventures, especially since the shortages of shipping and service troops experienced by Central and Southwest Pacific theaters throughout the war would have worsened with the Formosa-Amoy escalations. On the positive side, too, the securing of Formosa and Amoy would have given the allies a strategic chokepoint on the Japanese line of communications to Southeast Asia, cutting off more effectively the critical supply of strategic raw materials like rubber, oil, and bauxite from Malaya, Borneo, Sumatra, and Java.

The establishment of an allied beachhead around Amoy, whether or not it was enlarged appreciably, would have been a tremendous boost to Chinese morale, which after the Japanese offensive in the summer of 1944 had drooped badly and had led to talk of negotiations for a separate peace with Japan. On the other hand, the presence of an American army in Fukien province (Amoy) at the end of World War II might have provided the impetus the strong China Bloc in America wanted to justify intervention in the looming Chinese civil war.

The Joint Chiefs had initially considered possibilities other than invasions of the Philippines, Formosa, and the Amoy region. Some attention had been devoted to a direct assault on Kyushu or even Honshu, but neither Nimitz nor MacArthur, when queried by the Joint Chiefs, believed an invasion of the Japanese home islands would be feasible without a large and secure base of operations to the south as well as land-based air support. The operations in the Aleutians by the Japanese in 1942 and the Americans in 1943 were fraught with so many weather-related problems that no earnest consideration was given to mounting an axis of advance by way of the Kuriles and Hokkaido, especially since repeated efforts to get the Soviet Union to permit American planes to use its Siberian bases had been to no avail. In retrospect, it seems the northern assault route might have been given more attention; it appears ironic that the war began with the Pearl Harbor attack force taking advantage of the North Pacific, but that same avenue of approach to Japan later was discarded as laden with too many meteorological and logistical problems.

Other options that were discussed and dismissed were bringing about the capitulation of Japan by accelerating the blockade of the home islands or the strategic bombing program, with some American Navy and Army Air Forces leaders convinced that a ground assault was not necessary if the naval and air forces were augmented, used more efficiently, and employed patiently in a strategy of attrition. In the end, of course, Japan's actual surrender resulted from two developments that the Joint Chiefs and their planners had not considered prior to the final weeks of the war: the use of atomic bombs and the entry into the Pacific conflict of the Soviet Union. Indeed, the best hope of all for an earlier end to the war with Japan probably would have been more attention and better diplomacy devoted to engaging the Soviets against the Japanese long before 1945. In turn, the price for the West would have been an even greater Soviet presence in the Far East than was yielded in the Yalta Agreements. A most significant consequence would have been that the occupation of Japan, which became a virtually all-American show under MacArthur, would have been administered by allied zones as in Germany and undoubtedly with equally frustrating conditions for the conquered and the conquerors.

[1] Louis Morton, *Strategy and Command: The First Two Years. United States Army in World War II: The War in the Pacific* (Washington: Office of the Chief of Military History, Department of the Army, 1962), p.21.

[2] Pres. Franklin D. Roosevelt to Sec. of War Henry L. Stimson, Dec. 30, 1941, Box 5, Aid to MacArthur folder, Harry L. Hopkins Papers, Franklin D. Roosevelt Library, Hyde Park, N.Y.

[3] Roosevelt to General MacArthur, Feb. 9, 1942, record group 2, GHQ USAFFE records, MacArthur Memorial Archives, Norfolk, VA.

[4] Douglas MacArthur, *Reminiscences* (New York: McGraw-Hill, 1964), pp. 172-173.

[5] London *Times*, March 21, 1942.

[6] MacArthur to Gen. George C. Marshall, Aug. 3, 1944, in Grace P. Hayes, *The History of the Joint Chiefs of Staff in World War II: The War Against Japan* (Annapolis, MD.: Naval Institute Press, 1982), p. 611.

Chapter 8

The Mediterranean

Harold C. Deutsch, Carlo D'Este & Thomas L. Barker

A. What if Adolf Hitler in 1940-1941, instead of concentrating on an attack on the Soviet Union, had pursued an all-out Mediterranean strategy in continuing war with Britain?*

Harold C. Deutsch

"He keeps harping on Gibraltar." This was a frequent refrain in dinner table exchanges on a day's activities of interrogators and observers during evenings at the Grand Hotel in Nuremberg where they were housed. The reference was to the Fuehrer's paladin-in-chief, Hermann Goering, and to his reported insistence that Hitler's most fatal error of the war had been to attack the Soviet Union rather than to pursue a whole-hearted Mediterranean strategy after his triumph in the west.[1]

Obsessions about race and living space had fused in Hitler's mind during his stay in Landsberg prison. They found ample expression in *Mein Kampf*. They also tangled with rabid anti-Semitism, fanatical anti-Bolshevism, and vague but persistent concepts of a world condominium with the British Empire in which London played a tolerant or even supportive part as German power expanded eastward on the European continent.

By the late mid-thirties this latter illusion was fading. British hesitations and meanderings during the Ethiopian crisis and later during the civil war in Spain eroded Hitler's respect for London's drive and purpose. He also was losing hope that the western powers would stand by as he drove eastward. As German military power developed and opportunities to fish in troubled waters proliferated, Hitler, though still aiming at the 1942-1945 period for conclusive action, was increasingly impatient and irritable. The temptation, not only to exploit opportunities as they arose, but to seize the initiative in putting pressure upon vulnerable neighbors like Austria, Czechoslovakia, and Poland was becoming irresistible.

This tied in with Hitler's growing readiness to protect his rear before embarking on the drive to the east. In this sense the 1939 deal with Stalin was only the first vital step on the road to Moscow. Even as the 1940 campaign in the west proceeded, the Fuehrer was commencing to think in terms of launching an attack on the Soviets as early as the autumn on the same year.

Such a time-table depended largely on conclusion of the war with France and Britain, whether on the heels of the flight from Dunkirk or in association with Operation Sea Lion. But in striving to bring the British to heel, Hitler clearly lacked the killer instinct he had demonstrated in Poland or in dealing with the French. The explanation for this indecisiveness involved reviving hopes of an accommodation with London and growing preoccupation with an early attack on the USSR. Ostensibly, once the British rejected negotiation there was no alternative but to strike across the Channel. Yet many believe that Sea Lion was no more than a gigantic bluff. Eager to embark on the road to Moscow, Hitler was psychologically attuned to the notion that, by depriving Britain of her last hope of finding an ally upon the continent, an easier route to London would be opened up—a political path instead of a military one.

A chronological chart of actual events follows this section.

By mid-July 1940 Hitler was reaching the tentative decision to launch the eastern campaign early in the autumn. Before the end of that month he determined to prepare the necessary redeployment. On July 28, "Atlas," the special train of General Alfred Jodl's Operations Department (*Wehrmachtfuehrungsstab*) was directed to Bad Reichenhall. From there Jodl proceeded by car to the Fuehrer's Berchtesgaden retreat. When he returned to the train and summoned his four top subordinates, he sought to lessen the shock by making out that the attack was scheduled for the spring of 1941. Even then, there was a hub bub of consternation and protest.[2]

Jodl and Keitel were horrified by the idea of an offensive drive commencing at this late season of the military year. They had not been privy to plots of the previous autumn, when Hitler's insistence on attacking in the west, ignoring seasonal and terrain features, had brought top army leaders to within an inch of revolt.[3] But they had shared in the premonitions of virtually the entire *Generalitaet*. Even the most notorious of Hitler loyalists among the generals, Walter von Reichenau, had been so outraged that he had sent clandestine warnings of Hitler's intentions to the British government.[4]

Keitel and Jodl assembled what evidence and arguments they could on the hazards of a fall campaign in Eastern Europe. The final assault was made by Keitel on 2 September. According to him, Hitler listened quietly, merely said, "I agree," and passed on to other matters.[5]

Few have felt at ease dipping into the mind of the Fuehrer, least of all for a period when his utterances still were governed less by impulse than calculation. He was so subject to changes of mind and to vacillation that it is often difficult to distinguish between fundamental patterns of thought and meanderings of the moment. At time Hitler seemed to entertain contradictory notions at the same juncture. Thus immediately after Dunkirk, he foisted on army commander Walther von Brauchitsch a program of reducing the army ground forces to a "peacetime" basis. On 17 July, almost coincidental with the tentative decision to attack the Soviets that fall, Brauchitsch was told to disband 17 divisions and send the troops of 18 others to service in agriculture and industry. Between the abandonment of the autumn offensive in Russia and meeting with Foreign

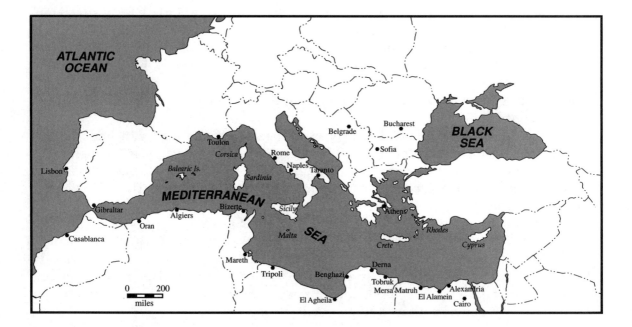

Minister Molotov in November, Hitler swayed back and forth between a Mediterranean program and moving against the Soviets in the spring.

If this interpretation is correct, the meeting with Molotov was no mere diplomatic exercise. Had Molotov proved compliant in the matters at issue, Hitler might well have put off his eastern volte-face and concentrated on dealing with Britain. But when the Russian confronted him on every regional issue from Finland to the Bosphorus, the decision to attack the Soviet Union in spring 1941 became fixed. This in turn dictated a policy of not permitting significant German resources, either to become mired in direct operations against Britain or to be absorbed in a peripheral assault on British positions in the Mediterranean. The Mediterranean string to Hitler's bow was also becoming frayed by developments in his relations with three Latin states: Italy, France, and, most crucially, Spain.

A true Mediterranean strategy for Germany at this juncture indeed demanded the skills of a political conjurer, the critical challenge lying in assuring the collaboration of states at odds among themselves. The core issue concerned the fate of the French empire in North Africa., Mussolini's predatory intentions focused on acquiring Tunisia and as much as possible of Algeria. The Spaniards aimed at absorbing all of Morocco and the Oran district of Algeria. Vichy France recognized that it was in desperate straits and perforce had to seek a protective hand in Berlin. The French surrender having been based upon the conviction that the war had been irretrievably lost, national pride forbade any thought that Britain could somehow survive and triumph by herself. The late June assault on the French fleet at Mers-el-Kebir and the abortive raid on Dakar in September also produced deep and general resentments. If the price was right and sufficiently certain, the entry of Vichy France into the war on the German side was no longer inconceivable.

Spain, just emerging from her civil war, was economically prostrate and correspondingly fearful about what the Royal Navy might do to her Atlantic communications. Franco could only be awed by the German victories virtually at his front door. The least the Caudillo could hope to get away with was to declare his country a non-belligerent ally of the Axis without commitment as to the time she would enter into hostilities.

Proposals for excluding Britain from the Mediterranean proliferated in high German quarters by mid-summer. Goering and Jodl advocated a vast pincer movement centering on a drive to Gibraltar and a simultaneous one through Turkey and Syria to Suez. Unquestionably, Hitler was for a time attracted to such a strategy. To keep his options open, however, he stipulated that any move into Spain must commence by early February in order not to collide with the projected eastern deployment.

This condition placed a heavy premium on full-scale Spanish collaboration, and correspondingly on a successful outcome of the meeting with Franco at Hendaye on 23 October. Spanish submission to his demands was more or less taken for granted. Though some haggling on economic and territorial issues was expected, Hitler could not contemplate the Caudillo failing to yield when it came to a showdown. The Fuhrer was the more confident because of his (correctly) high estimate of the influence in Madrid government quarters of Admiral Wilhelm Canaris, head of the Wehrmacht's intelligence (*Amt Ausland Abwehr*).

Canaris had played a prominent role in Hispano-German relations since the late thirties. Widely presented in history as an "enigmatic" figure and undoubtedly possessed of a highly complex personality, he really should not be the "man of mystery" that he appeared to so many contemporaries and historians. Fundamental to estimates of his political orientation should be the fact that virtually from the time he assumed office in 1935, he gathered in the Abwehr a leadership group of determined anti-Nazis, down to the level of secretaries. Franco knew him as a dedicated friend of Spain and he was on intimate terms with General Jorge Vigón, successively chief of intelligence, chief of staff, and war minister.[6] Vital for the situation then developing was his determination to, first, spare Spain the hazards and miseries of war, and second, prevent Hitler from winning the war.[7]

Much remains unclear about just when Canaris commenced his campaign in Madrid to thwart the Gibraltar project. Franco's brother-in-law and foreign minister Serrano Suñer testified that the Caudillo on at least two occasions expressed perplexity about Canaris' insistence that Germany was fated to lose the war.[8] To have been at all plausible, this advice can only have been advanced after Britain had evidenced her determination and some capacity to continue the war, and the United States had demonstrated an inclination to commit itself in some measure to the British cause. In other words, it must have been offered approximately by September 1940.

In reports to the Fuehrer, the admiral of course maintained a convincing pose of firm adherence to the Gibraltar project. Hitler never appears to have doubted his sincerity, but his Madrid embassy friends, Ambassador Eberhard von Stohrer, the Abwehr station chief, Wilhelm Leisner, and Erich Heberlein, the embassy's deputy chief of mission all knew better.[9] Even before Hendaye, the admiral was coaching Franco and Vigón in a sense directly contrary to the official pressure from Berlin.

The story of the encounter of the two dictators at Hendaye on 24 October is a familiar one and requires little elucidation Hitler's alternately patronizing and bullying tactics served only to permanently antagonize the proud Spanish leader. Outwardly the participation of Spain in the war with Britain was not at issue. Arguments centered on timing, what Germany could supply in the way of economic and military aid, and Madrid's territorial ambitions in Africa. As Hitler hoped next day at Montoire to persuade Petain to join also in the war against Britain, he was in no position to give hard assurances on the latter point. In effect, Spain's share in the loot would depend on the degree to which the French could be compensated from Britain's African empire.

Even if the German dictator could have made the desired territorial commitments without such strings attached, the outcome of the Hendaye meeting would scarcely have been very different. Franco and Serrano Suñer would most probably merely have haggled more on the types and measures of aid they required to commence hostilities.

Despite his diplomatic debacle at Hendaye, Hitler refused to believe that he had lost the game. German preparations for the peninsular campaign continued apace. The newly promoted Field Marshall von Reichenau was designated to command the attack on the Rock. "If required," enunciated Hitler, Spain would simply be forced into the war.

This latter thought must have vanished with the Molotov meeting and the resulting definitive decision to move against the USSR the following spring. It is questionable whether Hitler knew anything of SS machinations to topple Franco and replace him with the fanatically pro-German Muñoz Grandes, soon to command the Blue Division on the East Front. There remained pressures and persuasion, and here Hitler called on what he conceived his largest caliber Spanish gun — Wilhelm Canaris — for the final assault on the Madrid fortress.

On 7 December the admiral presented himself at the Prado palace in the company of General Vigón, with whom he appears to have concerted matters the previous day. Hitler, he related, counted on crossing the Spanish frontier on 10 January and on mounting the attack on Gibraltar on the thirtieth. The transcript of the discussion shows Canaris at his most persuasive, but Franco again stressing his inability to conform to such a timetable. The vital feature for the Spaniards was no doubt Canaris' private assurance that there was no longer a danger of Franco's hand being forced by outright German invasion. This almost certainly involved hints that the Fuehrer soon would be fully preoccupied elsewhere, further adding plausibility to Canaris' warnings that Germany was fated to lose the war.

Though Hitler per force cancelled the Gibraltar operation, he remained sufficiently hopeful to engage in further soundings in Madrid. When these proved failures, he closed discussion with an acid letter to Franco on 6 February. The collapse of the Gibraltar project also erased most of the interest he had shown in military collaboration with France. General Warlimont, who had made substantial progress in negotiations at Paris, was instructed to confine himself to a "receptive attitude" and was left out on a diplomatic limb by receiving no further instructions.[10]

Let us now assume that in 1940-1941 Adolf Hitler had totalled up his political accounts and decided to curb his impatience to attack the Soviet Union in favor of embarking on a full-scale Mediterranean strategy. The exact course of affairs would naturally have largely depended upon the timing of such a decision. It would conceivably have come either on the very morrow of his triumph in the west, when he was actually thinking of attacking the Soviets in the autumn or, more likely, in the period from early September, when he abandoned this plan, to the meeting with Molotov in early mid-November. The view enunciated here has been that during the previous weeks Hitler was wavering with respect to the timing of his swing to the east—whether it should come in the following spring or at some later date.

In the first instance it would have appeared all but inconceivable that Franco could have summoned the fortitude or the resources to resist a German thrust to the Rock. German prestige in midsummer stood at a dizzy height, Britain's finest hour had not yet struck. An American inclination to back the threatened island had not thus far become evident. Instead Franco had seized the diplomatic initiative to align himself ostentatiously with the Axis. In addition, the defenses of Gibraltar had not yet undergone the modernization that was soon to be undertaken. The mechanized drive recommended by General Heinz Guderian could have counted on ineffective Spanish resistance and a maximum of Spanish cooperation.

The fall of 1940 was also a time when the Balkan states and Turkey, intimidated by common assumptions about Britain's bleak outlook and impressed by Hitler's still ostensibly solid understanding with Stalin, would scarcely have opposed a German drive to Suez. Britain, assailed both in its home base and along its Mediterranean artery of empire, would have found it both psychologically and physically difficult to respond meaningfully. Hitler, in turn, would have felt the less delayed in his ultimate thrust eastward.

Our alternative scenario, positing the inauguration of a Mediterranean strategy by a thrust to Gibraltar at the beginning of February 1941, would have given events a considerably different aspect. Per force as yet lacking assurance from Canaris that Hitler was preparing a massive deployment in the east, Franco would almost certainly have caved in when confronted by a firm German intention to move against the Rock with or without Spanish cooperation.

In most calculations of the prospects of a determined German assault on Gibraltar, the success of the enterprise at comparatively low cost has been taken more or less for granted. While such an outcome appears probable enough, it should not be assumed to have been wholly inevitable. The logistic problems to be faced by the Germans in the move through Spanish territory were formidable. Rail communications had been left in a chaotic state by a civil war that had ended only in the spring of 1939. The Spanish rail gauge differed from that of France and would have imposed endless complications in transshipment. The cooperation of the Franco government would certainly have been grudging, and the presence along the routes of a sullen and hungry population would have produced significant difficulties for a Wehrmacht little interested in winning hearts and minds even among allies.

At Hendaye Franco had told Hitler that national honor dictated that any attack on the Rock should be primarily a Spanish enterprise. The German dictator had brushed the matter aside without condescending to argue, but it was bound to have remained an issue. Spanish pride would have been deeply offended if Franco's troops had been given no more than a supportive role. It might have led to a foot dragging that, though perhaps not resulting in outright sabotage, still could have impeded operations at various points.

British naval units in the Strait were not likely to have played a major role in Gibraltar's defense. The aircraft carrier *Illustrious* would have been an especially vulnerable target as was indeed demonstrated later at Malta.

German interest in Gibraltar extended well beyond impeding Britain's western entry into the Mediterranean. Seizure of the Rock would in its larger sense have proven preliminary to a thrust into Morocco and the erection of formidable air and naval bases that would have had both offensive and defensive significance in any potential conflict with the United States. For the same reason, Operation Isabella, for the proposed seizure of Portugal, could well have been preliminary to a leap to the Azores. British and American anxieties concerning the Spanish and Portuguese island possessions had already claimed the attention of London and Washington. German success at Gibraltar would undoubtedly have greatly accentuated the U.S. interest in the Caribbean manifested in the destroyers-for-bases agreement of the late summer of 1940.

Our scenario now shifts its focus eastward to consider the probably fate of Malta. The island had been recognized as an obstacle to Mussolini's expansive ambitions since 1936, when tension engendered by the Ethiopian war made an Italian conflict with France and Britain highly conceivable. Italian and German staff studies foresaw the seizure of the island as a first step toward a show-down in Africa. Several months after conclusion of the Pact of Steel (May 1939) the problem was also touched upon in staff discussions but was left in abeyance, war not being envisaged before 1943.

On the British side the prospect of hostilities with the Axis was not contemplated until after Munich. A quick lop-off of its Italian wing had many attractions. In such a framework, Malta was regarded as a launching pad rather than defensive bastion. Malta had been all but defenseless in the autumn of 1940. But as the focus of British resistance shifted from the home island to the Mediterranean, it underwent reinforcement that paralleled the revamping of British positions from Gibraltar to Suez. The defenses of Malta were considerably strengthened, notably in the form of its anti-aircraft capacities and its potential as an air base.

Hitler was not initially prepared to exert pressure on the island that could hinder his eastern deployment. However, if that concern became irrelevant only those factors associated with Mediterranean plans would have determined the timing and scope of an assault on the island. Later experience with the casualties suffered by elite troops in the taking of Crete had not yet engendered in Hitler his familiar phobia against over-the-water adventures. The Fuhrer, remembering thus far only the resounding success of the leap into Norway, would scarcely have hesitated to approve the venture. He was sure as well to have been spurred on by the Navy's Grand Admiral Raeder, a wholehearted devotee of the Mediterranean strategy, as well as by Goering, whose forebodings about a Soviet adventure led him to welcome any diversion. It may be assumed that Goering's talented chief of staff, Jeschonnek, whose deployment of the 10th Air Fleet a year later against Malta was to earn high praise, would have also put on a sterling performance in the spring of 1941 when there was no Russian campaign to distract him and claim the bulk of Luftwaffe resources.

A year later the Axis air offensive against Malta was to oblige the British to withdraw the bulk of their naval forces from the defense of the island. It may be assumed that developments in 1941 would have taken a similar course. With Gibraltar presumably all but closed since February by a German attack on the Rock, the resupply of Malta's garrison would have been reduced to a minimum, perhaps virtually ended. General Warlimont was later to negotiate with the French for Axis use of Tunisian bases. By then, since the 10th Air Fleet was needed on the Eastern Front, the air assault on Malta had largely petered out. If, however, an agreement with the French had been concluded by the spring of 1941, this would have greatly facilitated aerial operations and any parachute action that might have been involved in an invasion. Formation of Italian parachute forces, which at a later time impressed General Student, had a good way still to go in the spring of 1941. On the other hand, Student's elite XI Parachute Corps stood completely ready for such an operation.

This raises the question of a probable conflict over the use of German military resources against Malta, as opposed to Crete. High German quarters assumed that they were insufficient for simultaneous assault on both islands, and a major argument developed over which should receive priority. Student and Goering favored Crete whereas Jodl's operations staff opted for Malta. According to the scenario with which we are now concerned, however, it is questionable whether such a choice would have been required. As will directly become evident, it is doubtful whether Crete would have presented much of a problem. It might never have been garrisoned by the British. If, as appears probable in our scenario, the British had foregone their foredoomed intervention in Greece because of an all-out German offensive in the Mediterranean, Malta would assuredly have had priority over Crete in resource allocation.

Assuming that the full twenty thousand plus Cretan invasion force had been available for a descent upon Malta, in addition to any Italian units suitable for such an operation, the outcome could hardly have been in question. The invaders of Crete had played no part in the campaign on the Greek mainland, having been largely brought down to Greece during the final stage of that campaign. We shall eschew any detailed speculation about the course of such an assault. In view of the overwhelming strength of the invaders, the isolation of the island due to the virtual closing of Gibraltar, and the numerous shortcomings of the defenses (then not nearly approximating what they became later), it is difficult to escape the conclusion that British resistance would have been quickly overcome.

If we further direct our spotlight eastward, we encounter Italy's problems. Of concern in our scenario is the role that might have been played in developments by the Italian navy. In view of the time frame with which we are dealing, Mussolini's navy would already have suffered severely from the British air raid on Taranto (11 November 1940). On the other hand, if there had been no British intervention in Greece with corresponding German pressure for an Italian strike at British convoys from Egypt, there would have been no naval encounter at Cape Matapan to inflict additional damage.

One may further assume that with Hitler's adoption of a Mediterranean strategy, Berlin would have been more generous in allotting fuel to the oil-starved Italian fleet, with a commensurate gain in its mobility and morale. If the British, as appears probable, had decided against an all-out defense of Crete, it would have made for an easy German takeover. The Luftwaffe, anticipating no call on its resources for an early eastern campaign, could have played a primary role in sweeping the waters south and east of that island, inhibiting British naval operations beyond the immediate defense of Egypt or, in desperate case, that of Cyprus. The Italians might then have provided naval support for possible leaps from Crete to Cyprus and from that island to Syria.

Insofar as Italian contributions to Axis efforts in land warfare were concerned, a similar revitalization from evidences of a German decision to throw real weight into Mediterranean operations, particularly in North Africa, could be expected. If, as our analysis has presupposed, the Fuehrer's Mediterranean extravaganza had commenced with a drive to Gibraltar in February 1941, the move would have been too late to forestall the debacle suffered by Mussolini in the advance to the frontier of Egypt. But, although the disasters in Cyrenaica and Ethiopia could not be completely forgotten, the outlook for the Axis in the war with Britain would have so greatly brightened as to create in the Italians something like enthusiasm. More particularly, there should have been more weight in Italian efforts in the offensive against Egypt.

Given an alternative strategy, what in actuality was conceived as Rommel's rescue expedition would have assumed the formidable aspect of a major blow at Britain's position in the eastern Mediterranean. Hitler's aim would have been to strike at the vital centers of Britain's Middle Eastern position. For this a more formidable force than that initially assigned to Rommel would have been essential. In fact, it appears unlikely that a commander so junior as the soldier soon to be hailed the "Desert Fox" would have been placed in charge. One of the recently created field marshals would probably have been chosen. Had the siege of Gibraltar been successfully concluded, Reichenau might well have been shifted from that command, perhaps even while the siege was still under way. Another possible choice would have been Germany's pioneer armor leader, Heinz Guderian. With Reichenau in command, Berlin would have been assured of a campaign scarcely less enterprising than that actually waged by Rommel. The course of continuing hostilities in Northeast Africa would inevitably have depended in large part upon whether the British would have foregone intervention in Greece, an adventure rivalling in absurdity Franco-British plans for coming to the aid of the Finns in March 1940. Would they have appreciated in time the form and scope of Hitler's switch to a Mediterranean strategy? If this had become clear, most probably via Ultra, the folly of dividing Wavell's meager resources on behalf of what was at best a face-saving operation would surely have become evident.

Deprived of support from home, except for what could have been conveyed via the circuitous route around the Cape, Wavell's forces in North Africa would have met with overwhelming logistic problems. The most serious difference from the situation he actually faced in 1941 would have been in the realm of air-power. Even if Gibraltar had remained open for a while, Hitler's ability to increase the number of his war planes in the narrow waters of the Central Mediterranean far exceeded the current capacities of his opponents to match. For Hitler it was merely a choice in the allocation of resources. Britain was drawing from a nearly-empty pocket.

Could Wavell, once he had placed all possible weight behind O'Connor's drive westward, have taken Tripoli before the Germans arrived in force? The answer seems to be: perhaps, but barely. Wavell's success in holding his gains would have been contingent upon subsequent operations in North Africa. Even then, had the Axis sought to push eastward toward Egypt, the loss of Tripolitania to the British would not necessarily have closed that road for good. There was also the wholly conceivable route from Tunisia over the Mareth Line pursued later in reverse by General Montgomery—

a route that would take an already-overextended British army in its very exposed left flank.

Let us make the plausible assumption that the British could have forestalled a major landing in Tripoli and that the wide swing via Tunisia had not been an option either because of French intransigence or logistic difficulties inherent to the undertaking. Hitler might have chosen either of two alternative approaches. The one led via the stepping stones of Crete and Cyprus to French-controlled Syria. With Crete abandoned or lightly garrisoned by the British, conquest of the island should have presented no particular difficulty. With respect to Syria, General Henri Dentz was soon in reality to demonstrate his vulnerability to German blandishments: if Vichy had hesitated, Hitler would perhaps still have encountered a willing collaboration. Another likely path would have led across Turkey. Even before the German expedition to rescue Mussolini in Greece was launched, General Franz Halder's army high command had anticipated an eastern pincer parallel to that at Gibraltar; that is via Bulgaria and Turkey. The plan was approved by Hitler on 4 November 1940. The Turks, for their part, were, like the Balkan states in early 1941, intimidated by the German victories as well as hoping for German support against Soviet pressure with respect to the Bosphorus and Dardanelles.

The fate of a German drive against Egypt through the Balkans and Turkey can not be posited with any confidence. With British forces divided because of the imperative need to maintain a strong garrison in Tripolitania, the defense of Suez against a Nazi drive southward across Palestine would indeed have been difficult. There was the obvious alternative of a lunge to Syria via Cyprus, which had also been considered in Berlin before the heavy casualties of the attack on Crete had dampened German, and especially Hitler's, disposition for over-the-water operations. On the other hand, the British fleet at Alexandria in our scenario had not been called upon for the defense of an evacuation of Crete with the considerable damage suffered in that operation. It would have provided a formidable obstacle for which the Italian navy would have found it difficult to provide an adequate makeweight. As in actuality at Crete, the British would have faced grave risks to deny the Axis convenient stepping stones to their bulwarks in the Near East.

A British rout in Egypt could be expected to lead in domino-fashion, to the loss of the remaining British strong points in the Middle East. It was touch-and-go in Iraq during 1941 anyway, while the Palestine mandate would have been overrun in the German lunge southward from Syria. By the end of 1941 the Mediterranean would in effect have become an Axis lake.

Such German victories would have produced repercussions, in every sense of the word, on a world-wide scale. German domination of the Balkans would doubtlessly have been even more comprehensive than it actually was at this stage. The entire Mediterranean basin, including all of North Africa, would have fallen under Axis control. Yugoslavia would no longer have been a hold-out of sorts; in fact, the anti-Axis government of General Cusan Simovic would probably never have come to power. As a result, in the impending clash with the Soviets there would have been no Yugoslav partisan activity to claim Axis resources.

What can we assume concerning the impact of these Mediterranean developments on the calculations and policies of the Soviet Union, Japan, and the United States? As things stood in the spring of 1941, the Soviet posture with respect to Germany was rapidly taking on a form of abject cringing before the threat looming on the western horizon. There were no longer any signs of the firmness, indeed truculence, that Molotov had demonstrated the previous November. This shift of Soviet tactics had no mollifying effect in Berlin during May-June 1941. Any readiness on Stalin's part to yield on the issues that reached from Finland to the Straits, about which Molotov had seemed adamant, would scarcely have altered Hitler's bellicose intentions. Whether he would have struck in 1942 or held his hand until 1943 might well have depended on the course of relations with Britain. With British fortunes at their lowest ebb after the exhaustion of the Empire's offensive resources in the Mediterranean and the Middle East, even Churchill might have weakened in his resolve or have been replaced by an appeaser or a realist of the Halifax school. Had Hitler still been willing to grant the relatively generous terms he appeared prepared to offer in July 1940, an understanding might have been reached. As he still must have felt somewhat uncomfortable about a two-front war, the Fuehrer might have delayed his eastern deployment until the conflict with Britain had been terminated. How a war with the Soviet Union that commenced in 1942 or 1943 would have ended is considered elsewhere in this volume.

However, we should again point out that each of these essays in alternative historical outcomes is based upon the realities of the time in question. Here Hitler is assumed to have wiped the slate clean as far as Britain was concerned, and to have established virtual dominance of the Mediterranean and the Middle East. Both psychological and physical circumstances would as a result have been much more favorable to him than they actually were when he attacked the Soviet Union in 1941. Moreover, it is possible that a delay of a year or two in his move eastward could have enabled German army intelligence to correct its fantastic underestimate of the Soviet Union's military manpower potential before the actual attack in June of 1941. In the face of his obsession with eastern expansion, it is doubtful whether this would have given the German dictator sufficient pause in his aggressive stance. It might, however, have impaired the perceptions of his generals. Events in the Northeast African/Near Eastern theater might in a different sense have given pause to estimates of a more favorable outlook for a march eastward. Overcoming desperate British resistance there would have been a heavy charge on German military resources. The considerably larger investment in tank forces than those doled out to Rommel would have made for proportionately greater costs. Desert warfare is particularly hard on heavy armored vehicles. There would also have been far larger demands on the Luftwaffe that would have exacted their own heavy toll.

Undoubtedly, the world-wide repercussions of an elimination of the Axis' "soft underbelly" would not have stopped short of the Pacific. Most notably this would have been the case if the succession of catastrophes suffered by British arms had induced London to deal with Hitler's Germany. In that event and with the fading of any prospect of an early American intervention in European affairs, Hitler's interest in fostering Japanese pressures on the British Empire might well have gone sharply into reverse. The increased probability of a German victory over the Soviets would further have boosted Japanese interest in northern expansion. Hence, Tokyo might have been expected to be correspondingly more vulnerable to appeals to join in the anti-Communist crusade Hitler proclaimed.

And where would a successful conclusion of a full-scale Mediterranean strategy by Adolf Hitler have left the United States? Much, perhaps all, would have depended upon whether the damage to British power would have forced or pressured London to agree to some form of accommodation with a still Nazi-ruled Germany. In the latter event Washington would have been left holding the bag. By having ostentatiously aided Britain, it would have made a mortal enemy of Germany's megalomaniac dictator. That awareness surely would have led to an escalation of American rearmament. Depending on such circumstances as the course of operations after Hitler's attack on the Soviet Union, American aid to Stalin might either have been entirely withheld, or accelerated beyond what it actually became. In any event, the prospect of an eventual clash with Berlin and/or a direct threat to the United States would greatly have increased American concern about the Caribbean and Azores. Indeed, had the latter not already been under German occupation, an American takeover would have become probable.

In the opposite case of Britain's having held out, however tenuously, America's concern with its own defense would have been much accentuated. With the increasingly visible likelihood of an eventual clash with Germany, the preservation of Britain as an existing aircraft carrier and potential launching pad for invasion of the continent would have become proportionately more vital.

However, we shall continue with what appears to have been more likely: a scenario in which London would have reached some form of understanding with Berlin. With the support of a desperate Britain no longer a central concern, one conceivable, often alleged objective of the Roosevelt administration—entering the European war via an Asian back door—would have ceased to influence Washington policy makers. If, in addition, the Japanese, at least for a time, had abandoned their southern drive in favor of northward expansion, a major additional factor would have operated to smooth Washington-Tokyo relations.

Another of the essays in the present volume stresses the thesis that Britain would have done well from the beginning not to have mounted a major defense in the Mediterranean. The argument holds that she should have concentrated her naval resources in the Atlantic and Indian Oceans.[10] If this view is accepted, does it necessarily follow that Hitler by his Mediterranean strategy would have obliged his opponents to fall back on their best defensive posture? The answer might be "yes" had not the exhausting struggle for the Mediterranean and Middle East depleted British resources to the point where continuation of the war in any form would have become problematical. Thus, a Mediterranean strategy in 1940-1941 still would deserve to be labelled the most promising road to German victory in World War II.

Chronological Chart of Actual Events

1940

25 June	Franco-German armistice comes into effect
30 July	Hitler directs deployment for an autumn assault on the Soviet Union.
2 September	Hitler abandons intent to attack Soviets that fall.
15 September	Climax of the Battle of Britain.
23 October	Hitler and Franco meet at Hendaye
11-12 November	Hitler-Molotov meeting. The dictator determines to attack the Soviets in the spring of 1941.
7 December	Admiral Canaris acts out supposed conclusive persuasion of Franco. Hitler abandons Gibraltar project.

1941

12 February	Rommel arrives in Tripoli
3 April	German intervention in Yugoslavia and Greece.
20 May	Germans launch attack on Crete.

B. What if the allies had invaded Sardinia and Corsica instead of Sicily in 1943?
Carlo D'Este

In July 1943 the allies launched what later was at the time the largest amphibious invasion in history against Axis forces on the island of Sicily. After Operation Husky only the D-Day landings in Normandy in June 1944 would be of greater size and scope. The decision to invade Sicily was made at the Casablanca Conference In January 1943 by the Combined Chiefs of Staff and approved by Churchill and Roosevelt. However, what is little known is that prior to Casablanca, serious consideration was given to an invasion of the island of Sardinia. What follows is a scenario for what might have transpired if Sardinia had been invaded instead of Sicily.

The possibility of an invasion somewhere in the Mediterranean in 1943 first surfaced in London during the summer of 1942 when the War Cabinet's Joint Planning Staff began examining possible operations. Two important strategic objectives emerged: Sicily and Sardinia, and code-names for each were assigned, Husky for Sicily and Brimstone for Sardinia.

The joint planners found merit in both Husky and Brimstone. If both islands were to fall into allied hands, it would represent a serious threat to the Axis in both France and Italy. Sardinia offered the advantage of being far less strongly defended and thus capable of being captured several months earlier than Sicily, where a larger invasion force and considerably more complex planning was required. Although Sardinia was an excellent base of operations for the air forces, it had far less to offer ground forces other than as a base for commando raids against southern France, Corsica or the Italian mainland. The main drawback was Sardinia's lack of harbors and beaches suitable for an invasion or for staging amphibious operations against France or Italy.

What made Sardinia attractive was the fact that in 1942 and subsequently in 1943 the island was lightly defended compared to Sicily. Allied naval and air planners believed that the vital Strait of Messina could not be closed to Axis shipping regardless of the success of an amphibious landing. The Strait was a serious obstacle and from the outset the allied naval chiefs expected heavy losses if the Germans and Italians buttressed the already well-defended heights along the Italian and Sicilian sides of the Strait. The Joint planners predicted that an invasion of Sardinia could be mounted at least two months sooner than Sicily and the problems facing the naval forces could be resolved far more easily by an invasion of Sardinia.

Moreover, if the Germans reinforced Sicily prior to an invasion, the planners somewhat pessimistically believed Husky would fail. The same, they argued, did not apply to Sardinia. "Much as we should like to take Sicily, we feel that against the odds for which we must at present allow, the operation is not practicable. We therefore recommend the capture of Sardinia to be followed by Corsica as soon after as possible."[11]

General Sir Alan Brooke, the Chief of the British Imperial General Staff and the architect of British military strategy, was committed to an invasion of Sicily and strongly opposed to Sardinia. However, as a result of the recommendation of the Joint Planning Staff and its strong support from the naval and air chiefs, Admiral Sir Dudley Pound and Air Chief Marshal Sir Charles Portal, neither of whom had any enthusiasm for Husky, Brooke was eventually compelled to accept Sardinia over Sicily.

Thus at Casablanca the British Chiefs of Staff formally proposed that the major allied effort in the Mediterranean in 1943 be Operation Brimstone, the invasion of Sardinia. Although they opposed further large-scale operations in the Mediterranean, once pressured by the British and Roosevelt into reluctant agreement that there must be a continuation of what was started in North Africa in 1942 with the Torch landings, the

US Chiefs of Staff, led by General George C. Marshall, readily accepted Sardinia as the next allied target.

Its drawbacks notwithstanding, Sardinia was a tempting target. With the same meticulous planning accorded Operation Husky, the allies could have successfully carried out an amphibious invasion of the island in the late spring or early summer of 1943. The same, enormously successful deception operations that benefited Husky would have succeeded with Brimstone. The cornerstone of the deception effort took place in the spring of 1943 when allied intelligence carried out Operation Mincemeat, which in the postwar years became known as "The Man Who Never Was." On 30 April 1943 the body of a Royal Marine officer, later identified by the Spanish as "Major William Martin," a member of Lord Louis Mountbatten's Combined Operations staff, washed ashore in southern Spain. Attached to the wrist of Major Martin was a courier's briefcase containing authentic documents and plans that revealed that the target of Operation Brimstone was the Peloponnesian coast of Greece rather than either Sardinia or Sicily. In reality the corpse had been planted offshore by the British submarine HMS Seraph and the operation was designed to lure the German Abwehr into accepting the body of "Major Martin" and his briefcase as authentic. As planned, Spanish authorities turned the documents over to an Abwehr agent who immediately sent copies to Berlin, where the German high command accepted them as genuine Mincemeat and the massive disinformation program initiated by "A" Force, the British controlled deception organization for the Mediterranean theater of operations, left Hitler and the OKW predisposed to follow their instincts regarding where the allies would strike next.

Thus, not only did the Abwehr believe the corpse and the documents it carried were valid, but the intelligence arm of the Army High Command (OKH) described them as "absolutely convincing." As a result, for the next several months the OKW ordered that the defense of Greece be given priority over everything else. Although very successful, the deception operations were not the only reason why there were so few German forces in Sicily, Sardinia and Corsica. As the British official intelligence history notes, "by this time Hitler's lack of confidence in his Italian ally had developed into positive and well-founded suspicions about her willingness to remain in the war at all, and he was naturally reluctant to commit German forces in an area where they might be lost in the chaos of a general surrender." The Mincemeat documents in short, together with all the misinformation provided by "A" Force gave Hitler additional reasons for a disposition of forces to which he was already strongly inclined.[12]

There were few Axis forces on Corsica to have prevented capture of the island once Sardinia had fallen. Moreover, unlike Sicily where the Germans were able to reinforce the island via the Strait of Messina, there could have been no such reinforcement of Sardinia which would have been successfully blockaded by allied naval and air forces. It was one thing for the Germans to resupply Sicily across the narrow Strait of Messina; it was quite another for them to have run a gauntlet of the one hundred miles of open sea that separated Sardinia from the Italian mainland.

A recent study of the Sicily campaign argues that:

> If the Allies had to invade a Mediterranean island in the summer of 1943, their target should have been Sardinia …they would have faced only one partially formed German division …Once Sardinia fell, Corsica would have been untenable. When the major Allied landings on the Italian mainland came, they could have taken place one hundred miles north of Rome instead of one hundred miles south of it …this would have saved the U.S. 5th and British 8th Armies a year of heavy fighting up the Italian peninsula and would have put the industrial targets of Austria and southern Germany within easy reach of Anglo-American bombers a year earlier.[13]

Thus, if the allies had chosen to invade Sardinia and Corsica, they would not only have been successful but, in the process, the entire course of the war in the Mediterranean would have been irrevocably altered. The island of Sardinia was virtually indefensible, with less than a full German division to defend against an overwhelmingly superior allied air, sea and ground force. While it is true that the initial air support would have had to come from carrier-based aircraft, it would not have taken more than a few days for at least one airfield on Sardinia to have been captured by the invasion force.

Of equal consequence is that when the invasion of Italy inevitably followed, there would have been no justification for the two invasions of southern Italy which actually took place in early September 1943, at Salerno by Lt. Gen. Mark Clark's Fifth Army, and the boot of Italy (Operation Baytown), by the XIII British Corps of Montgomery's Eighth Army. As the capital of Mussolini's fascist state, Churchill had always regarded Rome a vital political prize for the allies and would have undoubtedly still demanded its capture, thus, the initial object of an allied target might well have been either the Anzio sector or operations at both Anzio and in the Civitavecchia sector to isolate and capture Rome. An operation at Anzio in the summer or early autumn of 1943 would have been very different from the near-disaster that took place in 1944.

Wherever they had elected to invade, allied possession of Sardinia and Corsica would have put sever pressure upon the German high command to defend Italy. The invasion of Sicily in July 1943 left the Germans convinced that a second landing on the Italian west coast would take place and that it would be no farther north than the operating range of allied aircraft based in Sicily, i.e., the Naples-Salerno sector. As one senior U.S. admiral said before the invasion of Salerno a week after Operation Baytown, "any officer with a pair of dividers could figure out that the Gulf of Salerno was the northernmost practicable landing place."[14] But with Sardinia and Corsica in allied hands a very different scenario materialized. The German commander-in-chief, Field Marshal Albert Kesselring, would have been faced with having to deploy his forces across hundreds of miles of coastline in order to prevent an allied landing in central or northern Italy that would inevitably trap all axis forces south of the invasion site. Moreover, Kesselring would never have been given the opportunity to create the great defensive positions at Cassino.

What is indisputable is that the invasion of Italy via Sicily led to a long and bloody campaign that began in Calabria and at Salerno in September 1943 and lasted until May 1945.

Allied strategy with respect to operations after the Tunisian campaign ended in May 1943 was conservative and lacked both imagination and boldness. Had the allies chosen the more daring Sardinian and Corsican option, there is no doubt that the way the Italian campaign was fought would have been fundamentally different. And, perhaps, the names of places like Salerno, Cassino, the Rapido and Anzio would today still be merely obscure names on the map of Italy.

C. What if the Allies had chosen the Ljubljana Gap rather than ANVIL in 1944 or 1945?[15]

Thomas L. Barker

The idea of invading northwestern Yugoslavia with ostensible purpose of forestalling Soviet hegemony in the Balkans and East Central Europe was seriously entertained, at least by the British, on two distinct occasions. The first was just prior to the August 1944 landing in southern France and the second during the painful autumn 1944 assault upon German defensive lines in north-central Italy.

Only on the first occasion did Operation Armpit, as it was then known, have much to do with reality. The general discussions, preliminary planning, and mainly theoretical preparations that took place on the second occasion, rested upon profound misconceptions. In due course the project's chief advocates — Churchill, who outdid himself in furthering it, and his client, Alexander, a better tactician than strategist — had to recognize the futility of trying to implement the scheme.

It is a commonplace that the British Prime Minister was powerfully predisposed to launch blows at Europe's "soft underbelly." While his use of the phrase can be traced to 22 September 1942, a telegram from the White House dated 11 November indicates that Roosevelt was thinking about the region on his own. Among the host of subjects more or less congenially debated at Casablanca was what actions should be pursued in the Mediterranean after the impending final expulsion of the Axis from North Africa. Churchill — at that time motivated not by fear of an expansionistic U.S.S.R., but concern for preserving Britain's traditional ascendancy in the region — was successful, if only temporarily in imposing a "Mediterranean strategy." It also seems that he was suggesting, however ambiguously, that one could get at the Germans through the Balkan back door.

The issue arose anew at the Cairo-Tehran-Cairo meetings in late November 1943. Roosevelt casually asked whether Istria or the Ljubljana Gap might not serve as a route to Vienna. Stalin, mainly concerned with propagating a "second front," shifted the discussion to a landing in southern France. Churchill, who had first mentioned Vienna as a possible campaign goal on 19 July and also knew beforehand what FDR would say, seized upon the president's initiative to counter Stalin's idea. However, the American military was opposed to any Balkan involvement, even on the peninsula's northwest edge.

Although Churchill was more or less reconciled to the Tehran decision for approximately five months, the unforeseen stalemate in southern Italy affected the thinking of his military associates. Anvil came to be regarded as a competitor for resources by British officers in both Italy and London. Responding to an initiative of Alexander's, Churchill, on April 6, 1944, weighed in strongly against Anvil and for the Ljubljana Gap, continuing his quixotic effort as late as 9 August, just six days prior to the actual landing on the French Riviera.

Despite the rebuff he had received, Churchill refused to relent. He flew to Naples, settled into a posh villa overlooking the bay, and closeted himself on 12-13 August with a pompously garbed Tito brought over from the island of Vis. The prime minister advised his guest that the allies might be able to smash through the Gothic Line into the Po Valley and then lunge northeastward into Istria. If a Dalmatian port could be secured and a large volume of supplies and equipment delivered, the Yugoslav National Liberation Army might aid the British Eighth Army's landward drive to Trieste and beyond. The chief effect of this ploy was to arouse the suspicions of Tito who vented his displeasure of an even temporary British administration of the ethnically mixed, politically disputed Venezia Julia as well as of western control of the Ljubljana-Maribor-Graz corridor.

Notwithstanding Tito's grumbling, Churchill, on 28 August, informed FDR that "Tito's people will be awaiting us in Istria." In a letter to Jan Christian Smuts, his South African confidant, he even posited a sudden Nazi collapse and reported that he had instructed Alexander "to be ready for a dash (to Vienna) with armored cars."

Churchill submitted his resuscitated scheme to the Second Quebec conference of 10-16 October. He did manage to extract from Admiral King a pledge to reserve an "amphibious lift" for ferrying men and material up the Adriatic to Istria. The Americans also promised to remove no more of their divisions from Italy. It had cost the Americans little to indulge their importunate ally's "Balkan" flight of fancy. Stalin also chimed in harmoniously at the Third Moscow Conference (8-9 October), secure in the assumption that withdrawal of Romania and Bulgaria from the German side and the Red Army's advance into Hungary would allow him to reach Vienna before anyone else. Encouraged, Churchill returned to his Neapolitan villa to parlay again with his military subordinates.

Forced to rethink the practical chances and perhaps even the necessity of his Ljubljana grand slam, Churchill had Wilson, Sir Henry Maitland, now the Supreme Allied Commander in the Mediterranean, develop a new, more restricted plan. Six frontline divisions, rested, refitted, and retrained, would be sent to Dalmatia. Three or four of them would be used for the initial February crossing with the rest to follow once Rijeka had fallen. However, the CCS were no more interested in the second proposal than they had been in the first. While he was probably still secretly hoping for a different outcome, Churchill had to agree with Brooke, in view of the delay inherent to Wilson's plan, that the Western Allies essentially limit themselves to increased aid for the partisans. Wilson confirmed this arrangement on 22 November. Most of the amphibious lift was released soon thereafter. Italy remained the exclusive focus of major Anglo-American military effort.

However, there is an addendum to the tale. Probably even more than Churchill, Alexander was loathe to renounce the idea of a Viennese end run. He made bold on 29 October to concoct a last minute plan of his own which he buoyantly christened Gelignite. What is remarkable about it is that "Alex" still conceived of a vast pincer movement that would dissect Kesselring's army: one claw would reach across the Brenner and the other to Vienna. However, the scheme was doomed by late November by a more stable German front in Yugoslavia, and by negative administrative-logistical reckoning.

Although as late as 17 October Churchill had been of good cheer about conditions in Italy, by 29 November he was forced to sanction Wilson's view that Istria ought to serve merely as the object of a 'feint attack.' Shortly thereafter Kesselring launched a counterstroke in the western Apennines, and non-integrated, despondent black American soldiers rapidly gave ground. This destroyed any residual optimism. The sole remaining utility of the project was a minor, Cisalpine hoax.

What if Churchill had prevailed?
Many years of automobile, train, boat, and foot travel in the region have familiarized the writer with the terrain conditions and communications infrastructure of Dalmatia, Istria, Slovenia, Carinthia, and Styria. When the theoretical question of the Ljubljana Gap plan's chances for success was first put to him, his spontaneous reaction was one of skepticism. How could anyone have seriously proposed dispatching a heavily equipped, mechanized army to such difficult countryside and have expected it to progress smoothly, swiftly, and far? The skimpy road network, at least compared to

The northern Adriatic

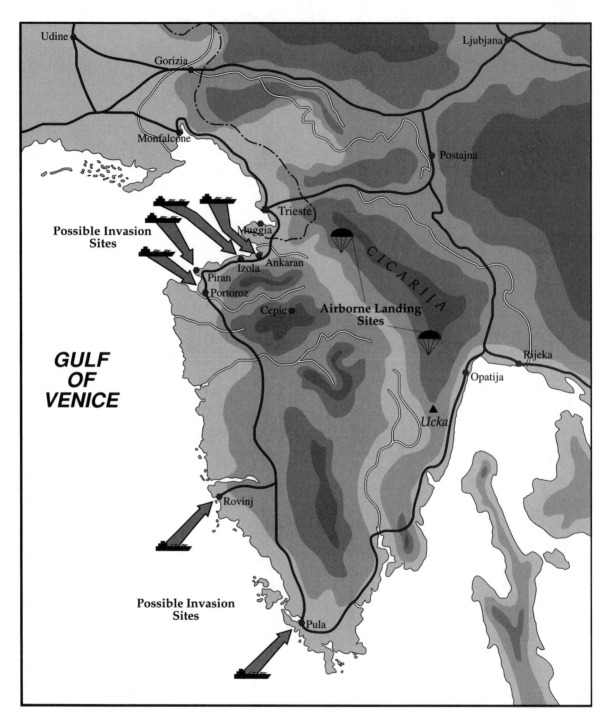

The Istrian Peninsula

northern France and the Lowlands, was in even worse shape before 1945. To seek to repeat Napoleon's infantry-oriented Inner-Austrian campaign of 1797 with the completely different implements of twentieth-century armored warfare seems a pipedream. This judgment is peremptory, but is it really justified? Was Roosevelt, who had accepted the counsel of his military associates, perhaps mistaken when he turned a deaf ear to Churchill on 29 June 1944 in emphasizing the logistical hindrances that would be encountered in so formidable a geographical environment?

The hypothesis of an Istrian landing may be reviewed first. The very steep shore between Trieste and the swampy delta of the Isonzo/Soča west of Monfalcone could hardly have been the site for it. In theory, the port facilities of Trieste were susceptible to assault, especially a coup de main. However, they were well protected by mine fields, coastal guns, and small naval craft. A number of locally moored, larger vessels could have been scuttled at sensitive spots. A later British study concluded that it would take a month to clear even one channel allowing limited discharge of urgently wanted supplies and three months to unblock the others. Though the quays were widely dispersed, demolitions would have had at least some effect. Stubborn street-by-street resistance, the infantryman's most terrifying nightmare, would almost certainly have ensued.

The western shore of the Istrian peninsula down to its tip at Pula (Pola), is made up of numerous cliffs, scattered coves, occasional anchorages, a few tiny beaches, one fjord-like bay, and a score of minor harbors, of which Rovinj (Rovigno) is the biggest. Nowhere is it suitable for a large-scale over-the-beach landing. The only possibility would have been so-called "scramble" landings in which boat ramps would have been let down right onto quays, moles, and jetties; a few wade-ins would also have been feasible. The coast from Pula northeastward to Opatija (Abazzia) is much worse, consisting largely of precipices impossible even for rangers to climb. Extended, sandy, Normandy-style beaches can not be found from Ravenna, south of Venice, onward. The sole exception is the Iesolo-Caorle resort strip (above lagoon-girded Venice) where shallows — heavily mined in 1944-45 — reach far out to sea and marshes lie inland.

The area west-southwest of Trieste stretching from the present Italo-Yugoslav border at Lazaretto/Lazaret to Portorož/Portorose, the post-World War Two "Zone B" and now Slovenia's exquisitely beautiful riviera, would have been better for a "scramble" operation and was in fact Wilson's ultimate, if hardly risk-free choice. There is a series of assailable, if very narrow, landing sites — at Lazaretto/Lazaret, Ankaran/Ancarano, Izola/Isola, Strunjan/Strugnano, Piran/Pirano, and, perhaps as the least problematical, at Portorož/Portorose. The intermittently rocky shoreline, however, directly abuts hills in many places, especially near Piran, a fishing port and genuinely world-class urban architectural monument. Where they could have pushed inland with a degree of ease — certainly not at Piran which would have been utterly destroyed had it been strongly held — the soldiers nevertheless would have found themselves fighting amidst vineyards as well as confronting well-prepared defenses. Moreover, the resultant overall footing, some twenty undulating Ripuarian miles, would have been dangerously limited. A landing in the Bay of Muggia/Milja, directly adjacent to Trieste, would have been subject to withering fire from the city itself and was therefore not even considered.

Pula, once the Hapsburg navy's home port, might also have been stormed, especially by paratroops, but posed the same difficulties as Trieste. Moreover, behind Pula and Istria's western rim lies the limestone Karst, a rough interior landscape pierced then only by a few unpaved, dust-choked roads and replete with sinkholes (made-to-order redoubts), underground streams, and caverns — a terrain that would have proved to be as difficult as Normandy's bocage country. To be sure, since he rejected it, Wilson did recognize the impracticality of this option.

The landing itself would probably have succeeded, albeit with heavy losses along the shore due to direct fire and house-to-house combat. The planners regarded a one-division airborne strike as the key to the operation. The parachutists would have descended onto the Čepić polje (Piano di Arsa) and a few other smaller drop zones in basically rather rough terrain in order to "seize important dominating features immediately southeast of Trieste" (the Brkini, Čičarija [Tschitschenboden], and Učka [Vena]). The rest of the corps, which according to contemporary calculations could have been adequately supplied through the local harbors, would have consisted of two seaborne divisions with motor transport and a reserve formation.[16] Another advantage would have been air superiority: though, the Allied bases were farther away than the Nazi ones, Wilson's vast preponderance in the number of planes would have been crucial in the context of good, late summer weather.

Success in "bounc(ing) the enemy out of some of the small ports which form these *landings*" would seem to have been all the more likely since the hostile forces immediately stationed in present-day northwestern Yugoslavia were a hodgepodge of perhaps no more than some twenty thousand men — albeit with one good division posted in Istria proper. The Slovene White Guard (Domobranstvo) would almost certainly have tried to join the allied side. Other local quislings, mainly Ustashi oddments and Fascist militia, while hardly formidable, would probably have opposed the invaders. In all events, the maritime assault would have been a mere adjunct to a landward thrust from the direction of Venetia.

The striking force, if it had not been stymied in the first place by tough opposition at the northern end of the Apennines or by the difficulties of vehicular movement in the well-watered Po valley (which would have left the dangerously distant Istrian corps bottled up), at least would have been able to bypass Trieste and the elevated Karst terrain to its east. It could then have proceeded along the somewhat easier, albeit partly montane, frequently constricted route from Gorizia/Gorica via Postojna (Adelsberg) to Ljubljana, the so-called "Gap." Nevertheless, the British could still have been threatened or stopped had the ever resourceful Kesselring sent major detachments due east as he withdrew north of the Po and into the Alpine foothills. Also, as the British in fact foresaw, Trieste itself would probably have been turned into an isolated but virtually impregnable fortress like Brest after D-Day: this would have made it very hard, though not impossible to effect Wilson's plan for the amphibious units to squeeze past the city on the sole highway that ran northward at the time in question.

If it is fair to assume that Alexander's army, strung out along the single road available to it, had managed to erupt into Slovenia's broad heartland, leaving the Julian Alps to its left, one must consider the next set of hurdles it would have met. To the north, lie the Karawanken mountains, which, if by no means impenetrable, are traversable only over three high passes. If Kesselring had meanwhile nestled into the natural defenses of the Alps, Carinthia would doubtlessly have received reinforcements sufficient to counter any allied incursion launched from the Ljubljana basin. Had the province's defenses somehow been breached, troops could well have passed throughout the Klagenfurt basin into the septentrional valley system of western Styria. Yet they still would have had to thread their way down the Semmering pass into Lower Austria. The sinuous Packstrasse led only to Graz. Moreover, unlike the "Old Reich," the Ostmark (ex-Austria) was then completely devoid of Autobahnen.

Should the allies have preferred to press ahead along toward Celje (Cilli) and Maribor (Marburg), they would finally have encountered open countryside, assuming that meanwhile their way had not been barred by the advent of frigid weather and snow-clogged roads. They could then have proceeded northward to the Graz basin where new mountain ranges bar the way to the Vienna plain, or eastward via Prekmurje into Hungary's Little Alfold. In both instances they would have found themselves roughly 250 kilometers beyond a Trieste not yet in their hands and another 100 from Venice and its mainland dependency of Porto Marghera. Moreover, though it was Italy's number two port, Venice was liable to easy blockage by a systematically retreating foe due to its mainland causeway and tight lagoon entrances.

The allied line of communications would thus have been stretched to the utmost. Indeed, it would almost certainly have snapped since Wilson was thinking not merely of sealing off Trieste but also Rijeka and, evidently, Pula as well: the necessary quays and daily tonnages would have been denied him semi-permanently. The logistical faculties of the Istrian landing fleet would never have sufficed for a host that would have grown to a size of more than three corps. Railway reactivation forecasts were equally dismal. The straitened situation of General Sir Charles Keightley's three-division-strong V Corps in Carinthia, which subsisted for some weeks from an only thin trickle of supplies arriving via the crater-pocked roads leading through the imposing canyons of Friulia and the Val Canale during the May 1945 Trieste crisis, likewise bears recalling, all the more so as it was the last echo of Churchill's Ljubljana Gap strategy. One simply cannot imagine how a trans-Slovene anabasis — a modern version of Xenophon's harrowing peregrination — could have brought about a significant Anglo-American military presence in western Hungary and/or the capital of the Ostmark in advance of the Soviets.

Were Wilson and Alexander to have forsworn an Istrian assault in the late summer of 1944 in favor of an opposed landing and a thrust inland across the Dinaric range — an admittedly entirely hypothetical variant of their respective autumn schemes — the consequences would unquestionably have been far worse, in fact probably disastrous, notwithstanding probably success in the initial amphibious operation against numerically inferior Nazi forces guarding the Dalmatian littoral and islands.

The left jab, accompanied by a second, lesser assault landing toward a presumably stubbornly defended Rijeka — the capture of which was the prerequisite for an advance upon Austria — was a particularly far-fetched plan. It would have had to be delivered along the highway that is tucked onto the generally declivitous and sometimes sheer coastal rim, a route improved only after 1945. Moreover, when one considers the travail of the abrupt, winding roads that rise from Rijeka to either Istria or Ljubljana, it seems clear that this approach would have turned out to be a military cul-de-sac altogether.

For its part, the main swing inland toward the Karlovac-Zagreb plain and back toward Rijeka would have constituted a detour of immense proportions across — as with the left jab — flimsily bedded, largely unsurfaced, often one-way, hairpin curve roads. Ten-tonners would soon have destroyed them, and Shermans would have had to slip into reverse gear in order to make it through the bends. Four-wheel drive vehicles would have been called for in quantities momentarily unavailable. Bad fall-winter weather would have brought the advance to a standstill, making the Apennines seem like child's play in comparison.[17]

It is also unlikely that the relatively small port facilities at and near Šibenik — many lighters would also have been needed — could have supported so huge a sweep. Moreover, even had they remained intact, the railways leading from Split, Šibenik, and Zara via the crucial junction of Knin, across Bosnia to inland Croatia are tunnel-studded and tortuous in the extreme. The Eighth Army staff apparently thought it pointless to project their repair and use. Indeed, the coastal mountains have always represented a major impediment to the economic well-being of Yugoslavia's commodious interior. It was a sensible course of military action only in the context of a lunge toward western Hungary.

Since every increase in geographic distance inevitably brings about a need for additional manpower and logistical effort, a further question must be asked, at least in the Istrian context. Had Alexander not lost the equivalent of two corps to Anvil/ Dragoon and had he received an increment of fresh divisions from abroad, however modest, would he then have been strong enough both to shove Kesselring into the foothills of the Alps and to carry off his and Churchill's east-central European gambit? The answer seems fairly obvious. In the first place, whatever help would have arrived from North America, western Europe, or another military theater would have been minuscule at best Exploitation of the Normandy breakout was SHAEF's paramount concern. To have delayed this enterprise in favor of the northwestern Balkans would have meant allowing the Germans to mount a stronger defense between Alsace and the Rhine delta. MacArthur while farther away, would not have been a less outspoken competitor than Ike.

An army the core of which would have been the seven divisions given to U.S. General Patch for his Côte d'Azur landing — in no case would de Gaulle have let the "French" ones be frittered away on a Pannonian wild goose chase — would have become so distended as to lose all impetus. Even if as many as fifteen divisions had somehow been scraped together from hither and yon, most would have found themselves pinned down in Istria, Primorje (the part of Slovenia "by the sea"), Venetia, Friulia, and Carnia or diffused along the slender protracted passage which in reality the Ljubljana "Gap" and its extension(s) beyond Slovenia's capital may be said to constitute. Quite literally, there would not have been enough troops, equipment, and stores to go around even if the supply pipeline had been assured by the conquest of Venice, Trieste, or Rijeka and reconstitution of the local railway network.

In pondering geographic snags and available military resources, the issue of presumptive enemy counter-moves has been mentioned only briefly. If one may postulate Kesselring having been able to menace the left flank of forces that had penetrated into northeastern Italy and Istria, how much more would the right flank of two or three Eighth Army corps have been endangered once they had reached Lower Styria, the natural escape route of the more than three hundred thousand Nazi troops under Field Marshal von Weichs (Supreme Commander Southeast) and his subordinate, Colonel General Alexander Löhr (Army Group E), who were then occupying the Aegean, mainland Greece, southern and central Yugoslavia and this at a time when the Bulgarians, Rumanians, and Hungarians were still fighting, however dispiritedly, on Hitler's side? Though, paradoxically, it did not deter him in the least — perhaps because by late summer he was becoming truly worried about the Russians.

While an allied thrust into the northwestern Balkans might well have provoked Germany's satellites into deserting the Fuhrer even sooner than they did, Löhr's professionally brilliant, stage-by-stage disengagement from the far south to northern Croatia must be taken into account in any rumination over Balkan might-have-beens.. The highly efficient Nazi security services could most likely have squelched any attempt by the Austrian-born German plenipotentiary in Zagreb, the rather strange, ideologically confused, General Edmund von Glaise-Horstenau, to instigate a switch to the allied side by fascist Croatia in conjunction with a mooted "Austrian" faction in the Wehrmacht's Balkan officer corps.

Roosevelt, whatever his motivation in directing Churchill's attention to the American public's potentially negative reaction to a Balkan adventure, was certainly perspicacious in portraying southeastern Europe as a morass. Although Churchill was not proposing to plunge into the very middle of it, even its fringes were soggy. It seems likely that the Slovene National Liberation Army, which was relatively weak in Istria and Primorje, would have greeted the advent of an allied host from Italy with mixed feelings: its collaboration would have been lukewarm at best. Wilkinson told Alexander and Brooke that assistance in holding off the foe at the moment of an Allied landing was "likely" but not to "be entirely relied on."

The guerrillas' Communist leaders, at any rate, had no love for the capitalist superpowers, distrusting them for their historical indifference to Slovene territorial claims and mistakenly suspecting them, as everywhere in the partisan camp, of wishing to intervene militarily in southeast Europe in order to help indigenous reactionaries. While Tito, who perhaps knew through the OSS that the Americans had frustrated Churchill's scheme, would have been too far away from Slovenia to be immediately involved — save in the case of a Dalmatian landing — his stance would almost certainly have been similar. A number of events subsequently made the British realize this. The first instance was Land Forces Adriatic's rather strained relations with the Yugoslav National Liberation Army during minor forays against Brač, Korčula, and Šolta in September of 1944. This was followed by the poor treatment accorded Floyd Force — an artillery detachment sent to aid the partisans in their vain autumn effort to block the retreat from Albania via Montenegro of the Wehrmacht's XXI Mountain Corps — and the chilly reception granted two British cruisers that put into Zadar on 18 November.

A further manifestation of Partisan suspicions was the contemporaneous deterioration in the status of allied liaison officers stationed in Slovenia and elsewhere. Had Wilson and Alexander harbored any lingering doubts about Tito's hostility, they must surely have been disabused by his rejection of Fairfax, a plan of 16 November to use British light forces — one armored and one field artillery regiment — in the northern Adriatic and to build a big airfield in the vicinity of Zadar. Other causes of Yugoslav fear and hence of trouble were Britain's anti-Communist intervention in Greece (December) and the Balkan activities of the United Nations Relief and Rehabilitation Administration.

What would have been the outcome of an offensive that debouched on the Ljubljana plateau or even reached as far as Maribor? On the assumption that by the late summer of 1944 Hitler was more receptive to suggestions of withdrawal than he had been previously, a consolidation of German defenses in the Alps based upon the three Army Groups from the Balkans and Italy would have left relatively weak, perhaps battered Allied forces in Slovenia in the position of functioning as little more than an exiguous connection to the Red Army in Hungary. To the south of them Yugoslavia might well have been caught up in ever more vicious civil strife with Soviet intervention required to tip the scales in Tito's favor, leaving the country far more in Stalin's debt than actually proved to be the case or even under his control as a satellite.

It is likewise possible that a Balkan substitute for Anvil/Dragoon would have prolonged the war by at least several months. Admittedly, the extent to which Eisenhower's exertions in western Europe would have been impeded by lack of the mooted seven-division Mediterranean building block is difficult to assess. Nonetheless, one may argue, in opposition to certain British historians such as Sir Arthur Bryant, that if SHAEF had disposed of fewer forces, the stalemate prior to Hitler's last-gasp Ardennes Offensive (Battle of the Bulge) would have been worse and the consequences of the latter far graver, perhaps even encompassing a Soviet penetration to the Rhine. One may also surmise that Vietinghoff's Army Group Southwest would not have been the first to capitulate.

A final observation is in order. The accuracy of Clausewitz's dictum about the concatenation of war and policy seems to undergo constant reaffirmation. In the present instance, after almost half a century of argument it may be submitted that political reasoning, however credible it may have appeared to some writers during the heyday of Moscow's former East European empire, had to give way to sound military judgment in mid-1944. As far as Churchill and the few soldiers who agreed with him were thinking in grand strategic terms — it may be reiterated that they were trying on both rational and subjective grounds to impose their own strategy for the agreed one of Mediterranean containment and attrition — they were overlooking or misconstruing technical factors. Had the Prime Minister succeeded, the result would most likely have been the inverse of his alleged goal of stemming the Red tide. It is well for his, as for Alexander's, reputation that the endeavor came to nought. In all events, the facts (and counterfacts) now give historians no choice but to quit making effective judgments in the matter.

Postscript

The bushwhacking of the Yugoslav Army by lightly equipped Slovene territorial militiamen at an especially constricted point south of the town of Brežice along the crucial central Sava river passageway (Atlas Slovenije, 155) during the summer, 1991 Independence War — a trap originally designed to snare a potential Soviet invading force — has again illustrated the hazards of moving motorized columns through the kind of terrain in question. Emulating World War Two's Slovene National Liberation Army (an autonomous branch of Tito's partisans) and under the guidance of Defense Minister Janez Jansa (a military history devotee), Ljubljana's weekend warriors exploited a hill position and forest cover adjacent to the deliberately truck-cluttered autocesta and destroyed Federal armor point-blank with hand held missile launchers. (Cf. the New York Times, 5 July 1991, A-7 and 7 July 1991, Section 1,6.) In the earlier historical setting the counterinsurgency SS Police Regiments and the Wehrmacht were the targets of similar tactics. The guerrillas suddenly felled thick trees across roadways with explosives and then blasted the foe with British PIATS and the more effective U.S. bazookas that the allies had air-dropped to them. The adaptable Nazis would almost certainly have used their own Panzerfäuste in order to stymie the British (and actually tried to in the Val Canale at the war's end). Of course, Eighth Army commander General Richard McCreery, unlike the present day, mainly Serbian general staff officers, presumably would have had enough foresight to link infantry and tanks: the foot soldiers would have fanned out in belated lateral ripostes or, more prudently have scoured the woods ahead of the vehicles. It is also worth noting that the Sava route, the main link between the Wehrmacht army groups in the Balkans and Italy, was annexed to the Third Reich from 1941 to 1945 and repopulated with Austro-Germans removed from their ancestral home, the ethnic island of Kočevje (Gottschee). Males had to serve as home guardsmen (brambovci, Wehrmänner).

1. Personal experience of the writer. His own scheduled interrogation of Goering in November 1945 had to be cancelled when he was called home because of a family emergency. In his place, two colleagues of the State Department Special Interrogation Mission, DeWitt C. Pole and Harold Vedeler, interrogated Goering.

2. Jodl's deputy, Warlimont, discovered in a roundabout way that Hitler's voiced intention was to move in late September 1940. Walter Warlimont, *Inside Hitler's Headquarters, 1930-1944* (Praeger: New York, 1964), 112, and conversations with Warlimont, September 1945 and in later years.

3. The story from the German side is related by Harold C. Deutsch, *The Conspiracy Against Hitler in the Twilight War* (University of Minnesota Press: Minneapolis, 1968).

4. Deutsch, 74-77. The author later conferred with the two British diplomats who passed on the information from Stockholm and Copenhagen. Interviews with Peter Tennant and Jasper Leadbitter

5. Interrogations by the writer of Jodl and Keitel, October-November 1945.

6. Interviewed by the writer in 1958, a number of Spanish generals who had been close to Vigón asserted that for him "Canaris could do no wrong." Notably General Esteban-Infantes.

7. Shortly after the armistice with France, dining with Josef Mueller in a Munich hotel, Canaris was so distressed when he was jokingly told that the British would most certainly come to some understanding with Hitler, that he quit eating. When the contrite Mueller apologized, the admiral replied that it was not a matter for joking. Britain must somehow hang on to become the future "aircraft carrier of the United States." Conversations with Josef Mueller, 1958 and subsequent years.

8. Interview with Ramón Serrano Suñer, April 1958.

9. Interviews with Wilhelm Leisner and Erich Heberlein, April 1958.

10. Discussions with Warlimont, September-October 1945 and subsequently.

11. War Cabinet Joint Planning Staff Paper J.O. (43) 18 (Final), "Brimstone" versus "Husky", 9 Jan. 1943, Public Record Office, Kew, London.

12. Michael Howard, *British Intelligence in the Second World War*, Vol.. V, "Strategic Deception," London, 1990, p 91.

13. Samuel W. Mitchum Jr., and Friedrich von Stauffenberg, *The Battle of Sicily*, New York, 1991, pp. 300-301.

14. Vice Admiral H. Kent Hewitt quoted in Samuel Eliot Morrison, *Sicily-Salerno-Anzio*, Boston, 1954, p. 249.

15. For a more detailed and annotated account of this topic see Thomas M. Barker, "The Ljubljana Gap Strategy: Alternative to Anvil/Dragoon or Fantasy?" in the Journal of Military History, 56 (1992), pp 57-86.

16. PRO PREM [Public Record Office, Premier] 3, 275/3. The Brkini and the Čičarija run from the southeast to the northwest; roads lead toward Trieste through adjacent (southeastern) valleys.

17. PRO WO 204/1832 (undated, circa 30 October 1944 AFHQ study, "Transadriatic Operations in the Spring of 1945"; the appended comments of U.S. Brigadier General G.L. Eberle (the G-3), were especially skeptical while the document itself reveals annoyance over Alexander's initiative; and PRO WO 204/8085 (Eighth Army "Memorandum on Operation Gelignite" of 12 November 1944).

Chapter 9

The June 1944 Invasion

Walter Dunn, Carlo D'Este, Harold C. Deutsch & Dennis M. Showalter

A. What if the invasion had been attempted in 1942? In 1943?
Walter Dunn

An invasion in 1942

During the summer of 1942 three plans were under consideration by the western allies: SLEDGEHAMMER, a limited invasion of France in September 1942 to aid the Russians should they be in need; ROUNDUP, a full-blown invasion of France to be launched in 1943; and GYMNAST, a plan to invade North Africa.

Churchill favored GYMNAST, fearing heavy casualties in a premature invasion of France, while Chief of Staff Marshall and Secretary of War Stimson based their planning of the American war effort on an invasion in 1943. During Molotov's visit to Washington in 1942 Roosevelt had promised him a second front that same year and was under heavy pressure from military advisors to avoid the North African venture. Nevertheless, faced with British refusal to support SLEDGEHAMMER, in July 1942 Roosevelt decided on North Africa.

What if Roosevelt had been able to convince Churchill that an invasion of Europe was essential to aid the Soviets? In July 1942 the Soviets were being driven back to the gates of Stalingrad and seemed in need of some action on the part of the west to divert German strength. What would have been the impact on the subsequent history of the war?

Although we must assume that any plan to land in France would not have been a complete surprise, and therefore German dispositions would have been different, the Germans had very few available divisions to add to the garrison in France. They had not been able to replace the losses from the Russian winter offensive and had been forced to reduce the infantry divisions in Army Group Center and Army Group North from nine infantry battalions to six, using the available replacements to build up the divisions in Army Group South.

The German strategy for the summer of 1942 was a breakthrough in the south with the twin objectives of cutting Soviet river and rail communications with the Caucasus oilfields by taking Stalingrad and of occupying the Caucasus, making the oil available to Germany. Stalin, concerned over the safety of the Moscow industrial and communications center, held large reserves in the center. In June 1942 there were six tank corps in the Western Front defending Moscow, seven tank corps in the Bryansk Front defending the southern approach to Moscow, and four tank corps in the Southwestern Front east of Kharkov. In addition, five more tank corps were held in the Stavka reserve, for a total of 22 tank corps. A tank corps was equal to a German two-tank battalion panzer division and twice the strength of the one-tank battalion panzer divisions in Army Groups North and Center. In the three Russian fronts and the reserve were 110 of the 175 tank brigades in the Soviet Army in June 1942. In addition, ten reserve infantry armies were forming in the Stavka reserve.

Given the existence of numerous Soviet reserves, it is doubtful that the Germans would have been able to move significant numbers of divisions from the east to the west.

The Germans were able to concentrate their forces, providing local superiority for the attack in the south, but once the Soviets shifted reserves, they were able to inflict a disastrous defeat on the Germans at Stalingrad. Even if the southern campaign had been cancelled and the German Army had remained on the defensive, without the presence of the powerful 6th Army and 4th Panzer Army in the south, the Germans would have been hard pressed to contain Soviet attacks.

The German forces in France probably would not have been reinforced heavily in 1942, regardless of a threatened invasion. However, the Germans already had considerable resources there. In June 1942 the Germans had 34 divisions in the west. The best divisions were fourteen formed in November 1940 for occupation duty. They arrived in France in May and June 1941, equipped with Czech artillery and captured weapons and vehicles. During the summer of 1942 these divisions were being reequipped with German weapons and trained for combat in the east. Four additional divisions were formed by taking combat-fit men from the occupation divisions and training them for the Russian Front. All four left the west in June and July 1942. Another division was formed from new recruits and also left for Russia in June 1942.

Nine of the German divisions were static (bodenstaendige) divisions. These divisions were formed specifically for defensive operations and lacked the horses, wagons, and limited number of motor vehicles assigned to German infantry divisions to move heavy equipment in combat conditions. Static divisions had only six infantry battalions and one artillery battalion. They were more or less tied to the areas, usually ports, that they were assigned to defend. A further seven divisions had suffered losses in the east and had been sent to France to rebuild. Six had arrived in May and June and the 10th Panzer came in April. None had been rebuilt by June 1942.

Therefore, of the 34 German divisions assigned to the west in June 1942, nine were tied to their fortifications, nineteen were ready for combat, and six were being reconstructed. The net result was a thin shell along the coast. This shell was weakened in the following months to provide reinforcement for the east. Ten divisions were sent from the west in June and July. By August 1942 German strength had dropped to 31 divisions, some of the departing divisions having been replaced by newly formed units. Additional new divisions brought the strength up to 33 in September, but the overall quality was dropping rapidly.

Marshall's plan for SLEDGEHAMMER, presented to General Sir Alan Brooke in April 1942, required eighteen divisions, of which five were to be American. After the initial beachhead had been established, Marshall promised 100,000 Americans per month (equal to about four divisions with service elements).

Marshall's plan was very conservative in estimating available troops. The British Home Army was still a potent force in June 1942. Included were seven armored divisions, 21 infantry divisions, three Canadian infantry divisions, two Canadian armored divisions, and the Polish armored division—a total of 34 divisions. In addition, the 2nd Infantry and 51st Infantry Divisions were sent overseas in June 1942 and would have been held back had an invasion been planned.

American resources were fifty divisions that had been formed by June 1942. In addition to twelve Regular Army infantry divisions, two Marine divisions, and two cavalry divisions in existence prior to Pearl Harbor, eighteen National Guard divisions had been activated by April 1942 and five armored divisions had been formed before December 1942 — a total of 39. Eleven more divisions were formed in the next six months. Of these fifty divisions, seven were in the Pacific and three had been sent to Britain. Of the remainder, thirty divisions had a year of training by June 1942.

Additional demands for the Pacific were not serious. Only two Marine divisions and two infantry divisions were sent there between June 1942 and March 1943, leaving thirty trained divisions as of June 1942. The combined forces of the British and Americans were 64 trained divisions, with three to five new American divisions completing twelve months training every month beginning in March 1943.

To move the divisions to Europe, the United States demonstrated its ability to combat load and lift divisions directly from American ports for the North African invasion. Combat loading wasted shipping because the troops were loaded on the same ships as their equipment and supplies to ensure availability when the landing took place. Items were stored in the order in which they were needed; for example, rations and ammunition would be immediately available, whereas replacement clothing would be at the bottom of the ship.

Once a port was secured, troops and supplies could have been shipped in a more economical fashion. The safest way to move troops was on the fast passenger liners, carrying as many as 15,000 men on a four-day trip to Europe. Relying on their speed to avoid submarines, the liners travelled alone. None were sunk during World War II. In August 1944 eight divisions were delivered to Europe, eight in September, and six in October, indicating the rapid rate at which troops could be delivered.

The problem in 1942 was the U-boat menace to the supply ships, which travelled in slow convoys, further complicated by the inability of the British to break a new German Enigma naval cipher during most of 1942. In February 1942 the German Admiralty introduced a fourth rotor to the Enigma machines used on submarines and at the same time introduced "Triton," with new keys for the Enigma machines. The new cipher was not broken until December 1942. During that period losses to the U-boats escalated to 652,000 tons in May 1942. After the cipher was broken in December the British were once again able to veer convoys away from the wolf packs and losses dropped. The period of heavy losses coincided with the time that a heavy build-up would have been in progress for SLEDGEHAMMER. However, the Americans were able to move heavily escorted convoys to North Africa in November 1942, and most of the supplies needed for the early months of the invasion were already in Great Britain. In case of dire need, cargo space for British civilian requirements could have been allocated to military use, resulting in a temporary reduction in the standard of living in Britain. Increased conventional methods of antisubmarine warfare would also have alleviated the situation, given the high priority of supporting an invasion.

The British and Americans had nearly double the number of German divisions in June 1942 and the western divisions were of much higher quality. Additional divisions would have been available each month as American divisions completed their training. Based on the North African experience the British would have been able to land at least four against the lightly held beaches in the Cherbourg Peninsula and establish an Anzio-like beachhead. The allies would have won the build-up race. The main contributor to such a landing would have been the British, and in a desperate fight to defend the beachhead, losses might have been heavy. It is doubtful that a major breakout from the beach would have occurred before the spring of 1943, when the continuous supply of trained American divisions would have been assured.

The major impact on the future course of the war would have been the loss to Germany of a rich source of fresh divisions for the Russian Front and a safe haven for the rebuilding of divisions bruised by battle in the east. The campaign in south Russia was a constant drain. Beginning in October 1941 there had been a steady flow of trained divisions from west to east. The west was refilled with new divisions or burned-out units from the east. Had there been active operations in the west in 1942, there would have been no fresh divisions for the east. Between October 1942 and February 1943, seventeen divisions left the west for Russia and one went to North Africa. These divisions played a major role in rebuilding the front after the Stalingrad disaster. Five panzer divisions from France played a major role in the counteroffensive in the spring of 1943. Had these divisions been tied down in the west, the Russians might well have liberated much of the Ukraine a year earlier, sparing many Soviet lives.

The commitment of the allies to France in 1942 would have eliminated the costly and strategically questionable campaigns in the Mediterranean. The war possibly would have been shortened by about a year. The implications of shortening the war are discussed below.

An invasion in 1943

The allies had sufficient forces in 1943 to launch the invasion. That summer the American Army was nearing its peak. By August ninety Army and four Marine divisions had been formed. Only two Marine divisions and no Army divisions were formed after that date. By June 1943 there were fifty divisions with twelve months training. During the next twelve months 37 more divisions would have completed their year. Only thirteen divisions had been sent to the Pacific by May 1943 and two more went in June, still leaving 37 for Europe. Had the invasion gone forward in 1943, the Army might well have formed an additional ten divisions as originally planned. On 25 October 1942 the War Department had ordered the process of forming divisions slowed down because there were no immediate plans then to make use of them. With a 1943 ROUNDUP, the formation process would have gone on. The American contribution to a 1943 landing and buildup would have been 37 on 1 June 1943, with three to five additional divisions becoming available each month.

The British contribution, as stated in the War Office plan of May 1942, would have been ten British infantry divisions, eight British armored divisions, two Canadian armored divisions, three Canadian infantry divisions, a Polish armored division, a mixed division of Czechs, Belgians, Dutch, and Norwegians, and one or two airborne divisions (the availability of the 6th Airborne was in doubt) — a total of 26 or 27. Although the British Home Army had been depleted by shipments to North Africa and elsewhere by June 1943, some of the divisions would have been returned. The total of American and British divisions available would have been about 63.

In June 1943 the Germans had 44 divisions in France, but the quality left much to be desired. Twenty-one were static divisions without transport. Four were new divisions, including two SS divisions formed from members of the Hitler Youth, too young for combat. The other two had been in existence three months and one month, respectively. Sixteen divisions were formed by giving training units the numbers of the units lost at Stalingrad. The divisions had been in existence only four months or so and were far below strength. For example, in mid-April the 376th Infantry Division had only 3,763 men, including men in hospitals and on detached service. The 16th Panzer Division had only sixteen tanks at that time. Two additional divisions had been returned from Russia for refitting in April and January. The 65th Infantry had been formed in August 1942 and was fairly well trained. Of the 44 divisions, only the 65th and the 328th were comparable to a British or American division.

The only question was the ability to deliver the troops to the combat zone. By May 1943 the battle against the U-boats had been won. The landing in Sicily in July 1943, a seven-division force, was stronger than the 1944 D-Day force. The beaches in Normandy were defended by a far less formidable German force than greeted the Allies in 1944. The defenses built by Rommel in 1944 — including underwater obstacles to fend off landing craft, the "asparagus" poles to close off potential glider landing zones, and coastline emplacements — would not have been in place. The establishment of the beachhead would have been accomplished quickly and the thin crust of defenders brushed aside.

With the rapid occupation of Cherbourg and Brest, the Germans would not have had time for systematic destruction, and these ports would have eased the supply situation. Even if these ports could not have been taken, sinking over-age ships would have provided the breakwaters, as did the Mulberry system in 1944. Without the destruction of the French rail system, necessary in 1944 to prevent the movement of German reserves, the railroads would have been much easier to restore and would have provided a major source of lift from the beach to the front after the breakout.

The Germans would have been hard pressed to find reinforcements, considering the immense pressure of the Russians on the Eastern Front and the need to defend the Mediterranean coastline. The allies probably would have reached the Elbe before the Russians. Given the German's justified fear of Russian retaliation, the Germans would have done their utmost to keep the Russians out of Germany, even at the sacrifice of territory in the west. The western allies probably would have taken Berlin.

The war would probably have ended by the spring of 1944, with far-reaching results. During the final twelve months of 1944-1945 the bombing offensive reached its peak, killing hundreds of thousands of civilians as well as costing the lives of thousands of British and American air crewmen. During the same period the process of annihilating the Jews was speeded up. Perhaps two million Jews were killed in the final year of the war. Furthermore, the terrible price that the Soviet Union paid for victory would have been reduced by at least several million. All of that bloodshed would have been avoided in exchange for possible heavy casualties in Normandy, which in the end might not have been much greater than those suffered in the futile campaigns in Sicily and Italy.

Of far greater long-term consequence, had the war in Europe been terminated earlier, the conference at Teheran would have settled the problems of the postwar world while Roosevelt was a comparatively healthy man and able to negotiate more forcefully with Stalin, especially with a strong Second Front in place. With British and American forces in control of most of Germany, there would have been no need to surrender eastern Europe to the Soviets.

B. What if the Germans had detected that Operation "Fortitude" was a ruse?
Carlo D'Este

In early 1944 the allied planners for Operation Overlord, the cross-Channel invasion of Normandy, initiated the most daring deception operation of the war. Under the code name of Fortitude, its purpose was nothing less than to convince Hitler and the German commanders in the west that the Normandy landings were merely a feint and that main allied invasion was to be launched against the Pas de Calais sector north of the River Seine by six allied assault divisions. Eventually this force was to establish a bridgehead that included both Antwerp and Brussels with 50 divisions.

By playing to the German propensity to believe that the main invasion would be against the Pas de Calais, the architects of Fortitude fulfilled the most essential ingredient of any successful deception operation: that there be sufficient elements of truth to reinforce an already existing belief. In the case of Fortitude, the Germans not only believed that the Pas de Calais was the most likely site of the cross-Channel invasion, but that the allies would be obliged to invade there in order to eliminate the V-1 and V-2 rocket sites. The German terror campaign against England (primarily against London) had left the Germans with an exaggerated sense of the effect these weapons were having against the British populace. In short, the German belief in the probability of the invasion coming against the Pas de Calais had by February 1944 reached a fixation that was aided and abetted by the Fortitude planners.

The crux of Fortitude was the creation of a fictional 1st US Army Group (FUSAG) under the command of the flamboyant Lieutenant General George S. Patton, Jr. The Germans had long feared Patton as the most able battlefield commander on the allied side and the most likely candidate to command the allied invasion force. Patton, who had only recently emerged from months of virtual isolation in Sicily after the slapping incidents the previous August, had been relegated to the command of the Third US Army which was secretly being trained in England during the spring of 1944 for a post-invasion role in Normandy. The Germans were encouraged to believe this because of their logical belief that Patton was the commander of the fictional FUSAG.

While the real Overlord force was assembling and training all over England, Scotland and Northern Ireland, this fictional army group was created in East Anglia. Dummy troop concentrations were established using cleverly designed wooden and rubber replicas of tanks, guns, boat and vehicles. Double agents working for allied intelligence were fed information that confirmed the presence of a large invasion force in East Anglia. To give even further credence to these fake installations, a signal network was established whose sole purpose was to transmit a steady stream of phony message traffic twenty-four hours a day. In this way the illusion was created that there were at least six divisions operational in East Anglia.

Between the fake intelligence and the equally fictitious message traffic the Germans soon built up the intended picture of an entire army group preparing to invade the Pas de Calais. By the spring of 1944 there was clear evidence that the Germans had fallen for Fortitude hook, line and sinker.

Let it now be assumed that it was not until well after the war ended that it was confirmed just how the allied invasion plan was compromised. Unknown to the allies, both Overlord and Fortitude came apart sometime in the final month prior to the cross-Channel invasion, which was now due to take place during the first week of June. As tempting as it had been to believe the wealth of information flowing through German intelligence channels into the headquarters of the Oberkommando der Wehrmacht (OKW) in Berlin, there were more than a few skeptics who had learned well the lesson of just how effective and tricky the allied deception planners had become. Thus, while it was generally accepted within OKW that the allied invasion would be in the Pas de Calais, there were some, most of them intelligence officers, who nourished doubts. Perhaps it was nothing more than skepticism borne from having been duped by previous allied deception tricks in the Mediterranean, but not everyone in Berlin had fallen for Fortitude. The drawback was that the skeptics had no evidence to contradict the prevailing thinking. To convince Hitler and the senior staff officers in OKW, solid evidence would soon have to be uncovered.

Fortunately for these German officers, an extraordinary stroke of providence caused the allied plan to become fatally compromised in the spring of 1944. For several months the allies had conducted a series of amphibious exercises designed to train the invasion forces for the Normandy landings. One of these exercises took place in late April off the Devonshire coast of southern England. Code-named Operation Tiger, it was one of the largest and most ambitious exercises yet attempted. Designed to simulate the forthcoming landings by the US VII Corps in the Cotentin peninsula, Tiger called for a corps-sized force to be landed on the beaches of Slapton Sands, an area of Devon southeast of Dartmouth. This force was to consist of the entire VII Corps and included an American engineer group whose task was land and clear the beaches for the invasion force.

Not only was Tiger a major failure as an exercise (everything that could have possibly gone wrong, did), but it turned into an unmitigated disaster when the naval force was unexpectedly attacked by a flotilla of German E-boats operating from Cherbourg. The E-boats attacked with torpedoes and automatic weapons just as LSTs were attempting to land the engineers on Slapton Sands. The result was death and chaos as the marauding German torpedo boats sank two fully laden LSTs and damaged two more. Men were machine-gunned in the water; others drowned and it was later determined that many had improperly fitted life jackets. In all, 749 men lost their lives in the icy seas off Slapton Sands and the incident became a postwar *cause célèbre* in the 1980s when it was learned that the dead had been secretly buried in mass graves and their loss covered-up to avoid tipping the hand of the allies.

Unfortunately, the attack had a wholly unknown effect that soon wrecked the secrecy of the Overlord plan. On the corpse of one of the dead, an American colonel, later fished from the sea by an E-boat, were found fragments of the real invasion plan. Against orders, the officer had been carrying a copy of the Overlord plan. To their surprise German intelligence learned that Normandy was the true focus of the cross-Channel invasion, not, as thought, the Pas de Calais. Within the intelligence directorate of OKW there ensued a series of probing re-evaluations of allied intentions. So secret was this endeavor that only a handful of the most trusted intelligence officers participated. Fearing Hitler's wrath, they worked around the clock painstakingly assessing every scrap of information known to them in what was later determined to have been the most intense intelligence effort of the entire war. Past assumptions were discarded, difficult questions were posed and every single piece of evidence, both pro and con, was closely examined. Had the dead officer been yet another plant, similar to "The Man Who Never Was," or had they fortuitously discovered intelligence of momentous importance? They soon ruled out coincidence when it was clearly established that the E-boat attack had come strictly by chance. Obviously the allies would not kill hundreds of their troops merely to perpetrate their deception operations.

After some three weeks the evidence was sufficient for them to conclude that Fortitude was an elaborate and clever deception operation. They had been able to establish by independent means that Normandy was not only the real invasion site but that there was to be no invasion of the Pas de Calais at a later date.

So sensitive was the German evaluation that only a single copy of the document detailing the true allied intentions was produced By the third week of May, nearly a month after the attack on the allied convoy, the report was secretly presented to General Alfred Jodl, the OKW chief of staff and the officer who briefed Hitler twice each day. By-passing Jodl's boss, the weak and ineffectual Field Marshal Wilhelm Keitel, the OKW intelligence staff had presented their report to the man most likely to convince Hitler of the momentous significance of their discovery.

Jodl waited to brief the Führer until Keitel was given a rare day off. Stunned by the report, Hitler nevertheless readily conceded its conclusions. Although he had long accepted the prevailing belief that the allies would attack the Pas de Calais, he had nevertheless nurtured a foreboding that perhaps Normandy was the real allied objective.

Although the Germans never learned that their Enigma cyphers had been broken more than three years earlier, Hitler was determined to guard against a leak of the report by establishing the most stringent security ever employed. Nothing was to be put into writing or communicated to others, even via the supposedly secure Enigma system. There was too much risk of a cypher-clerk or someone in the chain of command learning of the deadly secret of Fortitude and Overlord. Hitler hastily ordered the commander-in-chief West, Field Marshal Gerd von Rundstedt and the commander of Army Group B, Field Marshal Erwin Rommel to his mountain retreat at Berchtesgaden. The two officers had no idea why they had been summoned and expected the usual abusive harangue from Hitler.

Thus, on 31 May 1944, exactly one week before the allies would invade a fifty mile length of Normandy beaches from Caen to Cotentin peninsula, the two field commanders responsible for defending France were told the truth of what was expected to occur sometime within the next two weeks. Their orders from Hitler were clear: the Normandy invasion was to be defeated on the beaches. Under no circumstances were the allies to be permitted to gain a bridgehead in France.

What if the allied high command had learned that Fortitude had been compromised?

When it was learned that one set of Overlord documents was missing after Operation Tiger, there was near panic in the top echelon of SHAEF, the allied high command. A number of bodies had not been recovered from the Tiger disaster, among them the colonel, a member of Major General J. Lawton Collins's VII Corps staff, who it was determined had been illegally carrying a copy of the plan. It was finally concluded that even in the unlikely event the Germans had found his corpse, the Overlord document would have been water soaked and unreadable. There was little that could be done except to carry out the Overlord and Fortitude plans on the assumption that there had been no compromise. Eisenhower personally briefed Churchill and after considerable discussion the Prime Minister came to the same conclusion as his supreme allied commander. Despite his occasional wild schemes, Churchill's pragmatic side took over. More than a million troops had been brought into the United Kingdom and southern England had been turned into an armed camp. These men could not be sustained indefinitely in such cramped conditions. The only opportunity to invade Europe was during the full moon period of June. If the invasion were abandoned on the basis of incomplete evidence that the plan might have been compromised, it could not be remounted until 1945. Such a delay was unthinkable. There was simply no choice. Overlord would continue as scheduled. The show would go on.

The question also arises: if the Overlord plan had been compromised within two months or less of D-Day, would the allies have opted instead to invade along the Pas de Calais. The answer to this question must be an emphatic "no." Not only was there insufficient time to have altered the myriad of air, sea and ground plans and training required to launch Overlord, but nothing could change the fact that this region of France was simply the wrong place for an invasion on such a massive scale. Even a postponement of D-Day for a month or more would have been unlikely: Given the unpredictability of the English Channel in late summer, autumn and winter, it is doubtful the allied high command would have risked delaying the invasion until July or August when the moon was full and the tides right for an invasion. Thus, even if the weather with favorable weather in high summer, it was vital that it remain so during the months following the invasion in order. With its enormous logistical appetite, any prolonged bad weather was considered a serious risk to the allied expeditionary force.

The Pas de Calais was the closest point to Britain, provided the most direct route of advance into Germany and afforded maximum air cover from airfields in southern England. Its drawback was that the Pas de Calais was such an obvious invasion site that the Germans had heavily reinforced its defenses and concentrated the bulk of their troops in France in this region. More importantly, there were few adequate ports to accommodate the enormous flow of troops and material required in the post-invasion buildup and the potential landing sites were too small to accommodate division-sized assault forces. Even if Normandy had been compromised, the Germans would have retained sufficient defenses in the Pas de Calais to discourage any notion of switching the invasion site. In short, the allies were committed to Normandy no matter what might have happened.

If the allied high command had learned that Normandy had been compromised, there would have been significant changes to the Overlord plan in order to permit the invasion to have taken place as scheduled. For example, the air forces would have abandoned all pretense of bombing western France (to avoid giving away the invasion site) and concentrated instead on preventing the Germans from reinforcing their Normandy defenses prior to D-Day. Some examples are: around-the-clock bombing, including saturation bombing of German defensive positions and routes of approach to the invasion sites. Naval fire plans would have been altered to provide for increased seaborne fire support of the ground forces and the French resistance would have been asked to undertake sabotage efforts along the invasion front. And, the invasion force itself might have been beefed up with additional assault troops, weapons and possibly even a fourth airborne division (the British 1st Airborne) to land on the great plain behind Caen and in the hills of the Odon River valley.

What if Hitler had permitted Rommel to relocate his panzers near the Normandy beaches?

In our scenario, for Erwin Rommel, the knowledge that the invasion was to take place in Normandy was like a stone lifted from his shoulders. For months he had argued in vain with Berlin that he should be given control of the strategic armored reserves in France. On Hitler's orders, OKW had denied Rommel the control of these precious reserves and instead had placed them under the command of his rival General Leo von Geyr von Schweppenburg.

For some months there had been a fundamental disagreement between Rommel and Rundstedt and Geyr over the employment of the panzer divisions when the invasion came. In November 1943 Rundstedt had created Panzer Group West as a large mobile reserve capable of reacting to an invasion in either the Fifteenth Army (Pas de Calais) or Seventh Army (Normandy) sectors. Rundstedt positioned them near Paris and envisioned employing the panzers in a large-scale counterattack against the allied landings, wherever they were launched.

Rommel firmly believed that the only hope the Germans had of defeating the invasion lay in an immediate counterattack against the beaches *before* the allies could establish a bridgehead. Geyr's philosophy was the exact reverse. He maintained that only by means of a powerful, centrally-controlled armored counterstroke could the invasion be disrupted. The three officers had repeatedly clashed until finally Rommel exercised his authority as a field marshal and appealed directly to Hitler for control of Panzer Group West. At first Hitler agreed with Rommel, but then reversed himself in March 1944 when von Runstedt protested. The result was a compromise in which three of Geyr's panzer divisions were transferred to Army Group B as mobile reserves, while the other four were retained in Panzer Group West as a central mobile reserve. However, they could not be committed without approval from OKW, which meant Hitler had to give his personal permission. The result was that both von Rundstedt and Rommel were without tactical control and the means of influencing the forthcoming battles at the critical moment.

According to his chief of staff, General Hans Speidel, Rommel considered a minimum of five panzer divisions necessary for the defense of the Normandy coast and later quoted his chief as saying:

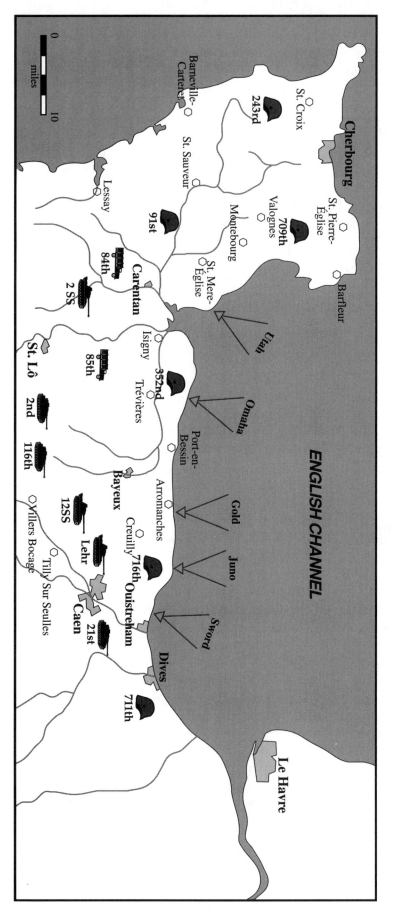

ENGLISH CHANNEL

Cherbourg

243rd

St. Croix

Barneville-
Carteret

St. Pierre-
Église

709th

Valognes

St. Sauveur

Montebourg

Lessay

91st

St. Mere-
Église

Barfleur

84th

Carentan

2 SS

Isigny

St. Lô

85th

352nd

Trévières

Utah

Omaha

Port-en-
Bessin

2nd

116th

Bayeux

Arromanches

Gold

Juno

12SS

Creuilly

716th

Lehr

Ouistreham

Villers Bocage

Caen

Tilly Sur Seulles

21st

Sword

Dives

711th

Le Havre

0

miles

10

151

"Elements which are not in contact with the enemy at the moment of invasion will never get into action, because of the enormous air superiority of the enemy …If we do not succeed in carrying out our combat mission of warding off the allies or of hurling them from the mainland in the first 48 hours, the invasion has succeeded and the war is lost for lack of strategic reserves and lack of Luftwaffe in the west."[1]

Geyr never conceded the validity of Rommel's strategy and saw the Atlantic Wall as little more than an outpost position, arguing that since the time of Hannibal decisive battles had never been fought in such positions and certainly could not be fought with the effect of mass and shock action within range of a great enemy battle fleet offshore.

Given his paranoia over the possibility of a coup by his officers, we can never know what Hitler would have done if the Germans had positive knowledge of the allied landings in Normandy. However, it is reasonable to believe that he would have permitted Rommel to at long last win the argument over the employment of the panzer reserves. If Hitler had signed an order transferring Panzer Group West to Army Group B, Rommel would have immediately ordered Geyr to begin moving his units toward Normandy. In order to avoid tipping off allied photo reconnaissance aircraft the divisions would have been ordered to move under strict blackout conditions only at night. During the daylight hours they were to find concealment. It is likely that Rommel would have placed both Fifteenth and Seventh Armies on full alert and immediately ordered reinforcements from the Pas de Calais to Normandy. Although most of the divisions assigned to Fifteenth Army were static and devoid of mobility, two mobile infantry divisions, the 84th situated near Rouen and the 85th northwest of Amiens, certainly would have been redeployed to Normandy under the same conditions of secrecy as the movement of the panzer divisions.

Thus, if Hitler had given Rommel a free hand to have disposed these formations, what would he have done? In the case of the six panzer divisions[2] displaced into the Normandy sector, Geyr would have likely established the HQ of Panzer Group West in a forest southeast of Caen, just as he did after the invasion in 1944. Rommel too would have installed an advanced field headquarters of Army Group B somewhere between Caen and Falaise. Rommel's priority would have been the defense of the most dangerous sectors in Normandy: the Caen-Falaise corridor and, in the west, the highways connecting the Carentan peninsula with Periers and St. Lô.

Here is one scenario that Rommel might have employed. The 12th SS Panzer Division was positioned north of Odon River to attack toward either Caen or Bayeux, while the 21st Panzer and Panzer Lehr Divisions were dispersed in wooded areas east and west of Caen. The two infantry divisions were sent to the west to prevent any breakout toward St. Lô and to counterattack any landings in the Carentan sector of western Normandy. When it arrived from southern France, the 2nd SS Panzer Division was to be placed in blocking positions along the key choke points — the highways leading from Carentan to St. Lô and Periers — to block any attempt at a breakout from the Cherbourg peninsula. The remaining two panzer divisions (the 2nd and 116th) were dispersed west of Villers-Bocage as Rommel's strategic reserve. When the shape of the invasion could be determined this force would be committed where and when necessary, but only under his personal order. By the early evening of June 5 these dispositions were completed. It only remained for the allied invasion to commence. Tensions ran high as every German soldier in Normandy was poised for the commencement of the battle that would decide the outcome of the war.

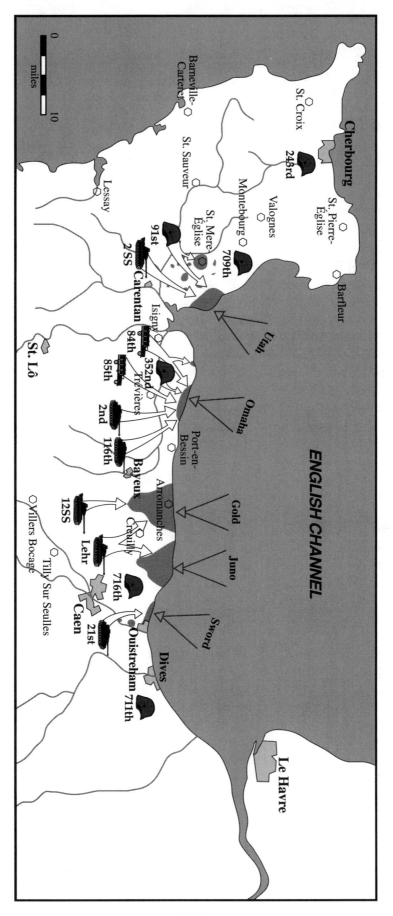

ENGLISH CHANNEL

Cherbourg

St. Croix

Barneville-
Carteret

243rd

St. Pierre-
Église

St. Sauveur

Montebourg

Valognes

Barfleur

Lessay

91st

St. Mère-
Église

709th

2SS

Carentan

Utah

Isigny

352nd

84th

Trévières

85th

St. Lô

Omaha

2nd

116th

Port-en-
Bessin

Bayeux

Arromanches

Gold

12SS

Creully

Juno

Lehr

716th

Sword

Villers Bocage

Caen

21st

Ouistreham

Tilly Sur Seulles

Dives

711th

Le Havre

0

miles

10

153

What if Rommel had been present in Normandy on 6 June 1944?

The single most important factor that might have changed the course of the invasion of Normandy was the presence on D-Day of the dynamic German ground forces commander, Field Marshal Erwin Rommel.

Like all soldiers, Rommel missed his family and had been looking forward to finding some way of taking a few day's leave in order to be with his beloved wife, Lucie, whose birthday was on 6 June. Commencing on 4 June the weather had turned rotten, with high winds and rain and the Channel became a cauldron of choppy waves and excessively high tides along the Normandy beaches. Although Rommel knew the invasion was imminent, it did not seem possible that a huge invasion armada could carry out amphibious landings until the weather improved. His meteorological officer reported that there would be no break before 7 June. Thus, as we now know from what happened during those crucial days of early June 1944 Rommel's absence from Normandy at the time of the allied landings was crucial.

Across the Channel, Eisenhower's Met officer, Group Captain J. M. Stagg had delivered such a pessimistic report on the weather situation that Eisenhower had no choice except to postpone for twenty-four hours the invasion scheduled for 5 June. Thousands of allied soldiers and sailors sweated out the delay in cramped conditions aboard the 7,875 ships that comprised the invasion force. At a meeting of the allied invasion commanders held at 10:45 P.M. the night of 4 June, Stagg offered a ray of hope when he predicted that there would be a slight break in the weather which, although marginal at best, would permit the landings to take place the morning of 6 June. With the concurrence of his invasion commanders, Eisenhower elected to proceed and his historic decision set into motion the greatest amphibious operation in the history of warfare.

Under our scenario, Rommel was tempted to request leave to make a quick visit to the family home in Herrlingen near Ulm. However, even though the weather was terrible he recognized that duty impelled him to remain in Normandy to await the inevitable allied landings. He believed, with considerable justification, that his presence was absolutely essential if the invasion force was to be defeated. Thus, despite the heavy seas and poor visibility in the Channel, Rommel ordered his Seventh and Fifteenth Armies on standby alert, one stage below the Code Red condition that would apply when the landings actually began.

Shortly after midnight on 5 June when the first reports emanated from Seventh Army of glider landings in both the Carentan and Caen sectors, Rommel would have immediately placed his entire army group on full battle alert. During the night the three panzer divisions in the Caen sector would probably have moved ever closer to the beaches: the 12th SS to positions north and west of Carpiquet airfield and the Panzer Lehr to the wooded areas north and northwest of Caen. The bulk of the 21st Panzer would have remained east of the Orne River. After dispersal from positions in the Bois de Bavent outside Dives-sur-Mer, infantry and panzers would have attacked the airborne troops that had landed along the east side of the Orne and the Caen Canal. Infantry elements of the Panzer Lehr and the 716th Divisions, supported by a tank battalion, would have attacked British parachute troops in the Benouville-Ouistreham sector.

Given the actual near-run battle fought by the British airborne and commando forces east of the Orne, it is reasonable to conclude that with such powerful reinforcements the Germans would have neutralized these forces and inflicted enormous (perhaps total) losses. Although a few stragglers might have managed to escape, the small, lightly armed allied force would have simply been no match for German firepower and quick reaction.

Would the allies have detected the presence of these panzer divisions in the Caen sector before the D-Day landings? Certainly, the French Resistance would have immediately noted their presence and attempted to alert the allies. However, more than a week before the landings the Resistance had sent a message to England that the guns thought to have been at the Pointe du Hoc had been dispersed inland in April and were thus no longer a threat to the landings on Omaha and Utah Beaches. That message did not arrive in time and the Ranger operation up the steep cliffs of the Pointe du Hoc were carried out. It is reasonable to conclude a similar notification of the presence of the panzers would have similarly failed to reach allied intelligence in time. Even if they had, the allies were irrevocably committed to the landings.

Assuming that the panzer divisions had managed to conceal their movements and presence, there is no assurance, even with intensive photo reconnaissance flights in the weeks leading up to D-Day, that allied intelligence would have detected the disposition of these divisions into the Caen sector — just as it failed to note that the 352nd Division had been defending the Omaha Beach sector since April 1944. Thus, it is quite possible the presence of these formations would have come as a nasty and likely fatal surprise to the allies.

During the actual invasion in the Caen sector the British 3rd Division ran into serious trouble along Sword Beach where the combination of excessively high tides and German counterattacks prevented the capture of Caen on D-Day. Add to a "what if" scenario the presence of Panzer Lehr and the 12th SS Panzer Divisions, and the results would have been nothing less than disastrous. The British 3rd Division and the 6th Airborne Division elements west of the Orne would have been roped off and, if not destroyed, contained in a narrow, thinly-held beachhead, perhaps a few thousand yards deep, between Sword Beach and the Orne. Casualties would have been very high. The Canadian 3rd Division and 2nd Armored Brigade might have been more successful in the Juno sector but would not have advanced as far as the Caen-Bayeux highway. Although prowling allied aircraft and naval gunfire would have kept the panzers pinned down in their concealed positions during daylight hours and thus prevented a counterattack on 6 June, the Germans would have launched serious attacks under the cover of darkness that night.

Despite the magnitude of their reinforcements, the Germans still could not have established a defense in depth in the time before the landings. Therefore, the greatest Anglo-Canadian success might have come on Gold Beach, where the veteran British 50th Division and the 8th Armored Brigade landed without heavy casualties. Nevertheless, their beachheads would have hardly been more than a mile deep before they encountered elements of the 12th SS Panzer and the 716th Infantry Division.

To the west, the US landings on Omaha Beach by the 1st Infantry Division and two regiments of the 29th Infantry Division ran into savage resistance from the 352nd Division which dominated the heights overlooking the seven-mile long beach. Losses were high as German troops poured fire on to the exposed troops. During the first six hours the invaders held only a few yards of beach, which remained under intense enemy fire. The situation on Omaha was so critical that Lt. Gen. Omar Bradley, the US ground force commander, seriously considered evacuating the beachhead and switching the follow-up units to the British sector or to Utah beach. Eventually, extraordinary leadership on the part of the American commanders carried the day as GIs stormed the heights and drove the German defenders from their fortified positions. Casualties on both sides were grave.

It was only on Utah Beach that the allies enjoyed a full measure of success. Despite the presence of the two newly-arrived infantry divisions in the Carentan sector, the 4th US Infantry Division successfully established a two-mile deep beachhead without serious loss. Here, the allies were able to take advantage of the marshy terrain which was unsuitable for mobile operations. Rommel was satisfied with a stand-off that would prevent allied forces from advancing to the south and southeast and posing a threat to encircle his defensive positions in the Caen-Bayeux sector.

Thus, despite losing strategic surprise the allies managed to establish three tenuous, but separate, beachheads across a sixty-mile front. The problem facing the allied commanders was how to link-up the three beachheads before the Germans could take advantage of their isolation and attack their vulnerable flanks. Rommel now had a clear picture of the extent of the invasion force and elected to concentrate his forthcoming armored counterattack against the US V Corps in the Omaha sector. If his panzers could crush Major General Leonard Gerow's two divisions south of Omaha, the remainder of the allied beachhead at Caen and near Carentan could be rolled up and the invasion defeated.

Both sides recognized that the forthcoming battle would determine the fate of the invasion. Rommel assembled a powerful armor-heavy task force consisting of the two reserve panzer divisions plus infantry elements of the 352nd and 716th Divisions. Their objective would have been the low hill mass that ran from south of Port-en-Bessin to Longueville in the east, where V Corps had established its beachhead line. During the first twenty-four hours the allies had rushed reinforcements ashore in a desperate effort to reinforce V Corps before Rommel's blow fell.

Would the end result have been any different under our "what if" scenario? Probably not. There would not have been time nor reason to invest the Omaha or Utah sectors with the newly arrived panzer and infantry divisions. The 352nd Division would have fought virtually the same battle on Omaha and although the 4th Division could have expected higher casualties on Utah Beach, both landings would ultimately have succeeded. The great distinction between what actually happened and our scenario would have been the battle by the allies to break out of their narrow beachhead at Omaha before the panzer counterattack came. Here is what might have occurred.

The morning of 7 June Rommel put into practice what he had preached: a powerful counterattack against the invasion before the allies were given an opportunity to establish a firm bridgehead from which they could not be dislodged. The full fury of the German attack would have fallen upon V Corps by as many as four German divisions: the 2nd and 116th Panzer Divisions, elements of either the 84th or 85th Divisions, rushed from the Cotentin sector to the east, the 352nd Division and the artillery fire of every gun in Normandy that could be brought to bear. To the east, secondary attacks would have been launched by the 12th SS Panzer, 21st Panzer and Panzer Lehr, while in the west, the 2nd SS Panzer would have arrived from southern France and have hammered the combined infantry-parachute force of the 82nd and 101st Airborne and the 4th Infantry Division. In many places the allied defenses could not have contained the German onslaught and their lines would have been penetrated by the violent panzer onslaught. The German drive could only have been stopped by a steel curtain of around the clock naval gunfire and close air support during daylight hours. In the end, the allied naval forces would have spelled the difference.

For the navy to have saved the day was a precedent established the previous September at Salerno, where only the timely intervention of the fleet prevented a tragedy. During the bloody struggle for Salerno, allied naval guns laid down barrage

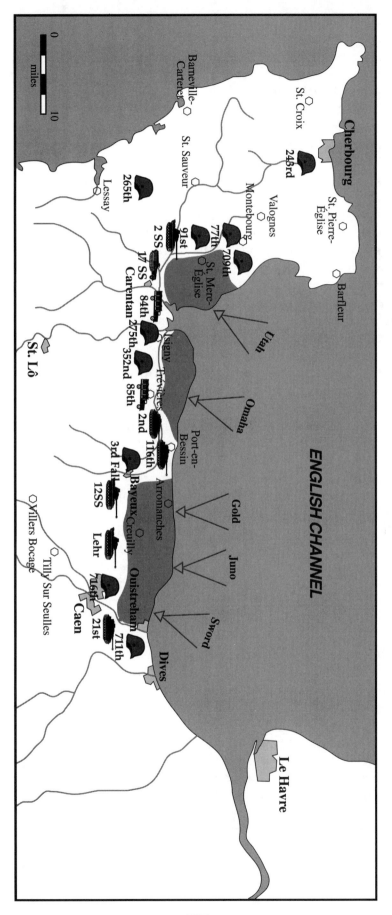

ENGLISH CHANNEL

Cherbourg

St. Croix

Barneville-
Carteret

St. Pierre-
Église

243rd

Barfleur

St. Sauveur

Valognes

Montebourg

265th

Lessay

St. Mère-
Église

709th

77th

91st

2 SS

Uah

17 SS

84th

Carentan

St. Lô

275th

352nd 85th

Isigny

Trévières

2nd

116th

Omaha

Port-en-
Bessin

3rd Fall

12SS

Bayeux

Creully

Arromanches

Gold

Lehr

Ouistreham

Juno

Villers Bocage

Tilly Sur Seulles

716th

Caen

21st

711th

Sword

Dives

Le Havre

miles

0

10

157

after barrage to disrupt and breakup the determined German attacks. The same would have taken place in Normandy.

Virtually every battleship — of which there were seven — and as many as twenty-three cruisers would have fired in direct support of the beleaguered invasion force. The 5 and 14 inch guns of the battleships USS Texas and USS Arkansas could deliver such withering fire that, once targeted, they could literally annihilate a German formation. Nevertheless, in places the panzers could have driven clear to the beaches and destroyed everything in their path. Fortunately the terrain of Normandy would have impeded any attempt to roll up the various isolated beachheads. Eventually, thanks to the navy, the perilous allied beachhead would have held — but just barely.

Casualties on both sides would have been appalling. Allied losses of over 25,000, with at least 10,000 dead would not have been unreasonable. German losses would have been equally costly, principally from naval gunfire and allied artillery. Many of the artillery pieces would have fired at point blank range, with their tubes depressed to act as direct fire weapons.

The determined Rommel would have continued pressing his counterattacks regardless of his mounting losses. Restlessly prowling the front line to offer encouragement to his men and a boot to commanders who showed signs of faltering. Rommel would have reminded one and all that this was their only opportunity to crush the invasion and that unless they were successful, they would most likely die.

However long the battle may have lasted, it would indisputably have been the most savage and costly engagement of the war in the west. Both Eisenhower and his two ground commanders, General Sir Bernard Montgomery and Lt. Gen. Omar Bradley, would have thrown caution to the winds and hastened every possible reinforcement available into the fray. Naval gunfire would have continued around the clock. Aerial attacks by Air Vice Marshal "Mary" Coningham's 2nd Tactical Air Force and heavy bomber support from Air Chief Marshal Sir Arthur Harris's Bomber Command would have pounded German assembly areas in the Caen, Falaise and Villers-Bocage sectors. The RAF would have also been employed at night, while the B-17 bombers from the US Eighth Air Force struck during daylight. The German death toll would have continued to climb.

Given his insistence on controlling all German forces in Normandy, Rommel would have had little choice except to continue counterattacking as long as he retained the initiative and there was even the slightest chance of success. Moreover, as he had done in the past, Hitler would have ordered a fight to the death and refused to accept any plea from Rommel to withdraw his forces out of range of allied naval gunfire. In the end, Hitler's bullheadedness, as it did later that year during the ill-fated Ardennes counteroffensive, would have ensured German failure. Rommel's eventual recommendation to withdraw inland out of range of the allied naval guns would have been scornfully rejected by Hitler's decree that there be no withdrawal, no retreat, under penalty of death.

In all, the German counterattacks would likely have consumed no more than five days, but they would have been the most desperate five days of the entire war. Churchill would later have modified his "finest hour" quote to include the inspired defense of the Normandy beachhead and Eisenhower would have hailed the men of the allied Expeditionary Force as "the most magnificent soldiers I have ever commanded."

At some point Seventh Army would have been obliged to withdraw behind the Rivers Odon and the Orne, but not without more fierce fighting in the defense of Caen, Villers-Bocage and the river crossings. In the end, the Germans would still have controlled the important Caen-Falaise plain and the road net leading to and from Caen.

There would have been no change in Rommel's conviction that the days of the German army in Normandy were numbered. The feeble efforts of the Luftwaffe to oppose the RAF and USAAF only made matters worse. Most of the Luftwaffe were blown from the sky on D-Day and D+1 and were thereafter little seen. They were greatly scorned by the ground troops who cursed them as cowards. Of the great aerial and naval bombardments Rommel has written:

> "Even the movement of the most minor formations on the battlefield-artillery going into position, tanks forming up, etc., - is instantly attacked from the air with devastating effect. During the day fighting troops and headquarters alike are forced to seek cover in wooded and close country in order to escape the continual pounding from the air. Up to 640 [naval] guns have been used. The effect is so immense that no operation of any kind is possible in the area commanded by this rapid-fire artillery, either by infantry or tanks."[3]

The German counterattacks clearly would have left the allies in no position to pursue aggressive offensive action until further massive reinforcements and follow up formations, and supplies and ammunition could be brought ashore. To make matters even more difficult, the allied build-up was literally crippled for three days by the great storm which pounded Normandy from 19 to 22 June. It was the worst gale in nearly forty years and caused severe losses to allied shipping in the fierce seas. Some eight hundred ships of all sizes were beached or lost. The Mulberry harbor being erected on Omaha beach was totally destroyed and never replaced; the British Mulberry at Arromanches was damaged but fortunately not lost. Resupply came to a dead stop.

The weather was so fierce that any intention by Rommel to launch another counteroffensive would have been thwarted by the savage weather. Although the allies were able to eventually replace their losses, Rommel's attacks would have insured that it would be well into July before they could have launched an offensive to break out of their narrow bridgehead. Until then, Caen and high ground south of the city would have remained firmly under German control.

Thus, until mid-August the two sides would have fought a battle of attrition on the eastern flank that varied little from what actually occurred in 1944. The enormous size of the battlefield meant that the Germans could not defend in depth against the inevitable allied offensive to break free of the Normandy bridgehead. In late July Bradley launched an offensive to break the German left flank in the Cotentin peninsula. St. Lo fell to the U.S. First Army on 19 July and when Operation Cobra succeeded in crushing the German left flank, Patton's recently landed U.S. Third Army was unleashed. By 1 August, Third Army had broken the final bottleneck at Avranches and both armies had swept into the open country beyond. For the Germans who had lost their inspirational commander in mid-July when his staff car was strafed by an RAF Spitfire, the genie was out of the bottle and the Normandy campaign was irrevocably out of their control.

Although Rommel had been able to wrest control of the German armored reserve from his rivals inside the army in time to carry out his strategy of attacking the invasion force while it was still vulnerable, his powerful tank-infantry forces were simply unable to overcome the devastating allied naval gunfire and air support. His critics, the most vocal of which remained Geyr, would have argued the German counteroffensive had been doomed from the start and that Rommel ought to have retained his armor well inland out of harm's way before initiating a counteroffensive. The question of who was right has never been resolved and to this day is the subject of spirited discussion and debate.

C. What if the Allies had been repulsed on D-Day?
Harold C. Deutsch & Dennis E. Showalter

In many ways things were touch-and-go with respect to the landings in Normandy on 6 June 1944. It was entirely possible that they could have been repulsed at the water's edge. According to his own testimony, Eisenhower would have felt obliged to dispatch his hastily-scribbled memo assuming full responsibility for the debacle. To some extent, events would then have been shaped by the nature of the battle itself. A defeat, with the allied forces essentially intact and potentially able to try again, would have had different consequences from a debacle on the order of Dieppe. Morally, however, D-Day was an operation that could only be mounted once—especially from a British perspective. Not merely had the last of the island empire's material resources been committed to the operation. Psychologically as well, a war-weary, debilitated population was playing its last cards.

Paradoxically, however, defeat in Normandy might have strengthened Britain's position in allied strategic councils. From Churchill downwards, doubts of the feasibility of a cross-Channel invasion had characterized British approaches to the operation. With U.S. emergence as the coalition's dominant partner, British hopes of eventually playing Greece to America's Rome had muted dissent. Certainly the issue would have once more come fully into the open as the corpses of failure washed ashore on Britain's south coast.

A possible operational consequence would have involved refocusing on the Mediterranean—rerouting new U.S. divisions to Italy instead of Britain, perhaps even opening a new front in the Balkans. ANVIL-DRAGOON, so long the bane of Churchill's life, might have seemed attractive from an alternate perspective, as a sop to those he considered the embarrassed amateurs of the U.S. Joint Chiefs of Staff. Even Norway conceivably could kindle new interest as a focal point for a flexible amphibious strategy, as opposed to the now-discredited American SLEDGEHAMMER.

This would not, of course, mean complete abandonment of a cross-Channel operation—only its postponement until Nazi Germany should be further, decisively weakened. That task in turn would fall, objectively, to the Red Army. On June 21, 1944, the third anniversary of Barbarossa, the Soviet high command unleashed Operation Bagration against Germany's Army Group Center. The German front did not collapse; it disappeared. By July 3, the Russians had advanced over 200 miles from their start lines. Not until autumn did the Soviet offensive stop at the borders of East Prussia and the gates of Warsaw. It was during these very months of desperation, however, that Hitler formed from the Reich's last resources the strategic reserves that, historically, were used in the Battle of the Bulge. Given the absence of a second front in Western Europe, these resources, or the bulk of them, would have been available for a counterstrike against the Russians in the same time frame: December, 1944.

That availability was likely to have been reduced by an intensified Anglo-American air campaign against German oil and transportation resources. A German victory on D-Day would have done nothing to reduce the overwhelming air supremacy of the western allies. Indeed the absence of a land front would have freed the tactical air forces for operational missions. Even with the limited range of many fighters and medium bombers, the Germans would have found large-scale troop movement difficult — but not impossible. Air power alone could not have stopped an "Eastern Bulge." The Red Army was another factor entirely. Given the high level of tactical operational skills achieved by Soviet forces, and given the extreme discrepancy in numbers between the combatants, a counter-attack eastward could have done nothing more than buy time — perhaps six months, no more.

The next crucial question in this scenario would have involved the westward advance of the Soviet steamroller. Given the absence of an allied presence in northern France or a token foothold along the coast, the Yalta Conference would certainly have taken a different tone. Most of the trumps would have been in Stalin's hands, and the Soviet dictator was a man who knew how to utilize high cards. A likely outcome would have involved a Soviet "zone" of occupation in Germany extending to the Rhine river, with the British, French, and Americans playing token roles in governing a Germany they had done so little to defeat. Roosevelt and Churchill would have had little choice in the matter. Given FDRs real-time hopes for noblesse oblige on Stalin's part, the American president might even have welcomed the settlement. In any case the USSR's victory would have been on a scale unthinkable in 1941.

One further possibility remains in this scenario: U.S. employment of the atomic bomb against Germany. Should the Reich have hung on into the late summer of 1945, Munich or Cologne rather than Hiroshima might well have been the first nuclear target. Contrary to some popular legends, there is no evidence that American military and political leaders were in any way reluctant to use the bomb on a European target for racial or cultural reasons. Militarily, had Germany proved able to hold up the Red Army and increase Soviet casualties by a last-ditch resistance—hypothetically continuing even after the fall of Berlin—destroying what remained of a major city in the west or south might have been reasonably expected to produce surrender even of a rump Reich dominated by Nazi die-hards. Diplomatically, the bomb's use would have offered a final form of compensation for a failed second front. It would have also served as a not-so-subtle warning to the USSR that occupation of Germany by no means guaranteed hegemony over Europe. The "atomic diplomacy" and "nuclear blackmail" that remain the constructions of historians would likely have been all too real given the absence of British and American ground forces at the final German capitulation.

This in turn leads to a final speculation. The anti-Soviet consolidation of western Europe under NATO was in large part facilitated by negative reactions to Russian behavior in the east. Becoming part of a Soviet imperium offered few attractions compared to Camel cigarettes, nylon stockings, and the Marshal Plan. But the radioactive rubble of a German city or two would have offered a powerful argument for the Communist parties of France and Italy, for British Labourites, and indeed for anyone of ordinary common sense and goodwill, that U.S. concern for Europe's welfare did not exclude willingness to incinerate in a particularly horrible fashion some tens of thousands of Europeans for political reasons. After 1945, Japanese propaganda in large part succeeded in making Hiroshima the defining event of the Pacific War. What might a far more powerful and sophisticated information/disinformation system have achieved with a European nuclear target? Perhaps Gorbachev's rhetorical vision of "Europe from the Ural Mountains to the Bay of Biscay" might have become a geopolitical reality a quarter-century earlier.

---

[1] Quoted in postwar interrogation of Lieutenant General Hans Speidel, German Report Series, Foreign Military Studies, Mss. # B-720, US Army Military History Institute, Carlisle Barracks, PA.

[2] These divisions were: Panzer Lehr, 2nd, 12th SS, 21st, and 116th Panzer. The 2nd SS "Das Reich" was en route from southern France and expected to reach Normandy by the morning of June 5.

[3] Quoted in B.H. Liddell Hart (ed.), *The Rommel Papers*, New York, 1954, pp. 476-77.

Chapter 10

July 20, 1944

Peter Hoffmann

A. What if the allies had offered more favorable peace conditions to a post-Hitler government?

What if the allies had responded to German opposition appeals in 1943 and 1944 by agreeing to grant more favorable conditions of peace to a post-Hitler government in which they had confidence? "More favorable conditions" is defined here as representing in the view of the opposition and potential recruits a substantial improvement on unconditional surrender. As only the Army could oppose Hitler effectively, its leaders had to be persuaded that Germany's position could be improved by the removal of Hitler and his henchmen.

This had been attempted in July and August 1938 by General Ludwig Beck, then Chief of the General Staff of the Army. Beck failed to convince Colonel-General von Brauchitsch, the Commander-in-Chief of the Army, and the other senior commanders, of his firm belief that most of the desired revisions of the settlement of 1919 and 1920 that Germany sought could be achieved through negotiations. Neither did the victors of 1918 offer any assurances in this regard until September 1938, nor did the commanders accept Beck's reasoning that "the soldier's duty to obey ends when his knowledge, his conscience and his sense of responsibility forbid him to carry out a certain order," in this case the invasion of Czechoslovakia.[1] They did not support his proposal to confront Hitler with a refusal to carry out orders in this case which Beck had expected would have led to Hitler's overthrow.

After 1 September 1939, most senior Army commanders continued to be skeptical in this regard. Their perception was that the war was imposed on Germany. Germany had just grievances against Poland, and Polish intransigence was made possible by a Polish-British pact. Britain declared war on Germany for the Balance of Power. France, Australia, New Zealand, South Africa and Canada followed with declarations of war; the United States immediately supported Britain and France with shipments of arms and other necessities of war.

Until the beginning of November 1939, the Chief of the General Staff of the Army, General Halder, was committed, verbally at least, to supporting a coup d'etat against Hitler's regime. But on 10 November 1939 he said to one of the conspirators who tried to press him to take action against Hitler, and to prevent the planned offensive against France: "1. It violates tradition. 2. There is no successor. 3. The young officer corps is not reliable. 4. The mood in the interior is not ripe. 5. It really can not be tolerated that Germany is permanently a "people of helots" for England. 6. Concerning offensive: Ludendorff, too, in 1918 had led the offensive against the advice of everyone, and the historical judgment was not against him. He, Halder, therefore did not fear the later judgment of history either."[2] Halder gave voice to sentiments widely held.

Further, there was the matter of loyalty to the legitimate Supreme Commander and Head of State. If someone removed him, the position would be changed; but until then, most military leaders were not willing "to act" to help eliminate the power bases and structures of the Nazi state. The question of the oath is left aside here. Suffice it to say that it was less an ethical issue than one of military necessity and tradition.[3] In January 1943, Manstein insisted that the Soviet Union could and should be fought to a draw. Even Stauffenberg believed in the summer of 1944 that Germany must be maintained as a power factor if she were to have any hope of negotiating for acceptable armistice conditions; only in the desperate weeks of July did Stauffenberg accept the necessity of unconditional surrender on all fronts.

In weighing retrospectively the impact that allied support to the German Resistance in the form of acceptable peace conditions might have had, one must keep in mind the long series of efforts to overthrow Hitler, beginning in 1938, all of which were made without any allied assurances to the German opposition. Equally, one must not overlook the events of the winter of 1939-40. When there was what had to pass for substantial encouragement to the conspirators, it failed to stimulate a coup d'état. An offer of more favorable conditions might well have led the opposition to redouble their efforts, later in the war, to win the military support they needed; but in view of the attitude of most military leaders, and of all those who commanded forces capable of military combat, nothing suggests that these efforts would have met with greater success. Allied assurances might have improved the circumstances in which a coup could have taken place in Germany. Whether or not they could have stimulated a coup d'état at other times than those of the known attempts, is subject to doubt.

B. What if Rommel had not become incapacitated on 17 July 1944, but had remained in command of Army Group B on 20 July 1944, with Kluge in command as Supreme Commander West?

Both Rommel and Kluge made fairly far-reaching commitments to the conspirators. In somewhat different ways and for slightly different reasons, neither Rommel nor Kluge could be fully relied upon by the conspirators. Rommel was opposed to assassination, and Kluge kept changing.

Rommel thought it "stupid" to try to assassinate Hitler because of the aura which surrounded Hitler in the eyes of the German people. He thought the revolt ought to have been launched in the west, by German retreat resulting in an unopposed occupation of Germany by the forces of the western allies. Thus Hitler would have been presented with an accomplished fact. Rommel and his chief of staff Speidel in the middle of July concluded that the German front in France would collapse within a few weeks. They decided to open independent peace negotiations and made preparations for them. According to Rommel's account to his family, they won over Kluge. On 15 July, Rommel drafted a message to Hitler in which he gave an account of the situation. He concluded by saying he felt in duty bound to speak plainly, and to say that "the unequal struggle is approaching its end," and that it was "urgently necessary for the proper conclusion to be drawn from this situation."[4] In Rommel's account, this message had the character of a "last warning": he did not want it said that he had stabbed anyone in the back. But the weight of Rommel's account is that he would have done just that if his "last warning" had gone unheeded. Rommel did not make clear how he and Kluge expected to carry this off without being sacked immediately at the slightest hint of disloyalty.

If Rommel had been in his position as Commander of Army Group B on 20 July 1944, if he had been informed of the assassination attack, and soon afterwards of its failure, it cannot be ruled out that he might have carried out his plan for a negotiated retreat in the west. As soon as this would have transpired, he would have been removed from command and arrested if he did not escape by shooting himself or by going into hiding. On the other hand, Rommel's opposition to assassination might have caused him to keep his distance from the plot. He might have decided to postpone carrying out his plan until the furor over the assassination attempt had subsided.

The possibility that Rommel might have carried Kluge along cannot be ruled out. But Kluge's commitment was always tentative.

Hofacker and his co-conspirators in Paris, particularly Gotthard Freiherr von Falkenhausen, all agreed that independent action by German forces in the west was impossible for the following reasons: it was clear to the conspirators that neither Rundstedt nor Rommel or Kluge intended to disobey an incumbent Fuehrer in any major way; it was also their perception that, had these commanders attempted to take the western front out of the war, there would have been internal warfare as Hitler undoubtedly would have called upon the Eastern Front and the home front to combat the western front!

Doubt about the likelihood that Rommel and Kluge would have tried to seek some sort of unauthorized arrangement on the Western Front is increased by a lack of reliable evidence that they had taken any steps in that direction. There is, furthermore, no indication that such steps had any prospect of success. Rommel and Kluge appear not to have had any evidence of an allied willingness to make some accommodation in the west. In December 1943, Helmuth Count von Moltke transmitted to Alexander Kirk in Cairo an offer, based on the condition of the continuance of an unbroken Eastern Front along an approximate line from Tilsit to Lemberg, of "military co-operation with the allies on the largest possible scale" which, the offer stipulated, must lead to a rapid occupation of Germany. There was no allied response to this offer. It appeared that the United States and the United Kingdom were determined to bring the war to conclusion only in conjunction with the Soviet Union, and only on the basis of the unconditional surrender of German forces on all fronts. Nor is there any indication who would have been prepared to honor Moltke's commitment, or how this could have been accomplished before Hitler and Goering had been removed. There is no evidence that Moltke's December overture was based on any firm understanding with a commander in the west; Rommel was appointed Commander of Army Group B officially as at 1 January 1944; it is conceivable that Moltke had some assurances through Lieutenant-Colonel von Hofacker, the conspirators' liaison with Rommel, and his cousin Stauffenberg. Kluge was not, of course, appointed to succeed Rundstedt until 2 July 1944. An account by Rommel's chief of staff, Speidel, that Colonel J. E. Smart, formerly of General Eisenhower's staff, had been shot down over Vienna on 10 May 1944 and had wished to be put in contact with Rommel with a view to an "independent conclusion of the war" remains unconfirmed.[5] Equally, nothing is known on the allied side concerning Otto John's Madrid connection. It is quite clear, on the other hand, that Adam von Trott's various efforts in Sweden produced no allied support for the German conspirators.

C. What if Hitler had been killed on 20 July 1944?

Hitler named Goering his successor on 23 April 1938; he declared this publicly in his speech of 1 September 1939, naming Hess as second in line of succession; after Hess's flight to Scotland, Hitler reconfirmed Goering as heir apparent in a decree on 29 July 1941 and excluded Hess whose position as Personal Secretary was now relinquished entirely to Martin Bormann.

Minutes after the assassination attack at 12.50 P.M., on 20 July 1944, a communications blackout went into effect, but not before the most important leaders, including Goering, had been notified by their various representatives in Hitler's headquarters. Goering hurried over from his own field headquarters in East Prussia to "Wolfschanze." Had Hitler been killed, Goering would have proceeded to take control as the Fuehrer's successor.

There is no reason to believe that anyone — Keitel, Ribbentropp, Himmler or Bormann — would have tried to prevent Goering from taking the reins initially. All would have been interested in maintaining the appearance of a stable leadership; in fact, the Fuehrer's death would have probably have been kept secret as long as possible, as indeed the communications blackout was meant to prevent news of the assassination attack from getting out.

The conspirators also wished to isolate the headquarters; one in their number, General Fellgiebel, Commander of Wehrmacht Signals Troops, was prepared to act to accomplish this. As it happened, the wishes of the conspirators and the interests of the surviving Hitler regime coincided on this point during the first two to three hours after the assassination attempt. Legends about a plan to destroy the communications centers in the headquarters had wide currency after 1945, but no substance. The new leadership was not likely to lose control of the instruments of the state as long as their reign appeared legitimate and legal. Neither the civil service nor the population at large were likely to deny them their continued support.

Mussolini's special train, due to arrive shortly to take him to *Wolfschanze* for a visit with Hitler, would have been delayed for an hour or two, as in fact it was. Probably the visit would then have gone forward, with Goering in Hitler's place.

Whether or not, and if so, how soon Goering would have thought of appointing a new commander-in-chief of the Army is difficult to guess. He was himself certainly incompetent to lead the Army; if the Chief of the General Staff, General Zeitzler, had been ordered to carry on as deputy commander-in-chief, it is doubtful that he could have managed the Army in the face of its greatest crisis thus far, the collapse of Army Group Center, with casualty numbers far greater than those incurred at Stalingrad. Moreover, neither Zeitzler nor Goering were the personalities to restore the primacy of the Army in matters of land-warfare. Ambitious OKW and *Wehrmachtfuhrungstab* men such as Keitel, Jodl and Warlimont might well have thought the moment come to combine control of all theaters of war in the OKW. In case of such conflicts, a compromise would probably have been struck, with the appointment of Rundstedt or Manstein as armed forces chief of staff or as commander-in-chief of all land forces.

Goering was heir apparent: the failed genius of the German airforce, a sporadically energetic organizer of men and materials, a morphine addict but still from time to time an efficient intriguer in the corridors of power, an extreme hedonist who took along on trips a pot of diamonds to play with. What is known of him does not afford reliable guidance for surmises about his actions in the situation envisioned. He would have understood that his negotiating position could only be based on his ability to do further damage to Allied forces, and on his willingness to use or forego the opportunity. He would have understood equally that his ability to do damage could be enhanced by sacrificing untenable positions. He might have followed the advice of Kluge on a partial withdrawal in the west, thus avoiding the pocket at Falaise. He might have even authorized the withdrawal of German forces from France entirely. As a man concerned with the economic side of the war, he would probably have held on to Norway and Denmark in order to secure the material resources of Sweden. But he would have probably permitted Army Group North to retreat to more tenable positions, and generally tried to consolidate the Eastern Front somewhere east or southeast of East Prussia. He might have given one or the other order, as that for the retreat of Army

Group North, during the day of the attempted coup d'état, but most of his military decisions would have been delayed by events more immediately pressing.

Later in the afternoon of 20 July 1944, the news of Stauffenberg's return to Berlin and the coup d'état attempt in the capital would have reach Keitel. The headquarters might have reacted by denying Hitler's death. The moment of truth would have come when Major Remer, commanding officer of the Berlin Guard Battalion and acting under orders from the insurgents, tried to arrest Goebbels. If Goebbels had by this time been informed of the events in *Wolfschanze* and of Hitler's death, he might have confidently rung up Goering to let Remer speak to him. Had Goebbels been in the dark, he probably would have sought to reach the Fuehrer, but would have settled, for the moment at least, for the Fuehrer's successor. Goering would probably have sensed the importance of reassuring Remer and would have done his best, which would very likely have been very good, to convince Remer that he was the victim of traitors. If Goering had succeeded, events would have gone as they did: the coup d'état would have collapsed in the capital.

The coup d'état party had little to set against the formidable constitutional and physical resources of the *Wolfschanze* command center, which also controlled the fighting fronts and their supply. The odds were that they would have lost the battle for control of the Reich if Hitler had been dead and succeeded by Goering. The Berlin conspirators controlled only a few secondary command centers and training troops of the Home Army; they controlled even these forces uncertainly. Had Goering succeeded Hitler, it would have been probably just as difficult as it turned out to be on 20 July to move any troops into Berlin. With Goebbels still in office, the coup d'état party would equally have failed to gain control of the radio stations and transmitters which are so important in a modern dictatorship. There would probably not even have been a civil war, although there might have been altercations between Army and SS units here and there.

The situation in the military districts and military governments in the occupied territories was hardly more favorable for the success of the coup d'état in the case that Hitler had been killed and Goering had succeeded him. Had Goering emerged quickly as Hitler's successor, the officers in the military districts would very likely have transferred their loyalties to him at once.

Due to the uncertainty among the conspirators in Berlin about the success of Stauffenberg's assassination attack until he returned to tell of it, orders went out to military districts and command centers in Germany and in the occupied territories only late in the afternoon of 20 July. The orders claimed that Hitler was dead, they directed the immediate assumption of executive powers by Army forces, and the arrest and removal of the Nazi leadership in all its forms. In a good number of cases, these orders arrived in the absence of the commanding general, and in the absence, after duty hours, of his chief of staff. This caused delays independent of whether or not Hitler was alive. When the responsible officers were eventually confronted, some as early as about 5 P.M. others much later, with the coup orders to seize control of Nazi Party and government installations, they would have already received, or they would have received almost simultaneously, urgent messages from *Wolfschanze* insisting either on Hitler's survival and continued control, or on Goering's legal succession, and they would have demanded unquestioning loyalty in the interest of maintaining the fronts. Such an appeal would very likely have succeeded.

Thus, some of the events would have unfolded as they did. In Berlin, the leaders of the coup d'état were likely to have been shot, the survivors of the initial hasty court-martial held by the embarrassed Commander of the Home Army, Colonel-General

Fromm, would have been arrested by the Gestapo; in Prague, Vienna and Paris there would have been moves towards a seizure of control, and they would have been aborted during the night, and followed by arrests.

Goering would have sought to rally all of the state's forces by an appeal to völkisch and national-socialist ideals, by vowing to fulfill the Fuehrer's legacy and to redouble efforts to fight the enemies in the east, west and south to a standstill. But, hoping to be accepted by the Allies as a negotiating partner, he would probably have halted the mass murders in the concentration camps. Taking into consideration Goering's character and his record of having attempted to prevent war from breaking out and later from expanding, one may expect that he would have spared the surviving conspirators and attempted to use some of them for overtures to the Allies. The former ambassador in Moscow, Schulenburg, would probably have played a role, and the former ambassador in Rome, Hassell, who was an in-law of Goering, would have played a role and might have replaced Ribbentropp. Goering would have been confronted with the unconditional-surrender demand. He might have tried to steer a middle course between surrender and continued fighting along consolidated fronts. In the course of the next two or three weeks after the attempted coup d'état, perhaps after the fall of Paris, he might have been persuaded to install a government including members of the conspiracy in the hope of getting better terms for Germany.

Speculation beyond the first few days or weeks is futile. Even the most accomplished chess-players can not foresee more than a few moves although they are concerned with a finite situation and only one brain with which to interact. The Second World War was infinitely more complex. There is, search as one might, no evidence to suggest any modification of Allied war aims in case a more acceptable government were installed in Germany. The military balance would not have changed at all in favor of Germany. Thus the ultimate outcome of the war would have been the same. But the war would very likely have been concluded as much as half a year before 8 May 1945.

[1] Wolfgang Foerster, *Generaloberst Ludwig Beck: Sein Kampf gegen den Krieg*, Munich, 1953, p.122.
[2] Helmuth Groscurth, *Tagebucher eines Abwehroffiziers 1938-1940*, pp.236-237.
[3] Captain (Res.) Hermann Kaiser, diary 20 Feb. 1943 in *Generale: Neue Mitteilungen zur Vorgeschichte des 20. Juli*, Die Wandlung l (1945/46), p.531.
[4] *The Rommel Papers*, ed by B. Liddell Hart, Collins, London, 1953, pp. 486-487.
[5] Falkenhausen to Dr. Clemens Plassmann 24 March 1947. Max Domarus, *Hitler: Reden und Proklamationen 1932-1945*, Verlagsdruckerei Schmidt, Neustadt a.d.Aisch 1963, p.1316.

Chapter 11

Allied Drive to Berlin, April 1945

David M. Glantz

SHAEF Headquarters: Rheims, France, 15 April

The long anticipated order arrived at Eisenhower's headquarters at 1600 hours 15 April 1945. The Supreme Commander spent an hour digesting its contents and anticipating its implications before assembling his staff. In a quiet tone he began reading the order to his staff. "Proceed to Berlin with all deliberate speed!" Eisenhower paused until the muted applause had subsided and then read on, "Your objective is to secure as much of Germany east of the Elbe River as possible and Berlin itself. Take care to inform the Red Army of your objectives and do not engage Soviet forces unless in self defense. Concentrate your forces on the Magdeburg-Berlin axis with secondary attacks toward Stettin and Leipzig-Dresden. Assemble reserves to assure against any Soviet actions against you, and, if necessary, cordon off German forces in the Ruhr region rather than reducing them. The Russians are being informed of our intentions through proper channels. Good Luck, Marshall."

Although he understood the enthusiasm of his staff for an advance on Berlin and had been urged for days by his subordinates to pursue such a course, Eisenhower faced the task with mixed emotions. As he returned to his quarters after the staff meeting, he mentally catalogued the problems he faced. The political issue was clear to all. For weeks acerbic messages had passed between Roosevelt, Churchill, and Stalin over the fate of liberated territories and peoples in eastern Europe. Churchill, in particular, concerned over apparent Soviet violations of the Yalta accord, argued that only a *fait accompli* engineered on the battlefield could have any chance of holding Stalin to his promises concerning the democratization of Eastern Europe. Before his death, days before on 12 April, Roosevelt privately began sharing the same sentiment. His correspondence with Stalin displayed greater impatience, although, to his death, he still adhered to the agreement. The new President, Truman, was an unknown quantity, but it was conceivable he could alter U.S. policy to accord with Churchill's concerns. Apparently he had.

The military ramifications of the new order were even more daunting and fraught with uncertainty. A dash for Berlin was indeed possible, and military commanders well forward described the increasing disorganization in German opposition as they argued for a drive on Berlin. Both Bill Simpson of Ninth Army and George Patton of Third Army for days had pressed Eisenhower to ignore political considerations and exploit German military weakness with a drive directly eastward to Berlin. In fact, since Soviet forces had stood idle along the Oder River for over two months, they argued such a thrust could assist the Soviets as well.

Eisenhower was unsure. Weeks before, he had entertained such thoughts, but he had concluded since that peripheral questions such as securing North Sea ports and dealing with a potential and rumored German national redoubt in southern Germany also warranted his attention. Most important, Eisenhower feared what might occur should U.S., British, and Soviet forces adopt plans whose main thrusts converged on the same objectives, moreover on an objective the Soviets believed they had "blood rights"

to secure. "No," he concluded, "a simultaneous drive on Berlin would be fraught with danger."

Soon after, Eisenhower had issued plans which ostensibly shifted major forces away from the Berlin axis. Montgomery's 21st Army Group was to swing north and northeast to complete clearing of the Low Countries, the north German ports and southern Denmark. Dever's 6th Army Group was to wheel southeastward and advance into southern Germany on a broad front from Coburg to Baden Baden. The right wing of Bradley's 12th Army Group, Patton's Third Army, was to shift its axis of advance southward as well to support Dever's drive, although the bulk of Patton's strength was still north of the Thuringer Wald within striking distance of the Elbe.

This left only the remainder of Bradley's 12th Army Group available for a strike toward Berlin, and Bradley's group was not ideally postured to undertake the task. Eighteen of Bradley's divisions, including all of Gerow's Fifteenth Army and two corps of Hodge's First Army were busy reducing German Army Group B, encircled in the Ruhr, while several of Ninth and First Armies' divisions were dealing with a smaller encircled German force in the Harz Mountains. While Eisenhower could change the Ruhr "reduction" mission to simply "contain," in so doing releasing as many as half of these divisions for the more important Berlin mission, the released divisions would arrive forward piecemeal and only after completing extensive marches.

Thus 12th Army Group had only the forward elements of Ninth, First, and perhaps Third Army to employ in an immediate drive on Berlin, a force of about twenty divisions. They could be reinforced within three to seven days by as many as ten additional divisions. These forces were almost evenly distributed on a front from south of Wittenberge on the Elbe to the Thuringian Forest. To conduct a concentrated drive on Berlin, these forces would have to concentrate along the Elbe-Mulde River line, pierce those water barriers, isolate or reduce the major cities of Magdeburg, Dessau, Halle, Leipzig, and Chemnitz, penetrate the seventy kilometers to Berlin, perhaps reduce that city, and do so in coordination with potential Soviet actions.

As these considerations raced through Eisenhower's mind, his thoughts returned inevitably to the largest question — what will the Russians do? That question haunted Eisenhower's remaining waking hours as he mentally planned the options he would have his staff commit to paper in the morning.

83rd Infantry Division Headquarters: Barby, Germany, 15 April

As the sun settled hazily over the western horizon, frantic activity continued to animate the picturesque little German river village of Barby. Two days before, the U.S. 329th Infantry Regiment of General Mason's 83rd Infantry Division had, in quite leisurely fashion, crossed the Elbe River, where by nightfall it was joined in its bridgehead by full tank and tank destroyer battalions. Mason's good fortune was matched by 2nd Armored Division operating further north, which secured a small bridgehead near Madgeburg. Although 2nd Armored's bridgehead had subsequently been eliminated, by 15 April the 83rd Division's foothold became even more secure since during the evening before Combat Command R (CCR) of 2nd Armored Division had joined the bridgehead defenders and extended the bridgehead eight kilometers to the east. A sign over the bridge entrance captured the troops' mood, "Truman Bridge. Gateway to Berlin over the Elbe. Courtesy 83rd Thunderbolt Division."

General Simpson, Ninth Army Commander, echoed his troops' enthusiasm. Having entrusted his staff with planning "to enlarge the Elbe River bridgehead to include Potsdam," early on 15 April Simpson flew to Bradley's headquarters to argue his case for a further advance. After frustrating, day-long discussions, which included a phone call to Eisenhower, Simpson returned to his headquarters and then to Barby with his hopes for a further advance dashed. Despite Bradley's and Eisenhower's arguments that military problems alone precluded such a reckless course, Simpson was convinced they failed to comprehend German weakness. His mission that evening was to buoy the enthusiasm of this troops, in particular the 83rd Infantry Division in their precious bridgehead. Characteristically, Simpson let his staff continue to develop their plans. He mused to himself, "In spring, hope springs eternal."

At 1900 hours, as Simpson and Mason watched further reinforcements filter across the treadway bridge spanning the Elbe in the twilight, Mason's chief of staff approached and passed Simpson a small folded message. He read it silently, smiled, handed it to Mason, and said, "Your Remagen will be remembered as the launching pad for the final drive in the war. We're going to Berlin from Barby." Simpson ordered the enthusiastic Mason to enlarge the bridgehead in the morning and prepare for passage of 2nd Armored Division. Wishing him good night, Simpson hastened back to his headquarters to join his planning staff. There he found an order from Bradley summoning him and his chief of staff to Bradley's headquarters first thing the following morning.

12th Army Group Headquarters: 16 April

At 0800 hours 16 April Bradley, Hodges, Simpson, and Patton met to map out plans in accordance with Eisenhower's instructions. There was unanimity among the army commanders that quick work could be made of remaining German opposition, and Berlin could be reached within a week. Patton added the impolitic judgment that Russian military opposition could be easily dealt with as well. He suggested that perhaps the Oder River would be a better objective than just Berlin.

Bradley listened to his commanders but tempered their enthusiasm with hefty doses of reality concerning the problems associated with achieving success in such a plan. German eradication of 2nd Armored Division's bridgehead across the Elbe cast doubt on his field commanders' sanguine view of crumbling German opposition. Clearly some regrouping and concentration of forces would also be required to generate requisite strength for a rapid drive on Berlin. To sustain the drive and meet any unforeseen eventualities, the bulk of divisions tied down in the Ruhr and Harz Mountain regions would have to join Ninth and First Armies' attack force. Some modification would also have to be made in Montgomery's northern thrust to afford protection to Bradley's left flank and provide strength for the ultimate assault on Berlin. Earlier that morning Eisenhower had already informed Bradley that Montgomery's attack axis would shift eastward south of Bremen toward the Elbe River south of Hamburg. Montgomery's right flank, VIII Corps of Dempsey's Second Army, would strike the Elbe near Wittenberge to protect SImpson's left flank and support Ninth Army's drive on Berlin. Patton's XX and VIII Corps would have to reorient their axes of advance northwestward toward Chemnitz and Dresden, leaving XII corps to cover his ever-lengthening right flank. Some provision would also have to be made regarding major population centers like Magdeburg, Leipzig, and Dresden, whose reduction would take time and sap the strength of the main Berlin thrust.

The full day of deliberations among the army commanders produced a plan agreeable to all (see map 1). The 12th Army Group would initiate the final thrust across the Elbe and Mulde Rivers along three axes. Ninth and First Armies would attack jointly toward Berlin. The main attack by the joined flanks of the two armies would have XIX Corps advancing from Madgeburg and Barby toward Potsdam and VII Corps from the

171

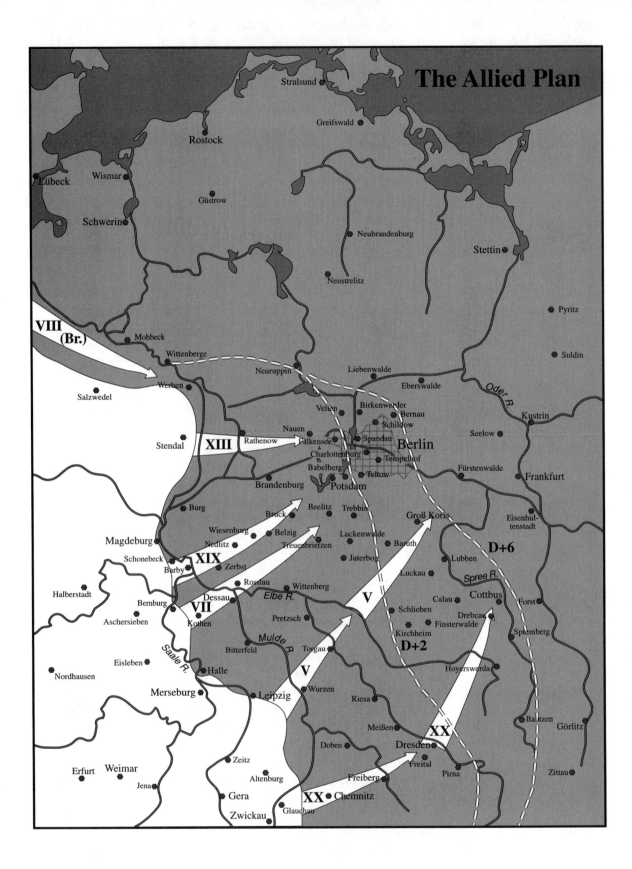

The Allied Plan

Dessau area toward Trebbin south of Berlin. Ninth Army's XIII Corps, followed and supported by XII British Corps would advance from the Wittenberge-Stendal region toward Rathenow and the northwest suburbs of Berlin. First Army's right flank V Corps would bypass Leipzig, cross the Mulde River at Wurzen and establish a bridgehead across the Elbe River at Torgau. On Bradley's right flank, Patton's XX and VIII Corps would advance via Chemnitz to establish bridgeheads across the Elbe in the Dresden area, while Patton's XII Corps would cover the long flank along the Erzgebirge (Mountains).

During the first phase of the operation, which was to last three days, 12th Army Group forces were to reach a phase line running from Neuruppin, through Potsdam, Trebbin, Luckenwalde, and Schlieben to east of Dresden. During the ensuing three days the operation would culminate in the seizure of Berlin and Cottbus. Ninth and First Armies would envelop Berlin from north and south, and Third Army would secure the Cottbus-Spremberg region. Bradley's forces would link up with Soviet forces occupying or advancing from the Kustrin bridgehead or across the Oder and Neisse Rivers. British XII Corps would establish security along Ninth Army's left flank from Wittenberge to Neuruppin and assist Simpson's envelopment of Berlin. The attack would begin at dawn on 17 April after only limited regrouping, and it would be spearheaded by forward forces. Other Ninth and First Army elements would deploy forward from the Ruhr and Harz regions as rapidly as possible to constitute a reserve and participate in phase two of the operation. All army commanders were ordered to bypass major cities if necessary to maintain the momentum of the advance.

The day of intense planning was punctuated in mid-morning by stunning news. Eisenhower radioed that the long awaited Soviet offensive had begun. Soviet forces were hammering German defenses along the Oder and Neisse Rivers from Kustrin to Gorlitz. He judged that the Soviet main efforts were from the Kustrin and Forst regions toward Berlin and Cottbus. Since quiet reigned north of Kustrin, it was apparent Soviet objectives coincided with those of the Western Allies. All immediately understood a race was on. Fewer understood the perils of that race. (see Map 2)

83d Infantry Division Headquarters: Barby, Germany, 16 April

At noon on 16 April an anxious General Mason received a cryptic order from Ninth Army headquarters. The news received earlier of the new Soviet offensive underscored the urgency of the order, which read, "Preliminary to launch of a general offensive toward Potsdam on 17 April, dispatch strong task forces to occupy Zerbst and Nedlitz and prepare for advance of division main force." Similar preparatory orders anticipating the new offensive were received by XIII Corps' 5th Armored Division, VII Corps' 3rd Armored Division, V Corps' 9th Armored Division, and XX Corps' 6th Armored Division. Mason quickly ordered formation and dispatch of a task force consisting of CCR 2nd Armored Division and two battalions from the 83rd Infantry Division. By nightfall this hastily assembled force had taken Zerbst and were preparing to move northwestward the following morning.

Soviet High Command (Stavka): Moscow 15 April

Stalin nervously paced his apartment in the Kremlin awaiting reports from Zhukov and Konev regarding the state of their offensive preparations. He had just received a report from Major General Shtemenko of the General Staff detailing Allied progress in central Germany. The news was disquieting, but Stalin congratulated himself that he

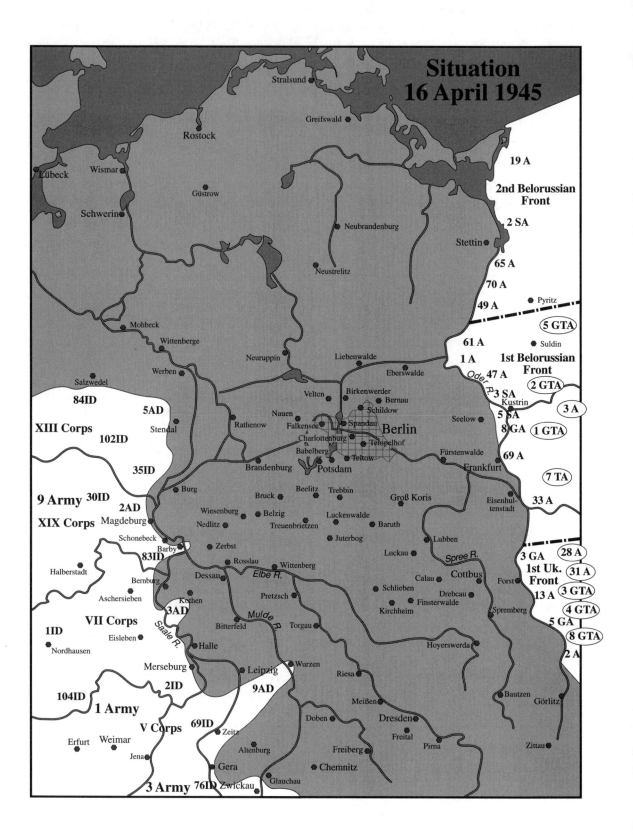

Situation
16 April 1945

had at least foreseen the shape and implications of Allied moves and was prepared to counter them.

In fact, since late January Allied strategy had been a subject of major concern. It was clear that once the Allies were over their shock in the Ardennes, the sheer weight of their resources would likely submerge Germany. And when forced to address the realities of the situation, it was clear that the Germans in general, and to an increasing extent their field commanders preferred to be overwhelmed by Americans and British rather than Soviets. It had therefore been prudent for Stalin to decide to halt his January offensive through Poland at the Oder River, although at that time his most forward forces were but 60 kilometers from Berlin. The excuse of long and vulnerable flanks was an adequate one to justify the halt and provide a smokescreen for his real motivation. Certainly, he reasoned, German forces in Silesia and Pomerania had threatened Soviet forces in their own right. They, however, had posed an even greater threat when considered in the context of another looming problem — that of growing Allied disagreement and the potential consequences should Allied armies move on Berlin.

The pause to regroup and eradicate German forces on the flanks, Stalin reflected, provided time to replenish manpower and equipment stocks for the final drive on Berlin. More importantly, it provided time to gauge Allied strategic intent and to gather sufficient strategic reserves necessary to deal militarily with any Allied attempt to violate provisions agreed to at Yalta.

Stalin mused to himself, "All that has now been done. The flanks have been cleared. German forces have been isolated in Courland, Zemland, and Danzig, forces are massing along the Oder River sufficient to crush the Germans and seize Berlin, and powerful reserves have been assembled to deal with Allied duplicity in this, the culminating period of the war." A pragmatist by trade, Stalin had proven his ability to define and ruthlessly pursue vital ends. Berlin was such an end.

Stalin recalled that less than two weeks earlier he and his commanders had put the seal on the final plan for termination of the German war. In meetings on 31 March and 1 April in Moscow, the assembled STAVKA and preeminent field commanders planned the Berlin operation, and coincidentally actions to be taken should Allied armies interfere. At the planning sessions he had remained preoccupied with Allied actions, noting a one point, "I think Roosevelt won't violate the Yalta accords, but as to Churchill, he wouldn't flinch at anything…"

How significant that comment had been. Now Roosevelt was dead, only to be succeeded by a political hack from the American outback who would be mere grist for Churchill's strong will. Those menacing Allied spearheads along the Elbe River bore ample witness that Truman had weakened and perhaps had already caved in to Churchill's desires.

Fortuitously, the planning session had anticipated such developments. The plan for a rapid two *front* thrust on Berlin incorporated operational variants for either Allied involvement or non-involvement. The delayed commitment of a third *front* to the north permitted freedom to shift forces into the Berlin-Cottbus sector to deal with Allied interference. Finally the large, superbly equipped Soviet strategic reserve assembled over several months would offer prospects for enforcing the Yalta agreement, by force if necessary.

Now on 15 April, Stalin mentally reviewed those measures and the plan for the Berlin operation as he awaited his *front* commanders' calls. Zhukov's 1st Belorussian and Konev's 1st Ukrainian Fronts would strike tomorrow toward Berlin and Cottbus. Zhukov's three center armies (3rd Shock, 5th Shock, and 8th Guards) would penetrate German defenses around the Kustrin bridgehead and march due west to envelop and reduce Berlin. Three right flank armies (61st, 1st Polish, and 47th) would bypass Berlin to the north and secure objectives along the Elbe River south of Wittenberge by the twelfth to fifteenth day of the operation. Zhukov's left flank 69th and 33rd Armies would plunge south of Berlin to the Beelitz and Juterbog region in the same time frame. Two tank armies (1st Guards and 2nd Guards) would support the main drive on Berlin. Once through German defenses, 2nd Guards Tank Army would shift north and reach the Liebenwalde region north of the city by D+4. Thereafter, depending on Allied actions, it would either swing south to envelop Berlin or continue westward leading the advance of Zhukov's right flank armies to their objectives.

Zhukov's reserve consisted of 3rd Army, 5th Guards Tank Army, and newly fielded 7th Tank Army, allocated from Stalin's strategic reserve. While Zhukov could employ 3rd Army as he saw fit, the other powerful armies were to be employed only on Stalin's personal orders in the event of an Allied attack on Berlin. Contingency plans called for 5th Guards Tank Army to cooperate with 2nd Guards Tank Army north of Berlin and 7th Tank Army to cooperate with 3d Army in support of Zhukov's forces operating south of Berlin.

Konev's front was to conduct its main attack across the Neisse River south for Forst toward Cottbus and Spremberg with three armies (3rd Guards, 13th and 5th Guards), while two armies (2nd Polish, 52nd) launched a secondary attack further south toward Bautzen and Dresden. The five combined-arms armies were to secure the line of the Elbe River from Juterbog south to Dresden by the tenth to twelfth day of the operation. Two tank armies would join battle after German defenses along the Neisse River had been penetrated. Thereafter the two armies would lead the drive westward, in one of two variants. If Allied forces halted along the Elbe, 3rd Guards Tank Army could shift its axis of advance northward to join Zhukov's 2nd Guards Tank Army in enveloping and reducing Berlin. The 4th Guards Tank Army, in this case, would sweep northwestward to the Potsdam area to assist in isolating Berlin and to support the combined arms armies' advance to the Elbe. In the event of interference, the two tank armies were to advance westward in tandem toward the Juterbog and Torgau regions, flanked on the right by 3rd Army and 7th Tank Army. Konev's reserve consisted of 28th and 31st Armies and newly formed 8th Tank Army from the strategic reserves. Like Zhukov, Konev could employ the two combined-arms armies as he saw fit, but could use the tank army only in the event of Allied intervention. In that case 28th Army would advance to support 3rd and 4th Guards Tank Armies north of Torgau, while 31st and 8th Armies drove to the Elbe between Torgau and Dresden.

Rokossovsky's 2nd Belorussian Front, with five combined arms armies supported by several separate mobile corps, had orders to delay its attack until 20 April. By that time Allied intentions should have become clear. If the Allies halted at the Elbe, Rokossovsky's front would plunge across northern Germany south of Stettin to secure the line Wittenberge, Waren, Demmin, Anklem by the twelfth to fifteenth day of the operation. If Allied forces moved on Berlin, Rokossovsky could shift his axis of advance southward to support Zhukov's drive to and beyond Berlin.

In the event of Allied interference, Stalin assessed that Zhukov and Konev had sufficient force to isolate Berlin and secure initial front objectives. The three tank armies from the strategic reserve (5th Guards, 7th, and 8th) would be sufficient to drive Allied forces beyond initial objectives lines through Magdeberg, Leipzig, and Chemnitz and perhaps further. In no case would Stalin order an advance beyond the demarcation line agreed to at Yalta. This he intended to declare openly to Churchill, Truman, and Eisenhower should conflict with Allied forces appear imminent.

Stalin's musings were interrupted as Shtemenko arrived with word that both Zhukov and Konev were ready to render their evening reports. Both declared that all was in order for timely commencement of the offensive. Before retiring in the wee hours of the morning, as was his custom, Stalin ordered intensified aerial and long-range ground *razvedka* (intelligence collection) west of Berlin and Dresden and along the Elbe to determine Allied intentions.

12th Army Group Headquarter: 17 April

All eyes were glued to the wall-size situation map as the 12th Army Group operations officer delivered the 1800 hour briefing to General Bradley and his staff. The officer laconically related the day's action from north to south in the army group's sector.

Ninth Army's XIX Corps had expanded its bridgehead east of Barby, seizing Zerbst and reaching the outskirts of Wiesenburg, where elements of German 349th Infantry Division, supported by a tank battalion, brought the advanced to a halt. XIII Corps consolidated its positions west of the Elbe near Stendal and prepared to cross the river on 18 April. First Army's spearheads (3rd Armored and 9th Armored) likewise secured bridgeheads across the Elbe and Mulde Rivers near Rosslau and Wurzen while Third Army's 6th and 4th Armored Divisions bypassed Chemnitz and reached the outskirts of Freiberg, halfway between Chemnitz and Dresden.

The process of generating reserves accelerated as 1st Infantry Division disengaged from its Harz Mountain battles and moved forward, and six of Ninth and First Army's divisions in the Ruhr assembled and prepared for forward movement with a tentative arrival date of 20 April. German resistance was spotty, with the best organized opposition in the Magdeburg, Wiesenberg, and Dessau sectors, where scattered German Twelfth Army elements were defending. Bradley concluded the session by ordering all of his armored spearheads, in particular those of XIII, XIX, and VII Corps of Ninth and First Armies, to accelerate their advance.

1st Belorussian Front Headquarters: Kustrin 17 April

Zhukov listened nervously to the evening situation reports. The carnage on his front was appalling as his forces repeatedly assaulted German positions on the Seelow Heights. His decision to commit both of his tank armies to battle in the small bridgehead on this, the first day of battle, only complicated the task of coordinating so large an assault force, and now the nearly 1,000 tanks at his disposal were dispersed in pockets and locked in close tactical combat with enemy strongpoints. With movement restricted, the tanks were being decimated by *panzerfausts* seemingly in the hands of every German old enough to carry one. At this stage, Zhukov reasoned there is nothing more I can do than smash the defenses frontally, once and for all.

That, of course, would take time, and Stalin's repeated queries did nothing to assuage Zhukov's growing bad mood. To his chagrin, reports from Konev's sector to the south were more optimistic. Konev's combined-arms armies had forced the Neisse River and were progressing well through the German defenses on the west bank of the river. And Konev had not yet committed his two tank armies. Zhukov could imagine the result when those armies went into a clean penetration. In essence, while his armor slugged it out for days with German defenders—losing strength by the hour—Konev's tank armies, once committed, would have a clear road forward. The implication was clear to Zhukov. Konev may well share in the seizure of Berlin.

But then Zhukov recalled the ominous report passed to his front intelligence elements from the GRU just an hour before. According to aerial *razvedka*, Allied armored columns had been detected moving east of the Elbe south of Magdeberg. "Is this an isolated incident," thought Zhukov, "or a portent of things to come?" Only time would tell, but at least, in this instance, it should give Konev cause for concern.

CCA Headquarters, 2nd Armored Division: Belzig, Germany 18 April

CCA 2nd Armored Division, reinforced by one regiments of the 83rd Infantry Division, finally overcame German defenses at Belzig at 1800 hours. Heavy afternoon showers had restricted movement along the roads. Although organized German resistance was light, the constant harassing fire of groups of Germans armed with the ubiquitous *panzerfausts* forced the column to repeatedly halt. Infantry, supported by tank and anti-tank gunfire, rooted the Germans from farmsteads, each of which functioned like a fortified strongpoint. VII Corps' 3rd Armored Division, whose gunfire could be heard to the south, was experiencing the same delays, but nevertheless kept pace with 2nd Armored.

By evening, news arrived that 9th Armored Division of V Corps had succeeded in seizing Torgau on the Elbe, and, further south, Patton's 4th and 6th Armored Divisions were within 10 kilometers of Dresden, although increased resistance now also slowed their advance. The 2nd Armored Division G-2 reported heavy fighting in the Soviet bridgeheads west of the Oder and Neisse Rivers, but apparently German defenders had prevented a precipitous Soviet breakout westward. The operations officer did some quick calculations and estimated that Potsdam was only 45 kilometers distant, while Soviet forces were still about 50 kilometers from the eastern suburbs of Berlin. It was clear the race could still be won.

1st Ukrainian Front Headquarters, along the Spree River (5km North of Spremberg): 2100 18 April

Konev, at his forward command post located near the command post of General Pukhov's 13th Army, noted the briefer's words with satisfaction. German defenses along the Spree River between Cottbus and Spremberg had been thoroughly ruptured (While Zhukov further north struggled for operational freedom). Throughout the day he had watched with pride for hours as Rybalko's [3rd Guards Tank Army] two lead tank corps crossed the water obstacle, fanned out in multiple columns, and sped to the west. Just kilometers south, Lelyushenko's [4th Guards Tank Army] mobile corps were making even better progress. His advanced brigades would penetrate 45 kilometers west of the Spree before calling a halt for a night's rest.

This, of course, made his immediate task even more urgent. Detailed orders would have to be dispatched to re-direct those armies' forward detachments in the proper direction before they were too deep in the German rear. "Good God," mused Konev, "It is certainly better now than it had been in the early war years, when scarcely any objective could be taken on time." The message causing Konev concern had been received but twenty minutes before. It read:

To Stepan [Konev's codename]
Allied forces crossing the Elbe River vicinity Magdeburg, Dessau, and Wurzen with apparent intent of moving on Berlin. It is imperative you secure *front* initial objectives without delay.

I order:

(a) Advance your two tank armies to line Potsdam, Beelitz, Wittenberge, Torgau and support with two combined-arms armies, while containing by-passed German forces and sealing off southern approaches to Berlin.

(b) Secure line of Elbe River from Torgau to Dresden and westward to Pretzsch with remaining combined-arms armies and mobile corps.

(c) Advance your second echelon armies (28th, 31st) to Luckau-Finsterwalde regions, but do not commit until receipt of STAVKA orders.

(d) 8th Tank Army remains under STAVKA control but will relocate to the Drebcau region to await further orders.

(e) 7th Tank Army will shift to your *front* sector, east of Neisse River.

(f) To speed your advance employ strong reinforced forward detachments in advance of your main force.

(g) Plan multi-brigade-size airborne assaults in the Beelitz and Torgau regions for evening of 19-20 April.

(h) *Front* boundary with Zhukov extended from Lubben to Potsdam.

Igor [Stalin]

Within two hours Konev's new orders were complete and had been dispatched to his armies. His orders reflected Stalin's desires:

I order:

3rd Guards Tank Army to advance via Calau, Luckau, and Luckenwalde to secure Beelitz-Potsdam region, block advance of Allied forces to Berlin and westward withdrawal of Berlin enemy group. Link up with air assault force vicinity Beelitz on 20 April. 3rd Guards Army — cover right flank of *front* advance on front Cottbus-Lubben-Gross Koris and support advance of 3rd Guards Tank Army. 13th Army — follow and support 3rd Guards Tank Army. With one corps isolate German forces in Berlin from the south. 4th Guards Tank Army — Advance via Finsterwald and Schlieben to Juterbog and Wittenberg on Elbe River. Secure Elbe River line from Wittenburg to Pretzsch. 5th Guards Army — support advance of 4th Guards Tank Army and secure objective along Elbe River between Pretzsch and Riesa. 2nd Polish Army — advance to secure Elbe River line between Riesa and Dresden. 52nd Army — secure *front* left flank from Dresden to Corlitz, 4th Guards Tank Corps precede the advance and link up with airborne assault force east of Torgau on 20 April. Begin advance effective 0500 19 April.

By separate orders, Konev arranged for the two airborne drops to occur simultaneously at 2000 on 19 April, hopefully before Allied forces had reached the areas.

One hundred kilometers to the north, Zhukov fumed over his lack of success. Despite constant goading from Stalin, his forces still wallowed deep in the German defenses. He too had received new orders "to push 2nd Guards Tank and 47th Armies westward north of Berlin to the Velten area by evening 20 April." Zhukov well knew that the order was impossible to fulfill. Moreover, Stalin seemed to realize that fact as he shifted 7th Tank Army southward into Konev's sector. Zhukov realized he was about to become subject to two indignities. First, he would likely share the glories of conquering Berlin with Konev. Second, his forces would play only a secondary role in the larger issue of the race with the Allies for Berlin.

2nd Armored Division Headquarters: Bruck, Germany 2400 19 April

Rumors of a Soviet airborne drop ran rampant through headquarters, although hard intelligence concerning such an event was difficult to come by. Ninth Army light observation aircraft and ground personnel detected heavy, low-level aircraft traffic in the Beelitz area. Radio intercept units shortly after 2200 hours picked up short radio transmissions in Russian, and what little could be translated indicated some Russian ground activity east of Beelitz.

Even more fascinating were sketchy reports from First Army, which told of Russian paratroopers landing in scattered fashion in the rear of 9th Armored Division's bridgehead east of Torgau. All that could be gleaned from these fragmentary reports was that some Russians surrendered peacefully, while others opened fire and were then shot.

To confirm or dispell these rumors or at least those in his sector, General White, 2nd Armored Division commander, ordered a reconnaissance in force be dispatched at 0300 to determine what action, if any, was going on east of Beelitz. The 2nd Armored Division's main force was to resume its advance at 0500 in tandem with 3rd Armored spearheads operating further south.

12th Army Group Headquarters: Magdeburg 0200 20 April

The long night for Bradley had become even longer as report after strange report reached his headquarters. The day's news, until evening, had been fine. XIII Corps' 5th Armored Division had secured Rathenow by 1500 hours and then had moved eastward toward Nauen with corps infantry following in its wake. XIX and VII Corps' spearheads were approaching Beelitz, V Corps had secured a sizeable lodgement over the Elbe River east of Torgau, and Patton's spearhead had done likewise northwest of Dresden. Then, at midnight, disconcerting reports arrived from both Ninth and First Armies.

Reports of a potential Russian airborne drop in the Beelitz region, although it could not be confirmed until the next morning, were consistent with reports which soon after arrived from First Army. Hodge's headquarters, shortly after 2230 hours, recounted how numerous Russian paratroopers, identified from the 3rd Airborne Brigade, landed in the center of its bridgehead about 2 kilometers east of the Elbe bridge at Torgau. Scattered groups of paratroopers opened fire on American logistical vehicles and moved along the highway toward the eastern approach to the bridge. Short of the bridge, a reserve armored battalion and a company of infantry engaged the force, killing or wounding thirty and capturing forty before the remainder fled. Other small groups of Russians offered resistance until convinced that the "German enemy" were really Americans. Disarmed Russians (including a major) reported their missions was to seize and hold the bridge against the Germans until the arrival of a Russian mobile ground force, expected to arrive in less than two days time.

Bradley was visibly upset by the reports and immediately contacted Eisenhower's headquarters. "What," asked Eisenhower, "are Russians doing along the Elbe? Their offensive is still struggling to escape the Oder and Neisse bridgeheads." Bradley assured Eisenhower these troops were really Russians and not Germans in Russian disguise (à la Kampfgruppe Peiper in the Ardennes). He added his opinion that perhaps Russian progress in the Cottbus sector was better than anticipated, and this airdrop was an attempt to forestall further American movement east. "If so," Eisenhower interjected, "it is a clumsy attempt. In any case proceed according to plan, Brad, and I will clear things with Washington."

Bradley at 0300 hours ordered Simpson to report as soon as possible on the situation at Beelitz. To Hodges, he wired, "Proceed according to plan, but with caution. Employ all means of reconnaissance."

The White House, Washington, D.C.: 2300 19 April (0500 20 April German time)

Marshall phoned President Truman as soon as he had confirmed news of the Russian paradrop along the Elbe. He related the evening's event to Truman and added his views regarding possible Russian motivation. After a pause Truman said, "I agree with your assessment. Stalin knows our intent and is signalling us his. I will find out what is at the bottom of this. In the meantime advance according to plan, but insure our movements are well-coordinated and properly supported."

Within an hour Truman dispatched a message to Stalin with a copy to Churchill. It read:

> I have clearly outlined our plans to you — that is to advance with all speed to assist your operations along the Oder and destroy German forces. We cannot do so if interfered with by Soviet parachute forces dropping in our path.
>
> Our operations will proceed according to the plans outlined to you. To preclude nasty incidents, I request you also share your plans with me and my senior commanders. We intend no harm to your forces and believe you share our concerns as well.

> Truman

Churchill's response arrived within one hour. It cryptically noted Russian intentions to take Berlin come-what-may and encouraged Truman to adhere to his plan and brook no further interference from Stalin. Truman took the additional precaution of wiring Eisenhower to alert all strategic air forces for possible employment in the near future on missions other than bombing Berlin.

STAVKA, Moscow: 1000 20 April (0900 German time)

Stalin, forced to interrupt his morning sleep by a message from the General Staff, was in a foul mood. He read Truman's message uttered an oath, and summoned Antonov and Shtemenko. "What is the status of our airborne drop?"

Shtemenko related that the Beelitz drop had been successful, and the 1st Brigade had occupied the village and blocked all roads through it. Unfortunately, he added, there was no communication with 3d Brigade near Torgau. Light aircraft had attempted to establish communication but were driven off by antiaircraft fire, presumably American.

"Has the situation changed at Kustrin?" asked Stalin.

"Zhukov reports slow progress, but a possible full penetration of German defenses by nightfall," whispered Antonov, who then volunteered, "but Konev's tank armies are moving at full speed toward their objectives. 7th Tank Army is due by midday in Konev's rear area east of the Neisse."

"I have provided Truman and Churchill my plan and objectives," growled Stalin, "but they have ignored them. And they now expect me to respect theirs. We shall see whose plan is most effective."

"And," he silently thought, "who has the will to carry it out."

Turning to Antonov, he directed him to radio Konev — but, thinking better of it, asked for the phone to Konev's headquarters. When Konev had been found, Stalin said to him, "Tell Rybalko [3d Guards Tank Army] and Lelyushenko [4th Guards Tank Army] to allow no one to hinder their march to my objectives." As if to purge his soul of the message's bad tidings, he rang up Zhukov to tell him, "You have two days to reach Berlin and no longer. When you do so, launch Sinenko's army [5th Guards Tank Army]

181

to link up with Rybalko near Potsdam." He menacingly added, "If you fail, there are other Marshals who would gladly do so."

3rd Guards Tank Army Headquarters: 10 kms NW of Calau, Germany 0800 20 April

Rybalko watched from his command post as the tail end of General Mitrofanov's 6th Guards Tank Corps would its way northwestward. It was a fine corps, led by the superb 53rd Guards Tank Brigade of General Arkhipov. Arkhipov was fulfilling the mission given personally by Konev to Rybalko, "Lead your advance with your best brigade. Reinforce it with all it needs to reach Beelitz within 24 hours. I want the rest of the corps to arrive within 36 hours." It was not an unreasonable mission. Mitrofanov's corps had performed similar feats on numerous occasions in the Ukraine and southern Poland — and against a more formidable enemy. Yet today there was a special tension in Konev's and Rybalko's orders. For a new enemy might be at hand.

12th Army Group Headquarters: 1600 20 April

"Damn those paratroopers," mumbled Bradley to his chief of staff. His anger was well founded for Hodge's spearhead 2nd Armored Division had been faced with a day-long dilemma. The Russian airborne force had seized a 2 to 4 kilometer square area around Beelitz and now blocked all the roads through the town. Although they had not fired on the American tank column, their menacing presence prevented the division from using the main road to Potsdam.

Both 2nd Armored Division and XIX Corps headquarters reacted to the dilemma cautiously but with imagination. Leaving two infantry battalions and two tank companies under 83rd Infantry Division control to isolate the Russians in the town, the remainder of 2nd Armored, supported by the 83rd Infantry, bypassed the town to the north and, by nightfall, reached within 8 kilometers of Potsdam. Inexplicably, German resistance lessened as the columns swept around Beelitz as if an open German invitation was being offered the Americans to enter the city. Bradley intended to continue the drive despite the Russians, and, to that end, he ordered Hodges to advance the 35th and 30th Infantry Divisions, whose lead elements were then just south of Brandenburg, to hasten forward and support 2nd Armored division. The armored division itself was to "secure Potsdam and the western suburbs of Berlin on the axis Potsdam-Zehlendorf-Charlottenburg."

The more vexing problem for Bradley was VII Corps' situation. Its lead 3rd Armored Division confronted Russian road blocks leading to Beelitz from the southwest, and no one was certain what Russian forces were moving to support the paratroopers. Intense reconnaissance in early afternoon over the Luckenwalde area to the southeast of Beelitz revealed no Russian presence. Radio intercept, however, picked up heavy Russian radio activity further southeast, but local cloud cover precluded aerial detection of any Russian forces.

Bradley's orders were clear, and both he and Hodges resolved to carry them out. In a calculated risk that Russian forces were still far to the southeast, Bradley and Hodges ordered 3rd Armored Division to bypass Beelitz to the south and march on the southwestern outskirts of Berlin via Trebbin toward Teltow. The division reconnoitered routes south of Beelitz during the evening, and the division, led by Combat Command A reinforced with 104th Infantry Division riflemen was to follow at 0500 hours the next day. While 3rd Armored advanced, the 104th Infantry was to contain Russian forces at Beelitz, reconnoiter southeast toward Luckenwalde, and await relief by 1st Infantry Division, then moving northeast from the Dessau area. 7th Armored Division, just returned from the Ruhr and assembled at Kothen under VII Corps control, was to hasten forward to the Beelitz area the next day.

Concerned about XIX and VII Corps' troubled progress toward Berlin, Bradley urged Simpson to add the weight of XIII Corps to the assault on the city. The 5th Armored Division, then approaching Nauen against slackening resistance, was to drive through Nauen toward Spandau and Charlottenburg to link up with 2nd Armored's thrust further south. The 84th and 102nd Infantry Divisions would provide immediate support, and both 75th and 95th Infantry Divisions were now racing forward toward and across the Elbe.

The situation on Simpson's left flank was unsettling and put his flank in jeopardy. Although 29th Infantry Division had seized an Elbe crossing at Werben, British VIII Corps had not yet concentrated in the area to commence its supporting thrust on XIII Corps' left. Although that advance was to materialize on the 21st, clearly Simpson was on his own in his attempt to seize Berlin.

Further south Hodges' V Corps and Patton's reinforced XX Corps were well east of the Elbe at Torgau and north of Dresden. With open country before them, only Russian interference could prevent a successful advance on Cottbus. Late intelligence reports from ground reconnaissance units of both corps indicated little opposition but intense Russian air reconnaissance activity.

1st Belorussian Front Headquarters: Kustrin, Germany 2000 20 April

Bogdanov's [2nd Guards Tank Army] message reached Zhukov as he consulted with General Kuznetsov of 3rd Shock Army. It read, "9th Guards Tank Corps secured Bernau and is approaching Schildow. 1st Mechanized and 12th Guards Tank Corps cooperating with 79th Rifle and 12th Guards Rifle Corps of 3rd Shock. Prepared to advance on northeast suburbs of city this evening."

Four days and only 40 kilometers of miserable German turf, thought Zhukov. But then Stalin had said twenty-four hours before, "You have two days to enter Berlin," and now Zhukov would do so. The problem, however, was not just entering Berlin. Intelligence reports indicated American movement on the city from the west was imminent. Only Zhukov's forces could forestall that move.

Zhukov delayed no longer. He phoned Stalin, reported the situation, and asked for release of 5th Guards Tank Army to his control. Stalin hesitated and then asked, "For what purpose?"

Zhukov replied, "To advance via Velten to Falkensee to envelop the city from the north and northwest."

"Can you reach Falkensee in 24 hours?" questioned Stalin.

A hot flash enveloped Zhukov as he replied, "Yes."

"Then do so," replied Stalin, "you have the 5th Guards Tank Army."

Putting down the receiver, Zhukov noticed a barely perceptible tremor in his hands. Turning to Sokolovsky, his deputy commander, he said, "Order Sinenko to assemble his army east of Bernau by noon tomorrow and then immediately advance north of Berlin via Velten to Falkensee. He must reach Falkensee by 0800 tomorrow."

As Sokolovsky departed to dispatch the message, Zhukov hoped Sinenko could repeat the feats his predecessor Rotmistrov had so often accomplished. He almost wished Rotmistrov, with his 7th Tank Army, was available to perform the mission. But then, he thought, Rotmistrov has an equally important mission to perform further south — in Konev's sector. Zhukov could barely suppress a sneer.

CCB Headquarters, 9th Armored Division: Kirchheim, Germany 0915 21 April

Two clusters of tanks awkwardly faced one another on opposite ends of a clearing along the road running east from Kirchheim. Both had prudently withheld fire long enough to discern neither was German. An American captain advanced down the road under a white flag accompanied by a sergeant and a private. There, in the middle of the road midway between the two forces, they met a party of four Russians, one apparently an officer. The captain turned to the private and said, "You're the only one here from Chicago. Do your stuff." It was fortunate the man could speak Russian, for it would take more than sign language to handle this affair.

The meeting went on under glaring sunlight for almost an hour. Halfway through the discussions an older Russian Colonel joined the entourage and introduced himself as Colonel Dushak of 12th Guards Tank Brigade of General Poluboyarov's 4th Guards Tank Corps. He explained his mission, and, after the American explained his, the two agreed to halt operations while seeking instructions from higher headquarters. As the tension abated, the Russian colonel's aide appeared carrying two bottles of vodka. There, in the clearing, the groups passed the bottle as apprehension ebbed, and the small cluster of Americans and Russians toasted the end of the war.

With the 53d Guards Tank Brigade, 3rd Guards Tank Army: 7 Kilometers south of Trebbin, Germany 1000 21 April

Whipped on by repeated orders for haste from Mitrofanov and even Rybalko himself, General Arkhipov drove his brigade mercilessly forward. Although he had faced little resistance since his march commenced before dawn, he realized he was but 20 kilometers south of Berlin and the same distance from his objective of Potsdam. Resistance was bound to materialize, and it would likely be fanatic. Arkhipov had survived long enough to realize only bold action could overcome resistance and reduce losses. Bypassing Luckenwalde to the east, his columns raced northward toward Trebbin. At exactly 1000 hours he heard gunfire to the north and soon after received a report from his brigade reconnaissance element. "Enemy forces with two tanks manning a road-block on the highway. I can outflank if the main body can deal with the problem."

Arkhipov approved the request and ordered his 1st and 2nd Battalions to destroy the enemy and continue the march. The fight was brief. In the morning haze, both enemy tanks were destroyed, the small force was overrun, and two prisoners were taken. At 1020 hours, as he approached the smoking hulks along the road, Arkhipov was greeted by a sweating captain who reported in nervous tones, "The lst and 2nd Battalions are continuing their advance. The road-block was an American one."

Arkhipov gasped, and after a moment of silence, said, "Halt the battalions and reconnaissance element and await further instructions. Where is my radioman?"

Headquarters 3rd Armored Division: 6 Kilometers West of Trebbin 1030 21 April

General Hickey was livid, but spoke in slow measured tones. The report which had arrived just fifteen minutes before read, "Under attack by large force of over 20 tanks. Am outflanked and taking heavy losses. The enemy are…" The transmission cut off in mid-sentence. Shortly thereafter, aerial reconnaissance reports from First Army reported Russian forces moving in force northward through and around Luckenwalde. Intelligence also noted peaceful contact with Russian forces near Kirchheim.

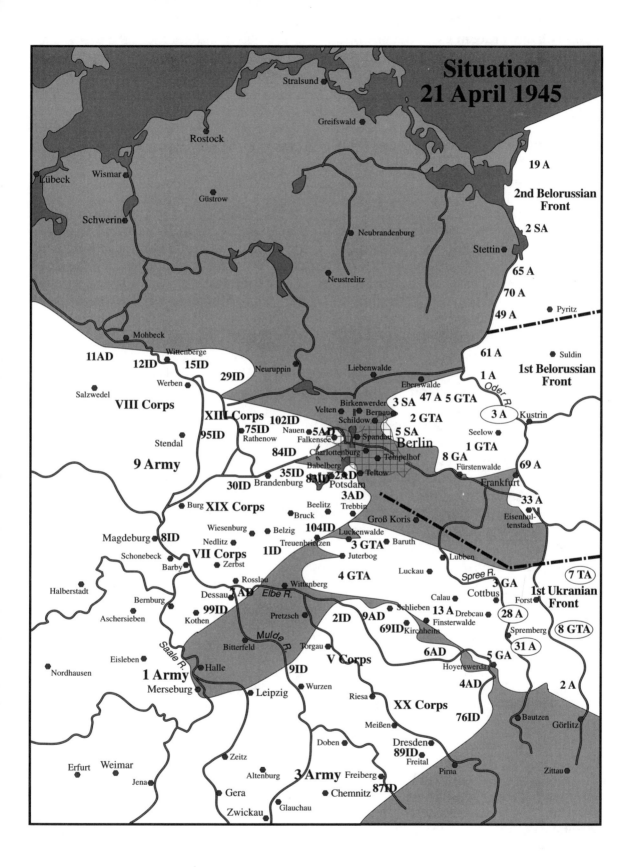

Situation 21 April 1945

Stralsund

Greifswald

19 A

Rostock

2nd Belorussian
Front

Lübeck Wismar

Güstrow

2 SA

Schwerin

Neubrandenburg

Stettin

65 A

Neustrelitz

70 A

49 A Pyritz

Mohbeck

61 A Suldin

11AD Wittenberge

12ID 15ID Neuruppin Liebenwalde

1 A 1st Belorussian
Front

29ID Eberswalde Oder R.

Werben

3 SA 47 A 5 GTA

Salzwedel

Birkenwerder 2 GTA

3 A Kustrin

VIII Corps XIII Corps 102ID Velten Bernau

Schildow 5 SA

95ID 75ID Rathenow Nauen 5AD Spandau Berlin Seelow

84ID Charlottenburg 8 GA 1 GTA

Stendal Babelberg Tempelhof Fürstenwalde 69 A

9 Army 35ID Teltow 2AD

30ID Brandenburg Potsdam Frankfurt

Burg XIX Corps 3AD Beelitz Trebbin 33 A

Bruck Eisenhul-
tenstadt

Wiesenburg Belzig Groß Koris

Magdeburg 8ID Nedlitz 104ID Luckenwalde

Schonebeck VII Corps 1ID Treuenbrietzen 3 GTA Baruth Lubben

Barby Zerbst Juterbog Luckau 7 TA

Rosslau 4 GTA Spree R. 1st Ukranian
Front

Halberstadt Dessau AD Wittenberg Elbe R. 3 GA

Bernburg 99ID Pretzsch Calau Cottbus 28 A 8 GTA

Aschersleben Kothen 2ID 9AD Schlieben 13 A Drebcau Forst 31 A

Nordhausen Eisleben Bitterfeld Mulde R. Torgau 69ID Kirchheim Finsterwalde Spremberg

Halle 9ID 6AD 5 GA Hoyerswerda

1 Army Wurzen V Corps 4AD 2 A

Merseburg Leipzig Riesa XX Corps 76ID Bautzen Görlitz

Meißen

Doben Dresden Zittau

Erfurt Weimar Zeitz 89ID Freital Pirna

Altenburg Freiberg 87ID

Jena 3 Army

Gera Chemnitz

Zwickau Glauchau

"Peaceful!" snorted Hickey, "ask my security outposts south of Trebbin." He immediately ordered CCB, then passing west of Trebbin to detour into the town and establish a defense line around its southern outskirts. CCR, then marching toward Trebbin from the west, was to halt and establish defenses facing south to await relief by the trailing 104th Infantry Division. Then the still angry Hickey reported the situation to VII Corps.

3rd Guards Tank Army Headquarters: Baruth, Germany 1115 21 April

Rybalko was shocked. It was as if all the adrenaline driving him for days had suddenly run out, leaving him utterly exhausted. The report from Mitrofanov lay limply on the hood of his *"Willys."* Certainly, Rybalko reasoned, Mitrofanov had acted properly. He himself had contributed to 53rd Guards Tank Brigade's action by underscoring the urgency of its mission. And wars seldom end cleanly. He approved Mitrofanov's request to halt and issued similar orders to General Novikov's 7th Guards Tank Corps. Novikov's corps had already reached the rail line running north from Juterbog, and his lead brigade and reconnaissance units were nearing Treuenbrietzen. Here they would remain.

Within minutes Rybalko was in contact with Konev's headquarters at Calau. He detailed what had occurred south of Trebbin and his subsequent actions. Konev, having been informed an hour before of the situation in 4th Guards Tank Corps' sector, approved of both Mitrofanov's and Rybalko's actions, but emphasized the continued importance of seizing Berlin:

" STAVKA does not wish confrontation with the Allies, but it does wish to take Berlin. All *front* forces are to continue their advance until contact is made with the Allies. Coordination measures in that regard are being worked out. However, in sectors where Germans are still in control, operations will continue. Regarding your army, move Sukhov's 9th Mechanized Corps northward to Berlin as rapidly as possible. There it will cooperate with Zhukov's forces in seizing the city. Expect support from 28th Army within 24 hours."

Konev sighed as he reconciled himself to what would probably be the end of the war. He felt personal affront lest in this, the last operation, he would fail to secure his original objectives. Only the knowledge that he still had a role to play in conquering Berlin assuaged his melancholy. He had an immense force at his disposal — seven combined-arms armies and two fully blooded tank armies. Backing them up were the superbly equipped 7th and 8th Tank Armies under the experienced Rotmistrov and Rodin. What more could a *front* commander ask for? But now Konev's fame rested in part on the actions of a single corps—Sukhov's 9th Mechanized.

As he walked away from the *"Willys,"* the thought occurred to him that perhaps it was not yet time to fight Americans.

12th Army Group Headquarters: 1400 21 April

Bradley had immediately passed Hodges' report to Eisenhower, who had, in turn, notified Truman and Churchill. The reaction to the news of Soviet actions south of Trebbin was simultaneous on the part of all three Allied players. Messages dispatched to Stalin lamented the actions, underscored the joint nature of these final operations, and conveyed a thinly veiled threat of the consequences of further such incidents. All three ended their transmission with suggestions for coordinated measures to be worked out between Eisenhower's, Bradley's, Zhukov's, and Konev's headquarters. All three underscored the fact that future political boundaries would result only from further negotiations and expressed a desire they not be settled by force.

STAVKA: Moscow 1800 21 April (1700 Berlin Time)

Ambassador Harriman delivered Truman's message to Stalin in person. Stalin had anticipated its contents, read it in silence, lit his pipe, looked directly at Harriman, and said,

> "I certainly share Truman's concerns and regret the day's unpleasant incident. However, this is war, and when Allies are not forthright in declaring their intent, soldiers often suffer. I have ordered my forces in the affected sector to cease operations and coordinate closely with American forces. This cannot, however, apply to areas where Germans still struggle — specifically Berlin which was, as I clearly stated, and still is our objective. We will pay in blood for its conquest, but we have also earned that right with our blood. Prudence and humanity argue the folly of American and British attempts to seize territory they by right and by previous agreement will have to relinquish once Hitler has been crushed. Zhukov is commencing the conquest of Berlin at this hour. If further incidents are to be avoided, Eisenhower had best coordinate closely with him."

Alone, Stalin paced the floor of his study after Harriman's departure. There were, he thought, no grounds for an apology over the incident at Trebbin. In fact, American impudence, goaded on by the British, could have produced more serious results. Rybalko could have rolled over the American forces, and had Lelyushenko [4th Guards Tank Army], Rotmistrov [7th Tank Army], and Rodin [8th Tank Army] intervened, the Americans would have had a taste of what the Germans had earlier experienced. I had only to give the order.

But here prudence and patience dictated otherwise. Four years of war at high cost had produced immense gains. With East Europe ripe for incorporation in the Russian camp, why squander the gains with an adventuristic policy? The Americans might risk further war with their reckless drive on Berlin, but he [Stalin] had more to lose. And, after the gains in eastern Europe, there was the Asian factor to consider. Russian intervention in the Japanese War and the conquest of Manchuria, and perhaps Hokkaido as well, could pave the way for an expansion of Russian power in China and Japan. Yes, he thought, instinct alone cautioned prudence in Europe at this critical time.

Stalin scribbled a note, handed it to Shtemenko who had just arrived, and ordered him to pass it to Zhukov and Konev. As he left Stalin's study, Shtemenko glanced at the note, "Take as much of Berlin as possible, but avoid conflict with Allied forces. All STAVKA reserve armies remain under my control. Rokossovsky [2nd Belorussian Front] will expand his attack on 22 April as planned, with his objectives unchanged. Stalin."

Stalin's parting words to Shtemenko were, "withdraw STAVKA reserve armies to original assembly areas under strict secrecy and await further orders."

5th Armored Division Headquarters: Falkensee, Germany 1900 21 April

The day's operations had resembled a triumphal march as resistance decreased to occasional desultory rifle fire. While the noise of heavy gunfire could be heard from the east, the open western approaches to Berlin beckoned the division's armored columns forward. CCA lead elements passed through Spandau and were deploying along the west bank of the Havel River. Patrols already probed along the road south of the Spree

River toward Ruleben and Charlottenburg. Word was that XX Corps' 2nd Armored Division had occupied Potsdam and Babelsberg and, itself, had reached the Berlin suburb of Zehlendorf. It would be a matter of hours before the two forces could link up and begin clearing the city itself.

1st Belorussian Front Headquarters: Kustrin 1900 21 April

Zhukov shouted into the phone, "Take the damn bridge at all costs!" and slammed the receiver into its cradle.

What more could go wrong? thought Zhukov. Sinenko's 5th Guards Tank Army was only 20 kilometers from Falkensee and was blocked by German forces holding a bridge across the Havel River west of Birkenwerder. Old men and boys could not have stopped Rotmistrov, and yet they had stopped Sinenko's army with over 500 tanks. The soldiers in him told him it was a small matter to stop an armored column along a narrow road, particularly across a river, but, on a day like this, emotion got the better of him. He reassured himself thinking that intimidation often spurred subordinates to superhuman efforts. This time only moderate efforts would suffice in putting the necessary force into the right place, at the right time. That place was Falkensee and there were still several hours left, or so Zhukov thought.

Two hours later Zhukov once again experienced nearly simultaneously all the glories and frustrations of a field commander as, in rapid succession, two reports arrived. The first was from Sinenko announcing the capture of the critical bridge. The second was from the *front* intelligence officer who declared that Falkensee was in American hands, and American patrols were operating as far north of Berlin as Hennigsdorf. Despite the shock of the news, Zhukov acted instinctively. He ordered Sinenko to secure a bridgehead over the Havel, send out patrols to meet the American, and turn the bulk of his army southward toward the Spree River and Berlin.

12th Army Group Headquarters: 2400 21 April

Quiet had descended across at least half of the front as an uneasy calm reigned over Russian and U.S. forces from Trebbin to Wittenberg and then southeast almost to Bautzen. Eisenhower had worked out crude coordination measures with both Konev and Zhukov, and Bradley was implementing them. All attention now telescoped into the immediate Berlin area and further north, where a final contest unfolded for the dwindling remnants of the once proud Third Reich.

While Eisenhower's orders echoed his earlier decision to seize as much of Germany as possible, they also incorporated an air of caution reflective of recent developments. Montgomery's 21st Army Group was to expand the operations into northern Germany as quickly as possible and advance as far east as feasible, while isolating German forces in Bremen and Hamburg. Meanwhile Bradley was to press on with the battle for Berlin.

Bradley's last orders of the evening were to Simpson and Hodges to occupy expeditiously as much of Berlin as possible. It was clear to Bradley that this final prize would be a shared one, for he well understood that Zhukov and Konev, whose forces that very hour were likely entering Berlin, shared his and his commanders' enthusiasm for this final battle.

Situation
25 April 1945

It was apparently clear to both Churchill and Truman that a fait accompli was in the making in central Europe. The decision to continue the Allied march toward Berlin had, in general, been politically and militarily proper. Allied armies had reached Berlin in advance of the Russians, had seized the key cities of Leipzig and Dresden, and would, it appeared, liberate a sizable portion of northwestern Germany, since the Russian offensive in that region had just begun and was proceeding slowly.

Stalin's reaction to events, despite the unfortunate incident at Trebbin, had been gruff but conciliatory, a good sign for future negotiations over the fate of eastern Europe.

Both leaders, however, were concerned about the consequences of a military race for turf within Berlin. City fighting is complex and confused at best, even when friend and foe are clearly distinguishable. Coalition fighting in a city where members of a coalition are not fully open with each other regarding how the enemy is to be defeated is another matter. In short, both Churchill and Truman feared a repeat of the Trebbin incident, which could occur on a larger scale. With both Allied and Russian forces fully concentrated and in contact with each other along almost half the front, no one could predict the consequences.

Moreover, Churchill was urging Truman to shift Eisenhower's reserves southward, to strip eastern Germany of armored forces so that Patton's Third Army could unleash a thrust into Czechoslovakia. Allied occupation of Prague, reasoned Churchill, could help prevent in Czechoslovakia the kinds of political monkey-business Stalin had undertaken in Poland. Truman seemed to agree.

Eisenhower's task, within the contest of messages sent by both Churchill and Truman to Stalin, was to negotiate with Zhukov and the Russian STAVKA a new demarcation line between Allied and Russian troops in regions where fighting was still underway.

As Eisenhower drafted his proposal, he thought that now was the time for some concessions. It was apparent that actual combat would propel U.S. and British forces to very favorable positions in Berlin and northwestern Germany. German resistance in eastern Berlin and along the Oder River south of Stettin was strong. Elsewhere it was less so. If combat ran its course, Allied armies could probably secure the bulk of Berlin south of the Spree River and probably seize sizeable portions of the city north of the Spree as well. Rapidly advancing British forces in the north would clearly reach the Ueeker RIver line west of Stettin. These gains would deny the Russians any sizeable share of Berlin and give them only Stettin and the Oder River's western bank in the north. Probably most grievous for the Russians would be their inability to participate in seizing what they called "Hitler's Lair," the Reichs Chancellory area of the city.

Eisenhower's message to Zhukov and Stalin accompanied a current Allied situation map as of 1600 22 April and Eisenhower's proposed halt line for U.S. and British forces. The text read:

> To preclude repetition of incidents such as occurred at Trebbin, and to insure equitable Russian participation in the reduction of Berlin, I propose to halt my troops on the boundaries indicated on the map. As you can see, this will require me to withdraw my forces in certain sectors to provide for more rational distribution of forces.
>
> Eisenhower.

Eisenhower was sure that Soviet understanding of time and distance problems alone, to say nothing of German resistance to her advance, would underscore that this was a clear concession on Eisenhower's part. In particular, it left most of Berlin north of the Spree River and a small sector south of the river in Russian hands. This would not be the case if the precipitous Allied advance continued.

As Eisenhower worked on the proposal, messages from Bradley indicated that the 5th, 2nd, and 3rd Armored Divisions were moving steadily toward the center of Berlin. Most important, 3rd Armor's seizure of the main road to Templehof blocked Rybalko's 9th Mechanized Corps' advance route northward into the city.

Stavka, Moscow 1900 22 April (1800 Berlin Time)

Stalin was once again visibly angered. First, there had been the report from Zhukov that 5th Guards Tank Army had met heavy resistance on the northern outskirts of Berlin. "It appears," he had said, "that the Germans will contest every inch of ground as they are doing against our troops elsewhere." Stalin had noted Zhukov's emphasis on "our" troops, confirming his suspicions that the Americans were being treated by the Germans as somewhat less than conquerors. The remainder of Zhukov's report was equally depressing as his two shock armies and two tank armies commenced a tedious process of clearing the northern and eastern suburbs of Berlin, block by block, house by house, and room by room. Konev's report only added to Stalin's discomfiture. Rybalko's 9th Mechanized Corps had made excellent progress in its drive north on Berlin until it reached the Teltow Canal. Crossing the Canal after a brisk two-hour battle Sukhov's tankers then encountered American road-blocks south of Templehof Airfield. Now Sukhov sought passage into Berlin further east, beyond the American lines, like water trying to pass around a barrier.

Stalin reviewed this information in the context of GRU reports from agents in Berlin and from reconnaissance-diversionary forces subordinate to Zhukov. These reports spoke of a rapid American advance and predicted American penetration into the heart of Berlin within forty-eight hours. When Stalin had demanded a timetable for Zhukov's troops to do likewise, Zhukov had said it would take at least seventy-two hours based on his current progress. It was now clear to Stalin that if combat was to determine the future map of Germany, Soviet forces would gain little more than they presently had seized — that is a narrow sector west of the Oder and table scraps in Berlin.

With Antonov and Shtemenko, Stalin drafted a new message to Eisenhower, which proposed that a new demarcation line be established to coordinate the junction of Allied and Russian forces. It ran due south from Stralsund through Neubrandenburg, along the Havel River to the Spree River, and eastward along the Spree to Russian lines east of Berlin. To this proposal was appended the demand, "We have earned the right to reduce the seat of Nazi power — that is the area between the Spree River and Unter der Linden. Request your forces stop short of that region. Stalin."

Shaef Headquarters: Rheims, France 2000 23 April

The message from Truman which read "Seal the deal" echoed that of Churchill. A day of near-frenzied negotiations with Stalin had seen both sides give ground, but, in the end, Eisenhower was satisfied with the fruits of his efforts. Eisenhower's and Stalin's respective proposals, made the day before, provided ample basis for negotiations. Stalin had bridled at the idea of surrendering more of northern Germany, while

Eisenhower was unhappy with the Soviet demand to seize the Reichs Chancellory area. What tipped the scales was the increased German resistance as U.S. forces approached the seat of Nazidom. It was obvious that the last several hundred yards would exact a huge price in blood on those who conquered it. "This," reasoned Eisenhower, "was the time to compromise." Besides, if Stalin's deal was accepted, Soviet forces were to relinquish their temporary control over this several square kilometers of disputed ground.

Affixing his signature to the message, Eisenhower directed his staff to issue copies to all of his force commanders.

Four Power Meetings: Potsdam, Germany 5 May

Allied negotiators had been meeting for two solid days to implement the temporary demarcation agreement and prepare the ground for future negotiations on a final peace treaty. The deliberations had become ever more rancorous as suppressed Soviet hostility surfaced time and time again.

Soviet forces were still refusing to abandon their prize territory south of the Spree River and had even refused to budge from the small scrap of land they were to pass over to Allied control northwest of Wittenberg, despite the fact that Allied forces had promptly withdrawn to the agreed upon line.

The Soviets failed to moderate their stance vis a vis Poland and eastern Europe and issued incessant press releases trumpeting Truman's and Churchill's duplicity in violating earlier accords. Meanwhile, both High Commands had immediately begun simultaneous drives into Czechoslovakia in what became a repeat of the race for Berlin. Tension remained high in headquarters on both sides and across the negotiating table.

At the news conference ending the day's negotiating session, reporters unleashed a barrage of hostile questions at Soviet, U.S., and British negotiators alike, many accusing them of sullying the memories of those who had perished in four years of war and selling out an exhausted world population, which yearned for peace.

During the late evening, Eisenhower walked into the hotel which served as his headquarters. As frustrated as he was over the tense and fruitless negotiations, he reflected that Allied actions had correctly anticipated the likely post-war Soviet stance. At least now, due to Truman's and Churchill's resolute action, the Russians had not been granted undue advantage. "The strong will the Western Allies had demonstrated in recent weeks as they won the war," Eisenhower thought to himself, "will be essential if we are to have any success in winning the peace."

He could not, however, avoid grimacing as he glimpsed the banner headline of a newspaper lying on the hotel main desk, "Allied Actions Substitute a Cold War for the Hot War!"

Postscript

The war in Europe endured for less than another month. Although American forces took Prague, they ultimately withdrew to lines approximating those drawn by Eisenhower. The Cold War did endure, its centerpiece a divided Germany and Berlin. Eastern Europe slid into the Soviet camp by coercion, occupation, and political manipulation. Two alliances came to symbolize the Cold War, and the armed stalemate which resulted kept a tense peace for over forty years. In the end, it was the imperative of internal political change that ended the Cold War.

In the 1990s a wave of economic and political reform shook the communist world. Revolution and reaction changed the face of Europe, altered political and military realities, and set world statesmen along a new path in search of a new concert of Europe. This new concert had to recognize a new reality — that of a unified Germany and Berlin.

Historians dissected the corpse of the Cold War and wondered among themselves, "To what extent were Truman, Churchill, and Eisenhower responsible for it." This question was duly added to the panoply of unresolved twentieth century questions.

Chapter 12

The Ultra Secret

Harold C. Deutsch

The introduction early in the 20th century of wireless communication stands high among factors that have had a revolutionary impact on warfare. By no means least in significance is the negative side of the picture: the inevitable vulnerability to enemy interception and decryption. The introduction and gradual extension during the twenties and thirties of cypher machines greatly increased the difficulties of penetrating the communications of potential or actual opponents. On the other hand, despite moments of doubt, the machines evoked a sense of security that led to a tendency to continue the use of systems that had actually been compromised. Particularly in the case of Germany and Japan, high level messages continued to be sent via compromised devices to the very end of the war.

So sensational was the impact of the revelations of Ultra during 1973-1974, that many students of the period for a time tended to regard it as decisive in the war's outcome. In effect Ultra, together with its Pacific counterpart Magic, was described as having won the war. This is a manifest absurdity in the sense that it ignored other factors without which the war could scarcely have been won. On the other hand, one can make a good case for the view that without "special intelligence" the war would have lasted much longer. The cumulative effect of operations which played a considerable part in allied successes contributed much to eventual victory and weighed the scales heavily against the Axis. The following will concentrate on the relation of Ultra and Magic to specific phases and operations of the second world conflict. As with all the essays in the present volume, it will be the general assumption that the course of affairs previous to those under discussion approximated the actual form of developments familiar from the general history of the period.

A. What if Ultra had not been available to the London government before the Battles of France and Britain?

Before the launching of the Second World War, Britain had been far from the leader of the pack in pursuit of either developing the mechanical devices in the field of wireless communication or penetrating such developments in other capitals. Germany and Japan were far ahead in constructing cypher machines of high quality—especially Germany's Enigma, and Poland, France, and the United States led the field in keeping close tab on the wireless communication systems of the expansionist powers. The British were enabled to make a great surge forward when the Poles, running short of resources to pursue their advanced program of penetrating Germany's machine cyphers, saw nothing for it but to turn over virtually the whole of their astonishing results to Paris and London a mere month before the opening of hostilities in 1939. This unearned windfall has been estimated as putting the British ahead at a single stroke a full two years from where they would otherwise have been.

It was now a matter of making up for lost time. That this was accomplished without stint is in large part the contribution of Winston Churchill. A major center for the decypherment of enemy wireless messages, notably those conveyed by the celebrated

Enigma cypher machine, was established at Bletchley Park on the very eve of the war. It developed apace as the conflict intensified, but would never have reached anything like its full compass if Churchill as prime minister had not thrown the full force of his great office and his extraordinary drive and imagination behind it. Without Churchill's personal intervention it is difficult to imagine the Bletchley community of over 7,000 persons and its absolute priority in the selection of personnel. This must be counted among his essential contributions to the eventual defeat of Hitler's Germany.

However great the score by which the western allies ultimately won the intercept race, it was the Germans who not only started well ahead, but maintained a substantial lead until well into the year 1941. The credit for this belongs less to Göring's Research Office (Forschungsamt) with its more than a thousand specialists than to the German Navy's superb B-Service. Together they gave Germany a head start and general lead in the area of wireless communications analysis. In the naval conflict associated with the German seizure of Norway the situation was so one-sided that the British commander in the North Sea complained that he never knew where the German units were, whereas they always seemed to know the location of his own ships.

In France the entire German offensive operation through the Ardennes was predicated on familiarity with the official code by which the Paris War Ministry communicated with its armies and army groups. Yet a single Ultra decrypt of the morning of 23 May largely restored the balance by saving Lord Gort's army from destruction. A signal from Army commander Walther von Brauchitsch to the advancing Army Groups A and B revealed the threatened encirclement of the British forces. The intercept is believed to have been vital in persuading Gort and Churchill to prepare the evacuation of Dunkirk, and thus the saving of an army without which the eventual allied victory over Hitler's Germany would appear inconceivable.

With respect to the Battle of Britain, it was fortunate that the first major breakthrough in solving the Enigma traffic of the period concerned the internal signals of Göring's Luftwaffe. Again and again the general pattern of the German air offensive as well as the size, timing, and targets of individual raids were revealed in time to permit the necessary adjustment of Britain's all too limited air defense. The offensives against the London dock area were known in time to permit the concentration of available fire fighting resources. Thus, whereas no single sensational decrypt can be said to have profoundly influenced the course of events, the sum total of their contributions to British defense is an impressive one. When the balance of forces in the Battle of Britain was posed on the razor's edge, the contribution of Ultra to the British cause deserves to be counted among the factors which in the end assured British victory.

B. What if Ultra had not been available for the war in North Africa?

There is much about the "intercept war" in Africa that is as fascinating as it is unique. Aside from the initial phases of the war in 1939-1940 it is the sole period of the conflict in which, for a time at least, something like a balance of forces can be said to have existed. A second unique feature that repeatedly and profoundly influenced the course of events was that on both sides the remoteness of the theater from the respective centers of command dictated the widest use of wireless communication, with a corresponding vulnerability that was exploited on both sides. For the Germans the situation meant a virtually full reliance on the Enigma. On the British side the enhanced value of Ultra was for a time paid for by German access to the code in which the American military attaché made daily reports to Washington.

Colonel Frank Bonner Fellers counts among the more extreme Anglophobes the writer encountered during his wartime experience. As he was also the type of person who troubled little to hide such sentiments, his British hosts could scarcely have failed to be fully aware of this. It may well have contributed to efforts to win him over that he was given extraordinary access to information on the daily course of affairs. This he duly reported in the "Black" attaché code which the Italians had purloined from the American embassy in Rome. Although they gave their German allies only the gist of the intercepted messages, this was sufficient to enable the Germans to break the code independently, with enormous benefits to Rommel's command. He was further assisted by a superb field intelligence unit under the talented Captain Alfred Seebohm. Together these two sources of vital information more than compensated for the advantages the British derived from Ultra.

A reversal of fortune that must have hit Rommel like a thunderclap came in July 1942 when an Australian commando raid overran the station of Seebohm's company. The captain was killed and his records seized virtually intact. It spelled the end of the Fellers leak. But before the curtain came down, the Germans had time for a final coup: the waylaying of the plane on which General "Strafer" Gott was coming to take over command of the British 8th Army in Egypt. Gott was killed and his place taken by Montgomery. Many of Gott's contemporaries believed him to be suffering from burnout. What if Montgomery had never become associated with British operations in Northeast Africa? The course of the war might well have been profoundly affected.

A number of Ultra victories had left major marks upon the confrontation in North Africa before the definitive shift of fortune that marked the late summer of 1942. In this category must be included the Battle of Cape Matapan of 27 March in which the Italian fleet, dispatched to the support of the German invasion of Crete, was once and for all eliminated as a significant factor in the Mediterranean operations. In the land war Ultra was generally successful in the interceptions and decryptions that determined or significantly affected the course of operations. As so often in this phase of the second world conflict, anxiety about security repeatedly hampered fullest exploitation of the medium. It was for example a vital aspect of the fumbling defense of Crete, where preserving the secret originally took precedence over saving the island and its garrison.

The enhancement in the role of Ultra that accompanied the solution of another German army Enigma key in August 1942, virtually coinciding with the coming down of an iron curtain on German intelligence operations, can be classed as the single most decisive factor in the reversal of fortune on the frontiers of Egypt. Montgomery, however false may have been his pose of extraordinary intuition in analyzing the situation, does no doubt deserve credit for his astute exploitation of the opportunities Ultra opened to him. His name is inextricably intertwined with the defeat of the German offensive at Alam Halfa and the following British victory at Alamein. As things were, Alam Halfa in particular was a bitterly contested battle whose outcome was for a time uncertain. Without the benefits of Ultra the possibility of Rommel's reaching the Nile delta is at least arguable.

In connection with both Alam Halfa and Alamein, Ultra was the single most vital factor that led to British victory. The most decisive consequence of the British intercepts was the sinking of virtually all Axis supply ships carrying vital cargoes to Africa—particularly tankers. Rommel's drive into Egypt and his defense at Alamein were crippled by these logistic disasters. With any lesser commander, the similar logistic blows that continued along his flight westward would have meant the obliteration of this retreating forces, even in the context of Montgomery's caution.

Ultra, even when handled with care, was likely to play strange tricks on its usual beneficiaries. The most notorious instance of such a backlash was the American debacle at Kasserine Pass, when Rommel overnight altered his plans and dispositions. The scales more than balanced, however, when Ultra revealed his subsequent shift southeastward to waylay Montgomery as the 8th Army emerged through the Mareth Line. Two days later the master of desert warfare left Africa for good.

What if Ultra had not been available to the allies in the Sicilian and Italian campaigns?

Aside from its role in keeping track of German reactions to the famed ploy by which a body of a supposed British courier was washed ashore on Spanish territory to divert attention from the approaching invasion of Sicily, Ultra played a comparatively minor role in the campaign on that island. Ultra performed its usual useful service of providing information on pending Axis movements and general order of battle. But it nowhere played a truly significant role in determining the course of operations. When it could have provided vital insight on such Axis moves as those preparatory to the evacuation of Messina, it was largely ignored by the senior Allied commander.

Part of the story involves an excessive concern about security that prevented the passage of vital information to front-line units from fear that their next moves might reveal familiarity with the Enigma messages. In some instances divisional commanders were left in ignorance of major developments on the Axis side of the line. Insofar as the American leadership in Sicily is concerned, General Patton's personal dislike of the British liaison officer attached to his command almost certainly played some part in the small heed which, in contrast to his later direction of affairs in France, he tended to give to Ultra during the campaign in Sicily.

It was only in the concluding phase of the fighting south of Rome that Ultra was able to live up to its full potential in deciding the course of the operations. Yet even before the allied landings at Salerno and at the toe of the Italian boot "special intelligence" proved enormously useful in showing the extent to which such diversionary efforts as Mincemeat (the "courier" corpse) had actually succeeded in tying down German troops elsewhere. Without these diversionary successes the allied situation at Salerno, for example, would have been a relatively hopeless one. If this is so, Ultra may be regarded as decisive in facilitating the landing and subsequent campaign in Italy.

Ultra made another contribution in that it revealed both Hitler's original intention to retire northward and continue fighting in northern Italy, and his subsequent rejection of Rommel's advice in favor of fighting on a strong line south of Rome on the level of Monte Cassino. Every German unit of any significance within or close to Italy was identified. Without the inside information the hazards of a landing on the peninsula would have been increased to a point where the entire enterprise would have become questionable.

Though Ultra continued to supply useful information, the stability of Monte Cassino front did not facilitate major impacts on the course of events during the months that followed. It was in the hope of breaking this deadlock and smoothing the path to Rome that General Alexander, strongly urged by Churchill, decided on the landing at Anzio. The beachhead was to be quickly exploited by a push eastward to the Alban Hills or a drive directly northward to Rome. Yet not only did General Lucas lack driving power in the two unblooded divisions assigned to him and which would have exposed his force to early annihilation. He made no effort to extend the perimeter of the beachhead to a point where German ordinance could not have dominated everything down to the water. What tactical information Ultra provided did save the entire enterprise in that it thwarted the German counterattack (*Fischfang*, February 1944) that might otherwise have succeeded in throwing the allies back into the sea. Thus, Ultra was a life saver at a critical moment of the campaign in Italy. Anzio can not be spared the label of failed operation. Ultra saved it from being a disaster.

So the virtual freeze of the front south of Rome and Naples continued through the spring of 1944. Then it was Ultra which paced the way north. Exact knowledge of the strength and location of every German unit in Italy facilitated a series of diversionary moves that fixed German strength as much as possible on the east and west coastal areas of the peninsula. Alexander finally initiated a breakthrough in the DIADEM operation not far east of Monte Cassino. The movement was well prepared, smartly executed, and associated with a full bag of deceptions, most of which were directed to attracting attention to the coastal areas. That DIADEM did not bring the war in Italy to a final victorious conclusion was in large part the fault of Mark Clark, whose vainglorious dash toward Rome allowed the German 10th Army to escape annihilation.

To summarize for the Italian campaign, without Ultra:
(1) the vital landing at Salerno would have been hazardous in the extreme and might well not have been attempted;
(2) the beachhead at Anzio might well have been obliterated in *Fischfang* (Feb. 1944); and
(3) the breaking of the Monte Cassino line by DIADEM and the thrust of the allies into northern Italy would scarcely have come in the late spring of 1944.

C. What if Ultra had not been available for the Battle of the Atlantic?

The contest in the Atlantic in the years 1940-1943 represents a phase of the war in which Ultra is frequently cited as the single most decisive factor in the allied victory. Air Marshal Sir John Slessor, who is emphatic in denying a major role to the medium in the Battle of Britain, here speaks of it as a "real war winner."[1]

Without its betrayal via an Ultra signal of Admiral Lütjens, the *Bismarck* would almost certainly have escaped to Brest. Thereafter in the maneuvering of allied convoys and German submarine wolfpacks, Ultra was a vital instrument on the allied side. It is no simple matter to allocate credit in allied success among it and the significant development of improved depth charges, D/F (radio direction finding) and the short-wave radar that enabled allied planes to come within easy range of surfacing U-Boats. The single close-to-decisive coup engineered by Ultra was its instrumentality in settling for once and all the dispute between the British Admiralty and its Submarine Tracking Room concerning German access to the code by which directions were conveyed to allied convoys.* Over night the curtain slammed down on the window which had given Dönitz a full view of convoy movements, obliging him after the unbearable losses of May 1944 (43 U-Boats) to abandon at that critical juncture the contest in the Atlantic. The inability of the Germans further to hold things even in the intercept war also determined the Atlantic contest.

There is considerable argument on how a less total allied victory would have affected their prospects for the invasion a year later. How much further depletion could the ships of the future covering armada have endured before it became prohibitive? Much of the merchant fleet assembled for the enterprise would assuredly have rested on the bottom of the sea, quite possibly leaving too few ships to support the invasion buildup in 1944. In the absence of an invasion a strong Soviet victory drive westward would have determined the war. But instead of ending as they did, somewhere between Berlin and the Elbe, the Soviets might well have extended their hold westward to the

Rhine or even the Channel, with consequences for the course of world affairs that would have reached down to the present day.

In our consideration of the role of Ultra in World War II some readers will perceive a gap concerning the impact of Ultra information made available to Moscow by London. Not that individual items or their sum total lacked significance. We know indeed that a mass of Ultra data was transmitted to Moscow from London, that in particular, months of such information was made available before the decisive encounter at Kursk of August 1943. But the Moscow archives have thus far been silent on the reception and exploitation of this information. Until the silence is broken we must confine ourselves to guess and logic, neither of which is much of a guide to an assessment of the true measure in which this aid was accepted and utilized.

D. What if Ultra had not been available for the invasion of the continent?

For Ultra, as for every program in allied intelligence, 1944 was scheduled to be the payoff year, in which carefully husbanded resources were to be expended freely to determine the conflict for once and all. Considerably more than even the large forces tactically assembled for the enterprise was needed to guarantee a successful landing and firm establishment. German strength, notably well-seasoned mobile divisions, exceeded all that could initially be brought against it. It was correspondingly imperative to divide Hitler's forces between the two areas conceivable for a broad-based invasion, Normandy and the Pas de Calais, if possible with the larger allocation to that which was not to be invaded. Imperative also in this scheme of things was deception concerning the size of the forces assembled in Britain so as to follow the initial landing with a continued threat to the Pas de Calais area.

By far the most decisive feature of this program of deception stemmed from the success, early in 1941, in breaking through the encypherment system employed in the Enigma communications of the Abwehr. In particular the instruction wirelessed to its advance post in Hamburg, from which directions were extended to its agents in Britain, exposed the entire network to British intelligence. It had the consequence of delivering every German agent in Britain to execution, incarceration or conversion. The so-called Double Cross system made the principal figures amenable to doubling of the highest order. The rest is a familiar story of the manipulation of the agents' reports from Britain, which were so managed as to totally deceive the Germans on all that pertained to supposed preparation of the invasion of the continent. Fictional divisions, a fictional army group (FUSAG) under the fictional command of General Patton, fake communications networks, fake staging areas, of which one appeared to point toward Norway, and a mass of other deceptive devices were employed with complete success.

When Ultra after the landing in Normandy revealed that Hitler was being persuaded to shift massive forces from the Pas de Calais to Normandy, he was induced to cancel the move by the report of one of the principal turned agents that the move against the Pas de Calais was imminent.

So the invasion progressed and took its course. Without the Herculean contribution of Ultra it might scarcely have been attempted. Under the best of circumstances it would have been touch-and-go. A final life-saver provided by Ultra in the Normandy campaign was tactical and associated with Mortain, General Bradley's conclusive victory against Hitler's attempt to smash through the comparatively thin American front before Avranches. Had Ultra not revealed the transfer of four armored divisions to that sector, the consequences notably for General Patton's army advancing into Brittany, could have been serious.

E. What if fullest advantage had been taken of the opportunities afforded by Ultra to conclude the war in Western Europe after the summer of 1944?

Commencing with the failure of the Falaise pocket to close its grip on the German armies fleeing from the collapsed fronts in Normandy, the remaining history of the war in the west of the continent is speckled with missed opportunities to bring it to a conclusion. There was Falaise itself, with the opportunity lost there to destroy Hitler's forces in France for once and all. There was the almost incredible failure to strike northward immediately after the fall of Antwerp to make sure of the control of the Scheldt estuary. Failure to do so made possible a logistic disaster of gigantic proportions. The whole of the Western Front was in some measure affected, not least the paralysis of Patton's 3rd Army as it stood poised for its first leap forward into German territory. It has been widely condemned as the worst, least excusable, error on the allied side during World War II, with Montgomery as the principal culprit but some share of the blame going all the way up to Eisenhower. The effort to cross the Rhine at Arnhem (Market Garden) was a disastrously failed enterprise for which a heavy price in lives and prestige was exacted. There was finally the surprise of the allies in the German offensive in the Ardennes. "The Bulge" did turn out a major allied victory, but exacted its own heavy price.

One would be tempted to cry, "Ultra to the rescue," if the true story did not convincingly demonstrate that in each and every instance, with only the partial exception of the Ardennes, special intelligence had not failed to speak loudly and clearly only to be ignored. Insofar as the situation in the following months is concerned, no poverty of information, but an extraordinary richness characterizes all of them previous to the Ardennes battle.

Contrary to what General Bradley at one point believed or wished to believe, the bulk of fleeing German forces was still in the Falaise pocket and could be further contained. It was simply a matter of Ultra being ignored at the critical juncture.

With respect to Antwerp, where the capable General Horrocks was kept champing at the bit by Montgomery while General von Zangen's 82,000 men were slipping through Walcheren and the Beveland peninsula, the greatest port of Western Europe was immobilized for three months, starving a good part of the entire front and halting in its tracks Patton's 3rd Army as it was poised to make its first leap into German territory. Meanwhile, Monty's hypnotic gaze was fixed on his cherished project of Market Garden. Yet there can be no real doubt about Ultra's message. It had clearly confirmed information from Dutch resistance elements concerning the two armored divisions refitting in the very area of the intended crossing of the Rhine.

As for Market Garden, Ultra had late but not too late conveyed this information and convinced leading figures of Eisenhower's staff that the project should be halted. Ike himself felt that he could scarcely do this peremptorily after having so often urged Montgomery to show more enterprise. But he did authorize Bedell Smith and Brigadier Young to urge Montgomery to reconsider, only to have their doubts swept airily aside, and the attack launched with its disastrous results.

The story of the role of intelligence in the background of the Ardennes offensive differs in a number of respects. Hitler, in addition to other extraordinary security measures, had decreed a temporary black out of the use of the Enigma. This alone should have alerted allied intelligence to something extraordinary being planned. Moreover, the Führer had not reached down far enough to alert all smaller units and some use of Enigma was continued. It did not tell much, but truly meticulous analysis would have revealed something.

Moreover, the alert Special Service Officer with U.S. 7th Army, Donald Bussey, had noted the movement of various smaller German units northward and speculated whether something was being prepared by the Germans on the Ardennes front. He went to alert the G-2 officer of 7th Army, Colonel Quinn, but was fobbed off with the comment that undoubtedly the information had already been noted by 1st and 2nd Army intelligence. In sum, though the message of intelligence on the coming German offensive cannot be described as having been loud and clear, it should have been sufficient to alert its recipients if there had been a listening ear.

It is not easy to explain or even to grasp this staggering series of failures at the operational level to conclude the war months before it was finally brought to a victory. One is forced to reach back to the explanation that over the last decades has been reiterated in many studies of the period — an attack of "victor's disease" so virulent that it swept through the allied leadership in response to the resounding triumph in the fighting in France. Doubts about the eventual outcome of the conflict having been basically resolved, Ultra simply no longer occupied the primary consideration of the allied leadership in the decisions which followed.

F. What if communication intelligence had not been available during the Pacific War?

This section is inevitably a coda to the discussion of the role of "special intelligence" in Europe. The ultimate discrepancy in the forces available to the combatants made Japan's defeat a matter of "when" rather than "if." In such a context, Ultra and Magic, the code name for the operation that broke Japan's diplomatic codes, were facilitators rather than enablers. The immensely successful campaign against Japan's merchant fleet, for example, was greatly assisted by the ability to read shipping codes. Submarines could be directed to their targets with a precision that nullified the Pacific's vast expanses. They could also be used economically. Three boat groupings were the norm, in contrast to the large "wolf packs" Dönitz required in the Atlantic. With Ultra or without it, Japan's neglect of convoy escorts combined with U.S. construction capacity would eventually have achieved the same results.

A similar case can be made for virtually every aspect of Ultra's and Magic's roles in the Pacific theater. Their information on Japanese defense preparations certainly reinforced the decision to use atomic weapons rather than risk invasion. But experience from Guadalcanal to Okinawa certainly provided enough data on Japanese behavior to generate the same decision had no signal intelligence data at all been available. Nevertheless, U.S. successes in breaking Japanese diplomatic and military codes represented both a major intelligence triumph in itself and a significant contribution to the war at tactical and operational levels. Three specific areas stand out.

1) **Pearl Harbor**: The success of the Japanese attack in the context of U.S. ability to read Japanese mail has generated a virtual cottage industry of conspiracy theorists accusing Roosevelt and Churchill, together or separately, of deliberately withholding from commanders on the spot information that might have averted the disaster. Conspiring to bring a united America into the war is depicted as worth the price of a few thousand lives and a few obsolete battleships. The major specific intelligence problem at Pearl Harbor, however, involved "white noise" — the discrepancy between the amount of information available and the ability to evaluate it accurately. In this sense, the U.S. was the victim of its own success, which allowed the interception and translation of over 7,000 Japanese messages in the six months before the Japanese attack.

A related problem involved the intelligence bureaucracy distributing relevant material to appropriate parties. A corresponding case might be made that absent the information derived from broken codes, Admiral Kimmel and General Short might have trusted more to professional common sense in adjusting to the increasingly-tense diplomatic situation. Short would probably have remained more concerned with sabotage than a surprise attack. His aircraft would still have been parked wheel to wheel for security purposes. The Navy would still have suffered from the effects of six months of false alarms that eventually diminished alertness. But without the tempting narcotic of intelligence regularly supplied from Washington, which had to be taken on trust to preserve the secret, the commanders on the spot, both competent officers, might have kept their subordinates sufficiently galvanized to give Nagumo's pilots at least an unpleasant surprise and a bloody nose on that December Sunday morning.

The consequences would probably have been more political and emotional than military. The Japanese attack would still have done significant damage. But American morale would have been higher had the fight been less one-sided. What then? Perhaps a major counterattack into the western Pacific, a larger version of the abortive operation to relieve Wake? Husband Kimmel was no Chester Nimitz. Could he have avoided a Midway in reverse? Perhaps by its involuntary role in an initial defeat, special intelligence contributed to a final victory.

2) **Midway**: By the spring of 1942, U.S. cryptographers had their credibility at CINCPAC. They had also established the nature of Japan's plan for the Midway operation, including dates, times, and diversionary targets. That plan has so often been criticized as too clever to be wise that it is easy to overlook the high level of probability that without cryptanalysis Nimitz and his subordinates, heavily outnumbered and coming off a virtually-unbroken series of defeats, might well have been drawn into Yamamoto's strategic web. Special intelligence did not win the Battle of Midway. It did contribute to victory by enabling U.S. commanders to focus on winning while fighting at a numerical disadvantage, and by facilitating optimal use of limited physical resources.

In an alternate scenario, Midway could have become a U.S. defeat of sufficient magnitude to delay a U.S. counterattack until new ships came into service and new air groups could have replaced those lost. While a successful invasion of Hawaii remained a remote possibility, the results would certainly have included even more desperate island fighting, Japan would have had time to develop its outlying "barrier" while still possessing the "javelin" of its First Air Fleet. In that context would the U.S. have devoted greater resources to the Pacific at Europe's expense? Or would Roosevelt, King, and MacArthur have bided their time, awaiting the outcome of the Manhattan Project and the development of aircraft with the range to deliver the bombs from Hawaii? Would two nuclear devices have been enough to convince a Japan whose people and leaders might evening 1945 have justifiably regarded time as still on their side? If not, what then? More bombs, with the accompanying risk of the U.S. becoming the major postwar villain once the effects of atomic explosions became known? Or an invasion mounted by armed forces already war-weary and seeking to return home? Unpleasant alternatives certainly—but ones that remain in the realm of speculation.

3) **MacArthur's Southwest Pacific Campaign**: Douglas MacArthur's return to the Philippines between 1943 and 1945 featured a series of deceptions and maneuvers so universally successful at the operational level that even the general's critics tend to accept them as proof of his military talents. Yet MacArthur's successes depended heavily on Ultra. What might have been the consequences had he been forced to operate

without special intelligence? The Southwest Pacific theater ranked above only China-Burma-India on the priority list for resources. As early as December, 1942, Ultra served as a force multiplier by reporting Japanese air deployments to the area, and the routes and schedules of Japanese supply and invasion colonies. Initially U.S. submarines and aircraft were only able to whittle down their enemies. By the time of the Battle of the Bismarck Sea in March, 1943, however, air power alone could destroy whole convoys.

Ultra served MacArthur in other ways as well. It confirmed the effectiveness of the deception campaign that kept Japanese eyes turned away from the 400 mile leap to Aitape and Hollandia in April, 1944. It provided information on Japanese reinforcement of the Philippines later in the year. Tactically, Ultra kept MacArthur's forces informed of orders of battle and plans for aerial counterattacks during the Leyte invasion, and even provided the first clear knowledge that the kamikaze attacks involved more than a few desperate pilots acting on their own initiative.

None of these contributions were decisive by themselves. Without Ultra the Americans and Australians would still have made reinforcing Japanese positions in the Southwest pacific increasingly difficult — but by degrees instead of exponentially. MacArthur would therefore have faced stronger forces, better supported and supplied. Would he have been so successful in finding undefended landing sites? Would his losses have been heavy enough to discredit the concept of a two-pronged strategy in favor of an all-out drive across the Central Pacific? Both scenarios appear plausible. And had they been played out, might not the image of "Dugout Doug" have resurfaced? Might the general even have been relieved of his command — an option certain attractive to the Roosevelt administration, one, in fact, averted only by his developing image as a national hero? Even without such a decision, might MacArthur have been discredited enough to deny him the major post-war roles he played in the Far East? Great events sometimes turn on small ones, as the massive door of a vault depends on a single ball bearing. What if...?

[1]   Conversation with Sir John Slessor, 1956.

Chapter 13

Hitler's Role

Gerhard L. Weinberg

A. What if Hitler had not held up rocket research?

One of the issues often raised after World War II concerns the more radical innovations in weaponry introduced during the conflict. Among the most dramatically different of the new entries were the so-called secret weapons, or "V" weapons employed by the Germans. Of the four actually put into service, the V-2, originally referred to by its German developers as the A-4, was in some ways the most important because it pointed clearly to a future in which ballistic missiles, carrying nuclear warheads, became the major weapons system of the Cold War. Impossible to intercept in flight, the V-2, the world's first liquid fuelled, gyroscopically stabilized, ballistic missile, began to be fired by the Germans at London in early September, 1944. Fourteen hundred were fired at the United Kingdom, most of them toward London, and sixteen hundred more were aimed at Belgium, with a majority aimed at Antwerp, a major port captured intact by the British and, after considerable delays, the most important Allied supply port in western Europe.

Because the early development of the rockets which led to the A-4, as it was then called, had been pushed by the German army weapons office with support from two successive commanders-in-chief of the German army, the question could be raised: what if this project, instead of being something of a pet scheme of the army leaders in the face of Hitler's doubts, had been pushed much more vigorously? Even without that push in the 1930s, the target date for V-2 employment had been in the winter of 1943-44 but set back primarily by the results of Allied bombing and the teething problems of the new type of weapon. Had Hitler, who only became seriously interested in the weapon in 1942, pushed for it earlier and assured the A-4 project a higher place in the German priority allocation system to match that urgency, would it not have been possible for the Germans to straighten out the weapon's problems earlier and move it into production in 1943 rather than 1944? And what would have been the impact on the war of such a weapon brought into action at a time before the Western Allies had landed in France in June 1944 and possibly even before they had landed on the mainland of Italy in September 1943?

These questions need to be considered from two quite different perspectives before they can be answered. First, what would have been the effect of such a speed-up on the Germans? Second, what would have been the effect on the allies of an earlier employment of the new weapon? On the German side, any massive earlier push for the refinement, production, and employment of the A-4 would by 1942 have required substantial reallocation of resources within the German war economy. In 1942 and 1943, the key years of the war in this regard, the German war economy was dominated by the needs of three broad categories of weapons systems: air planes, armored fighting vehicles, and submarines. It would certainly have been possible to shift resources from these programs to the A-4 project, but it is doubtful that such a reallocation would have helped the German over-all war effort substantially.

The one great opportunity for Hitler to make a major reallocation of resources during those years came with the defeat of the U-Boats in the Battle of the Atlantic in the early summer of 1943. Instead of continuing a massive commitment of men and materials to the continued U-Boat war, Hitler could have disregarded the advice and hopes of his newly appointed Commander-in-Chief of the Navy, Admiral Dönitz, and invested the resources freed by such a decision in other aspects of the German war effort such as the A-4. Whatever the other effects of such a decision, it would have increased the volume, not the timing of the new weapon's employment. Any earlier decision for a major reallocation of resources would have required substantial reductions in other programs. It seems correspondingly doubtful that such a change would have benefited the German war effort.

The lower marginal utility of the A-4 as compared with airplane, tank, and submarine production was a function of the weapon's nature. Very early in the rocket program it became evident that its original purpose had changed. The program had been initiated in the first place as a way to send a precisely aimed warhead (initially to be loaded with poison gas) further than conventional artillery; the shift from a form of long-range but accurate artillery to a ballistic missile meant abandonment of accuracy for range. One could reasonably expect to hit a target the size of a large city like London, but not small though more critical targets like the embarkation ports for the planned allied invasion of France. Since the Germans did not know that their espionage network in England was in reality controlled by the British, the procedure eventually utilized by the latter to mislead the Germans about the impact points of their missiles could have been employed to even greater effect against any effort of the Germans to hit small rather than huge target locations.

As for the delivery of explosives to London, the A-4 was in any case a highly inefficient system. The one ton warhead of the rocket could and did arrive with essentially no warning, but the effort required was quite out of proportion to the physical effect. Almost half the rockets were rejected as defective by those who were to fire them. There was, in addition, a high proportion of misfires. The major effect of sending a ton of high explosive to London (or other cities) by a procedure that was vastly more costly in resources than airplanes involved morale. This was the primary purpose of the weapon in the first place. As we shall see, it certainly had some effect in this regard; but whether a substantial increase in the numbers would have had a proportional effect in lowering British morale is at least open to question.

This point brings up the other side of the question. What if the V-2s had been either ready earlier or had been fired at targets in Britain in larger numbers? Three points can be made in this connection. Had the new weapons been ready earlier, the British leaders, especially Churchill and Brooke, might well have given up far earlier than November 1943 in their opposition to an allied landing in Northern France. Even after the conferences at Cairo and Teheran, Brooke in particular was still trying very hard to have the invasion postponed for several months in favor of greater effort in Italy; such a postponement would quite probably have aborted any invasion in the West in 1944 altogether. Certainly the German employment of the V-2 provides some food for thought to those who criticize American insistence on an invasion at the earliest possible invasion of northern France — from where the missiles were launched — and would have had a major effect on the Teheran Conference where the majority of the available time was pre-empted by Churchill's continuing opposition to any firm spring 1944 invasion commitment.

Any significant increase in the volume of the V-2 bombardment, as opposed to an earlier employment of the weapon, might well have increased its already substantial morale impact on a war-weary British population. Whether that increase would have been proportional to the greater German investment of resources seems very doubtful. We do know that Churchill was sufficiently concerned about the German weapons, both the V-1 unmanned jet bomber and the V-2 ballistic missile, to urge the use of poison gas in retaliation. The resort to gas was aborted by the strong contrary advice of the British chiefs of staff and an American veto. It is, of course, conceivable that in the face of a very much heavier bombardment these restraints would have been withdrawn. A more likely scenario is an even heavier bombardment of German cities, if necessary, by the allocation of greater American air resources to the European at the expense of the Pacific theater. In any case, more civilian lives would surely have been lost on both sides, but the broader contours of the war would not have been altered.

Although the other "V" weapons can not be discussed at equal length, there is no evidence to suggest that their earlier appearance or their availability in larger numbers, would have had repercussions any more substantial than the V-2. All three: the V-1, a jet-propelled pilotless plane; the V-3, an ultra-long-range cannon powered by series of sequential explosions as it shot out of a gun barrel hundred of yards long; and the V-4, a small four-stage solid fuel rocket, were designed with the same purpose in mind. They were to be means of carrying conventional explosives to London, hitting somewhere in that enormous urban area. The last two were actually never fired at London, being available too late in the war as a result of both development problems and Allied interference, primarily in the form of air raids. Whatever the temporary boost to German morale and deleterious effect on British morale, the delivery of a few hundred, or even a few thousand, tons of additional explosive to England by these devices would hardly have made any great difference in the war. All four weapons systems, each of them originally designed to be fired from fixed installations requiring additional massive resource investment, and each of them designed with London as the target in mind, serve primarily to testify to the thoughtful observer that Hitler placed a very high priority indeed on finding ways of striking at the island kingdom.

B. What if Hitler had not held up the Messerschmitt 262?

Another issue involving new weapons in World War II is that of the introduction by the Germans of operational jet powered air planes. A German prototype jet had flown for the first time just before the beginning of the war, and several models of jet planes, as well as a rocket-propelled plane, were under development in Germany during the war. Of these, the twin-engined Messerschmitt 262 seemed to be the most serviceable. In spite of great development troubles, numerous crashes, a very brief flight endurance, and a host of other troubles hardly surprising in a completely novel type of airplane, the great speed of the Me 262 and its reasonable stability in flight as compared with other jet planes suggested that here was the plane with which the German air force could have reclaimed the skies over Germany.

As the swarms of British and American bombers grew ever larger, and as their ability to find their targets improved, the danger to Germany was obvious. The massive destruction of German conventional fighter planes, especially by the Americans flying the P-51 Mustang, brought a return of large-scale bombing of Germany, dramatically reduced the effectiveness of the surviving German fighter squadrons as more and more experienced pilots were shot down, and pushed this downward spiral further by facilitating the bombing of German synthetic oil and other petroleum installations, thereby forcing a dramatic reduction in the fuel available for pilot training. It was in this set of circumstances that the possible appearance of a fighter substantially faster, not only than the allied bombers but also than their fighter planes, seemed to offer the possibility of Germany driving the allied bombers out of the sky.

It was in this general context that Hitler, when informed of the speed of the new plane after its first flight in July 1943, decided that it should be developed and produced with the capability of bombing, not simply as a fighter. It was his judgment that Germany had no other bomber which could in practice interfere substantially with Allied operations in the West The Me 262 was a potentially effective pinpoint parallel to the rockets and pilotless jets being planned for indiscriminate terror attacks on London; a plane, in other words, that could swoop out of the sky and hope to score hits on ships, tank assemblies and artillery positions somewhat the way the "Stuka" dive-bomber had done to such great effect in the early years of World War II.

Since the redevelopment of the Me 262, which had been designed without a bomb load or bomb-release mechanism in mind, would certainly take time and hence delay the introduction of the first completed jets into combat, most high-ranking German air force officers who knew of the issue objected to the conversion concept. They argued that the Me 262 should be built as quickly as possible in the largest possible numbers in its fighter configuration in the hope that this could close the gaping hole in Germany's roof. This was the first priority in their eyes; offensive air support for their ground troops, to say nothing of hit-and-run bombing at greater distances, seemed to them an issue to worry about later, if at all.

There is likely to remain a considerable amount of debate about the impact of larger numbers of German jet planes on the air war had these been available earlier. The ones which did enter the conflict may provide at least a clue, however. The dispersal of the whole German aircraft industry, decided upon by the Germans as a counter to the Allied air offensive, was the major factor in retarding German aircraft production in 1943-44. The Me 262 therefore, did not enter battle until the late spring of 1944. Once the Americans turned to the oil targets in that year, the whole jet program became largely a waste of effort. The pilots could not be trained properly and numerous new jet planes were destroyed on the ground, unable to fly for lack of fuel. When they tried to defend the synthetic oil works, their mechanical deficiencies and the overwhelming strength of the American escorts produced failure.[1]

Characteristic of German development conflicts during the war was the fate of the two-engined jet actually designed and built as a bomber, the Arado 234. First brought into service in 1943, its main utility was its ability to evade fighters on reconnaissance missions over England by its speed of up to 500 m.p.h.. Here was a plane which Hitler had not interfered with, but its substantial production was also delayed until 1944 because the factory had to be moved to avoid the strategic bombing offensive. All of two hundred had been produced when the Red Army overran the evacuated factory in the supposedly safe eastern portion of Germany to which production had been moved.

The jet airplanes, like the first two of the "V" weapons, may well have pointed to future technological developments in warfare, but their military utility in these early stages was minimal. The verdict of the most careful German analyst of the "V" weapons may justifiably be applied to the jet as well: "In this sense [as effective weapons] the V-weapons came not too late but too soon..."[2] Requiring substantial investment in technical as well as construction manpower, scarce materials, and all sorts of other resources, they constituted a poor allocation of resources in the strained economy of a country fighting a multi-front war, one in which most of the fighting was taking place on the Eastern Front where none of the new weapons were ever deployed. Germany's enemies, especially the United States, could afford to put substantial resources into projects which might or might not be useful and in time for employment during the war;

207

Germany could not. The most dramatic illustration of this last point is the American development of the atomic bomb; had the German rockets and jets prolonged the war in reality rather than imagination, they would have kept the Third Reich at war long enough to become the target for the first of these new weapons.

C. What if Hitler had left soldiering to the soldiers?

The library of German post-war memoirs is filled with an enormous array of accounts by those who had faithfully served Hitler for years, happily accepting his promotions, decorations, and huge bribes, but explaining in detail how the brilliant advice of the authors had been disregarded by the Führer to the detriment of Germany's military effort. The title of one of the memoir volumes of Field Marshal Erich von Manstein, *Lost Victories*, can be used to summarize the burden of much of this literature. The implication of most of this literature is clear: had the advice of the professional military leaders been followed all would have been well for Germany, or, at the very least, the defeat it suffered would have been considerably less messy.

In any examination of this issue, several matters of definition must first be clarified. There is not only the obvious fact that Hitler did not live to write his memoirs, but that in many instances in which a major difference between Hitler and military professionals is mentioned, there was substantial division as well among the key military themselves. Several important examples may serve to illustrate this point.

The halt of the German armor in May, 1940, as it was approaching the port of Dunkirk was advocated, and quite possibly originally proposed, by the commander of the German Army Group to which the relevant German units belonged, Colonel General Gerd von Rundstedt. In the August 1941 debate within the German military hierarchy about the next best step in the campaign on the Eastern Front, there was division as to the best next objective, a debate which a major German study has shown to have been irrelevant because for logistic reasons no offensive on the central portion of the front was then feasible anyway.[3] Opinion among German general officers in November about a final effort to seize Moscow was even more divided; certainly the most extreme optimist at that time was not Hitler but the Chief of the General Staff of the Army, General Franz Halder, the personification of the army professionals. Finally, when in November 1942 the decision had to be made whether to hold Stalingrad or order a breakout attempt, it was von Manstein himself who sided with Hitler in the debate.

It is, therefore, most appropriate to turn to examples in which Hitler insisted on a course to which all his professional military advisors (with the possible exception of Keitel and Jodl) objected. Two further preliminary observations are in order. Some things will have to be said about the air force and the navy as well as about the ground war, and something will need to be said about those major decisions — by far the majority — in which Hitler and his military advisors were in agreement.

The relationship between Hitler and the highest commanders of the German air force was complicated by the role of that force's commander, Hermann Göring. A highly decorated World War I flyer, Göring was initially relied on by Hitler. Even as the Führer's confidence in both Göring and the air force waned, the personal tie between the two was reinforced by the fact that the Deputy Führer, Rudolf Hess, had literally flown the coop and had to be declared mentally unbalanced by the German leadership. This made it extremely difficult to Hitler to contemplate dropping the second man in his state. What would the German public say to such a change?

Furthermore, the two key individuals under Göring in the decisive early years of the war were hardly men to divert Hitler's views or plans. General Hans Jeschonnek, the air force chief of staff, was a devout National Socialist without the slightest comprehension of what Germany was headed for. When he found out, he committed suicide. The chief of air force development and production at the beginning of the war, the former fighter pilot and stunt flyer Ernst Udet, was clearly beyond his depth in his administrative position, and had preceded Jeschonnek in suicide in the face of mounting difficulties. The fourth key figure in the Luftwaffe, Field Marshall Erhard Milch, held an ambivalent position in the Nazi hierarchy, having maintained his role by getting his mother to swear that she had committed adultery as a means of "straightening out" his otherwise unacceptable Jewish ancestry. That with such an assortment of characters at the top of the German air force there would be no general disagreement with Hitler on major issues should not be surprising. And doubts would, in any case, generally be removed by the longtime chief of German air force intelligence, General Josef ("Beppo") Schmid, who practically always saw things the way Hitler wanted them seen.[4]

Unlike the air force, the German navy was headed throughout World War II by a professional officer who had been promoted from inside the regular naval hierarchy and who was recognized as the navy's spokesman both inside and outside the service. Hitler kept the navy chief he inherited in 1933 for a full decade, and generally he and Admiral Raeder worked in harmony. There were, however, three major issues on which the two differed. The first was the admiral's insistence, beginning in the fall of 1939, that Germany should immediately resort to unrestricted submarine warfare, accepting the assumption that this would be likely to involve almost immediate war with the United States. Hitler preferred to wait with war on the United States until he had either had the opportunity to build the huge blue-water navy he believed Germany needed for war with the United States or secured the participation on Germany's side of such a navy from an ally.

It is at least conceivable that Germany's drawing the United States into the war in the winter of 1939-40, as Raeder's proposal contemplated, would have enabled the Germans to sink somewhat more tons of shipping in the first year of the war in spite of the small number of submarines then available to the German navy. It is also quite possible that an earlier involvement of the United States in an all-out war with Germany might have stimulated the Japanese into moving forward in the Pacific earlier, thus providing the Germans with the allied navy that removed Hitler's hesitation about war with America in December 1941, but it is very difficult to see what long-term advantage any of this would have brought Germany. It is certainly true that in late 1939 the United States was even less prepared for war than two years later. The converse of this is that for the Germans to draw the United States into the war two years earlier would also have implied a far more dramatic American rearmament effort earlier than was in fact the case. It would presumably not have come in time to preclude the defeat of the Western Powers by the Germans in the spring of 1940, but it would very likely have changed the reaction of France to such a defeat. Would the French have pulled out of the war in June, 1940, if at that time the United States had already been in the war several months? The contours of the war would indeed have been different if Hitler had agreed to Raeder's proposals in October 1939 or in the subsequent months when the two differed about essentially the same subject. It is, however, extremely doubtful that there would have been major changes in Germany's favor as a result.

A second major difference between Hitler and Raeder concerned the role of the Mediterranean in German strategy. Raeder regularly argued for some agreement with Vichy France, a concentration of German power on driving the British out of the Mediterranean, and continued cooperation with the Soviet Union which had been especially helpful to the German navy. This was indeed a fundamental difference in strategy, but it rested on an equally fundamental erroneous perception on Raeder's part.

The National Socialist movement led by Hitler had come to power in Germany promising to expand Germany's living space by conquests of land in Eastern Europe. It was determined to carry out such a policy or perish in the attempt. Hitler was no more likely to abandon his project for the simple, quick and easy attack in the East than he had been willing — as Raeder well knew — to forego the operation which had been proclaimed the necessary preliminary: the major war in the West. If Germany was not to seize land in Eastern Europe, what was the point of the National Socialist government and of the war in the first place? It is doubtless probable that the war would have become a very different one had Germany concentrated on the Mediterranean instead of launching an invasion of the Soviet Union, but any such shift presupposed not merely a change of direction in the military effort but a complete change in the top leadership of the country — and this Raeder was never prepared to contemplate.

The third major difference of opinion between Hitler and Raeder began in the summer of 1941 and continued until early 1942. It concerned the stationing and employment of Germany's remaining major surface warships after the sinking of the battleship *Bismarck* in May, 1941. Raeder very strongly preferred to leave the battleships *Scharnhorst* and *Gneisenau* as well as the heavy cruiser *Prinz Eugen* at Brest with the basic intention of continuing to employ them in the war against Allied shipping, primarily in the Atlantic Ocean. It was his belief that in this role the ships could both provide an important addition to the sinkings being inflicted by German submarines and demonstrate the significance of surface ships to the German navy of the future. Hitler, on the other hand, was convinced, after the loss of the *Bismarck*, and in the face of repeated British air raids on Brest, that the German ships would be hunted down and sunk or wrecked by bombs in port if employed as Raeder preferred and that the same fate awaited the new battleship, *Tirpitz*, being readied for inclusion in Germany's operational fleet. Instead, Hitler wanted the big ships transferred to Norway because he believed that continued control of Norway was of the highest importance to Germany and that the British would be likely to attempt an invasion of that country once the German invasion of the Soviet Union, already set for the late spring of 1941, was under way.

The dash up the English Channel, in which the three ships successfully made their way through the Channel under the noses of the mortified British, was to lead the two battleships onto mines which the Royal Air Force had quickly laid in lanes previously swept of mines by the Germans. It took months to repair the *Scharnhorst*, while the *Gneisenau* was hit by British bombers as she was undergoing repairs and never returned to active status. It can certainly be acknowledged that if Hitler had followed Raeder's advice, the two ships would not have been mined on the way to their eventual destination in Norway. The fact that the *Gneisenau* was wrecked in port, however, suggests that Hitler's belief that the ships would sooner or later be demolished by bombers if they continued to be based on Brest had a solid foundation.

Furthermore, Raeder's expectation that the ships could play a major part in contributing to Germany's effort in the Battle of the Atlantic rested on very dubious premises. In May and June of 1941 the British swept the northernmost reaches in the North Atlantic of the weather and supply ships which the German navy had stationed there primarily to support its surface warship operations.[5] Thereafter, sorties by warships from Brest were very likely to end very much the way that of the *Bismarck* did. It is, of course, possible that before being sunk in action or wrecked by bombers while in port, the German ships would have inflicted some substantial damage on allied shipping, but given the greatly increased British ability to read German radio messages in the latter months of 1941, partly as a result of cypher material captured in the sweep of weather and supply ships, it would seem much more likely that the dispatch of the surface ships into the North Atlantic would rather have resembled the suicide mission of the *Scharnhorst* from its Norwegian base in December, 1943. The responsibility for that German naval disaster rests with Raeder's successor, Admiral Dönitz.

On practically all major issues, the enthusiastic National Socialist Dönitz agreed with Hitler, and it could in fact be said that Dönitz not only agreed with Hitler on all essential points, but actually influenced the Führer very considerably. On the employment of the Navy, and particularly on the continuation of the submarine campaign after the German defeat in May, 1943, and again in the fall of that year, it was Dönitz who urged on Hitler the policies and priorities that were actually adopted. Furthermore, the high priority which Dönitz persuaded Hitler to give to the hopes of the German navy for a resumption of the submarine campaign with new types of submarines played a major role in getting Hitler to adopt a military strategy on the Eastern Front in the last year of the war which, with its effort to protect the Baltic training ground of the German navy, brought him into one of the bitterest of his conflicts with the professional soldiers to be taken up in the following section.[6] In any case, it was a reflection of Hitler's enormous confidence in Dönitz as a devoted follower and a man like-minded about the conduct of the war that he appointed the admiral to be his own successor.

It is at this point that we can turn back and look at Hitler's relationship with his generals at key points during World War II. Certainly in initiating that war, he and his professional military advisors were of one accord. With very few exceptions, they were not just willing but even eager to go to war with Poland in 1939. The subsequent push into Scandinavia was at the instance of the German navy, and of Admiral Raeder in particular. (Raeder claimed otherwise, but during the war, he always pointed to this enterprise as the great feather in the navy's cap which he himself had been wise enough to advocate *before* the events to which he attributed the decision in post-war apologies.) The planned German attack in the West was undoubtedly one of the few instances of a major disagreement between Hitler and most of Germany's military leaders. Hitler wanted to launch the offensive through the Low Countries into northern France already in the fall of 1939, preferably in early November. A large number of the German army's leaders did not agree.

It was Hitler's opinion that the time for Germany to strike was when she still had a headstart in armaments and before the British and French could utilize their extensive resources to catch up. Furthermore, he argued that the international situation was as favorable for Germany as it was likely to get: the Soviet Union might not always be so helpful; Mussolini might not always be in charge of Italy; and the United States was still neutral and very weak. Confident that Germany, fighting on only one front, could beat France and England, he wanted to strike in the West, the sooner the better. As for the violation of the neutrality of Holland, Belgium and Luxembourg, that was something he had been planning to do for a long time and gave him no pause. That such an action might lead others to change *their* approach to war and to Germany clearly either did not occur to him or did not bother him if he thought about it at all.

On this last point, a second violation of Belgian neutrality compounded by the violation of Holland's, several of the generals were quite uneasy. Others, under the influence of their World War I experience, were very much concerned about a possible repetition of the deadlock on the western front in which Germany had eventually succumbed. They preferred to let the allies try to attack. Still others were at least somewhat hopeful that after an interval, it might still be possible to work out some sort of compromise peace with the Western Powers by which Germany could keep much of what she had conquered in Poland but would avoid a new major war altogether, while many held to varying combinations of all these opinions.

It is extremely difficult to develop a convincing scenario for what would have happened had the Germans not attacked in the west. There are, however, three complications with this set of speculations. In the first place, the success of the Scandinavian venture both changed the attitude of the West, especially Great Britain, to the prospect of continued war, reducing rather than increasing any possible willingness to consider a compromise peace. On the other hand, that same campaign certainly emboldened the Germans. Secondly, the repeated postponements of the planned attack in the West provided the opportunity for the Germans to change the initial plan from a thrust primarily in the northern sector into the plan eventually adopted, designed to cut off the allied troops hastening to assist the invaded neutrals. In the process, the confidence of Germany's military leaders in the likely success of the operation steadily increased, and their objections against an offensive in the west as steadily decreased.

There had been some among them who during the winter had toyed with the idea of displacing Hitler. Representatives of some of the opposition had contacted the British government about such prospects. With a minute number of lower level exceptions, all fell into line in the end and played a major role in the violation of the neutrality of the Low Countries instead of overthrowing Hitler, thereby forever destroying their own credibility as opponents of Hitler in the west. In the third place, one must question whether the rejection of the idea of an offensive in the west was not in many ways similar to the later objection of Admiral Raeder against an invasion of the Soviet Union which has already been discussed. Hitler had always planned a war in the West to enable Germany to seize vast stretches of land in the East. If the generals did not agree with this program, their only alternative was to remove Hitler altogether, and this the overwhelming majority was not prepared to do.

No significant divergence between Hitler and his military leaders developed in the campaign in the West thereafter. There was also no substantial disagreement with Hitler's summer 1940 decision to invade the Soviet Union, or with his drastic under-assessment of that country's military power.[7] On the contrary, Hitler yielded to the advice of those among the military who urged against Hitler's preference for an attack still in the fall of 1940 for a postponement until 1941, so that the transfer of German forces from west to east and the preparations of an adequate logistic base for an eastern campaign could be accomplished more easily. Several officers had doubts about the attack on Greece, but there were no substantial divergences on the general issues of the Balkan campaign of the spring of 1941. From the available evidence it would appear that the decision to utilize the available German airborne strength for an assault on Crete rather than Malta was very much in accord with the preference not only of Hitler but of General Student, the commander of German airborne troops. In the later arguments over a Malta operation in 1942, Hitler's opponents were the Italian, not the German, generals and least of all Rommel who always favored rushing forward regardless of logistic and other considerations.

Once the campaign in the east had been launched there were periodic differences of views, but as already mentioned, in most instances these saw the German military split among themselves rather than simply wanting to go a different path from Hitler's. With few exceptions, they agreed with his concept of this campaign as an ideological war of annihilation rather than a conventional military conflict. The circulars issued by German higher commanders to their troops justifying the mass murder of the Jews and of other categories of individuals reflect uneasy rumblings among the soldiers rather than objections from the field marshals and generals who signed those terrible documents — and who were not normally in the habit of explaining themselves to their men.

Whether a vigorous effort actually to take Leningrad on the run in the fall of 1941 would have resulted in the seizure of the city — or a long and bitter street battle — will have to remain an open question. Here there appears to have been a real difference of opinion, but whether a different tactic would have made a major difference is difficult to decide. Hitler and his commanders did begin to have very serious differences once the Soviet winter offensives had driven the Germans on the defensive, first in the north and south and then, most dramatically, before Moscow. Again it is difficult, with few exceptions, to see in retrospect where a different choice would have made for a substantially different outcome. At the southern end of the front, the German troops undoubtedly had to pull back to the Mius river as Rundstedt argued. In the central and most critical portion of the front, the differences of opinion between Hitler and certain of his field commanders are far more difficult to analyze because in several instances the army group commander, first Field Marshal von Bock and then his replacement, Field Marshal von Kluge, agreed with Hitler.

In the dramatic situation of the winter 1941-42, three things were obvious. All had little to do with any difference between Hitler and the professional military. In the first place, whatever strategy was followed in the East hereafter, the German army would never again be able to attack simultaneously on the whole front; the basic plan to defeat the Soviet Union in short, swift blows had failed.[8] Second, German military intelligence on the Soviet Union had failed abysmally, predicting just before the Red Army's offensive that it was incapable of launching one; and this record of practically invariably making erroneous predictions would remain the hallmark of "Foreign Armies East" as the agency was called.[9] In the third place, the crisis in the East coincided with the German declaration of war on the United States, a course toward which Hitler had been steering and against which not a single German military figure voiced any objection.

The extraordinarily irregular shape of the front at the end of the fighting that winter was undoubtedly in part due to Hitler's insistence on holding ground regardless of Soviet breakthroughs in adjacent sectors. In specific local situations it is certainly possible to argue that those who advocated retreat were correct and Hitler's insistence on holding on mistaken. On the other hand, it can also be argued that retreats generally involved the loss of equipment and supplies Germany could ill afford to lose, and that shortening the front curiously enough had the same shortening effect for the Russians. More important, it seems to me, is the fact that unless the coalition against Germany, which the Germans themselves had created, fell apart, there was practically no way that Germany could still win; and the differences within the German command structure which became much more vehement and clear-cut from 1943 on were related to differing perceptions of this issue. The point is most easily illuminated by attention to three major disputes in which the military professionals were indeed largely opposed to Hitler's choices.

Before these differences are analyzed, something must be said about the extraordinary crisis in Hitler's relations with his military advisors in September, 1942. It was in this crisis that the army group commander in the Caucasus was relieved (with Hitler temporarily taking the position himself), Army Chief-of-Staff Halder was replaced, and Hitler intended also to replace his closest military assistant General Jodl (but eventually did not carry out this change). Not long before this upheaval, Hitler had also relieved the commander of the other army group in the 1942 summer offensive.

There cannot be any doubt that this set of closely inter-related personnel changes, and Hitler's altered view of his immediate entourage, reflected a certain shocked realization that the great summer offensive, on which so much depended, was not going the way Hitler wanted and expected. The war in the West was also taking a decided turn in new directions, with the first thousand plane raid occurring three months earlier. Hitler could, it would appear, see by now, the possibility of the whole enterprise of war not coming off successfully. It was not so much a specific strategic or tactical difference with the generals, but rather a recognition that the whole effort might end badly, that must, in my judgement, be adduced to explain the otherwise incomprehensible discrepancy between the question in dispute — how best to get through one of the passes in the Caucasus — and the intended total reshuffle of the German military command structure. On the one hand, if Hitler had not interfered in the Caucasus operation in the slightest, it would have gone forward essentially exactly the way it did. On the other hand, the possibility of total defeat as an alternative to the hoped for total victory may make it easier to understand the major differences of opinion between Hitler and his generals in the following years of fighting in the East.

The major issues in the Stalingrad operation were ones on which, as earlier indicated, Hitler and his main ground forces advisor, Field Marshal von Manstein, were in agreement. The question which arose after the repulse of Manstein's relief effort and on which there was a major difference of views was that of the withdrawal of the German army group which had been sent to the Caucasus. Manstein, along with other German generals, wanted it completely evacuated to assist in the rebuilding of the German southern front. Hitler, on the other hand, insisted on a substantial portion, essentially the German 17th Army, remaining in the North Caucasus area and holding a bridgehead there. What was this argument all about and what did this difference mean?

Hitler still planned to win the war. To do that, he expected to have to seize the Caucasus oil fields both to deprive the Soviet Union of that major source of petroleum products and to fuel the German (as well as the Italian) war machine. As long as that looked to him like even a remote possibility, it made sense to him to hold on to a bridgehead across the Kerch Straits as a basis for future operations. Why give up voluntarily such a bridgehead only to have to seize it again? And if the remaining German troops were transferred to the southern end of the main front in the Ukraine, the Red Army units facing them would similarly be available for transfer elsewhere.

Manstein and other German generals, on the other hand, had given up on the possibility of seizing the Caucasus altogether. If the Germans had not been able to go that far either in 1941 or in 1942, there was surely no chance of doing so in 1943 or thereafter. Hence in their eyes it made more sense to pull the troops out and place them in the line where they would be more effective in defending continued German control of the Ukraine. What would follow such a success, however, was something none of them appears to have thought about. If it worked, what then? Did they expect the Soviet government to abandon one of the richest portions of the country to permanent German occupation? It appears more likely that this was expected to be a step toward losing the war in a less messy way than the one Hitler appeared to be heading for. Certainly there is no evidence to suggest that the subsequent campaign in the East would have gone very differently had the advice of the military been heeded.

A second major difference between Hitler and his generals occurred soon after at the same southern end of the Eastern Front. It involved the question of evacuating German and Romanian troops cut off in the Crimea by the advance of the Red Army. Hitler wanted to hold on to the area, partly because he hoped that a land connection could be reestablished by a German counter-offensive, partly because he was afraid that Red Air Force planes from there could attack the important Romanian oil fields, and partly because he was worried about the repercussions of any evacuation on the position of

Turkey. The German commanders thought that the first of these prospects was unlikely, that the second could not be helped, and that the third was outside their area of competence. The Romanians, and especially their leader, Marshal Ion Antonescu, believed that the evacuation was essential because it involved the only reasonably well armed and trained Romanian troops available for the defense of the home country after the Stalingrad disaster, with its tremendous loss of Romanian forces.

This is one case where an excellent case can be made for the position of the generals and of Antonescu (whose views Hitler generally listened to with considerable attention). Had the Axis troops cut off in the Crimea been evacuated in time, the defection of Romania and the destruction of the Germany army group in that country, followed by the rapid Soviet occupation of Romania and Bulgaria, would quite likely have been somewhat delayed. The Soviet units involved in first containing and the conquering the Crimea would, of course, also have been available for duty elsewhere, but the Germans and Romanians would probably have been better served by an early evacuation.

When one asks, however, what the longer term implications of such a change would have been, one would have to say that it all made little difference. Once the Red Army shifted its center of attack from the central portion of the Eastern Front to the southern and northern segments in the fall of 1944, the Germans were going to be driven out of the Balkans, and Romania and Bulgaria occupied, one way or another. More of the German and Romanian soldiers captured by the Red Army first in the Crimea and thereafter in Romania would presumably have been killed in the fighting. The whole process would have taken some weeks longer. The Red Army's offensive into Hungary would, likewise, have been delayed. There would also have been vastly more destruction in Romania in the fighting over that country. It is, however, difficult to see that all this would have altered the basic contours of the war in any substantial way; ironically, it probably ended up meaning that large numbers of German soldiers ended up in Soviet captivity instead of being killed in the fighting.

The same equally unanticipated result would issue from the even more heated difference between Hitler and his generals at the other end of the Eastern Front. In October, 1944, the Red Army succeeded in cutting off German Army Group North by driving to the Baltic Sea behind its front. The previous occasion had been under circumstances where it was still possible for the Germans to muster the reserves needed for a major counter-attack which reopened land communications with the army group; by October such an operation was practically impossible. Under these circumstances, the Chief of Staff of the German Army, by this time General Guderian, urged the evacuation of the two armies cut off in western Latvia so that the units could be utilized to reinforce the desperately-fighting German forces along the border of East Prussia and further south. Hitler agreed to the evacuation of many of the divisions but insisted that the equivalent of one army hold on to what the Germans called the "Kurland" (Courland) bridgehead. What was the point and what difference did it make?

Hitler was hoping at first that contact could again be reestablished, but his insistence on holding on when it had become obvious that this was not feasible was based on considerations relating to his broader view of the war at this time.[10] One concern was that Germany's critical iron imports from Sweden might be cut off by a Soviet naval advance in the Baltic attendant upon the loss of western Latvia. Even more important was his view of future strategy in the war as a whole, a view most strongly and consistently endorsed by Admiral Dönitz. It was Hitler's hope that the new types of submarines being built in large numbers in Germany would enable the German navy to return to a program of successful activity in the Atlantic. Faster even under water than the convoys of the Allies, able to stay under water almost indefinitely to avoid Allied planes and escort ship, the new submarines would turn the tide in the Battle of the Atlantic in Germany's favor. The American and British armies on the continent would be left without supplies and reinforcements and would therefore be either immobilized or pushed back. Such a victory in the West would enable Germany to transfer massive forces to the Eastern Front and strike effective blows against the Red Army. But if these rosy prospects were to be realized, the new submarines had to be worked up and their crews trained in the only body of water readily accessible as a training ground for the German navy: the Baltic. If every effort were not made to hold on to as much of the southern shore of the Baltic as possible, the new submarines about to come off the assembly lines could never be properly employed.

It can certainly be argued that this strategy rested on the shaky foundation of an assortment of illusions, and that Admiral Dönitz was at least as unbalanced as Hitler in steadily insisting that these fantasies were real prospects. One could, however, as readily ask whether Guderian's views were any more realistic. Would a relatively small number of additional divisions, almost entirely without armor, have made any substantial difference on the Eastern Front in the winter of 1944-45? He certainly argued with Hitler most vehemently over this issue, and it was in connection with this dispute that he was dismissed from his position as Chief of the General Staff of the German Army, but what would have happened if Guderian had his way?

In this case the evidence is reasonably clear about the alternative. The German navy was still in a position to evacuate the remaining troops from Latvia. These could indeed have been assigned to the front in East Prussian and Poland. There they would certainly had added to the immense German casualties incurred as the Red Army launched its winter offensive. The addition of the Courland troops to the German side, and the transfer of the Red Army units facing then might have prolonged the bitter fighting for a couple of days in January or in April, 1945 — depending on whether they had been evacuated in time for the first or the second Red Army offensive. But there is not the slightest evidence that the course of events on the main front in the East would have been any more different than that. As it was, the Courland divisions marched off into Soviet prisoner-of-war and labor camps in May, 1945, instead of being decimated in the winter fighting. The Soviets in fact had come to think of Courland as an elaborate POW camp maintained for them by the Germans. It all certainly made a big difference for the individual German soldiers, but not to the course of the war.

Let us return now to the Western Front in 1944 and 1945. The most important arguments affecting the German conduct of operations in the face of the anticipated invasion by the allies were among the German generals, not between them and Hitler.[11] After the allies were ashore, once again the immediate differences of opinion were of a similar sort. This was due to the fact that the German leaders had all been essentially equally fooled by the main allied deception operation. The first major difference occurred once the Americans had broken through the German front at its western end near Avranches and were pushing the newly activated American Third Army southward and into both Brittany and the rear of the German troops still holding in Normandy. The choice issue now was between an offensive operation toward the coast, designed to cut off the advancing Third Army and restore the old line, what came to be called the Mortain offensive, or trying to pull back the rest of the German front so as to avoid the massive encirclement for which the German 7th Army and the Panzer Group West associated with it appeared to be headed.

Hitler definitely favored the offensive as against both the army group and army commanders who favored extricating the German troops from the threatened encirclement (which came to be known as the Falaise pocket). There cannot be any doubt that the Mortain offensive failed in part because the Allies had learned about it from Ultra, and that the resulting German defeat was of great proportions (and would have been greater had General Montgomery closed the encirclement from the north). The question must be asked, however, whether the outcome would have been substantially different had the advice of the generals been followed.

It is certainly possible that a withdrawal would have enabled more of the German troops to avoid being killed or captured in the Falaise pocket. The German armor utilized in the Mortain attack would have been available to protect the withdrawal. Given Montgomery's proclivity for chasing rather than cutting off and destroying the German forces he faced, it is at least conceivable that a new line would have stabilized temporarily somewhere in France with vast additional destruction accompanying the fighting around such a new series of front lines. What must be recalled, however, is that the Allies had decided on the invasion of southern France, regardless of British protests. The success of that landing, which the Germans were in no position to prevent, guaranteed that the allied forces in France could be adequately supplied regardless of whether or not the ports on the Channel and North Sea ports were liberated. Under these circumstances, there was no way in which the Germans could evict the Allies from France. With the growing strength of the American forces, there could also be little doubt that any new lines established across France would also be broken. It certainly made some difference precisely where and under what circumstances the battle in the West came to something of a standstill in the winter of 1944/45, but once again we are talking about matters of detail rather than broader significance.

The next significant difference over the conduct of the war in the West came with the Ardennes Offensive. One concerned the concept of a major offensive in the West under any circumstances; the other about its direction if it were carried out at all. On the first issue, we are really looking at a difference of opinion between General Guderian, who was primarily responsible for the Eastern Front, and the commanders in the West. Guderian believed that Germany's reserves should be concentrated on the Eastern Front in defense of German home soil against the expected Soviet winter offensive. Hitler believed that the situation in the West offered the best hope of making a major impact with the last reserves Germany had scraped together because a force which could have such an impact in the West would never have an analogous effect in the vastly greater eastern theater.

It is undoubtedly possible that if the mass of the two German panzer armies which provided the bulk of the offensive strength in the December 1944 offensive had instead been committed to the Eastern Front, that would have resulted in making the final stage of the campaign in Europe harder for the Russians and easier for the Americans and British. It is also barely conceivable that this would have meant a meeting of the Allies in central Europe even further east than proved to be the case, but that is more speculative since the Germans would hardly have kept as large a contingent in the East — and would certainly not have sent such massive reinforcements to Hungary — had the Americans, British, and Canadians arrived on the middle and lower Rhine earlier and with their strength unaffected by the Battle of the Bulge. But the Red Army would have punched through any way, and the final result would have been primarily a larger Soviet bag of prisoners and a smaller American one.

The same thing applies to the arguments in April over the employment of the Wenck Army. Originally designed to drive a land connection westward to the German army group surrounded by the Americans in the Ruhr pocket, this army was turned around to fight in the opposite direction after it had lost most of its punch. Its new direction eastwards was designed to reopen connections to Berlin instead, but had it been given that assignment from the start, more of it would have been destroyed by the Russians rather than the Americans. It is true that its actions against the Americans further discouraged the latter from pushing on to Berlin, but there is little to show that without that discouragement such a move would have been made or that, had it been made, the Americans would have acted differently about Berlin than they did about Leipzig. The agreements about occupation zones had been made long before, and certainly the Americans, who wanted Russian assistance in the ongoing war with Japan, were not about to diverge from lines which the British had devised and which that country jointly with the Soviet Union had pushed the reluctant Americans into accepting the preceding fall.

Another disagreement concerning the German December offensive was between Hitler and commanders in the West. The latter were in favor of a sort of preventive offensive designed to throw the Allies off balance and improve the German position. Hitler insisted on a larger and more ambitious operation aimed at reaching and seizing the port of Antwerp with the expectation of bringing about a major shift in the whole situation in the West.

Had the preference of the military leaders in the West, led by Field Marshal von Rundstedt, prevailed, there would have been a more limited and somewhat differently designed operation. Once again the details of battle would surely have been different from those which followed on the type of offensive Hitler ordered, but the overall effect would hardly have been very different. The Americans would not have been shaken up as much, and Montgomery would perhaps not have been placed in charge of the northern portion of the affected American front, thereby being deprived of the opportunity for the notorious press conference in which he made a fool of himself, but it is difficult to discern any other major difference in the final stages of the war on the Western front.

This rapid survey of the war in Europe can not touch on all instances in which German military leaders differed with Hitler. It may, however, show something of very great significance for any understanding of World War II. In spite of the impression sometimes given by German post-war memoirs, especially those written by former military men, the most striking thing about that war on the German side is the existence of a broad consensus at the highest level. There were arguments and differences of emphasis; and because of Hitler's increasing tendency to intervene in the minutiae of military affairs, those differences became more numerous and sometimes more heated in the later stages of the war. But except for the decision to attack in the West, a decision on which most of the military slowly came around to Hitler's point of view, on the most fundamental issues there was an extraordinarily high degree of agreement. Going to war in the first place, invading the Soviet Union, waging that conflict as a war of extermination rather than a conventional military one, and going to war with the United States, all these were decisions on which there was general agreement with only the most minute exceptions. On those points on which there were serious arguments, it generally made rather little difference which of the alternatives Germany followed. If all were beaten together, it was perhaps because they deserved it.

[1]   Werner Girbig, *Mit Kurs auf Launa: die Luftoffensive gegen die Treibstoffindustrie und der deutsche Abwehreinsatz, 1944-1945* (Stuttgart: Motorbuch Verlag, 1980), p.148.

[2]   Dieter Hölsken, "Die V-Waffen: Entwicklung und Einsätzgrundsatze," *Militargeschichtliche Mitteilungen*, 38 (1985), p.116.

[3]   Klaus A. Schuler, *Logistik im Russlandfeldzug: Die Rolle der Eisenbahn bei Planung, Vorbereitung und Durchführung des deutschen Angriffs auf die Sowjetunion bis zurKrise vor Moskau im Winter 1941/42* (Frankfurt & New York: Peter Lang, 1987).

4   Horst Boog, "German Air Intelligence in the Second World War," *Intelligence and National Security*, Vol. 5, No. 2 (Apr. 1990), 350-424.

5   David Kahn, *Seizing the Enigma: The Race to Break the German U-Boat Codes, 1939-1943* (Boston: Houghton Mifflin, 1991), chaps. 12-14.

6   Howard David Grier, "Hitler's Baltic Strategy, 1944-1945," PhD dissertation, University of North Carolina, 1991.

7   There is a helpful examination of this whole issue by Andreas Hillgruber, "Das Russland-Bild der führenden deutschen Militärs vor Beginn des Angriffs auf die Sowjetunion," in the Festschrift for Fritz T. Epstein, *Russland - Deutschland - Amerika* (Wiesbaden: Steiner, 1978), pp. 296-310.

8   An excellent analysis in Klaus Reinhard, *Die Wende vor Moskau: Das Scheitern der Strategie Hitlers im Winter 1941/42* (Stuttgart: Deutsche Verlags-Anstalt, 1972).

9   Two reviews of the blunders provide plenty of examples: Hans-Heinrich Wilhelm, "Die Prognosen der Abteilung Fremde Heere Ost 1942-1945," in *Zwei Legenden aus dem Dritten Reich* (Stuttgart: Deutsche Verlags-Anstalt, 1974), pp.7-75; and David Thomas, "Foreign Armies East and German Military Intelligence in Russia, 1941-45, "*Journal of Contemporary History*, 22 No. 2 (Apr. 1948), 2611-201.

10   See the work cited in note 6.

11   A good review of these arguments is in Alan Wilt, *The Atlantic Wall: Hitler's Defenses in the West* (Ames, Iowa: Iowa State University Press, 1975).

<h1>Chapter 14</h1>

<h1>Conclusion of the Pacific War</h1>

Paul R. Schratz

When a piece of the sun struck Hiroshima on 6 August 1945, the world changed, never to turn back. The atomic genie entered our lives, and for good or evil it came to stay. In the words of William Laurence of the New York Times, an observer of the Hiroshima blast,

> "At exactly 0815 this morning, Hiroshima stood out under a clear, blue sky. One tenth of a millionth of a second later, a time imperceptible by any clock, 45,000 inhabitants had been vaporized — men, women, children, their homes, deeply private possessions; the city had been swallowed by a cloud of swirling fire as though it had never existed. The best watches made by man still registered 0815." [Edited]

One might ask if less cataclysmic alternatives were not available.

A. What if the U.S. had responded favorably to Japanese peace overtures from the emperor's entourage in late 1944 and early 1945?

From 1937 to 1945, half the provinces of China and the whole of the American, British, French, and Dutch possessions in the Far East fell to Japanese conquest. The Imperial Army believed that the difficulty of piercing the defensive perimeter would cause the allies to lose heart and make peace. Japan would be in total control of the Southern Resources Area for which she went to war, and would concede a few islands in the defensive perimeter, by then redundant.

Several Japanese admirals favored negotiations for peace after the battle of Midway on 6 June 1942. Other officials joined the peace movement in July 1944 after the key loss of Saipan and penetration into the inner defense zone brought down the hawkish Tojo government. A transition government under Koniaki Koiso, inclined toward peace, struggled until April 1945 when the USSR terminated her 1941 treaty of neutrality with Japan. Baron Suzuki and a dovish coalition came into power, headed covertly by the emperor himself. But throughout, the real control of the government lay with the army.

Stalin played an important role in delaying any peace offer. Japanese leaders deluded themselves that they had a special relationship with the Soviet Union based on the neutrality treaty of April 1941; Stalin preyed on Japanese fears to prevent an approach to the western powers.

In late 1944 Premier Koiso planned to send Prince Konoye on a peace mission to Switzerland and Sweden. It came to nothing. A flurry of peace feelers to Portugal, Sweden, Switzerland, and the Vatican also failed. Because of fanatic opposition by the army and die-hards surrounding Emperor Hirohito, the trial balloons conveyed no government position, only a desire to end the war without sacrificing the dynasty. The only direct proposal to the United States came from Commander Fujimura, the Japanese naval attache in Bern, Switzerland. On his own initiative in April 1945, he informed Allen Dulles, the U.S. intelligence chief there, that Japan desired negotiations toward surrender. He then reported to Tokyo that Dulles had originated the dialog. His frequent follow-up messages were suppressed by the navy and came to nothing.

National moods in the United States were anything but favorable to peace overtures. Xenophobia and revenge against the Pearl Harbor attack dominated American thinking. Seventy percent favored execution, imprisonment or exile of Hirohito; only seven percent favored retention. But heavy allied losses on Iwo Jima and Okinawa added to the growing desire to stop the killing and bring an end to the most terrible war in history. Nearly half the total American battle casualties in three years of war in the Pacific occurred in the first three months of the Truman presidency. Yet America's allies strongly opposed compromise on unconditional surrender. The Commonwealth nations had suffered extensively in the war, particularly Australia, and urged total surrender, sacrificing the dynasty, trial or execution of Hirohito, and harsh terms for the Japanese.

Preserving the dynasty was non-negotiable to the Japanese, but its importance was little understood in Washington or the allied capitals. In the United States, the failing hand of FDR and his demise in April 1945 created a deadly hiatus in American policy making. A tyro president and two successive secretaries of state with no experience in foreign affairs left American foreign policy at its weakest in the five months from Yalta to Potsdam. Yet Japan's peace feelers did elicit some response in high quarters as the costs of the war mounted. As early as May 1944, State Department officials led by the assistant secretary and former ambassador to Japan, Joseph Grew, sought to compromise unconditional surrender to allow retention of the dynasty. The JCS defined it as pointed essentially at the military, and that national suicide was not demanded.

A further boost to peace sentiments was provided when a naval intelligence unit led by Captain Ellis M. Zacharias, USN, with strong backing by Secretary of the Navy James Forrestal, was given authority to use psychological warfare against Japan by short-wave radio. This masterful campaign succeeded beyond expectations in setting the stage for a new Japanese attempt at peace. It influenced the 18 June peace message by Premier Admiral Suzuki asking Moscow to intercede with the U.S. on peace with assurance only on preservation of the dynasty. His appeal naively assumed that Stalin desired an early conclusion of the war in the Pacific. This demarche served only to force the Soviet dictator, whom a premature truce would have left fuming on the sidelines, to step up his plans for an attack on Manchuria.

The U.S. knew of Suzuki's cable through Magic. Perhaps there might have been a more positive response if sentiment in Washington had not come largely under the influence of the atomic bomb, soon to be completed. Both the U.S. and U.K. saw increasingly less to gain and more to lose in a negotiated peace. If negotiations meant peace without the bomb, the western allies no longer believed it to be in their interests. Thus both Stalin's striving to get into the Pacific war and the U.S. and U.K. striving to use the bomb meant that Japan's message came to naught.

In assessing the probably results of a positive U.S. response had specific Japanese overture been made, much, perhaps all, depended on the factor of time. It seems highly improbably that even modification of unconditional surrender and assurance of preserving the dynasty could have ended the war in late 1944 or early 1945. The Japanese popular delusion on the state of military affairs might have made it impossible for the still weak peace party surrounding the emperor to bring about a surrender. Very probably, as Hirohito later told MacArthur, there would have been a civil war and a wave of assassinations including the emperor himself. Elements of the army, augmented by countless fanatics, would continue to fight in the mountains and outlying islands. Such an eventuality, MacArthur claimed, would require doubling the occupation forces and ten years to master.

More realistic considerations govern the outlook concerning a possible conclusion to the war in June 1945, when Washington learned via the Suzuki cable of Tokyo's readiness to sue for peace. Had the U.S. interpreted unconditional surrender to allow retention of the emperor in June rather than July 1945, it remains likely, but far from certain, that the emperor and his confidants could perhaps have engineered an earlier surrender without an unmanageable army uprising. But it might have been touch-and-go. The Imperial Army had controlled Japan for 700 years and when in August the emperor made his unprecedented decision to order surrender, fanatic officers attempted a bloody coup to prevent his address to the nation.

Stalin was not yet able to enter the war on more than a token basis. Peace talks in June, to Japan's advantage, might have found him without a seat at the negotiating table. He would inevitably have shared, as would France and Britain, in the division of East Asia into spheres of influence. Without the bomb, without the precipitate demobilization of the superb U.S. war machine, the Russians might have achieved a stronger position in the Far East and weakened the American position worldwide. Those eventualities, however, depended largely on U.S. efforts to bribe Stalin to enter the war and avert the bloodshed in the invasion of Japan.

B. What if the U.S. had not bribed the Soviets to enter the war?

The JCS stated emphatically on 23 November 1944 that a Soviet commitment to enter the Pacific war was not only desirable but necessary for victory without the greatest blood-letting of the war in the invasion of Japan — perhaps a half million allied casualties. Before the Big Three meeting at Yalta in February 1945, the U.S. and British Combined Chiefs estimated the war would last eighteen more months. General MacArthur, slated for command of the invasion, considered it inevitable that the Soviets would take all of Manchuria, Korea, and possibly part of North China. He though the U.S. should press Russia to pay her way by invading Manchuria at the earliest possible moment, thereby tying down the Kwantung Army to prevent its use against the invasion. Soviet participation was seen as necessary as long as invasion appeared unavoidable — and until the bomb became a factor in the decision.

At Yalta Stalin made vitally important concessions toward setting up the machinery of the UN and agreed to enter the Pacific war two or three months after the German surrender. He had already been promised the southern half of Sakhalin island, the Kurile islands off Alaska, and a warm water port at the end of the South Manchurian railway at Dairen. The U.S. terms, unfortunately — based on faulty military intelligence a grave underestimate of the effect of the atomic bomb and overestimate of the state of Japanese morale — were widely regarded as a sellout by the U.S. president. Roosevelt's decisions at Yalta at least hastened the fall of China into the Soviet orbit, and legitimized Soviet domination of liberated Eastern Europe, Poland, and the Baltic.

Unfortunately, President Roosevelt was negotiating from weakness. The U.S. forces in Europe were recovering from the German Ardennes offensive threatening Antwerp in December 1944: The Polish government in exile was sacrificed because Soviet army control made Lublin a de facto government. Soviet armies already had all the capitals of Eastern Europe in their hands and the three great capitals of Central Europe within their grasp. In the Far East, restoration of some Russian territories lost in the Russo-Japanese war of 1904-05 sought to create a Soviet bulwark against a resurgent postwar Japan — a bulwark much to be desired at that time. But these territories were available at any time to Stalin for the plucking. He needed little encouragement to go to war against Russia's historic enemy. He was driven to avenge Russian defeats by the Japanese; he had his own plans for Asia and entry into the Pacific war guaranteed him a seat at the peace table. With or without a territorial grab, it did not necessarily mean, then or later, that the USSR would have become a Pacific power.

The question again was the timing. The American desire to get a Soviet commitment worked almost in reverse. The long delay by the U.S. before opening a second front in Europe despite Stalin's pleading was believed by many, including Stalin, to allow the Soviet and German armies to bleed each other to death on the Central Front. The shoe was now on the other foot. Inviting Stalin to become a belligerent in Asia conceded him the initiative so that he could delay his entry until the last moment while the Americans bled.

What if FDR had offered no territorial concessions at Yalta? Allied submarine and air power had destroyed 93 percent of the Japanese merchant marine, but sizeable troop movements to Japan were believed to be neither possible nor necessary. Ultra portrayed a Japan in extremity but also showed its military leaders as being blind to defeat, bending all remaining national energy to smash the invasion of their divine home islands. Feverish efforts to withdraw men and material from Manchuria, Korea and North China produced seven new divisions in Kyushu between April and July 1945. Mobile combat strength almost tripled, soon outnumbering the Allied invaders at the critical landing sites, a cause for increasing concern by General MacArthur. Ordinary prudence seemed to dictate a need for a Soviet invasion of Manchuria to prevent Japanese withdrawals to beef up the home defenses. It also indicated a strong need for the USSR to enter the war in her own interest.

Other possibilities effected Soviet entry. Stalin had only 150,000 troops on the Manchurian border on VE day. If the war in Europe had lasted a few weeks longer, the Russian land armies could not have been moved to the Far East in time. Second, every day saved in rushing the A-bomb to completion brought the Japanese surrender a day closer. If the western leaders and their planners had been properly briefed on the bomb, the rudimentary Hiroshima gun-assembly type could have been rushed to completion and dropped well in advance of the Nagasaki plutonium type. Third, an earlier concession on unconditional surrender to allow retention of the dynasty would have brought an earlier surrender, probably without Soviet participation, without invasion, and perhaps without the bomb.

What if the Hiroshima bomb had been completed sooner? Shortly after Truman became president, the atomic bomb promised to become a major factor in making Soviet entry no longer necessary. All important problems of the two bomb types had been solved. But few people realized that the Hiroshima gun-assembly type, proven in the first chain reaction achieved in the Chicago Pile 1 experiment in 1943, needed no field test. Only the Nagasaki plutonium bomb was tested at Alamogordo. Lt. Gen. Leslie R. Groves, head of the Manhattan District which produced the bombs, promised Truman a 1 August ready date for both types. But Truman never knew that the Hiroshima bomb could have been ready possibly weeks earlier, before any likely date for a Soviet entry into the Pacific war.

The bomb caught the planners with their pants down. Vague details given the president, Leahy, Nimitz, and MacArthur were wholly inadequate. A formal role for the JCS was largely circumvented by Groves; secrecy and lack of imagination kept them skeptical or indifferent. If key officials including Combined Staff planners had been briefed adequately to develop operational parameters, plan to end the war and limit Russian gains in Asia would have been more advanced. Over-secrecy seriously limited political exploitation. Further, when a last minute glitch developed in the plutonium

(Nagasaki bomb) detonator, the Hiroshima bomb was delayed until both were ready. With minimal knowledge at operational planning levels, invasion plans could have been scrapped, the first bomb readied, and a Japanese surrender demanded by late June or early July.

Laying like a palsied hand over American leadership in these critical weeks before Potsdam was the problem of obtaining political guidance on important issues relating to the war. If the new president were less heavily engaged in domestic problems, if issues in terminating the war had not have fallen to the free-wheeling Secretary of State James F. Byrnes, the path of history may have followed a different course. Byrnes neither welcomed staff assistance nor informed his subordinates that the war might come suddenly to an end. Washington was wholly unprepared for the overwhelming political and military problems on the eve of surrender. There was no approved surrender document, no surrender proclamation nor general order on urgent problems of how the allies, particularly the Russians, were to divide the Japanese empire during the initial occupation — matters of supreme importance to the future of Asia.

The Japanese proposal of 18 June referred to above sought Stalin's mediation of Japanese-American peace talks. Since the message revealed the abject condition of Japan and the Japanese belief that the USSR had no plans to enter the war, Stalin delayed several weeks, until the meeting at Potsdam, before informing the Americans. Since Truman had known of the offer through Magic, he realized that Stalin was foot-dragging to prevent peace negotiations until he could become a belligerent.

When Truman told Stalin of 24 July, also at Potsdam, of the new and unusually destructive bomb soon to be used on Japan, Stalin was non-committal. When the Hiroshima bomb fell on 6 August, however, he fully realized that the precarious condition of Japan, plus the A-bomb, might produce a sudden Japanese surrender with the Russians still on the sidelines. Quickly, and without notifying the allies, Stalin struck across the Manchurian border and declared war on Japan on 8 August.

Stalin claimed that the Politburo was concerned about the ghastly bloodletting in Europe and found little enthusiasm for a new war in Asia. Hence his eleventh-hour declaration of war on Japan sought to capitalize on a belligerent status in the peace negotiations with minimum bloodshed. If the Japanese fought with the same ferocity they had displayed at Iwo Jima and Okinawa, a surprise offensive against the 750,000 troops remaining in Manchuria risked disaster without major reinforcements from Europe. Yet if he stayed out completely, there was no basis in the peace negotiations for Truman to uphold the concessions made by FDR.

If Stalin had not entered the war, the bribe at Yalta would have been unnecessary. Since Soviet entry was important only as long as a U. S. invasion of Japan was unavoidable, the need for a Soviet attack on Manchuria ended either on 18 June 1945, when Japan asked the Soviets to mediate U.S.-Japanese peace talks, or a few weeks later, if the Hiroshima bomb had been used earlier. In either case, Japan would almost certainly have surrendered before Stalin entered the Pacific war, with consequent limitations on his postwar influence in Asia. A new vision would open for Harry Truman, soon to ride the atomic bomb toward a dominant American power position in Asia.

Had Stalin not entered the war, the tense balance in Asia promised new opportunities. Japan was prostrate; the European colonial empires were gone; China was in turmoil. Stalin's vision of the "Russo-Chinese Empire" of czarist days stimulated postwar political initiatives targeting China, Korea, and Indonesia. He wanted Sakhalin and the Kuriles to control the Okhotsk Sea and guard access of the fleet to the Pacific. His pet idea, the creation of a great navy in the shipyards of Japan, Manchuria and Russia, plus

Japanese and German fleet remnants, promised expansion into the blue Pacific as a future naval power.

C. What if no A-bomb had existed or, if so, none had been dropped?

The U.S. Strategic Bombing Survey concluded that Japan would have surrendered probably before 1 November 1945, without the bomb, without Russian entry, and without invasion. There is little reason to question that judgment today. In P. M. S. Blackett's words,

> "If the bombs had not been dropped, America would have seen the Soviet armies engaging a major part of the Japanese land forces in battle, overrunning Manchuria and taking a half million prisoners. All this would have occurred while American land forces would have been no nearer Japan than Iwo Jima and Okinawa. One can sympathize with the chagrin which such an outcome would have been regarded.[1]

If the A-bomb had not existed, the military effects of a possible delay in the surrender of a few weeks would have been minor. Unrestricted air and sea war plus mining of inland waterways, sharply increasing after May, would soon have cut off the home islands from significant movement of troops, food and raw materials and forced a surrender. The need for invasion would have passed and the added cost in allied lives, without the bomb, would have been superficial.

The political effects of the bomb in establishing an American postwar power role were far-reaching, however. Unrestricted use of the bomb against non-combatants raised serious moral questions. A Truman decision against its use, for legal or moral reasons, would have gained stature for American restraint but a major crisis in Washington would have erupted. The vengeful mood of the American people toward Japan, the enormous talent, treasure and resources spent in developing the bomb, the presumption of shortening the war and saving lives by its use, and the public outcry if the bomb were shelved left little room for maneuver. Insiders could not believe that "the world's greatest scientific achievement," pursued with a maximum national effort, could be put aside while the war still raged.

Lt. Gen. Groves urgently sought operational use of both the Hiroshima and Nagasaki types and was scared the Japanese would surrender before both bombs could be dropped. He schemed to speed up the process before a possible surrender, even to the point of trying to circumvent the Joint Chiefs to do so. Use of both bombs was assumed by almost all — a decision without actually deciding — and never analyzed for the monumental short-or long-term effects. The bombs shocked the enemy into surrender and galvanized the peace faction around the emperor to intervene decisively in the peace process. Dropping the bomb shortened the war, gave Tokyo a face-saving device to surrender, and reversed the urgency to get Stalin into the war. It allowed Japan to face the new era as one nation under an emperor symbolizing unity. It changed the whole structure of postwar Japan. It prevented the communism from sweeping through Japan and her conquests. It provided the leverage to obtain a postwar settlement largely on American terms, and it put new muscle behind the American power position worldwide.

What if only one bomb had been dropped? Several authorities noted that Japan's Supreme War Council was still split 3-3 after the Nagasaki bomb drop and claim that both were necessary. But on 8 August, on receiving the horrifying details of Hiroshima and before the Nagasaki bomb, Emperor Hirohito told Prime Minister Suzuki Kantoro that he wanted a prompt surrender "on whatever terms were necessary." He prevailed over the cabinet dissenters in an unprecedented initiative to break the stalemate. It was his decision — to accept Potsdam but retain the dynasty — ratified unanimously by the full cabinet at 0300 on 10 August. President Truman had the news in Washington 21 hours later, at 0900 local time on the tenth and, while debating acceptance, sent a message to MacArthur and Nimitz to prepare for a sudden surrender.

The second bomb was not necessary. It merely compounded the destruction and loss of life, primarily for a combat test of a new weapon. The single bomb brought a quick surrender but it did not save the countless thousands of American lives often claimed. Before historians gained access to secret files, the myth of huge numbers of American, British, and Japanese lives saved had already achieved the status of accepted history. Recent analyses, however, found that the number of allied lives saved by the two bombs almost certainly would not have exceeded 20,000 and would probably have been much lower. The vaporization of a city was not a primary factor. Nevertheless, the shock effect clarified the issues, and, in Emperor Hirohito's quoted words, "gave us an excuse to surrender earlier without losing face."[2]

At the last minute, use of the A-bomb might have been avoided by a Japanese surrender. The emperor deemed the Potsdam ultimatum acceptable from the beginning; on 3 August Prime Minister Suzuki and the cabinet advisors unanimously recommended acceptance. If Japan had been less lethargic in pursuing this last chance for peace, less obtuse in failing to recognize Soviet treachery, less naive in expecting Soviet mediation without a price tag, and less short-sighted in assuming that Stalin would favor keeping the emperor when toppling him was wholly in the Soviet interest—then hope could have stayed alive to avoid the atomic holocaust.

The Japanese response to the Potsdam ultimatum tied surrender to preservation of the dynasty. Had not an allied decision been forced as a condition of peace, would the dynasty have survived? Soviet pressure and American and allied public opinion clamoring for execution or imprisonment of Hirohito as a war criminal might have prevailed. Waves of fanaticism in Japan would spread turmoil through the Far East. Stalin's rampant march into Manchuria and Korea would have strengthened his demands for partitioning Japan with Russian troops sharing occupation duties. If no bomb had existed, the military effects of a few more weeks of war would have been minor. But the political effects on the American postwar role and her power position in Asia would have been far-reaching. It kept the emperor on the throne to preside over a unified Japan and prevented the cancer of communism from paralyzing the country. A last-minute surrender might have prevented the bomb—but was not the world better served by its use?

D. What if a Japanese surrender had been sought by "demonstrating" the bomb?

Roosevelt and Churchill at Hyde Park in 1944 casually discussed a "non-combat demonstration" of the bomb but agreed that the idea was premature. A demonstration would have greatly reduced the loss of life, eased the surrender process, and achieved the same timely result at far less cost. Significantly, the stigma on the U.S. for a violation of the laws of warfare, or for using the bomb "only against Asians," would not have arisen. If a demonstration were desired, some suggested avoiding public revulsion by bombing a desert or barren isle before the eyes of the allied nations. Some wanted a drop on an isolated Japanese forest such as Nikko or on the fleet remnants in Kure, to limit the death and destruction of non-combatants. Physicist Edward Teller suggested a high altitude night blast 20,000 feet over Tokyo where the awesome sound and light effects with minimal loss of life and property might have been persuasive. These suggestions were never considered seriously by policy makers.

For a demonstration to succeed, the desired psychological effect required direct visual evidence. The high altitude night blast over Tokyo would have maximized the number of observers whereas few in Hiroshima survived to tell the tale; reports trickling in to Tokyo carried little impact on people already devastated by more extensive loss of life and property in fire bombings. The Hiroshima blast destroyed communications with Tokyo immediately; the army tried to hide the ghastly evidence, refused to accept the bomb as atomic, and claimed to have countermeasures through proper shelters. Earthworms a few inches below the surface survived the atomic blast, they claimed.

The most practical type of demonstration received no consideration. If a prestigious international committee, including Japanese had been invited to witness a special detonation of the Hiroshima bomb at Alamogordo—not the plutonium type actually tested there—what harm could have resulted? Would it have been better or worse if Japan knew? It was far too late for the Japanese to capitalize on any technical information gained; their own atomic research program long before had ended in disaster. Why should the United States waste time and resources on a demonstration overseas merely to tell Japan we had the bomb? An additional detonation using the Hiroshima type bomb at Alamogordo ran no risk of failure and would certainly have influenced the peace. If it failed, there was no uranium available for another Hiroshima type bomb and manufacture of two plutonium bombs would delay use until about September 1945. But because of excessive secrecy senior policy makers knew little beyond the mere existence of the bomb. The non-combat demonstration was dismissed erroneously as "unduly risky and not compelling." Official Washington reached a virtually unchallenged consensus on targeting non-combatants in cities.

A deliberately targeted Japanese city, with prior warning, had been tentatively endorsed by Roosevelt and Churchill. Truman, however, feared that a warning might impel the Japanese to move POWs into the target area. He objected to using the bomb against civilians and opted for a drop, without warning, on a military target.

Would a nuclear demonstration be an effective deterrent in future crises? In the short term it might have ended World War II and soon been forgotten. But the ghastly loss of life and property at Hiroshima and the continuing hazard of radiation and genetic damage a half century later, unique in world experience, brought a revolutionary change in the relations of man to the universe etched indelibly on the human conscience. The stricken city became the world peace center where for almost 50 years, 1½ million visitors each year file past the perpetual flame, to burn until the last nuclear weapon disappears from the globe.

In sum, the various non-combat demonstrations discussed were never considered seriously by policy makers. The most practical idea was never thought of—inviting a prestigious international committee, including Japanese, to witness a test of the Hiroshima (gun type) device at Alamogordo. This type was not tested before dropping it on Hiroshima. It might have succeeded in ending the war. But more importantly, the ghastly loss of life and continuing horrors of radiation froze the experience in the world's memory as a vital and continuing deterrent to nuclear war. The horror of Hiroshima was a lesser price to pay for an everlasting deterrent than a far more catastrophic initiation into nuclear war at a later opportunity.

E. What if the allies had invaded the Japanese homeland?

The Japanese people never experienced an invasion. Drops falling from the swords of ancient gods created the sacred Land of the Gods. But the calamitous Imperial Navy losses plus fall of the Marianas, Iwo Jima and Okinawa, changed invasion estimates from remote to inevitable. Japanese intelligence predicted an Allied assault before 1 November in the Kagoshima and Ariake Bay areas of southern Kyushu to gain naval and air bases for a knock-out blow to the industrial and political heart of Japan in the Tokyo-Yokohama area. This happened to be a precise who, what, where, when, and how of the allied plan.

Under the Japanese defense plan *Ketsu-Go* ("Operation Decisive"), 5,000 kamikaze and perhaps 3,000 conventional aircraft of varying airworthiness were dispersed at 70 airfields, 24 seaplane bases, and 200 concealed takeoff strips throughout Japan; 19 destroyer types, hundreds of midget submarines, and 2,000 small, fast suicide craft prepared to attack the invasion fleet at night. Makeshift floating bombs were ready at 98 secret Shinto bases. To save food and release prison guards for duty at the front, all U.S. and U.K. POWs were to be executed. Lastly, Japan had used chemical weapons against China and allied planners anticipated extensive use of biological weapons in the final campaigns. A shipload of plague-infested fleas and rats enroute to the battlefields of Saipan in July 1944 was sunk by the American submarine "Swordfish" off Chichi Jima with the loss of almost all hands. (None of the rats left the sinking ship.) One can only guess at the dire consequences had delivery been made. The vast Japanese biological warfare plant hidden near Mukden, Manchuria, allegedly had the materials to destroy half the people on earth.[3]

If invaded, the Japanese envisioned a whirlwind counter-attack engulfing the allies on the beaches; hourly waves of 300-400 kamikaze attacks would overwhelm the naval air defenses; 15 to 30 percent of the invasion fleet of 5,000 ships would be put out of action before the first American soldier hit the beach. (In the Okinawa campaign, 402 Allied ships were sunk or damaged by kamikazes—twenty times the naval losses at Pearl Harbor—and 10,000 killed or wounded, five times the Navy losses at Pearl). The 700,000 defenders were backed by the entire population prepared to die "at the water's edge." Interlocking fire from high ground, camouflaged from air and sea observation, dominated the beaches. Critical hills were networks with tunnels, deep underground rooms, command posts, food and ammunition storage, even wells for fresh water. The ferocious defenses aimed to make the cost high enough in blood to force an allied withdrawal and a negotiated peace settlement. The entire nation would fight to the last ditch, then in the ditch with bamboo spears.

All Japanese planning emphasized the glory of suicide attacks. Home guards, including children, were trained in anti-tank war to throw themselves underneath advancing tanks with explosives strapped to their backs. (They were called "Sherman carpets.") The emphasis was on death rather than defeating the invader. Yet despite a homeland army of 2,350,000 men and four million para-military fighters, accurate intelligence estimates, a clear terrain advantage, the kamikazes, and the tenacious qualities of the Japanese soldiers fighting for their homeland from fixed cave networks, the defenses were not as formidable as appeared.

The buildup lagged. Chaotic Japanese logistics and lack of either a highway or rail network forced reinforcements to move by oxcart or human power over one-lane, rutted roads and mountain trails. Communications from division level used commercial telephones, below division level, runners or hand signals. The defense in depth created a tough outer shell but the impossible task of reinforcements and total lack of mobility over the mountainous terrain showed that once the invader cracked the shell, the battle was over. U.S. losses might have been catastrophic but the operation could not have been repulsed.

Could the massed Japanese build up have survived unopposed, pulverizing bombardment? MacArthur assured Marshall that the naval and air blockade would cut off all reinforcements or imports from China, Korea and Manchuria. ULTRA, however, disclosed that several army divisions left Manchuria and Korea for Kyushu from April to July 1945, and new divisions raised in Japan sharply increased the number of troops in Kyushu. But unquestionably allied air would wreak near-total havoc on the defenses in the three months remaining between Potsdam and D-Day, even without resort to nuclear weapons tactically, as General Marshall had suggested, to wipe out the defenses. The Japanese believed the invasion could not be repulsed. The leadership, including the war weary emperor, believed it would never take place.

Since the invaders could not be thrown back into the ocean, much of Kyushu would have become a vast American air and troop complex with major naval facilities at Sasebo for the final assault against Tokyo in March 1946. Beset by suicidal fanatics, guerrillas, and various other diehards, severe losses could be expected to the very last day of hostilities.

If the allies had invaded, the major unknown was the question of casualties. Could the promised bloodbath on the beaches of Kyushu force abandonment of the final phase, the invasion of Honshu to force a negotiated peace? At Yalta, FDR vaguely suggested a million, Churchill "a million American lives and half that number British." To clarify his decision on the invasion, President Truman requested a study in June 1945 of the cost in money and people. For various reasons, the study was never completed. The Joint Chiefs estimated casualties for Kyushu in the range of 30,000 to 50,000 dead and 100,000 wounded. Admiral Leahy estimated losses at 35 percent of Okinawa's 63,000. The president, carrying the responsibility, was horrified by another planning estimate of 58,000 dead in the first eight days and by General Marshall's estimate at Potsdam of a quarter of a million American casualties before overcoming the last of Japanese resistance. American dead in all of World War II totaled 292,000; atomic bombing to force a surrender seemed far preferable to a Pyrrhic victory on the battlefield.

If the invasion were launched it meant committing major cleanup forces after the surrender to a ten-year war in the mountains. As part of the surrender terms, the Russians would expect to occupy Hokkaido. If the dynasty were not retained, the added consequences were unpredictable. Japan would be destroyed as a unified state with far-reaching effects on future Pacific affairs. Lastly, would the American people have sustained a prolonged and bloody campaign with victory so near at hand?

Would the invasion have been carried out? Hardly. The evidence strongly supports the USSBS (U.S. Strategic Bombing Survey) conclusion that Japan would have surrendered before invasion. On 7 June, Emperor Hirohito and the cabinet gave up on the idea of moving to the redoubt in the Nagano Alps to fight to the end, indicating perhaps that there would be no "final battle"; Japan would surrender first. On 18 June — the same day as the fateful telegram from Japan to Moscow asking Stalin to mediate a U.S.-Japanese peace—a crucial White House conference was called to develop the strategy for invasion. Truman approved the attack on Kyushu for 1 November but held in abeyance the decision on the Honshu phase. As the meeting was breaking up, Assistant Secretary of War John J. McCloy was asked for his views. He suggested that serious attention be given to a political solution to end the war. In the resulting turmoil, the president and Admiral Leahy supported his proposal. It carried the day and led to the Potsdam Declaration within six weeks. After the Potsdam ultimatum, invasion was no longer an alternative. With or without the bomb, a negotiated peace would end the most destructive war in history.

If early peace initiatives had generated an American response, it is quite likely that the war would have been foreshortened. Or perhaps the war could have been terminated sooner by delivering a surrender ultimatum after capture of Okinawa in mid-July and dropping the Hiroshima bomb as quickly as possible thereafter. Completion of the Nagasaki bomb might have been delayed as a result but the early drop would likely have prevented Soviet entry. As a non-belligerent, promises at Yalta conditional on Soviet belligerency would be out the window. Alternatively, had the Hiroshima bomb been used instead as a demonstration at Alamogordo for world leaders including the Japanese, it might have ended the war at a much reduced cost in lives, but it would not have been an effective deterrent to a future nuclear war in any way comparable with the catastrophe of Hiroshima.

[1] P.M.S. Blackett, Fear, War, & the Bomb: Military & Political Consequences. NY, Whittesley House, 1949, pp. 130, 137.

[2] David Bercam, Japan's Imperial Conspiracy. NY: Morrow 1971, p. 1041

[3] After the Saipan incident, the Japanese leaders became fearful of the threat of allied retaliation and, aware of her vulnerability, pledged not to use gas except in retaliation, recalled gas munitions from the field and allegedly stopped production and destroyed the entire CBW arsenal in Manchuria and scattered the people.

Chapter 15

The War at Sea

Robert W. Love, Jr.

A. What if Britain had rearmed earlier in the 1930s or had adopted a wartime naval strategy consistent with her fleet strength?

The British Admiralty's greatest problems in World War II were rooted in decisions taken during and after World War I aggravated by the unwillingness of British statesmen, including Prime Ministers Stanley Baldwin, Neville Chamberlain, and Winston Churchill, to adopt foreign policies and grand strategies that the Royal Navy might reasonably uphold. The establishment of an independent Royal Air Force in 1918 with control over the Fleet Air Arm led directly to the loss of the navy's early lead in carrier-and land-based naval aviation with the result that the fleet entered World War II with too few carriers, a small inventory of obsolete naval aircraft, an indifferent naval air doctrine, not one high-level flag officer with a background in naval aviation, and few naval aviators senior enough to assume higher commands.

The pre-World War II Admiralty itself badly misread the meaning of the 1914-1918 war against the U-boat. It reposed excessive confidence in its newly-invented echo-ranging sonar, or asdic, system, and paid little attention to developing new escort and anti-submarine doctrines, weapons, and tactics that took into account the improved endurance, ruggedness, and tactical flexibility of Germany's recently constructed U-boats. Little thought was given to devising ways to counter U-boats by deploying long-range, land-based maritime patrol planes or air-or seaborne radars. This was greatly complicated by Churchill's commitment in June 1940 to the defense of Malta, Suez, and the eastern Mediterranean, a strategy that sought out the enemy wherever he happened to be, spread out the British fleet entirely too thin, and repeatedly and unnecessarily exposed Royal Navy warships undefended by combat air cover to Axis land-based air forces in restricted waters.

What if the Royal Navy had maintained its early supremacy in carrier-based naval aviation throughout the interwar years and had entered the war with a powerful land and sea-based naval air arm? More and heavier British carriers, better armed, faster, and more rugged naval aircraft, and a reasonable naval air tactical doctrine surely would have made more difficult the German occupation of Norway, and considerably reduced the danger of cross-channel invasion shortly thereafter. All British estimates of German invasion plans concluded that some invasion flotillas would have to venture at least ninety miles out to sea, at which point their land-based air cover could easily have been disputed by mobile carrier-based fighter and bomber squadrons.

But no amount of British naval air could have compensated for Churchill's disastrous insistence on holding Malta and Suez rather than falling back to Gibraltar and Aden, a strategy the Americans urged on him in 1941 and early 1942. A powerful multi-carrier-battleship task force based on Singapore and supported by squadrons of land-based fighters and maritime patrol bombers surely would have forced the Japanese to concentrate their carriers in the South China Sea in 1941, and made the occupation of Malaya and Singapore a quite contestable proposition. Instead, the small British Far

Eastern Fleet had to rely on a mere handful of overtaxed land-based bombers on 10 December 1941.

The loss of that fleet made it possible for the Japanese to quickly isolate Singapore and the Philippines, and advance headlong into the Dutch East Indies, the Marshall Islands and Gilberts with no thought of danger to their southeastern flank. A substantial British carrier force, even one forced to withdraw from Singapore to Ceylon, would have confronted the Japanese Navy with the intractable problem of a two-ocean war in the Indian Ocean and the Pacific.

Had the Japanese Navy been faced with a real prospect of conducting a large-scale naval war on two fronts in 1941, its support for Prime Minister Hideki Tojo's war policy surely would have been less vocal. A two-ocean front was what Admiral King intended to create when he urged the Admiralty on the eve of the action off Midway to use their old battleships and carriers in the Indian Ocean to conduct a quick raid on Timor. The mere presence of a British modern "fleet-in-being" in the Indian Ocean would have caused even more one-sided outcomes in the Coral Sea, off Midway, and in the South Pacific in 1942 and 1943, and so led to a considerable acceleration of the U.S. Pacific Fleet's great Central Pacific offensive along the Gilberts-Marshalls-Marianas-Formosa line.

Had the Admiralty recognized earlier than late 1939 the German U-boat threat and prepared for it accordingly, the course of the war would have been materially altered. A large-scale destroyer and light destroyer escort program and a supporting program to develop powerful land-based maritime patrol plane forces were easily within Britain's means in the mid- and late-1930s, although it would have come about at the expense of the Royal Navy's battleship and cruiser programs and the Royal Air Force's bomber program — but not at the cost of the naval aviation program.

Building austere escorts consumed fewer resources than constructing U-boats, and the British possessed throughout the war a far larger shipbuilding capacity than the Germans. If Churchill and the Admiralty had dedicated themselves first and foremost to the defense of the British Isles and its sea lines of communications to the Empire in North America, Africa, the Persian Gulf, and South and Southeast Asia, then the construction and organization of powerful ocean escort groups, land-based maritime patrol squadrons, and light carrier anti-submarine hunter-killer formations would have been their top priority. Early success in defending convoys and counterattacking U-boats, especially after the Germans began to operate from bases on the Bay of Biscay in late 1940, might have persuaded Hitler that Admiral Karl Dönitz's U-boat arm was as useless and costly as Admiral Raeder's battleships and heavy cruisers. Had the U-boat been defeated in 1941, as it well might have been had Churchill adopted a different policy, most American shipyards could have been used to produce shore-to-shore landing craft with the result that the date of the re-entry of the Allied forces onto the Continent would have been advanced by at least a year or two.

B. What if the British had not acquired Ultra and the ability to decipher the German U-boat command traffic?

The Royal Navy's capture of the U-110 and its codebooks and grid charts in May 1941 enabled British cryptanalysts at Bletchley Park to read German message traffic in *Hydra*, one of thirteen ciphers used by the German Navy during the war. *Hydra* carried many of the command directives from Dönitz to his deployed U-boats. Ultra also enabled the British to read German traffic concerning German heavy unit operations, deployments to the Mediterranean, and U-boat training in the Baltic. Ultra clearly provided the Admiralty with the means to conduct several evasive routing operations in mid-and late 1941, but the U-boats' success in turning back SC.52 — the only convoy turned back during the entire war — suggests that radio intelligence was by no means the most important key to defense of the transatlantic convoys. It must also be remembered that at the same time German Navy codebreakers had successfully attacked British Naval Cipher No. 3, an older U.S. Navy code which the Admiralty had adopted at American insistence in 1941 to carry Anglo-American-Canadian convoy and routing messages.

In the absence of an extensive and more thoroughly-researched scholarship on the importance of these two intelligence coups — research made virtually impossible by the British Minister of Defense's refusal to declassify the most critical Allied message traffic based on Ultra for the better part of 1943 — two good working propositions are that the Admiralty want to conceal some dreadful mistake or misappreciations; and, that the British, the Americans, or both made poor use of Ultra that year. In short, it is likely that some of the work of the rival special intelligence services cancelled one another out. Moreover, at best — when *Hydra* and later, after February 1943, when *Triton*, a replacement cipher, were being translated concurrently — the level of confidence in Ultra naval traffic was surprisingly low. Lag time constrained evasive routing and anti-submarine operations throughout the war, the Germans were skilled in the use of deceptive techniques that often spoofed the Admiralty, and many successful U-boat concentrations were simply the product of chance encounters and Dönitz's quick-thinking responses.

The one obvious tactical lesson of the Battle of the Atlantic was that convoys strongly defended by large numbers of powerful, well-equipped, well-trained, and well-led ocean escort groups, and supported by nearby land-based maritime patrol aircraft and hunter-killer carrier task groups, could not be seriously menaced even by very large, skilfully handled diesel submarine concentrations. The large number of heavily defended, uniformly successful American-escorted transatlantic troop convoy crossings demonstrated this as well. It now appears, therefore, that the value of radio intelligence in defeating the U-boat offensive has been greatly exaggerated by some scholars. Its importance was probably negligible by contrast to that of more the traditional elements of convoy warfare, such as the available escort pool inventory, the commitment of land-based and carrier-borne aircraft to covering and anti-submarine operations the overall level of materiel availability and quality, and the tactical efficiency of the ocean escort groups and their supporting air and sea elements.

C. What if the Germans had adopted a naval building policy and strategy before and during World War II more consistent with their resources and political objectives?

The German navy's major problem in World War II stemmed more from its failure to appreciate the naval lessons of World War I than from Hitler's alleged 'land-power' outlook. German victory in 1914-1918 hinged on defeating France and Russia, not on challenging Britain. Hitler's World War II policy of favoring his ground and air arms was therefore quite reasonable. What was unsound was to deny the German Navy any control over the design, production, or operation of most land-based maritime patrol bombers. Equally mistaken was German failure to provide for a truly unified anti-shipping command with naval officers exercising control of anti-shipping aircraft and coastal defense operations. Even more self-defeating was the German navy's prewar

Z-plan, a shipbuilding program that aimed at rebuilding the Wilhelmine navy, a balanced fleet policy that distributed scarce shipbuilding resources too widely and failed utterly to take into account the velocity of Hitler's diplomacy and grand strategy. The result was to leave Germany in 1939 with a handful of superb capital ships, but few screening escorts, obsolete naval weapons systems, too few long-range submarines, no truly effective anti-warship bombing capability, and an inadequate inventory of small coastal defense vessels such as swift torpedo boats and minelayers.

Having lost World War I in part owing to a U-boat fleet that was too small to isolate Britain or prevent the U.S. Navy from transporting the American Expeditionary Force to western France in 1918, the German Navy, nonetheless, planned in the 1930s to build a balanced fleet without much regard for what those ships might do to advance Hitler's foreign policy objectives other than enhancing Germany peacetime prestige. If the German Navy, instead of diversifying its naval construction, had devoted these resources to building more and better U-boats, and after 1940, a huge fleet of swift, radar-controlled coastal defense torpedo boats and mine craft, it would have more rationally applied its limited industrial resources. The steel, skilled manpower, tools, gear-cutting resources, electro-mechanical output, and shipyard capacity used to build the battleships *Bismarck* and *Tirpitz*, and the cruisers *Gneisenau*, *Prince Eugen*, and *Scharnhorst* would have paid for at least another two or three hundred U-boats, a lethal frontline force which would have forced the allies to devote even more of their resources to ocean escort groups and anti-submarine operations and thus delayed even longer the cross-channel movement. The active presence of very large numbers of fast torpedo boats on the French coast in 1944, supported by night-fighters and maritime patrol bombers and backed up by a large fleet of minelayers, would not only have menaced the establishment of an allied lodgment on the Cotentin Peninsula but also would have diverted Allied resources that were devoted to transatlantic and cross-channel shipping into costly escort and minesweeping forces.

If the German Navy had adopted a prewar and wartime building policy that eschewed battleships and heavy cruisers and instead stressed U-boats, submarine tankers, E-boats, coastal minelayers, shore-to-shore landing ships, and maritime patrol bombers armed with modern air-launched anti-ship bombs and torpedoes, Britain might truly have been endangered. Once France capitulated and Britain rejected Hitler's peace terms, the war at sea was clearly to be won or lost within the war zone in the English Channel, around the British Isles, and along the coast of occupied Europe.

Inasmuch as British industry, agriculture, and military operations depended greatly on imports, Admiral Dönitz's "tonnage warfare" strategy was a reasonable way of wounding Germany's most persistent enemy. But Dönitz had fewer than sixty U-boats in September 1939, and only a fraction of that number to deploy into the war zone. Aircraft and submarine anti-shipping operations were wholly uncoordinated. Even at the supposed height of the Battle of the Atlantic, the pseudo-crisis of March 1943, the German Navy had fewer than 100 frontline line U-boats dedicated to the transatlantic anti-shipping campaign, and fewer than half of these vessels were actually in or near the main area of operations. The epic cruise of the *Bismarck*, the gallant 1942 Channel Dash, and the raids of the *Scheer* and the *Hipper* boosted German morale, but building manning, and operating these extremely expensive ships cost the U-boat arm and the German coastal defense commands hundreds of vessels and uncounted hours of steaming time. Like the Danes and the Confederates in the 19th century, Germans in World War II learned that building a small capital ship fleet and engaging a superior naval power without arranging for offsetting assets is a recipe for strategic disaster.

D. What if the Japanese had adopted an entirely different building policy and strategy before they opted for war with the western naval powers in 1941?

The Imperial Japanese Navy which struck the first blow against Pearl Harbor was a polished weapon forged specifically to wage war against either the United States or Britain in the western Pacific or the South China Sea. It could not, however, fight both in the Pacific and the Indian Ocean at the same time, nor could it defend itself against a major campaign of attrition and still guard its interior sea lines of communications against anti-shipping raids by powerful, long-range submarine forces. The Japanese rearmed more quickly than their rivals in the 1930s, and the opposing alliance systems which evolved in 1941 forced Japan's foremost enemy, the U.S. Navy, to divide its ships between two distant theaters. The Japanese had some materiel advantages. Their *Fubuki*-class destroyers were superior to prewar American types, and their two *Yamato*-class superbattleships had the largest guns, heaviest armor, and greatest displacement of any contemporary warship. Japanese cruisers, slightly faster and more heavily armed than comparable American classes, had tubes to fire the Long Lance torpedo, an accurate, long-range, lethal weapon designed with night surface actions in mind.

On the whole, however, the Japanese were unprepared to wage modern naval war. Above all, quarrelsome, backward-looking military leaders wasted limited resources. Tokyo's faction-ridden national government lacked a single strong leader, being run instead by superstitious fanatics. An almost complete lack of economic intelligence blinded the Japanese high command to what its military and naval forces faced in the combat theaters. Political, strategic, and tactical coordination at a national level, and strategic and tactical collaboration at theater levels between the Army and Navy was virtually non-existent. Naval leadership was inspired but foolish. The commander of the Combined Fleet, Admiral Isoroku Yamamoto, had spent years in Britain and the United States before the war, but his wartime strategy suggest that he had really learned very little from these experiences. He totally misread the U.S. Navy's strategy on so many occasions in 1942 that the American decision to ambush his plane over the Solomons in early 1943 seems questionable in retrospect. Yamamoto's insistence on attacking Pearl Harbor must rank as a strategic blunder without modern parallel. It is mystery why he failed to understand that the Pacific Fleet's slow World War I-era battleships and trio of "treaty-class" carriers posed no serious threat to the Japanese offensive in the Western Pacific. Yamamoto's handling of his carriers before the battle off Midway almost assured their destruction, and his acceptance of an air war of attrition with the Americans in the Lower Solomons in September 1942 simply invited defeat.

Surprising as it might seem, the Japanese Navy had devised no realistic industrial policy to support its far-flung overseas military and naval operations. The result was that materiel shortages, deficiencies, and defects led to repeated setbacks. The Japanese designed some fine aircraft in the 1930s — although the vaunted Zero fighter has been vastly overrated — but the Imperial Navy's war planning was so deficient that it had arranged no workable system to compensate for the inevitable attrition to frontline planes or experienced naval aviators. Japan's I-class submarines were unequal to the demands of the Pacific War and the Imperial Navy's use of them was wasteful. Although Japan imported most of her raw materials, she never developed an effective convoy system, an appropriate escort doctrine, and adequate escort force, or a small, mobilization-class escort and anti-submarine ship comparable to the mass-produced Canadian corvette or the American destroyer escort.

Had the Japanese more carefully evaluated their opponents and acted accordingly, the outcome of the war might have been very different. As it was, Japan's understanding of her predicament was exceptionally primitive. The contents of the 1940 Two Ocean Navy Act were well known. Any reasonable appreciation of that shipbuilding program should have convinced the Imperial Navy's high command that war with the U.S. Navy would be suicidal. But Japan had other enemies: the Soviet Union, Britain, the Netherlands, and above all, China. Japan's best hope of destroying the British Empire in Asia and acquiring the Dutch East Indies lay with the success of the German campaign against Russia. Once the Soviets had collapsed, the Germans were certain to turn their attention back to Britain and further concentrate American resources on that conflict. Had the Japanese Navy been less insular, less parochial, its leaders would have pressed after June 1941 for the "northern strategy" against Russia and admitted that the Combined Fleet could not hold the South and Central Pacific against the Americans in a protracted war. It seems doubtful that the Soviets would have survived the resulting pressure on both flanks.

An alternative, but riskier strategy would have been to recognize and exploit the divisions within American politics by avoiding war with the United States while engaging the Thais, the British, and the Dutch. The time to have done this was after soon after June 1940. The Dutch East Indies fleet was negligible, and the British fleet was tied down by the neutral French Navy, the Italians in the Mediterranean, the defense of the English Channel, and the U-boat offensive in the Atlantic. The United States had no treaty commitment to defend Europe's colonial empires, and the Japanese should have reasoned that Washington's failure to come to the defense of the Netherlands or the British Isles against Germany meant that the chance of American entry into a war by Japan against the European colonial powers was highly unlikely. The 1942 campaign in Southeast Asia and the South Pacific suggests that such a war would have been short and decisive. This was, of course, what the Americans feared, and the reason that the U.S. Navy devised a 1939 plan to shift the U.S. Fleet from its bases on the West Coast to Pearl Harbor and implemented it in the spring of 1940. By failing to properly evaluate the obsolescence of those World War I-era American battleships and the hollowness of the political threat they were supposed to represent, the Japanese failed to take advantage of one of the two maritime strategies that might have seen their country among the victors in World War II.

Having decided to go to war with the United States in late summer 1941 anyway, the Japanese should have adopted a different strategy than opening their southern campaign with a pre-emptive strike on Pearl Harbor. As it was, the Pearl Harbor attack proved to be a military fiasco. The Japanese failed to understand that, for industrial reasons, the best reason for attacking a naval base in World War II was to cripple the facility, not to sink ships. Had Admiral Nagumo remained off Hawaii for another day or two, or even for an afternoon, his air groups could have easily worked over the ammunition dumps, fuel farms, submarine pens and other fixed installations on Oahu. Simply by bombing the ammunition dump at the entrance to the lochs would have shut down the naval base for months. As it was, Nagumo limited his bombing operations to only ninety minutes, and concentrated on sinking ships and destroying aircraft.

The damage inflicted on the Pacific Fleet on 7 December was inconsequential in that the slow World War I-era battleships could not cooperate with newer fast carrier task forces anyway. The loss of a few of their number had no significant effect on American strategy or operations in the early months of the war. Prewar U.S. Navy fleet doctrine was to operate the new fast *North Carolina* and *South Dakota*-class battleships in company with the speedy attack carriers, and the old battleships had no role to play in these powerful, highly mobile formations. They served bravely during the war, not as mobile capital ships but as nearly stationary offshore naval gunfire bombardment platforms. On the other hand, damaging Hawaii's fixed installations surely would have impeded the conduct of Admiral Ernest J. King's blocking, barring, and raiding strategy in the South and Central Pacific in early 1942. Constructing large, overseas military bases was, however, one of America's great wartime fortes, and it seems unlikely that the delay imposed on the Pacific Fleet's counteroffensive would have been meaningful.

Attacking Pearl Harbor clearly solidified American opinion behind Roosevelt's war policy and had the effect of so enraging Americans that they went to war with Japan with unprecedented unity and determination. Japanese strategists might have reasonably regarded a sneak attack on Pearl Harbor as one of the few steps they might take that would make immeasurably more difficult the task of negotiating a later settlement of the war that left the enlarged Empire intact, which was, after all, Japan's basic war aim.

Having engaged and enraged the United States, the Japanese should have chosen to follow a conservative strategy, ignoring pinpricks like Admiral Halsey's early raids on the Marshalls and the April bombing of Tokyo. Unless they were absolutely certain of crushing local superiority, they should have refused fleet actions as in the Coral Sea and off Midway, and instead devoted their limited resources to improving and perfecting the Empire's defensive outposts. As it was, the Japanese reacted to the Tokyo Raid by exposing almost their entire carrier force to potentially superior land-and-sea-based enemy air forces merely to overrun Midway Island, a fairly worthless outpost useful neither as an advance fleet base nor as a staging point for long-range strategic bombing operations against Hawaii.

Yamamoto's decision to enter the eastern Pacific in June 1942, like his move soon after to defend the Solomons, offered Admiral King the opportunity to engage the Japanese fleet in battles of attrition that destroyed the enemy's sea-and-land-based naval air forces. After Japan's frontline air power was wasted in the South Pacific and its destroyer force decimated in over sixty battles of attrition, the Imperial Navy lacked the means to implement any strategic decisions that would influence the course or outcome of the war.

The more conservative strategy of preserving the Combined Fleet as a "fleet-in-being" to protect Southeast Asia and the Dutch East Indies, operating the carriers and battleships only within supporting range of powerful submarine and land-based air forces, and securing the interior sea lines of communications between every major strongpoint within the empire's defensive perimeters through the use of convoys strongly defended by land-based maritime patrol aircraft and powerful ocean escorts, surely would have delayed the Pacific Fleet's progress, would have greatly increased the cost of the war to Japan's opponents, and might have made more possible a negotiated peace had Tokyo realized the value of the Philippines as a bargaining chip. King, alone among allied strategists, understood from beginning to end how much delay worked disproportionately to Japan's advantage.

Instead of pursuing a conservative strategy, the Japanese risked their formidable air striking capacity with the aim of sinking the Pacific Fleet's three carriers off Midway. This fleet action was obviously one of the turning points in the Pacific war, but it was not truly decisive in the classic sense. The U.S. Navy's long-term advantages were so great that the Japanese, regardless of the result of any single battle or campaign, lacked the resources to alter the overall balance through wartime shipbuilding, or even to inflict enough damage on the Americans to influence significantly the eventual outcome of the conflict.

When King committed his three Pacific Fleet carriers to the Midway ambush he was fully aware that they all might be sunk. His concerns were heightened after Admiral

Halsey, whom he trusted, fell ill and was replaced by Admiral Fletcher, whom King already wanted to relieve. But King was risking the U.S. Navy's prewar ships, not its wartime construction. He understood that the twenty-four *Essex*-class fast attack carriers, which did not begin to arrive in the Pacific until early 1943, would deliver the main blows against Japan. In short, had all three Pacific Fleet carriers been lost off Midway, Yamamoto would have found himself in possession of a worthless outpost and in need of a huge fleet to defend a new, long, highly vulnerable sea line of communications between Midway and the Marshalls. Japan could do little to replace wartime ship losses. King could simply shift resources to the *Essex* and *Independence*-class heavy and light attack carrier programs — probably at the expense of the *Iowa*-class battleships and the Lend-Lease merchant shipping programs — with little long-term effect on the course of the war.

The struggle for Guadalcanal in the fall and winter of 1942 provided yet another opportunity for the Japanese to adopt a conservative strategy. King sent the Pacific Fleet and the 1st Marine Division into the South Pacific in August of that year not to retake real estate but to keep the enemy off-balance, predicting wrongly that the Japanese would fall back on more defensible lines around Rabaul. Instead, Yamamoto reacted by throwing his fleet-and-land-based air forces into the maw of American air power, one of the worst mistakes of the entire Pacific war. This created a crisis for the Americans on the eve of the November 1942 Congressional elections, and forced Roosevelt to order the Army to support the Navy Guadalcanal campaign. Roosevelt was worried that if the Japanese evicted the Marines from the Solomons, then the Republicans would win those elections and return to Congress in January 1943 with a majority in at least one House. Their stated intent was to curtail the president's powers as commander-in-chief, put a brake on Roosevelt's unstinting support for the Soviets, balance the war effort more evenly between the Atlantic and Pacific, and so dilute even more the already-corrupted grand strategy of Germany-first. Domestic politics moved Roosevelt to order the Joint Chiefs to spare no resources to hold Guadalcanal. Thus, the paradoxical outcome of a Japanese victory on Guadalcanal would have been to focus even more resources on the Pacific Theater and less on the Atlantic, all to the disadvantage of Japan.

E. What if the U.S. Navy had fully rearmed in the 1930s and had been truly prepared in December 1941 to fight a two-ocean war?

American fleet strength fell somewhat below the benchmark of "treaty" limits in the 1920s, but what really retarded the prosecution of the war in 1942 and 1943 was Roosevelt's failure in 1935 to realize that the naval disarmament system had collapsed and his insistence that, with a few exceptions, American naval shipbuilding conform to the 1936 Second London Treaty until as late as December 1939. The White House, not Congress, retarded naval rearmament under the New Deal. The 1934 Vinson Act aimed only at building up to a "treaty fleet" by 1942, the 1938 Second Vinson Act stretched this out to 1946, and even the enormous 1940 Two Ocean Navy Act was not to be completed until 1948. As late as the spring of 1940, on the eve of the fall of France, Roosevelt slashed a Navy Department request for an increase of twenty-five percent in authorized fleet tonnage to eleven percent, although it was clear at the time that Congress would vote for the larger figure.

American naval rearmament in the decade of the Great Depression was not retarded by a shortage of skilled manpower, raw materials, or unused industrial or shipyard capacity, nor indeed by opposition in Congress. Every major naval shipbuilding program between 1933 and 1941 was initiated by the Navy Department, supported by overwhelming majorities on the Hill, and slashed by the White House. Roosevelt vacillated between negotiating further naval disarmament treaties and building up to treaty limits in the 1930s, with the result that the Navy in 1941 had no frontline battleships or post "treaty-class" carriers afloat, a bare handful of modern, long-range maritime patrol planes, few fighter, bomber, or torpedo squadrons operating heavy, all-metal, single-engine monoplanes, and almost no modern austere escorts or ship-to-shore or shore-to-shore landing craft. A powerful, balanced fleet capable of conducting major offensive air, sea, and amphibious operations in both the Atlantic and Pacific theaters concurrently in 1941 probably would not have deterred Hitler, but the effect on Japan might have been significant. Admiral Yamamoto supported the decision to go to war on the basis that the Combined Fleet could hold off an American offensive for about two years, but even his stance might have changed had he believed that he could not defend Japan's far-flung empire for more than a few months.

The U.S. Navy's prewar "balanced fleet" policy was widely criticized by many early historians of World War II. More recently, however, the "balanced fleet" policy has been seen in a less harsh light. With few exceptions, the Navy developed the tools to fight before the war. By 1941, plans were in place to build the ships, weapons, and aircraft, and to train the sailors, airmen, and Marines who would fight the war. Early setbacks, while spectacular, were truly marginal; indifferent presidential leadership, the lack of a coherent national industrial policy, and Allied disputes over strategy delayed offensive campaigns and operations more than enemy action. And, at the end of the war, every foe had been beaten. No other military organization produced such an extraordinary cast of grand strategists and fighting admirals of the first rank. Fleet Admiral Ernest J. King, the wartime Commander-in-Chief of the U.S. Fleet and Chief of Naval Operations, supervised the largest warship and naval aircraft building program in history, devised strategies that defeated his enemies and held his own losses to a minimum, and picked combat commanders for the numbered fleets who uniformly possessed exceptional skills. It is instructive, for instance, to remember that the historical controversies that swirled around Admirals Halsey and Spruance concerned tactical decisions during battles — Midway, the Philippine Sea, and Leyte Gulf — generally counted as among the most pivotal sea victories of all time. The charge that the "battleship admirals" dominated the prewar Navy Department ignores the fact that the interwar Navy laid down more carriers than battleships, a policy that culminated in 1940 with the decision to construct the mobilization-type *Essex*-class carriers so that each vessel might embark a powerful, flexible five-squadron air group.

But the entry of the *Essexs* into the fleet in 1943 did not by itself upset the balance of power in the Pacific. What made the U.S. Navy's carriers so potent in World War II was not only their large air groups but also the accompanying anti-ship, anti-air battleship-cruiser screens. Wartime carriers could not conduct 24-hour, all-weather flight operations and there were no reliable nightfighting squadrons embarked until late 1944. In short, the air group, all-powerful in good weather during the day, was itself wholly exposed, as was its flight deck, to enemy gunfire or torpedoes once the sun went down or a storm came up. Positioning his carriers so that they might escape at night from opposing battleships and heavy cruisers or lurking submarines was one of the major skills an admiral brought to his command in the war. Yet, as a result of the 1935 decision to build the 35,000-ton *North Carolina*-class fast battleships — an illustration of the balanced fleet policy — and to arm them with 16-inch main batteries, the Navy entered the war on the verge of deploying battleship-carrier-screen formations superior to anything afloat.

Roosevelt's addiction to naval disarmament — the United States did not renounce the 1936 London Naval Treaty until December 1939 — but the policy that produced this ultimate outcome, and the decisions that led to the construction of the follow-on four heavy *Iowa*-class battleships and the three heavy *Midway*-class carriers, were rooted in a belief in the strategic correctness of a balanced fleet and a conviction that mass production methods might somehow be applied to wartime capital ship construction.

Had the prewar U.S. Navy been dominated either by "battleship admirals" or "brown-shoe" naval aviators who totally disregarded the needs of the other community, the results would have been costly. Most Navy men agreed on a "balanced fleet" policy, however, regardless of their warfare specialty. The plan to build eighteen *Essex*-class carriers, embodied in the 1940 Two Ocean Navy Act, was devised by a submariner, Captain Charles M. "Savvy" Cooke, who hated to fly, and the penultimate "battleship admiral," Harold R. "Betty" Stark, whose entire career was a testimony to primacy of the prewar "Gun Club" or [Bureau of] "Ordinance gang." With the collapse of the 1922 Five Power Naval Disarmament Treaty in 1936, the pressure within the Navy to replace the World War I-era battleships — the vessels attacked at Pearl Harbor — was intense. Indeed, battleship replacement headed the Navy's priority shipbuilding lists for four years thereafter and no carriers were laid down between the last of the "treaty class" carriers, the 19,200-ton *Hornet*, and the first of the mass production *Essexs* in 1940. Had the Two Ocean Navy Act not shifted the focus back to a balanced fleet policy by emphasizing large-scale heavy carrier construction thereafter, the war against Japan surely would have been prolonged considerably. Fletcher and Spruance defeated Yamamoto's Combined Fleet at Midway with "treaty-class" carriers. Land-based naval aircraft provided the margin at Guadalcanal. By the end of 1942 attrition left only one undamaged, operational carrier in the South Pacific — at the very time when the *Essex* was putting to sea for her shakedown cruise. In the absence of a balanced fleet policy, the delays in prosecuting the war in the Pacific beyond the Lower Solomons would have been disproportionate to the time necessary to undertake heavy carrier construction.

American shipbuilding assets in World War II were remarkably flexible. Skilled labor, machines, tools, raw materials, especially steel, and shipyard capacity, were constantly shifted from building one type to another on a "crash" basis. The adoption of the First Landing Craft Program in 1942, its suspension in favor of the Destroyer Escort Program late that year, and its resumption in the fall of 1943 at the expense of escort shipbuilding demonstrates the proposition. The competition for those industrial assets applicable to shipbuilding from the Army, the War Shipping Board, and the British was intense following the passage of the 1941 Lease Act. As it was, by that time contracts for the *Essex*-class carriers had been let, shipyard time allocated, and labor, machines, and materials identified. Until it was well underway, the program never fell below the top of the Navy's priority list for manpower and materials. Inasmuch as Nimitz's Pacific Fleet could not force an entry into the Central Pacific without carriers and Admiral Thomas Kinkaid's 7th Fleet could not break the Bismarck's barrier and lift MacArthur's Southwest Pacific armies from New Guinea to the Philippines without covering carrier-based air power, delaying the *Essex*-class program would have prolonged the dual offensive, allowed Japan to stiffen her defensive perimeter, and made far more costly the inevitable American progression into the Western Pacific.

F. What if the Allies had invaded France in 1943? (The naval aspect.)

The U.S. Navy first proposed an Allied landing in northwestern France before Pearl Harbor, and Admiral King loyally supported General Marshall's concept for the

240

SLEDGEHAMMER and ROUNDUP plans in 1942. ROUNDUP called for a huge Allied fleet to land five divisions at the base of the Cotentin Peninsula in May 1943, and the British agreed to it when Marshall visited London in April 1942. One object of the plan was to concentrate all allied forces on one great, single object, to defeat Germany quickly, and then to turn on Japan. This was the essence of Admiral Stark's November 1940 Plan Dog strategy. But King and Marshall had another war aim, to prevent the Russians from overrunning Europe after Germany capitulated, and ROUNDUP served this end as well. King was fully prepared to support ROUNDUP without stint until 5 June, when he first learned from Admiral Mountbatten, then on a visit to Washington, that Churchill was backpeddling on the April accord. Aware on the 6th that the Japanese Fleet had just been mortally wounded off Midway two days earlier, King was eager to concentrate his efforts against Germany — until he learned soon after for certain that the British intended to renege on their agreements.

As early as 1941, U.S. Navy strategists sensed that the British would have to curtail their operations in the Mediterranean in order to invade France. Had the British been willing to abandon Malta, hold Gibraltar, and fall back to Suez or the Red Sea, the shipping to build up the army and tactical air forces for a late 1942 or an early 1943 invasion of France was available from the allied pool. The object of opening up the Mediterranean to British imperial shipping was surely not worth the cost to Britain of the North African war and the campaign against Italy. The major deficiency in the Roundup plan was in large landing ships and beaching craft, but the need for combat loaders and assault shipping was far less than it was for ROUNDUP than for Overlord — the 6 June 1944 landing — owing to the considerable differences in the state of Normandy's beach and coastal defenses as between early 1943 and June 1944. Greatly enhanced offshore gunfire support for the assault shipping and the total dedication of the Allied fighter and bomber forces to the beachhead would have more than offset the appearance of the German Air Forces over the invasion beaches and shipping anchorages. The Germans had little coastal artillery in place in the spring of 1943, and almost no fixed beach obstacles or deep sea mining. Neither in 1943 nor in 1944 could German heavy artillery or tanks operate within range of the allied battleships, and the German divisions defending France in 1942 and 1943 were poorly equipped by contrast to their 1944 counterparts.

In many ways, ROUNDUP was a less daunting operation than Overlord. More auxiliary and combat shipping would have been lost, but in 1943, by combining resources from the Pacific and Mediterranean, the Allied navies already possessed a formidable shore-to-shore lift and logistics capability. ROUNDUP would have changed the character of World War II and considerably improved the Western posture in the Cold War. ROUNDUP would have instantly shut down the German U-boat bases on the Bay of Biscay, brought nearly immediate victory in the Battle of the Atlantic, and permitted direct logistic support for the lodgment by using Norfolk to Normandy convoys. Germany's economy was not yet harnessed to its war effort, and Normandy's defenses were still in a sorry state.

OVERLORD quickly demonstrated that Germany was incapable of waging a two-front war. This was as true in 1943 as in 1944, no matter how Hitler had reacted. While the German Army had not been worn down on the Russian front in 1942, German industry had not geared up to supply a two-front war. These factors were probably offsetting. Had Churchill and General Alan Brooke not ingeniously sabotaged the ROUNDUP plan in July 1942, the major beneficiary would have been Japan. ROUNDUP's overriding priority was already draining ships, land-based aircraft, and troops from scheduled Pacific deployments in mid-summer 1942. An allied agreement to conduct the cross-channel movement in 1943 surely would have brought to an end the entire Pacific counteroffensive until at least 1944. What slowed the Pacific Fleet's grand thrust into the Central Pacific and MacArthur's slow-paced ascent from New Guinea to the Philippines was the two-ocean war, however, and the defeat of Germany in 1944 would have merely delayed Japan's day of reckoning. While this might not have much changed Asia's postwar political landscape, surely the fault line of the Cold War in Europe would have been situated much farther to the east. Indeed, ROUNDUP might have brought it right up to Russia's western frontier, thus immeasurably easing the burden on the western democracies of the long postwar struggle.

Chapter 16

The Air War

Richard J. Overy, Bernard C. Nalty, & Herman S. Wolk

A. What if the British had not devoted a major portion of their war effort to strategic bombing?
  Richard J. Overy

There is a widely held view that Britain's bombing of Germany in World War II was not worth the effort. The strategy took time to develop, and was technically deficient until better aiming devices and long-range fighters brought an increase in bombing accuracy and fighting ability in the last year of the conflict. The campaign cost a great deal in lives — almost a quarter of all Britain combat dead — yet it failed to bring Germany to its knees on its own. Critics of bombing make the point that Germany was defeated in the end by ground forces and that German war production continued to increase until the autumn of 1944 in the face of ever heavier bombardment. The moral argument, that bombing was simply an unethical form of warfare for a liberal state, was given greater force because of the failure to attack the primary objective, German war-making capacity and morale, with any decisive strategic effect.

This view begs a great many questions, not least that of what might have happened if Britain had never embarked on a bombing offensive in the first place. What would have happened if the resources used in the campaign had been diverted to other purposes? Or if different strategic options had been chosen in 1940? In practice such an outcome was never very likely. Since World War I British statesmen and military leaders were wedded to the idea that bombing would play a major part in any future war: bombing forces would either deter an enemy in peacetime, or, if used, wear down the enemy will-to-resist through devastating attacks on his home morale and the economic resources on which his armed forces thrived. Chamberlain, to be sure, had serious scruples about using the bomber program which was another source of friction at a time when the army wanted more production to help build up its offensive forces. Yet in the event these criticisms were never clearly focused enough and bombing was allowed to continue. Nor are the arguments much clearer with hindsight. Certainly the army could have done with more tanks and equipment in the desert, though it still needed the trained men to man them. A faster rate of build-up for army materiel might have produced a quicker assault on Europe, though there were other considerations also producing delay. More shipping and fewer bombers might well have made sense; but since a great deal of shipping was coming from American yards from 1942 onwards, bomber production did not trespass damagingly on the naval effort. Indeed, a switch from producing bombers to producing something different in 1941-2 might well have disrupted British war production rather than merely re-directing it. Those who argued for more army and navy weapons exaggerated the degree of flexibility in a war economy when it has to make large-scale changes in mid-stream.

There is some case for saying that the bombing effort actually helped the general mobilization of the British economy for war by providing it with the challenge of producing in mass what were large and complex pieces of engineering. Without the pressure for increased aircraft production, we can not be sure that the government would have faced the same need to divert resources away from consumer industry to armaments; nor would the other supply ministries have been faced with supply problems so severe that rationalization and conversion of civilian plant became a necessity. In other words it did not automatically follow that fewer heavy bombers would mean more tanks and ships. Instead it might well have meant fewer sacrifices from the civilian population.[3] Even if it is assumed that resources could have been used differently, it is not certain that they would have been used so productively. The large aircraft programs forced the pace in the rationalization of factory practice and labor use and dragged much of the rest of the industrial economy along with it. There were numerous technological and scientific spin-offs from the bombing program, including the search for the atomic 'super-bomb.' Without the bombers the British war economy might well have been less heavily and less efficiently mobilized: tank and ship production were notoriously less efficient users of resources than the aircraft industry. As it was, heavy bombers were not only the most cost-effective bombing aircraft produced (the Lancaster required on 9½ man-months of labor per 1,000 pounds of bombs dropped against 27½ for the Wellington medium-bomber), but by the middle of the war the Ministry of Aircraft Production considered heavy bombers to be the easiest kind of production to expand quickly.

Without the heavy bombers the RAF would have looked a very different force. It might well have been supplied with larger numbers of other kinds of aircraft. What would the air force have done with them? RAF strategy in the 1930s was based on the use of a bomber strike force to attack the enemy economy, and a fighter defense force to stop him doing the same to Britain. The development of a tactical air capability was in its infancy in the late 1930s. Only too late did the RAF and the Chiefs of Staff realize that Britain had almost nothing to contribute to the joint tactical air force in 1940, no dive-bombers, a number of feeble light bombers, and fighter aircraft not trained in battlefront warfare. Without a heavy bomber program the RAF would almost certainly have remained committed to twin-engined medium bombers, which were not capable of reaching distant targets in Europe, but which might have been used in a tactical role in the Mid East, or anywhere that British and Axis troops were in contact.

What is far less certain is whether the RAF would have gone on to develop and produce in quantity fighter bombers and ground-attack aircraft instead of strategic bombers. No dive-bomber was on the books in 1939, and after the Fall of France a battlefield air force was not an obvious priority. If instead the RAF had stuck with medium-bombers and fast fighters it might still have prevented invasion and facilitated the later assaults on Europe, but for much of the war it would have been left with large numbers of aircraft and not a lot to do with them. There is little evidence to suggest that the RAF and the army would have got together to produce the battlefield air armies that Germany and the USSR used on the Eastern Front. It was not simply the influence of the strategic bombing enthusiasts that inhibited the development of British tactical air power, but the fact that British strategists in the 1930s had failed to anticipate the kinds of aircraft and planning a continental war would require.

If air strategy would have looked less effective without bombers, British strategy as a whole would have looked positively anaemic for much of the war. The pre-war plans concerted with the French anticipated a war of attrition against Germany in which bombing would play a part in the blockade of Germany's economy, wearing down German resistance once allied air striking power had been sufficiently built up. The British liked the idea because it avoided the trench stalemate of the First World War. In terms of manpower and equipment the bombing offensive was regarded as a more efficient, cost-effective form of warfare. After the fall of France bombing took on a new lease of life; it was the only way left for the British to get directly at Germany. Without strategic bombing there was no way to retaliate; without retaliation a negotiated peace might have seemed more inviting. Without bombing there seemed little prospect of a direct assault on German-held Europe. In July 1940 Churchill wrote in somber mood to Lord Beaverbrook: "When I look round to see how we can win the war, I see that there is only one sure path. We have no continental army which can defeat German military power …there is one thing that will bring Hitler down, and that is an absolutely devastating, exterminating attack by very heavy bombers from this country upon the Nazi homeland."[4]

Britain's strategic options in 1940 and 1941 were extremely narrow. Churchill's support of bombing must be understood in the context of the time. He did not know that bombing would take as long as it did to become really effective. The switch to 'area' bombing in place of attacks on 'precise' military and economic targets developed only slowly between 1940 and 1942. Much more was expected of bombing in the dark days of 1940 than it could yet deliver. It was hoped that bombing would disguise the obvious decline in Britain's strategic position after Dunkirk. At this critical juncture Britain was still very unsure of direct American assistance. Bombing was the only way that Britain could stay in the war with any serious purpose without America. However many tanks Britain produced, the British army could not hope on its own to carry out a successful assault on Fortress Europe. But once American and the Soviet Union were in the war the situation altered. Bombing became instead a substitute 'Second Front' to show Stalin that he was not facing Hitler alone. After some initial misgivings the Soviet leadership became enthusiastic about bombing and even suggested suitable targets for Bomber Command to attack. At this delicate point in the war it was important for Britain's survival that she could show some action against Germany, for fear that Stalin might seek a separate peace and end Britain's chances of achieving her primary aim, the defeat of Hitler.

Bombing was also an essential instrument to ease Anglo-American re-entry to the Continent, by attacking German air power and isolating the invasion areas to prevent German reinforcement in the west. This was a hazardous and unpredictable enterprise. It was not what the bombing commanders thought the force was for; but the fact that a large heavy-bomber force with wide combat experience was in existence in 1944 proved a remarkable boon for a combined invasion force that lacked the battle experience of their German army opponents. If that force had not been available, D-Day in 1944 would have involved a great risk and the chances of achieving a successful continental landing much reduced. This higher element of risk might well have played into the hands of those who wanted the Anglo-Saxon powers to attack the Germans through the soft underbelly of southern France, Yugoslavia or the Balkans. Without bombing the shape of the war in the west would have been very different.

There was also a political element behind the bombing campaign. It helped to buoy up public morale at home at a time when the war had gone badly wrong, and when German aircraft were bombing British cities. There is scant evidence of a widespread desire for vengeance pure and simple. The bombing offensive was presented to, and accepted by, the British public as a successful and scrupulous attack on German military and industrial targets. Its real limitations (and the inaccuracy of bombing in particular) were kept from the public for fear of denting the morale that bombing was suppose to shore up. It seems clear that the German failure to retaliate against allied bombing later in the war provoked widespread disillusionment, and reflected badly on German propaganda. Bombing had the big advantage that it was, above all, newsworthy. The big set-piece battles on land and sea came few and far between and were quickly over. Bombing brought regular news items and victories. It helped to remind the public of the military side of the war in the long slack times between land and sea engagements, and its propaganda effect was carefully monitored by the Air Ministry and the Home Office. The bombing campaign played the same part in the projection of Britain's image abroad. The victims of Nazi aggression and Britain's foreign friends and potential allies could clearly see Britain's continuing commitment to the war. With bombing Britain was not just a lost cause.

This fact was brought home to the Axis powers as the bombing campaign moved from its ineffectual origins in 1940 to the massive destructive power of the later war years. The effect of bombing on the Axis states helped to shape their strategy and war capability: however that effect is measured, Axis strategy would have been different without bombing. Here the case of Italy is instructive. Bombing of Italian cities led to widespread demoralization and hostility to Fascists and left the Italian economy in a state of near collapse by 1943. Bombing speeded up the dissolution of the Fascist system. It did not have such an immediate effect in Germany, but it did force changes in strategy and the allocation of resources. Bombing brought about the diversion of productive capacity and manpower from other essential activities — two million men in anti-aircraft defense, many more in the task of clearing up the destruction, hundreds of thousands of workers producing anti-aircraft equipment, which by 1944 amounted to one-third of heavy gun, optical and electro-technical production. In addition the German war economy lost a great number of man-hours from air alarms and the poorer productive performance of tired and worried workers. Bombing even in its early phase compelled the German authorities to begin a strategy of industrial decentralization to safe areas at just the time that the centralization of production was beginning to bring dividends in better productivity. The significant thing is not that German war production continued to increase, which it did, but that the increase was not substantially greater. By the end of the war bombing did produce terminal crisis in war production — in 1945 production loss in aircraft was 48%, in tanks 42% — but since 1943 there had been accumulated losses in output, disruption to long-term planning, a scramble for improvised solutions, a situation in which German managers and ministerial officials found themselves running to keep still.[5] It is difficult not to accept that dropping 1½ million tons of high explosive and incendiary bombs on a sensitive industrial system will prevent it from producing its optimum.

Without bombing, German producers would have been ready to develop Germany's formidable productive potential, inside and outside Germany, to the full. More material could have been supplied to Germany's own armed forces and more manpower made available at the front and in the factories. Germany's combat effectiveness would have been considerably greater. The German reaction to D-Day is a good example. Without the heavy bombers the Luftwaffe would have been much stronger in 1944; without the interdiction and transportation plan German forces would have arrived in Normandy in larger numbers and at the right time. Without the bombing of the German homeland with ever greater intensity during the last eight months of the war, the retreat would have been much slower and the losses of western and Soviet combat forces much higher. A more numerous Luftwaffe would have meant more effective German campaigns everywhere in 1944; the German air force was pushed back onto the defensive by bombing, a role for which it had not been well prepared. The Big Week bombing attacks in February 1944 drove the German air force down to attrition levels from which it never recovered. If instead the Allied air forces had been obliged to meet the Luftwaffe head-on in a tactical battlefield contest, they would have fought much more on German terms; if the Luftwaffe had been left the freedom to stockpile aviation fuel and the synthetic oil industry had not been attacked, German forces have been allowed another important margin at a critical stage of the war. The oil attacks left German airmen short of fuel and forced cut-backs in training which severely inhibited the performance of the force in the last years of war.

In the British case there is room for doubt about whether or not the lack of a bombing campaign would have pushed British strategy towards building a large continental army with tactical air fleets for a frontal assault on Europe — which was essentially the American plan produced in 1942. But in the German case there is little doubt that without bombing and the subsequent build-up of extensive home defense forces and equipment, German forces would have continued to fight the war they preferred, with an offensive battlefield air force, effective medium-bomber support, and large well-equipped armies. This was, after all, the strength of the German war machine in 1940. German forces were not developed to provide a defensive perimeter or umbrella, though they got better at this as the war went on. German forces during the 1939-1941 period were essentially very good combined offensive forces. Bombing arguably succeeded in cutting down the margin in military effectiveness between the two sides to proportions which the inexperienced but well-equipped Allied forces in the West could cope with.

On the other hand, bombing played to British strengths. It was economical with combat forces; it placed emphasis on Britain's large manufacturing capacity; it fitted with British strategic traditions of blockade and 'indirect' warfare; and it made use of Britain's one area of real technical advantage, the scientific radio war. Without bombing the cost in lives and equipment for the Allies would have been greater, the outcome of the Second Front less certain, and the possibility that Stalin would have sought a separate peace with Hitler stronger. Bombing did reduce the dangerous margin in fighting power between the two sides in western Europe, while it supported the Anglo-American view of war as a war of economic resources. Given such differences in aptitude and outlook, bombing made considerable strategic sense for the western Allies. It is not clear that an alternative would have produced a quicker or more effective result. Indeed, it has been plausibly argued that if strategic bombing had been carried out more effectively the war might have been shortened considerably. Strategic bombing did not win the war on its own, but it was the price the western allies were prepared to pay to reduce the risk of their defeat.

Bombing did one other thing. It became a way of demonstrating that democracies were willing, if pressured hard enough, to use any weapon in defense of the democratic way of life. It was the other side of the deterrent coin, the willingness to use the unthinkable weapon. Chamberlain fought shy of bombing; Churchill and Roosevelt had no such qualms. The moral argument seemed at the time to be clearly on the allied side; appeasement gave way to firmness. It could be argued that without the evidence of western willingness to use the bombing to break the enemy home front and destroy civilian lives *en masse* (Dresden or Hiroshima), the strategy of deterrence in the post-war world might not have worked. For all those who doubted western resolution in the 1930s, there was now the awesome evidence of what liberal states would do with their backs to the wall. It is a sobering thought that without conventional bombing in World War II the world might have been spared the rapid onset of a nuclear arms race. In this sense bombing not only sustained Britain's war effort and inhibited Germany's, but it also helped to transform the international military order after 1945.

B. What if Hitler had pushed the development of the jet-powered Messerschmitt Me 262 as an interceptor rather than a fighter-bomber?

Bernard C. Nalty

The Me 262 flew for the first time in July 1942, using jet propulsion only, without the aid of an auxiliary piston engine turning a propeller. Among the pilots who tested the twin-jet aircraft was Adolf Galland, who scored 104 aerial victories during the war. On May 22, 1943, after wringing out a prototype, Galland predicted that the turbojet interceptor would "guarantee us an unbelievable advantage during operations, if the enemy keeps flying piston-engine aircraft." The new airplane so impressed him that he recommended cutting back on the manufacture of conventional fighters to make resources available for production of the Me 262.

In December 1943, another demonstration of the jet aircraft made a similar impression on Hitler, but the Führer decided to employ it as a fighter-bomber rather than an interceptor. He had logical reasons for his choice. D-Day for the invasion of Europe had to be fast approaching, and an assault from the west would bleed away military strength needed to fight the Red Army. Although Allied bombs were falling on the Third Reich, the Luftwaffe had not yet lost the control of the daylight skies demonstrated earlier in the year when inflicting crippling losses on the Bomber Command of the American Eighth Air Force, as it penetrated as far as Regensburg and Schweinfurt. Moreover, only four German cities — Lübeck, Cologne, Rostock, and Hamburg — had felt the full fury of the Royal Air Force Bomber Command. In these circumstances, Hitler concluded that the Me 262 could better serve Germany by bombing and strafing the invasion beaches than by intercepting British and American bombers.

Galland and Albert Speer, Hitler's minister of armaments, have argued that the Führer's decision prevented the Luftwaffe from acquiring the clouds of jet fighters that could have overwhelmed the P-51s and the other piston-engine fighters which began early in 1944 to drive German interceptors from the skies. Was their assessment correct? Whether correct or not, exactly what difference would this truly deadly fighter have made?

To single out Hitler's decision as the reason for the tardy appearance of the Me 262 is to overlook the difficulty of developing a radical new airplane and a revolutionary kind of engine. Indeed, Speer has acknowledged that he managed to subvert the Fuehrer's directive and bring out an interceptor version. Problems of aerodynamics and propulsion, rather than official policy, prevented the jet interceptor from entering combat before the summer of 1944. Finding a satisfactory turbine engine posed the most difficult challenge. Two models failed, and the third, which was finally adopted, never attained the goal of 50 operating hours between overhauls.

As if the problems of aircraft development were not enough, the Luftwaffe had run critically short of pilots. Sustained aerial warfare from North Africa to Norway, from London to Moscow, had cut deeply into the corps of fighter pilots; furthermore, the bombing of oil production facilities soon began drying up the supply of fuel for training replacements. When the first operational Me 262s emerged from the factory, pilots who had been flying conventional fighters made the transition to the new aircraft. At most, they flew the jet for six hours before entering combat; at the least, they received a cockpit checkout as they waited to take off.

Suppose that the development of the Me 262 had gone smoothly, that skilled pilots were available in adequate numbers, and that the jet interceptor entered service early in 1944 in sufficient strength to battle for control of the air over western Europe. The immediate result would have been the slaughter of American bomber crews — and of their British counterparts, if a radar-equipped night fighter version was available — but the German edge in quality would not have been enough. The enemy's success would certainly have spurred the development of jet aircraft in the United Kingdom, where an experimental prototype had flown in 1941, and in the United States. Without the urgency that the early appearance of the Me 262 would have caused, Gloster Aircraft of Great Britain produced a combat-worthy fighter, the Meteor, which took to the air in March 1943 and became operational 16 months later. Lockheed, an American firm, developed a first-class jet fighter, the P-80, which went from drawing board to prototype in just 143 days and was ready for combat testing in Italy when the war in Europe ended. Although the German jet was probably the best of these aircraft, it could never have rivaled the allied fighters in numbers. American productive capacity was so overwhelming that, if the skies over Europe were indeed blackened by jets, the fighters would have been P-80s, and the resulting attrition would have worked to the advantage of the allies.

For a time, despite its short range and unreliable engines, the Me 262 could have stopped the bombing of Germany's urban industrial heartland, forcing the Combined Bomber Offensive to attack targets in Nazi-occupied Europe that the Luftwaffe did not consider worth defending with the new jets. While the Americans and British built the necessary number of P-80s and Meteors and trained pilots to fly them, an invasion of France might well have seemed too risky and been postponed, but once the Allies had gained air superiority, the amphibious troops would have swarmed across the beaches of France. The advantage conferred on the Luftwaffe by the Me 262 would have proved temporary, rather than decisive: the jet fighter could have bought time for the Third Reich, but it could not have prevented the eventual invasion of western Europe or halted the Soviet advance from the east.

The indirect postwar effects of the German jet interceptor might well have been more important than its impact on the course of the fighting. While the Me 262 was disrupting the Anglo-American timetable for invasion, Soviet troops could have fought their way farther west, although at a grievous cost in lives and suffering. Because the Combined Bomber Offensive had been redirected against targets in the occupied countries, the nations of western Europe might have emerged from the war resentful of the destruction and loss of life the bombing had caused. As a result, it would have been far more difficult to rally these nations in an Anglo-American sponsored alliance like the North Atlantic Treaty Organization to meet the danger of aggression by Soviet troops poised not in eastern Germany but on the Rhine.

C. What if Allied strategic bombers had attacked German electrical power rather than the oil industry?
Bernard C. Nalty

In the war as actually fought, the strategic bomber made its greatest contribution to the defeat of Hitler by destroying the oil industry that fueled the German war machine. In May 1944, when the oil offensive had scarcely begun, Speer warned his Führer that: "The enemy has struck us at one of our weakest points. If they persist at this time, we will soon no longer have any fuel production worth mentioning." Because of the need to divert the American heavy bombers to help pave the way for the invasion and to neutralize the V-1 flying bomb and V-2 rocket, the allies could not follow up immediately, but the systematic bombing soon resumed, choking off the flow of fuel to airfields and battle fronts. Air Marshal Sir Arthur Harris, who headed the Royal Air Force Bomber

Command, participated only reluctantly in the oil offensive, but he admitted that it had succeeded, comparing it to betting on a longshot and winning.

For the Americans, oil had always been a target, but not necessarily the most important one. During the summer of 1941, in response to a request from President Roosevelt for an estimate of the armaments production needed to win a possible war against the Axis, a group of Army airmen exceeded these instructions and drafted a plan for bombing Germany into submission. After seizing control of the skies from the Luftwaffe, the American bomber force would destroy 154 targets in a variety of categories, including oil production. Near the top of the list, however, immediately after the neutralization of the German fighter force, stood the nation's electric power grid, for its destruction was expected to cripple almost the entire industrial base—oil production, shipbuilding, and aircraft manufacture.

In spite of the priorities set forth in this prewar plan, neither the Eighth Air Force nor the Fifteenth Air Force, which joined the daylight strategic offensive from bases in Italy, ever attacked the power grid. The Royal Air Force Bomber Command did try to shatter three of the hydroelectric dams that supplied current to the factories of the Ruhr valley, but the main purpose was to flood the heavily industrialized region. Looking back upon this attack, which breached one dam and damaged another, Speer again talked of a missed opportunity for the allies; follow-up strikes, he believed, could have deprived the entire region of electric power. There were no further attempts at dam-busting, however, for special bombs were needed, and the highly trained squadron that conducted the first raid suffered 50 per cent losses.

Speer was not alone in wondering why the attacks on the hydroelectric system did not continue until the power grid was shattered. Maj. Gen. Haywood S. Hansell, one of the officers who turned Roosevelt's request for production estimates into a blueprint for strategic air warfare, insisted long after the war that bombing could have destroyed the power network without interfering with the offensive against oil production. Rather than attack dams, he wanted to batter the generators, switching stations, and transformers. A number of factors, however, dissuaded the Americans from pursuing the kind of air campaign that Hansell championed. The generating plants tended to be compact, the largest of them measuring only a thousand feet on a side. Consequently, they were no easier to locate and hit, using radar, than the synthetic fuel plants. For best results, attacks on both the oil and electrical industries required visual aiming in cloudless skies, weather conditions that were rare during north European winters. Even so, Hansell remained convinced that roughly 7,000 bombing sorties could have severed the key links in the power grid, but the invasion had taken place and the oil offensive begun before the skies cleared and the Eighth and Fifteenth Air Forces had enough bombers and escorting fighters for such an undertaking.

Despite Speer's comments and Hansell's belief that the allies had indeed missed a great opportunity, the bomber force could not have attacked electrical power any sooner or with deadlier effect than its assault upon oil production. Not only did the weather refuse to cooperate until the spring of 1944, the Americans did not have air superiority before that time, and control of the daylight skies was essential, whether battering synthetic fuel plants and refineries or the various components of the power grid. Not until the early months of that year did an ever increasing number of bombers, escorted by long-range fighters, wear down the German interceptor force so that the oil offensive could begin. The allies could not have saved time by attacking a different but equally well defended target like electricity. The need to gain control of the air, neutralize the V-1 and V-2 (insofar as bombing could do so), and support the invasion would have determined the timing and intensity of an offensive against the power grid, just as these considerations influenced the onslaught against the oil industry.

Clearly, the Eighth and Fifteenth Air Forces could have gone after electrical power at the time they attacked oil. The Bomber Command of the Royal Air Force might have assisted them, assuming Harris overcame his antipathy toward "panacea targets" as he ultimately did in joining the attack on oil. The shortage of fuel, however, had a direct and almost immediate impact on military operations. Attacks on electrical power would have taken effect more slowly, since the grid, by its very nature, permitted the diversion of current from undamaged or repaired generating plants to areas served by bombed-out facilities. Germany might thus have staved off industrial collapse by manipulating the power grid to sustain for as long as possible the production of oil and armaments.

D. What if General Kenney had persuaded General Arnold to deploy the B-29s to the Southwest Pacific?
Herman S. Wolk

The uncertainty of when the force might enter combat operations was not the only question concerning the B-29 that faced General Arnold and the American high command. There was also the issue of where best initially to deploy the bomber. In the summer of 1943, just a few months after the crash of the second prototype, this question became a searing issue between Lt. Gen. George Churchill Kenney, commander of the Fifth Air Force, and the Allied Air Forces, in the Southwest Pacific Area, and General Arnold. Arnold was determined to use the B-29s against the Japanese homeland even if initially he had to base them in India and stage them through China. However, what if General Kenney's plan had been accepted and the B-29s were first used to strike Japan's oil producing and refining facilities in the Netherlands East Indies? Kenney was convinced that this "most decisive set of targets for bombing anywhere in the world" would have resulted in delivering a "fatal blow" to Japan.

The question of the use of the B-29s was played out against the overall strategy for the Pacific adopted by the U.S. Joint Chiefs of Staff. In the spring of 1943, the Joint Chiefs decided upon twin Pacific thrusts. General MacArthur would pursue a southern Pacific strategy, a series of envelopments from New Guinea's north coast through the Bismarck Islands to the Philippines. Admiral Chester W. Nimitz, heading the Pacific Ocean Area Command, would direct his thrusts across the central Pacific, through the Marshall Islands to the Marianas and then to the Philippines.

By the fall of 1943, when the B-29 issue erupted between Kenney and Arnold, the allied forces in the southwest Pacific had turned the tide against the Japanese. The early New Guinea campaigns had been completed with the capture of Buna, Lae, and Salamaua; the Fifth Air Force was administering a thrashing to the enemy air forces; and in March 1943 the Japanese had suffered enormous losses in the battle of the Bismarck Sea. Kenney's forces were impressively supporting MacArthur's drive along the north coast of New Guinea.

Thus, it was in this strategic and operational context that Kenney implored Arnold to send him the B-29s. Kenney's strategy for employing the big bombers was comprehensive, as might be expected from an air leader of his intellectual and strategic capacity. Kenney informed Arnold that his plan to decimate Japan's oil capacity ("the one essential commodity which she must have to carry on the war") would be a "war winning" strategy. General Kenney's big problem without the B-29s was simply that his B-24 Liberator bombers were limited in both range and bomb-carrying capacity. They could reach only refineries that accounted for less than one-fifth of the total capacity of

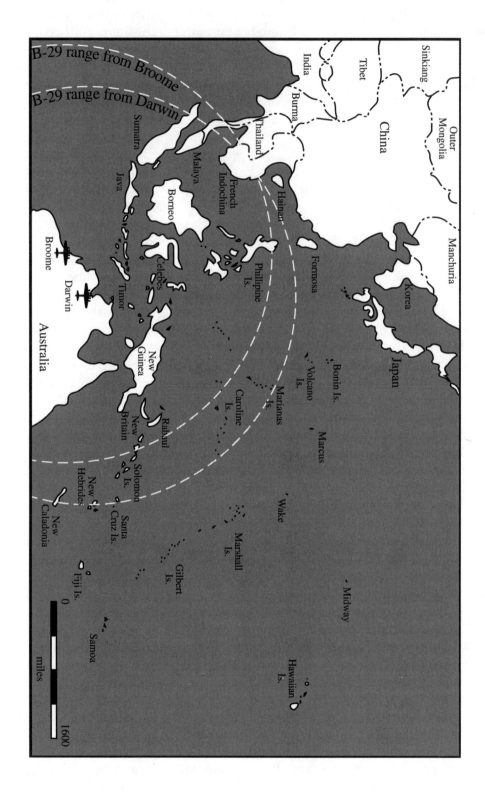

Deployment of B-29s to Australia

the Netherlands East Indies. And over the distance required to strike Sourabaya and Balikpapan the B-24 could only carry a maximum load of 3,000 pounds of bombs.

Japan had no synthetic fuel facilities and Kenney's plan was to base the B-29s in Australia where they would have the range — and carrying capacity — to attack ninety percent of Japan's oil producing and refining capacity: "Every single oil field, oil well and refinery is within range of the B-29 carrying a minimum load of ten thousand pounds of bombs and operating from existing fields along the north coast of Australia between Broome and Darwin." Sumatra, Singapore, Borneo, Mindanao and Palau were all within range of the B-29 as was the huge Palembang complex in southern Sumatra, producing half the crude and over half of the refining capacity. And realizing that plans were in the making to base the bombers in China, Kenney emphasized to General Arnold that Darwin was closer to the Sarawak and Brunei oil fields in Borneo than was Kunming, China.

Kenney's strategy contained another dimension. This would be a blockade by the mines laid by B-29s inflicted upon the enemy's shipping lanes stretching from Singapore to Saigon and Manila to the Marianas and the Marshall Islands. Airdromes would be used not only in northern Australia but also at Dobodura and in the Markham Valley of New Guinea. By October 1943, Kenney already had five airdromes in northern Australia ready for 25 B-29s. He believed that approval and implementation of his plan could result in the arrival of allied forces in Mindanao in 1944. "Japan," he informed Arnold, "may easily collapse back to her original empire by that time, due to her oil shortage alone. It is conceivable that she may be forced to sue for peace with certain overwhelming defeat staring her in the face."

In Washington, there was no question about eventually basing the B-29s in the Marianas. The argument centered on where to operate initially. Kenney's strategy was supported by Arnold's own Chief of the Air Staff, Lt. Gen. Barney M. Giles — and also by Admiral Ernest King, Chief of Naval Operations. Giles had visited Kenney in the southwest Pacific and was impressed with his logic and preparations. King supported striking oil and Japan's shipping lanes because it would have aided the Navy's central Pacific thrust.

Arnold however, was firm in his conviction that the B-29s should be directed against the Japanese homeland. He thought that ultimately Japan could be defeated without mounting an invasion with its enormous casualties. He also wanted the Twentieth Air Force bombers to remain under his direction from Washington and not be parceled out to area commanders. Thus, Arnold decided first for the China plan, with the subsequent B-29 offensive from the Marianas.

The B-29 raids from the Marianas began in October 1944, under the command of Brig. Gen. Haywood S. Hansell, but it was not long after Maj. Gen. LeMay's arrival in January 1945, that the B-29s began to wreck Japan's cities, and with help from the blockade and the Soviet entry into the war, forced the Japanese to surrender.

What if Kenney's plan had been adopted? What might have been the result? There was no doubt that Arnold's determination to attack Japan's industrial and population centers paid off, culminating with dropping the atomic bombs on Hiroshima and Nagasaki. It is clear that Operation MATTERHORN, the costly B-29 missions flown from China in the summer of 1944, were of little import. In this regard, Kenney's plan would have been far preferable. Striking the great oil refineries, mining Japan's sea lanes, and attacking her shipping would have been more effective than the China-based operations. The deployment of B-29s to the southwest Pacific would not have resulted in the "fatal blow" that Kenney had predicted, but it might well have contributed to knocking Japan out of the war earlier.

The Dutch East indies

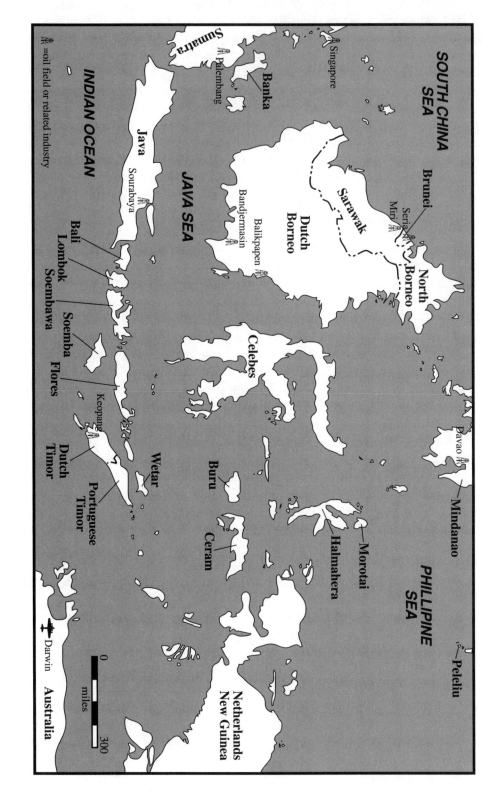

So Kenney's concept would have been appropriate for the June-October 1944 frame, but Arnold's conviction to throw the weight of the B-29 campaign against the home islands in late 1944 and 1945 was absolutely correct and played a decisive role in forcing the Japanese surrender.

Of course, had B-29 deployment been delayed for more than six months due to production problems, the entire question of Kenney's plan versus Arnold's concept, would have been academic. The B-29s would have gone directly to the Marianas.

In retrospect, the really key questions related to the developmental and production phases — so-called "Battle of Kansas." This is where the force of one man's determination made the difference. Arnold's obsession that the B-29 Superfortress should be hurled against the home islands was a crucial decision in the Pacific war and ultimately — in combination with the Blockade — it spelled victory without an enormously costly invasion.

E. What if, due to critical engineering and production difficulties, the B-29 had not become operational at all in 1944?
Herman S. Wolk

In World War II, the Boeing B-29 Superfortress very long range bomber was the only weapon bringing the destruction of total war to the Japanese home islands. The onslaught of the B-29 strategic bombing offensive from the Marianas Islands in 1945 ripped out the heart of the urban centers of Japan, resulting in awesome destruction and culminating in August 1945 with the dropping of atomic bombs on Hiroshima and Nagasaki. A long-sought goal of General Henry H. (Hap) Arnold, Commanding General of the Army Air Forces (AAF), had been achieved — the defeat of Japan without having to invade the home islands.

The defeat and surrender of Imperial Japan, of course, was due to a number of critical factors aside from the B-29 campaign. These included the Central Pacific drive that captured the islands that based the B-29s; the effective mining of Japan's sea lanes; the virtual destruction of Japan's combat and merchant navies; General Douglas MacArthur's successful Southwest Pacific offensive; and the ultimate entry of the Soviet Union into the war against Japan.

The most terrible price however, that the Japanese people had to pay for launching the war in the Pacific was the awesome destruction visited on the homeland and the enormous loss of life resulting from the B-29 offensive unleashed by the XXI Bomber Command of the Twentieth Air Force, commanded by Maj. Gen. Curtis E. LeMay.

The inception of the B-29 development program can be traced to 10 November, 1939 — two months after Hitler's onslaught against Poland — when Arnold, Chief of the Army Air Corps, in response to a recommendation of the Kilner Board, requested authority of the War Department to let contracts for experimental development of a four-engine bomber superior in all elements of performance (range, speed, bomb load) to the B-17 and B-24. A number of aircraft companies submitted proposals, but the Boeing Company's design for the XB-29 was judged by the Air Corps to be superior and the contract was awarded in September 1940.

Thus began an almost four year stretch of frustrating ups and downs in engineering, testing, and production in which some AAF officers doubted that the program would succeed. Hitler's invasion of Poland and the low countries lent urgency to what became known as the Very Long Range Project. General Arnold decided to take the large risk of cutting developmental and procurement corners in order to accelerate production. In simple terms, he ordered the bomber into production before it had been sufficiently tested. Usually, it would have taken five years to put a plane into production, but with war already in Europe, Arnold was determined to shorten this cycle. The XB-19, for example, a predecessor of the B-29, had been contracted for in 1936, test-flown in 1941, but never placed into production.

Even in 1941, many B-29 developmental problems remained to be solved. There were some in the Air Corps Materiel Division who doubted that this radical project could succeed. One of the earliest questions concerned the unusually high wing loading ratio which some thought would make the B-29, like the experimental B-26, dangerously heavy for the designed wing area. A Special Committee, which included Brig. Gen. George C. Kenney and Lt. Col. Kenneth B. Wolfe of the Materiel Command, recommended that no design change be made.

Special plants were constructed to build the gigantic, revolutionary bomber with the three-story tail assembly and 2200-horsepower Wright Cyclone R-3350 turbo-supercharged engines. Among other firsts to be built into the Superfortress were a radar navigation system and pressurized crew compartments. A new fire control system was also installed.

By May 1941, the Air Corps planned to purchase 250 B-29s; following the Japanese attack on Pearl Harbor, the purchase order increased to 500 and after a February 1942 production meeting in Detroit, over 1,600 were placed on order. This meeting also marked the formation of a B-29 Liaison Committee headed by Brig. Gen. K. B. Wolfe, who became a key official in the developmental program and in 1944 would lead the B-29 into combat from Chinese bases.

For over two years following the Detroit meeting, grave difficulties were encountered which earlier had prompted the program to be labeled "the three-billion dollar gamble." The XB-29 first flew in September 1942, piloted by Boeing's distinguished test pilot, Edmund T. Allen. Between September and December 1942 however, test flights clearly indicated serious trouble with the plane's R-3350 engines which frequently failed or broke out into fires.

On February 18, 1943, disaster struck. With Allen at the controls, two engine fires broke out during a test flight from Seattle, the fire spreading into a wing. This second prototype plane crashed into a meat-packing plant three miles from the end of the Boeing runway, killing Allen, his entire crew of ten and 19 people in the building. Subsequent investigations ordered by General Arnold and Senator Harry S. Truman determined that the engines were defective and that the manufacturer's quality control was inadequate. This shocking development resulted in Arnold's creation of the B-29 Special Project under Wolfe and Col. Leonard Harman to supervise all testing, training, and production. Incredibly, a third prototype almost crashed because of crossed aileron control cables, another disaster and potential end of the program barely being averted.

Many more accidents, most caused by engine over-heating, occurred through September 1944, and the B-29 was still not operational for combat even when deployed in April 1944 to the China-Burma-India theater of operations. During a single week in April 1944, five B-29s went down near Karachi due to overheated engines, the worst week in the history of the plane's overseas deployment including the subsequent movement to the Marianas islands. The basic problem — overheating due to tremendously high ground temperatures on the subcontinent — was eventually controlled for the most part by a crash engine-cooling project designed by engineers at Wright Field and the National Advisory Committee for Aeronautics.

Could the B-29 program have failed? There seems little doubt that had not these developments taken place during the intense pressure of a global conflict that the B-29 development and production program would have been halted. "In normal times," observed General Curtis E. LeMay, "the assembly line would have been shut down." In fact, even in early 1944, there was pressure to call a halt which was only overcome by General Arnold's iron determination to see the development and deployment through no matter what.

It is important to recall that this was in a real sense a far advanced, almost revolutionary, aircraft development program. Moreover, Arnold literally rolled the dice when he opted for concurrent experimental testing and production phases — unprecedented in the history of Air Corps development of major weapon systems. No doubt Arnold would have bulled ahead no matter how many accidents occurred and no matter how many officers had to be fired. Ironically, K. B. Wolfe, who survived development and testing, was later sacked by Arnold, who thought that Wolfe was failing to order sufficiently heavy attacks from the Chinese bases. When he replaced Wolfe with Maj. Gen. LeMay, Arnold noted: "K. B. did a grand job, but LeMay's operation made him look like an amateur."

What if the B-29 program and deployment had been delayed by from six to twelve months? This could have happened and indeed in 1943 loomed as possible or even probable. Had the program taken the five years ordinarily required, the start of the B-29 strategic campaign against Japan would have been postponed perhaps well into 1945. This delay might have been sufficient to trigger the planned invasion of Japan with its attendant enormous toll in killed and wounded on both sides. This would have depended upon how long it would have taken the B-29 offensive to hit its peak. In reality, in 1944 and 1945 it took over six months and the replacement of Brig. Gen. Haywood Hansell with LeMay for the effort to hit peak operations.

The two-stage ground invasion of Japan had been approved in June 1945 by President Harry S. Truman. The first phase invasion of Kyushu (OLYMPIC) was scheduled for November 1945 with a second phase invasion slated for March 1946. Truman was, of course, greatly concerned about the human cost of an invasion, reflecting about a possible "Okinawa from one end of Japan to the other." Chief of Staff Marshall told Truman in June 1945 that "airpower alone was not sufficient to put the Japanese out of the war." Marshall was supported by General MacArthur, who urged an invasion.

Significantly, also in June, Arnold visited LeMay in the Marianas, and LeMay informed the commander of the Army Air Forces that by bombing and blockade, Japan would be forced out of the war by 1 October 1945. The B-29 offensive, intensified between March and June, had Japan on the ropes, LeMay emphasized.

In retrospect, it was a close thing that there was a crushing B-29 campaign in 1945; the big bomber itself had been on the ropes in 1943 and 1944.

1 Public Record Office, Kew, London (PRO), AVIA 9/9, Churchill personal minute to the Lord President of the Council, 7.9.1941.

2 PRO, AIR 10/3866, "The Strategic Air War against Germany 1939-1945," report of the British Bombing Survey Unit, pp. 36, 38-9. R. Beaumont, "The Bomber Offensive as a Second Front," *Journal of Contemporary History* 22 (1987), pp. 5-8.

3 For problems of supplying aircraft industry labor see PRO, AVIA 9/9, Sir John Anderson to Churchill. "Bomber Production," 9.10.1941; AVIA 10/269, Ministry of Aircraft Production, "The Supply of Labour and the Future of the Aircraft Programme," 19. 5. 1943, esp. pp.4-6.

4 Churchill to Minister of Aircraft Production, 8.7 1940, reproduced in W. S. Churchill, *The Second World War: Vol. I, The Gathering Storm* (London, 1948), p. 567.

5 PRO, AIR 10/3871, British Bombing Survey Unit, "Potential and Actual Output of German Armaments in Relation to the Combined Bombing Offensive," pp. 7, 11, 23.

Chapter 17

What if Hitler had won the War?

Harold R. Deutsch & Dennis E. Showalter

Prologue: When and how Hitler might have won.

Any evaluation of the prospects of a German victory in World War II must be based on consideration of the Third Reich's race against time. Hitler's decision to risk a European conflict in September 1939 was less the product of a reasoned calculation than of his conclusion that it was time for Germany to fulfil her destiny as he conceived it. The Wehrmacht, however, far from being ready to implement a comprehensive, coherent Blitzkrieg strategy, was in the throes of a rearmament program characterized by inter-service rivalries and concentration on hardware at the expense of doctrine. Even in 1940, Germany lacked the means to destroy Britain from the air, to cripple her trade, or to assure isolation from outside (American and/or Soviet) support. By December 1941 Hitler had spread Germany's already-thin resources over Poland, Western Europe, much of Scandinavia, the Balkans, a part of North Africa, and vast expanses of the Soviet Union. Then, on 11 December 1941, he added the United States to the list of enemies, convinced that the entry of Japan would preoccupy the Americans, a people he conceived to be incapable of producing much beyond "refrigerators and razor blades" until his war in Europe had been successfully concluded.

Most historians stress this increasing gap between ends and means. National Socialism, unlike Communism, was an ideology essentially limited in its appeal, with accession to upper hierarchical levels determined by "objective" factors of race as opposed to the "subjective" element of class. By multiplying his enemies without having consolidated his power, the argument runs, Hitler doomed his cause to defeat virtually from the start.

It is thus not easily conceivable how Adolf Hitler could have "won" the war in any conclusive sense. Certain points in time, however, did offer at least a theoretical possibility of a German victory taking shape even against such odds. The most likely, indeed the only, stages where this would have been possible appear to have been four: (1) June-July 1940, when peace with Britain was almost within reach; (2) mid- and late-summer 1940, when an invasion of the British Isles immediately after the French surrender or in Operation Sealion might have succeeded; (3) the summer and autumn of 1941, when a combination of sincere efforts to make allies of the Soviet peoples and continuation without interruption of the drive on Moscow might well have produced the collapse of the Stalin regime, and (4) 1942-1943, when some kind of "peace" or truce could have been concluded if Hitler had refrained from war on the U.S. and pursued a more effective strategy.

A. What if Hitler had been able to negotiate peace with Britain in June-July 1940?

Much as the concept may today appear repugnant, the possibility of a British accommodation with Germany directly after the French surrender was not far fetched. A government under Lord Halifax that assuredly would have at least explored the chance of peace with Germany, failed to come into existence after the departure of

Chamberlain mainly because Halifax himself shrank from the responsibility. Also, as demonstrated earlier in this volume, Churchill himself was considerably less committed to fighting to the bitter end than his ringing appeals and postwar testimony implied.

Hitler himself confidently expected overtures from London. In line with his grudging admiration of the British Empire as an instrument of worldwide white supremacy, he was prepared to offer what, under the circumstances, would have been generous terms. For prestige reasons the Fuehrer would have had to insist on the return of Germany's lost colonies. He not only would have probably guaranteed the rest of the Empire but at the same stage might have been willing to offer Britain "compensation" in the form of French colonial territory. In the fall of 1940 he certainly showed no reluctance about the opposite tack, preparing to offer the French British possessions in return for collaboration against the island kingdom and for French territorial concessions to Spain and Italy. A grim feature of this scenario would have lain in the almost inevitable rivalry for Hitler's favor between the London and the Pétain government. Whether by military coup as in November 1942, a deal with the French, or a formal denunciation of the armistice of Compiègne on one pretext or another, Hitler was bound to make some attempt to gain control of the French fleet. With Britain out of the war, Pétain might well have submitted, recognizing the greatly reduced hope of France regaining her independence. The French fleet was a major piece on the European and world chessboards, and in Hitler's hand, this would have had a bearing on Anglo-American relations. On the other hand, it would push the British hard to secure a maximum of American support in an effort to avoid reduction to client status. On the other hand, it might inhibit appeals to Washington that would infuriate the Nazi dictator.

Hitler's now unchallengeable hegemony over Europe would have been particularly firm in Norway, Denmark, and the Low Countries. Any Anglo-German treaty would be sure to repudiate the governments-in-exile that had nested in London. Leopold of Belgium would have appeared in many quarters as the archtype of farsighted statesman, one who made the best terms possible for his country after having put up an honorable armed resistance. From Norway to the Bay of Biscay, indigenous Fascist type and collaborationist movements would have flourished in contrast to Churchill's injunction to "set Europe ablaze." Vichy France and Nationalist Spain would assuredly have been less hesitant than they proved to be in seeking places at the table of the "New Order."

The diplomatic conflict waged by the two totalitarian powers in Eastern Europe would have been more one-sided than it already was without Britain to play the role of Banquo's ghost. Deprived of any hope of using Britain as a makeweight, the Balkan states would have fallen that more easily into the German camp given their choice between that and depending on Stalin. It scarcely required knowledge of the region's post-war experience to appreciate where the harder lot lay. There would have been scant prospect of the anti-collaborationist coup of the late March 1941 in Belgrade and thus no extended Balkan war to distract Hitler in the spring of that year.

Would acceptance of German hegemony have extended to greater submissiveness toward Hitler's Axis partner, Mussolini? It is at least questionable. The tough Greeks would probably have resisted in much the same way as they actually did when the Italians struck from Albania, but might have contented themselves with *baroud d'honneur* as Vichy France did in late 1942. The variables here are too numerous to judge whether there would have been an Italian debacle in Cyrenaica. An armed clash over there would have depended on whether Mussolini had been included in the peace with Britain and whether the British would have put up a fight to show they still had teeth.

Hitler, given no Italian disaster in North Africa, would probably have felt it less necessary to bail out his Axis partner and allowed the Duce to stew in his own juice. If he had been spared the Balkan campaign with its heavy loss to elite troops and transport airplanes in the Cretan venture, the Wehrmacht would have been considerably better prepared for the great showdown with the USSR which directly followed.

It remains highly controversial whether the Balkan campaign of 1941 was a major factor in delaying the assault on the USSR for a month as has often been claimed. Seasonal considerations probably had much more to do with this. Whatever the reasons for the postponement, it surely contributed to the ghastly debacle of a campaign that ended in 40 degree minus weather before Moscow in December.

Particularly difficult to assess are the changes an Anglo-German peace would have portended for the plans, prospects and projects of Mussolini. The Italian dictator cannot be dismissed as Hitler's jackal, having twenty years worth of independent ambitions in the Mediterranean, Balkans, and North Africa. Absent the Libyan disaster of late 1940, his forces were a factor that could not be ignored. Hitler was faced by a serious diplomatic challenge in balancing Italy's claims as an Axis power against the interests of the clients that a peace with Britain would have brought into this camp. The internal politics of the New European Order were bound to be shaky for several years. Would Britain with so much else to concern her simply have given up in the eastern Mediterranean? Would Mussolini have been more or less hesitant about invading Greece? Such are among the more puzzling aspects of the political map of Europe as it would have been left by an Anglo-German accommodation.

A further area where a 1940 peace with Britain was likely to be significant concerns Germany's continental economic position. Integrating the resources of Europe into the Reich's further military buildup was a *sine qua non* for future success whether based on stabilization or expansion. The failure in this area is a matter of record. But could what Richard Overy has aptly called "The Era of Egotism and Incompetence" have followed a different path in the context of peace with Britain? There is small chance of Hitler's eventual goals having been changed. For Hitler peace with Britain would be no more than an opportunity to buy time to complete preparations for further war.

This leads to the key question of how peace with Britain could have influenced the course of German-Soviet relations. As things were, Hitler, as the campaign in the west was winding down in June, perhaps as early as the 1st days of May with victory in sight, began to itch for the earliest possible bound eastward, the ultimate goal of his dreams and policies. So overpowering was this impulse that by the second half of July and with Britain still to contend with, he determined to assail the Soviet Union *that fall!* Only with some difficulty was he dissuaded about 1 September by his closest military advisers who stressed seasonal difficulties.[1] Any elimination of lingering anxieties about a two-front war by peace with Britain could only serve to enhance the craving to strike eastward at the earliest possible moment. He could then have counted upon a Luftwaffe unscathed by the drastic attrition of a Battle of Britain, as well as liberated from the task of guarding the coastlines of Europe west and north of Germany. The erasure in occupied areas of all hopes of a British return to the continent and the acceptance of German domination as an unavoidable fact of life would have facilitated a drastic reduction, here and there perhaps an elimination, of occupation forces. It must further be assumed that there would be fewer obstacles to raising volunteer support among Fascist-type elements eager to join in an anti-Communist crusade.

What were prospects for more fully and effectively mobilizing German and collaborationist resources for the war in the east? So far as Hitler's personal role is concerned, the prestige gained from his victories in the west and north would have reached its true zenith with a peace with Britain. He would have been hailed as a great war leader who was also a true statesman, able to exercise moderation and restraint in the gathering of the fruits of victory. It was then a time when internal prospects to bring an end to the regime — very real before Munich and again in the fall of 1939 — were all but non-existent. For the time being the nation was prepared to follow him blindly on any path of his choosing. The question that remained was a very real one of his ability to assess realistically and attack purposefully the problems that impeded the fullest deployment of available resources for the task at hand.

The difficulties were considerable. Inter-service rivalries, the bane of the pre-war period, were not likely to diminish. No doubt, in the context of peace with Britain both the Luftwaffe and the *Kriegsmarine* would have received significantly larger resource allocations. Whether they would have made optimal use of them is at best debatable. With respect to the navy, Dönitz's ambitious plans for submarines would, with the end of the British blockade, have been more than ever subordinated to Raeder's—and Hitler's — dream of a world-challenging surface fleet, especially in view of the looming showdown with the United States, for mastery of the Atlantic. Progress with the Z-Plan would no doubt have become closely intertwined with prospects for the possible utilization of the French fleet.

The German army in this scenario might well sacrifice numbers for technology, perhaps demobilizing divisions of the later *Wellen* while improving the equipment of the rest. Hitler, unfortunately for his prospects in the east, was not inclined to build up a head of steam that would have utilized available resources to the limit. His underestimation for the task at hand was so extreme that he gave no attention to the somewhat feeble urgings of his generals to prepare for an eventual winter campaign. In any event, with the attack of the USSR scheduled for no later than the spring of 1941, time was lacking for fundamental changes.

Any successful German mobilization of the economy of dominated European areas demanded *focus*. Without the ongoing problem of continuing the fight with Britain, the Reich's administrative talents would be in a better position to concentrate on consolidating the conquests of 1940. This process would no doubt have been much facilitated by the enhanced cooperation resulting from Germany's western triumphs. With nowhere else to turn, client governments and local administrations would have concentrated on conciliating their new masters. Once again, however, the Third Reich lacked time to deal with fundamental weakness in the measurement of strength with the USSR.

In sum, it may safely be assumed that peace with Britain would have substantially though indecisively, added to German striking power eastward. One cannot fail, however, to take into consideration the other side of the coin — strengthening of the defensive capacities of the Soviet Union for meeting the deadly threat. The shocks and disappointments of the Winter War with Finland were already dictating something like a crash program in Soviet armament. This might have been stepped up further if Stalin had thrown himself more unreservedly into the task at hand. His obtuse refusal to take seriously the innumerable signs of a coming showdown with Germany was based in largest part on the stubborn conviction that Hitler would not permit himself to become involved in a two-front war. That consolation would now have fallen by the roadside through an Anglo-German peace. Thus, at the very least, the surprise factor would have been eliminated once and for all.

Joseph Stalin had long regarded war with Nazi Germany as inevitable. The Soviet dictator hoped, however, to delay its outbreak, both to give the USSR time to restore a military shaken by the purges, and to give the Nazi dictatorship time to foster consequent hatred among its subject people. No evidence has as yet emerged that Stalin planned a preventive war against the Third Reich. A month before Barbarossa, he spoke of May, 1942, as a probably beginning date for the final grapple between Fascism and Communism. On the other hand, Soviet doctrine and force structures were geared to wide-reaching strategic offensives. It would have represented no major change in the Russian way of war for Stalin to reconsider his strategy in the contest of a British defeat.

To allow Hitler time to consolidate his position in the industrial heart of Europe was to stack the cards heavily against the USSR, at least in the initial stages of an all-out future war. It is unlikely that Communist-inspired resistance to Nazi rule west of the Vistula would have had significant effect, even with all-out clandestine support from Moscow. Stalin would likely have sought improved relations with the U.S., but his prospects in that quarter were limited as well. A president and a society still reeling from the shock of Britain's fall were more likely to pursue a "Fortress America" strategy—one perhaps even involving assent to Japanese aggrandizement in the Far East—than to seek an alliance with a Communist state still officially bound to Nazi Germany by the Non-Aggression Pact.

Stalin, in short, might well have made the rational decision, sometime in late 1940 or early 1941, to convert the defensive forward deployment of the Soviet army and air force undertaken after Poland's collapse into an offensive concentration. A preventive war launched against the Reich in the spring of 1941 would have utilized the "window of opportunity" that existed as Germany was still working to assimilate her conquests. It would also take advantage of the strategic dislocation generated in the Reich by Britain's surrender. Instead of leaving the initiative in Hitler's hands, Stalin might well have chosen to settle Europe's destiny by a Barbarossa in reverse, such as the future Marshal Zhukov indeed had been urging.

There remains consideration of what an Anglo-German peace would have implied for German-American relations. The absence of a developing American aid program on behalf of Britain would have done something to relieve the more immediate tensions between Berlin and Washington. On the other hand, the erasure of illusions about an Anglo-French ability to erect an effective barrier against Nazi German expansionism on the other side of the Atlantic would have contributed much to more long-range American anxieties. A British deal with Hitler would have contributed much more to this. There is much to argue that the crash rearmament program already under way would have been stepped up even further. Among the more ominous closely observed developments of the European scene would be those concerned with the disposal of the French fleet. There might have well been an inclination in Washington to go easier in obstruction of Japanese expansionism. The more and specific the threat from Berlin, the more it would bear in one way or another on the disposition to further exacerbate relations with Tokyo. With Britain falling by the wayside as potential aircraft carrier and launching pad for American intervention on the European continent, the view in Washington could only have become more strictly defensive with more unified national support.

Japan , of course, would have been even more tempted to exploit to the full in the southwest Pacific the eclipse of French, Dutch, and British power. On the other hand, with Germany freed of the hazards of the two-front war and able to exert its full power against the Soviet Union, Japan's longstanding perception of Moscow as a mortal enemy could have encouraged seeking revenge for Nomanhan by participation in the destruction of the USSR. The probability of a Pacific conflict would have been proportionally limited.

B. What if Germany had conquered Britain, most probably by invasion, in the summer of 1940?

Our scenario here hypothesizes a German military "bounce" across the Channel after Dunkirk or following the French surrender, conceivably also a more complex, more formal invasion along the lines of Operation Sea Lion. It might even have been the consequence of a strategic victory of the Luftwaffe: a stripping of Britain's air cover, the Royal Navy shattered or driven to cover, and a government able to count the odds and capitulate before an actual invasion.

What in our previous scenario must undergo alteration if the war in the summer of 1940 had climaxed with military action against the British Isles rather than with political accommodation? The weight of historical opinion is certainly arrayed against the success of an assault upon the British Isles following Dunkirk or the French surrender. The loss or immobilization of much of the German fleet during the Norwegian adventure is one factor that speaks against this. That, however remote, it was still a possibility is supported by the contemporary urging of a number of German military leaders. Thus General Guderian proposed it at the time and maintained this view after the war.[2] But for the Fuehrer's mindset regarding Britain and his assumption that a peace proposal would soon be on the way from London, the project might well have received consideration.

Operation Sea Lion had better prospects though many continue to believe that Hitler was never entirely serious about it. In any event, a successful invasion or a knockout of Britain from the air would probably have had much the same consequences for the European and world scene as a peace treaty following the French surrender. The principal difference would have been whether, despite a brave show and talk of continuing the war in Canada, the Churchill government would have resigned or been voted out of office. If the government had gone through with the trans-Atlantic shift, there was, of course, every likelihood that Hitler would have sought to install a puppet regime, probably under a restored Edward VIII, and concluded with it a formal peace, perhaps even an alliance.

In either case, Hitler and his lieutenants would have been confronted with a complex set of challenges. Above all, what to do with the British Empire? In the context projected here, Canada, Australia, and New Zealand were virtually certain to turn to the United States. South Africa, which had entered the war by a single vote of its parliament, nearly as likely would seek an accommodation with the Reich. Mussolini, of course, would have pounced on Egypt, the Sudan, and the Somalilands, now stripped of much of their defenses. There were certain as well to be serious disturbances in India and Burma, perhaps a loss of these jewels of the imperial crown.

Much of these developments would conflict with ideas and aims of Adolf Hitler. He might well have decided that, even after conquering Britain by military force, it might be prudent to install his erstwhile foes as junior partners. Such a decision would have been supported by elites in both countries. From its beginning, the Anglo-German rivalry had been stoked by German insecurities. Now, with victory a fact, was the time not ripe for the two great "Germanic" peoples to compound their differences? Generosity was hardly a characteristic of National Socialism or of Hitler personally. Nevertheless, it would have been far easier to grant concessions to British relatives than to such as the Slavs in Eastern Europe. If pronounced on time, so moderate a policy might even have forestalled or neutralized the desperate shift of resistance to Canada that threatened so many complications for German policy. It would have greatly enhanced whatever reputation Hitler might thus far have achieved as a statesman, notably in the Western

Hemisphere. No doubt it would also have contributed something to allaying American anxieties about threats to trans-Atlantic aggression.

Alterations in American policy are even more difficult to predict than in our previous scenario. Internal political conflicts on aid to Britain, much exacerbated if the Churchill government had shifted to Canada, would in the above case have quieted. They would almost certainly have accelerated once Hitler's war machine turned against Russia. Even then, however, aid to the Soviets was unlikely to become a major issue, given the ideological and geographic distances between Moscow and Washington.

Some have perceived that Hitler at this juncture might have been poised between a decision to launch a "hot pursuit" across the Atlantic if the British moved to Canada or to embark on the long dreamed of quest for living space in the east. But for the Nazi dictator to conceive the problem in such terms would appear to contradict all we know about his actual thinking at the time. It was one thing to strive, as he had in going to war in the first instance, to clear his rear in Western Europe before launching the great enterprise. It was quite another to extend this concept to the other side of the Atlantic. Both timewise and from the standpoint of not affording the inevitable costs, everything appears to speak against it.

This is not to imply a hesitation of Hitler's part to devote some thought and resources to "what next" after the anticipated triumph in the east. He was likely enough to start immediately with stepping up the Z-Plan and with gaining allies and supporters in South Africa. There is little doubt about his thought of an eventual showdown with the United States, the center, as he conceived it, of a Jewish world conspiracy. After all, in some measure, the assault upon the USSR was something of a way station on the road to global supremacy. Thus he would have been ready to allot some resources to ultimate purposes derived from his illusions about the challenge just ahead. Not that he thought of being able to deal with the USSR, as it were, with one hand tied behind his back. But he was certainly guilty of a colossal underestimate of the difficulties of the task ahead.

As things were, in the event of a conquest of Britain or a failed attempt to accomplish it, the consequence would be a significant depletion of resources needed for deployment eastward. There was the cost of a trans-Channel leap in purely military terms, notably with respect to the Luftwaffe. If the British continued the war from Canada, such defiance would scarcely threaten an early return to Europe. In the eyes of Europeans, however, it could hardly fail to augment the likelihood of the United States of America eventually taking a hand. Thus any feeling that the final word in the war had now been spoken would have been considerably weakened. Both the ability to reduce occupation forces drastically and any hope of raising substantial volunteer armies from the Reich's new clients, would have been proportionally affected.

Altogether, then, commencement of the war with the Soviet Union in the context of this scenario would have found Hitler in a weaker military position than it proved to be in reality. The single plus would have been the absence of the attrition of the Balkan campaign, notably in Crete. Whether Barbarossa could have been launched earlier in the war depends once more on one's evaluation of other factors that bore thereon.

With Britain knocked out militarily from the war in Europe, situations on the continent and in the Middle East would not have differed substantially from those resulting from an Anglo-German peace treaty. Once more there would most probably have been no need for a Balkan campaign, no Belgrade coup or Italian debacle in Cyrenaica. Could Mussolini have been induced to refrain from attacking Greece, or had the Greeks failed to resist, Italy would have become an infinitely more effective ally on the coming Eastern Front. Conceivably the Yugoslavs could even have been intimidated into joining the anti-Soviet coalition.

264

If the British had refused to yield Gibraltar to Spain, Franco would have been virtually sure to assail this historic bastion of the British Empire. There would have been no German project for seizing the Rock and then proceeding beyond the Strait to Morocco. Thus there would also have been no particular reason for a meeting of the two dictators at Hendaye with the resulting personal rift between them. Hitler would have had no occasion to complain to Mussolini that for him the meeting had been like a drawing of teeth And Franco, ever more awed by Hitler's victories, might well have contributed more than the single Blue Legion to the war in the east. Indeed, it requires no great stretch of the imagination to assume that, with the United Kingdom knocked out of the war or flailing away feebly from Canada, Spain and France might have fallen completely into the German camp, giving the war against the Soviets the aspect of a truly European anti-Communist crusade. For Hitler there would have been no great inconvenience in paying the price of the release of two million French prisoners that Vichy would certainly have exacted. With Britain prostrate or out of serious contention, he should indeed have thought it a good bargain.

C. What if the Wehrmacht had defeated the Red Army in the summer and autumn of 1941 in Operation Barbarossa?

This scenario postulates a decisive German victory in 1941. It is based, of course, on the assumption that Britain had survived her ordeals of the previous year, and that events thereafter would have taken their actual course until the tanks rolled forward on 22 June. The notion of a German victory within the first six months of the war on the Eastern Front becomes plausible only if Hitler in mid-August had refrained from shifting the armored forces of Army Group Center southward, and had instead pushed onward with all available means in the direction of Moscow.

Whether such a concerted drive on the Soviet capital would have achieved its purpose of knocking the USSR out of the war has long been a subject of lively controversy among historians. Most recently it has been maintained vigorously by R. H. Stolfi.[3] In the current volume the contrary opinion is presented by David Glantz. Be that as it may, the conceivability of such a course of events cannot be ruled out. Plausibility becomes virtual certainty, however, if one can assume that Hitler had joined a sounder strategy with the type of appeal to Soviet populations detailed earlier in this volume by Samuel H. Newland.

If the Fuehrer of the German Reich had sincerely promulgated and implemented such a program, he would of course not have been Adolf Hitler. Except in the form of front propaganda which would really not commit one to anything, he strictly prohibited any hint of so enlightened a policy either for his fellow Germans or the populations of invaded areas. It is a bitter fact that he was determined to forestall false hopes in the latter or any inconvenient "soft" sentiments in Germany. To give our scenario full plausibility, however, there is no choice but to assume at least an initial show of good will on Hitler's part, one that he intended to repudiate with his usual cynicism when the time seemed ripe for him to throw off the mask.

The immediate consequence of German forces reaching something like the coveted Archangel-Astrakhan line would probably have been the deposition of Stalin by a loose coalition of generals and party leaders, none of them with the charisma or the track record to emerge as "the first among equals." Would in that case the USSR have survived as a state, or dissolved into chaos as Heinrich Himmler predicted? The explosion of centrifugal forces that dissolved the Soviet state at the turn of the final decade of our century argues strongly for the latter prospect. In any event, however, the external threat from the east to the Nazi empire would have been marginal. The real test of 'victory' would now have been internal: could the Hitler regime have stabilized its rule in the occupied territories?

Among the more tantalizing might-have-beens of the Russo-German war, especially from a German perspective, concerns the transformation in a matter of months of widespread good will among Soviet populations into rejection and bitter hostility. German tanks had been garlanded with flowers as they drove through the emancipated Baltic states of Lithuania, Estonia, and Latvia. In Belorussia and the Ukraine they were welcomed as liberators and fellow-Christians by men and women terrorized by Stalin's purges and impoverished by a quarter century of Communism. All this without, on the German side, the slightest pledge or even implication of generous treatment or a policy of true "liberation." But this early enthusiasm was short-lived. Behind the front-line units came the "Action Groups" of the SS, and a horde of Nazi bureaucrats determined to exploit the occupied lands without mercy. "The party succeeded in driving people back into the arms of Stalin," declared the later Ambassador Hans Herwarth von Bittenfeld, before the war a junior official in the Moscow embassy.

Nor was "the party" the sole offender. The Wehrmacht itself had been deeply permeated by the racist ideologies of National Socialism, which provided a razor-sharp cutting edge to an already-widespread sense of German superiority over Slavs of any type. To the ordinary *Landser*, the everyday experiences of life in Russia only reinforced a sense of the Russian people as a different species. To their superiors, the fate of civilians and prisoners of war alike tended to be matters of indifference compared with the pressures of the combat operations.

Could the Reich have changed its tactics, if not its principles? Here again the prospects for an alternate occupation policy would have depended on the interaction of two factors: the protean, if not completely random, nature of National Socialist ideology, and the relatively powerful internal position that would have accrued to a Wehrmacht victorious by December 1941. While the army's high command would certainly not have revised existing impressions of Slavic inferiority, generals and staff officers freed from the responsibility of winning a war might well have concluded that neither morale nor discipline were best served by treating the conquered east as a gigantic free-fire zone where anything was permitted to a wearer of German uniform. In this scenario the SS would have reached nothing like its levels of influence, political and military. Administrators, moreover, could have been expected to be more closely scrutinized in an environment of peace than was the case given the actual circumstances of the Reich's increasingly random, increasingly frantic war effort on the Eastern Front.

From the other side of the power relationship, the Soviet Union's collapse as a significant factor would have done much to remove the partisan alternative in occupied Russia. This in turn would limit the most commonly-cited excuse for the everyday atrocities which did so much to alienate the Germans from their subject peoples. Local notables with nowhere to turn but Berlin, at the same time freed from the practical threat of Soviet reprisals, might well have developed greater "appeasement skills." *Gauleiters* like Erich Koch, scarcely notable for their craft and cunning, were likely candidates for manipulation.

Would the Reich have had sufficient motive for such a major paradigm shift? With Russia destroyed and the U.S. neutral, any military threat still posed by Britain would have been merely vestigial. The Reich's security was assured. In such a context, the physical and ideological pleasures of an overlord's life style in the east could do much to submerge more sober, longer-ranging calculations of gain through cultivating Russian good will.

An influential element in forming opinions was likely to be the Final Solution. It is difficult to see this aspect of the Nazi system changing significantly in the context of a decisive military victory over the Soviet Union. The essential decisions had been made before Barbarossa's opening rounds; an Ostimperium of the kind projected here would merely have facilitated the process. Perhaps a certain community of blood-guilt might have been forged between the murderers and those eastern peoples who, where they did not participate, also did not regret. It seems more likely, however, that the annihilation of Europe's Jews in the newly-conquered territories would have served as a permanent reminder of just what the Nazis were capable of doing—and a corresponding warning against trusting them too far.

Victory in Operation Barbarossa, in short, was likely to bear indigestible fruit—indigestible, that is, in the context of a National Socialist system that would have been strained to the maximum by *occupying* the territory, and that would have had to change *essentially* in order to *assimilate* its eastern conquests. Energy that in earlier scenarios would be available for consolidating a New Order in the west was most likely in this alternative to be absorbed in sustaining a conqueror's role.

D. What if peace or perhaps an open-ended "truce" had been negotiated between Germany and the Soviet Union in 1942-1943?

German military success in 1942 impressive enough to induce Stalin to seek peace with the Reich requires a considerably greater stretch of the imagination than hypothesizing a victory gained in the previous year. A vital feature of such a scenario would be Hitler's refraining from declaring war on the United States in December 1941 and the associated likelihood, discussed by the present writers earlier in this volume, that, lacking the German dictator's initiative, Roosevelt would not have been able to maneuver his country into the war in Europe for a considerable period. Given the absence of whatever encouragement was provided by the assurance of a rapid mobilization of American power against Germany and of a steady increase of American material aid, there would have been no psychological tonic to step up Soviet morale. There would also have been no commensurate reinvigoration of Britain's war effort, or a buildup of British performance in North Africa to distract the Germans. The Soviet war leadership would further have had to reckon with reduced resistance in German-occupied countries, with more effective Italian participation in the war on the Eastern Front, and with no diversion of Hitler's military resources to guard the "soft underbelly" of the continent.

A vital part of the scenario would further be a sounder German strategy in the 1942 drive toward the lower Volga, and avoidance of the gross military errors that led to the disaster of Stalingrad. Most particularly here, there would have had to be an omission of the bifurcation of the south-eastern German offensive in the form of the push toward the Caucasus.

The continuation of American "neutrality" would have presented Stalin with a particularly critical grand-strategic dilemma. Even with direct U.S. involvement in the war, the Soviet dictator distrusted his western partners, suspecting them of seeking to use the Soviet Union as a catspaw, to destroy Hitler at the price of its own exhaustion. Stalin's repeated demands for a second front in northeastern Europe in part reflected his ignorance of the complexity of large-scale amphibious operations. They also manifested concern with keeping his allies honest by forcing them to increase their direct stake in the war. At the same time, Stalin never forgot that he had successfully cooperated with Hitler on a short-range, instrumental basis in 1939/40. Periodically between 1942 and

1944, Soviet diplomats in such neutral countries as Sweden made tentative overtures to their Nazi counterparts about the prospects of negotiating an end to the Russo-German war. In "real time" these initiatives came to nothing. Presumably — final determination can only be made with the opening of the ex-Soviet archives — nothing serious was intended. But suppose American aid had remained confined to lend-lease doled out sparingly by a neutral? Suppose Stalin had decided a drastic unilateral initiative was necessary to secure the U.S.S.R.'s continued existence? What if... ?

The most logical time for such an initiative would have been in the summer or early fall of 1942. With German armies driving ever-deeper into Russia, with nothing like a "second front" even a remote prospect, it was not beyond the limits of possibility for Stalin to seek terms. From his perspective it would buy time ...time for the new trans-Ural factories to increase their output; time for the Soviet Union to assimilate the brutal shocks of 1941; and time, not least, for the ramshackle Nazi empire to self-destruct under the inevitable pressure of an emerging proletarian revolution. Stalin, after all, had accepted the argument "the worse, the better" in 1932 — meaning that the more repressive was the Nazi rule, the more likely German workers and peasants were to rise against it. His attitude was unlikely to have changed drastically in the next decade.

Hitler's willingness to accept a settlement would have been more questionable. But at this time the Fuehrer had not yet quite become the intransigent warlord of the post-Stalingrad years. He was likely to receive comprehensive encouragement to negotiate. His generals would have urged the necessity of replacing the Wehrmacht's huge losses of men and material in the months since Barbarossa's inception. His diplomats would have stressed the advantages of a continental power block under German domination. "Bordeaux to Baku" was not quite as imposing a concept as "Bordeaux to Vladivostok" — but it was impressive enough to be going on with. Hitler's economists and "race scientists" might well have added their voices to the chorus, stressing the desirability of "coordinating" the resources and peoples of the new German empire.

Just where a line of demarcation would have been drawn would depend upon the exact state of military affairs. It could, for example, have been based on the Dniepr. What we may be sure of is that Hitler would have insisted on some form of access to Soviet oil. It is also clear that the terms of such a peace would have left the German armies so deep in Russia that neither of the principal contracting parties was likely to regard such an agreement as anything more than a truce.

With a negotiated settlement one must assume that the Soviets would retain substantial military potential. Hitler would have been obliged to observe considerable restraint in dealing with the areas left in his control. Though perhaps far from exercising a benevolent protectorate, he would have had to go slow with the enslavement of the East he outlined in his table talk. In view of the prospect of renewed war at a not too distant date, the Germans could scarcely afford to be sitting on a perpetual powder keg.

The conclusion of hostilities in Eastern Europe would have had a drastic impact on the British. With the Russian front quiescent, the Wehrmacht would be in a position to reinforce German and Italian troops in the Mediterranean to the limits of Axis logistical capacity. Vichy France and Franco Spain, moreover, were far more likely to trim their sails to the wind blowing from a Germany victorious in Eastern Europe. Within a relatively short timespan, Britain's military position in the Mediterranean and Middle East could have balanced on the edge of disaster.

What then? A belated U.S. entry into the war? A negotiated peace by a Labour-Tory coalition seeking to save what could still be salvaged of Britain's global position? A Soviet Union biding its time and rebuilding its strength for another and final round? In any case, a Soviet-German truce, even at the late date of 1942 or 1943, would have exercised significant influence on subsequent courses of World War II.

1   Information from Generals Jodl, Keitel and Warlimont. Interrogations by Harold C. Deutsch, October, 1945.
2   Interrogations of Guderian by Harold C. Deutsch, September-October 1945.
3   H.S. Stolfi, *Hitler's Panzers East: World War II Reinterpreted* (University of Oklahoma Press: Norman and London, 1991)

About the Authors

Walter J. Dunn, Jr. was director of 5 museums from 1956 to 1989, including six years at the museum of the State Historical Society of Wisconsin and sixteen years at the Buffalo and Erie Country Historical Society. He taught part time at the State University College of Buffalo. His book Second Front Now 1943 (1981) examined the possibility of launching the second front earlier and concluded that the decision in 1944 reflected political rather than logistical concerns. A work on the mobilization of the Red Army, Hitler's Nemesis, The Red Army, 1930-45 appeared late in 1994.

Colonel David M. Glantz was founder and Director of the Foreign Military Studies Office, Combined Arms Command, Ft. Leavenworth, Kansas. A Graduate of the Defense Language Institute, the U.S. Army Institute for Advanced Russian and Eastern European Studies, the U.S. Army Command and General Staff College (CGSC), and the U.S. Army War College (AWC), he has served on the faculty of the United States Military Academy, the Combat Studies Institute (CGSC), Ft. Leavenworth, Kansas; and the U.S. Army War College. Among the articles and books he has authored on Soviet and Russian military affairs are August Storm: The Soviet 1945 Strategic Offensive in Manchuria, 2 Vols.; A History of Soviet Airborne Forces; Soviet Military Deception in the Second World War; Soviet Military Intelligence in War; The Role of Intelligence in Soviet Military Strategy in the Second World War; Soviet Military Operational Art: In Pursuit of Deep Battle; From the Don to the Dnepr: A Study of Soviet Offensive Operations, December 1942-August 1943; The Soviet Conduct of Tactical Maneuver; and Soviet Military Strategy. He is editor of The Journal of Slavic Military Studies; he has just completed a single volume history of the German-Soviet War (1941-1945), and is working on a study of the failed Soviet offensive at Khar'kow in May, 1942.

Peter Hoffmann is Professor of History at McGill University, Montreal, Canada. His reputation as the principal authority on the German opposition to Hitler has been long established. Among his major works are The History of the German Resistance, 1933-1945, Claus Schenk von Stauffenberg und seine Brueder, and Widerstand, Staatsstreich, Attentat.

D. Clayton James is the John Biggs Professor of Military History at Virginia Military Institute. He has also held distinguished professorships at the Marine Corps University and Mississippi State University. He has occupied chairs at the Military History Institute of the Army War College and the Army and General Staff College. His three volume, Years of MacArthur, is the acknowledged leader in the field of biography of our World War II Pacific area leader. Among his other seven books are Antebellum Natchez and South of Bataan, North of Mukden.

Robert W. Love, Jr. has taught American naval history and recent military history at the U.S. Naval Academy since 1975. He is the author of a two-volume History of the U.S. Navy, author and co-editor of The Chiefs of Naval Operations, and editor of Changing Interpretations and New Sources in Naval History. His forthcoming books include Passage to Pearl Harbor: The U.S. Navy, 1939-1941 and The Chiefs of Staff of the U.S. Army.

John Kim Munholland is professor of history and director of the Western European Area Studies Center of the University of Minnesota. His special interests are in modern French history with particular reference to French imperial expansion, military history, and diplomacy of the 1930s and World War II. Among his publications are Origins of Contemporary Europe, 1890-1914, and articles on trials of the Free French in New Caledonia, The French Army and Intervention in Southern Russia, 1918-1920, and The French Response to the Vietnamese National Movement. During the past academic year he has been working in France on De Gaulle and the Free French Movement during the Second World War.

Bernard C. Nalty retired in January 1994 after almost 40 years as a historian in the federal government. He worked for the historical programs of the United States Marine Corps and the Joint Chiefs of Staff before transferring in 1964 to the United States Air Force Historical Liaison Office, which evolved into the Office of Air Force History and today's Center for Air Force History. His government publications include Air Power and the Fight for Khe Sanh, a monograph in a series of studies dealing with the history of the Air Force in the Vietnam War. He collaborated with Henry I. Shaw, Jr., and Edwin T. Turnbladh on Central Pacific Drive, a volume in the history of Marine Corps operations in World War II. The Marine Corps has circulated a number of his studies. He has written, collaborated on, or contributed to 1001 Questions Answered about Aviation History, Tigers over Asia about the Flying Tigers of World War II, and The United States Military under the Constitution of the United States, 1789-1989, to illustrated volumes on the Vietnam War and World War II in the Pacific and in Europe. He is co-editor of two collections of documents dealing with African Americans in the military—the thirteen-volume, Blacks in the United States Armed Forces: Basic Documents and its one-volume abridgement, Blacks in the Military: Essential Documents. He also has written Strength for the Fight: A History of Black Americans in the Military.

Colonel Samuel J. Newland served in the Kansas and (since 1989) in the Pennsylvania National Guard. He is currently Professor in the Department of Advanced Studies of the U.S. Army War College. Among his scholarly publications are books on Inside Hitler's Germany (co-author), Cossacks in the German Army, 1941-1945, and The Inevitable Partnership: The Franco-German Security Relationship (co-author).

Richard J. Overy is Lecturer in History at King's College, University of London. He is widely recognized for his mastery of the history of the European air war of World War II. Among his books are The Air War, 1939-1945, The Road to War, and The Iron Man. He is currently working on books dealing with the history of the Nazi economy and a general study of World War II.

Frederick D. Parker retired from the National Security Agency in 1984. He has worked in the Center for Cryptologic History at NSA since that time and is the author of two official histories on the role of the U.S. Navy communications intelligence in the Pacific War, particularly how it influenced navy decision-makers. The first book, Pearl Harbor Revisited: United States Navy Communications Intelligence, 1924-1941 contains the source material on which these books are based. His second book, A Priceless Advantage: U.S. Navy Communications Intelligence and the Battles of Coral Sea, Midway, and the Aleutians, is also available from the Center. He served in the U.S. Marine Corps from 1943-1945 and from 1950-1952.

Captain (ret.) Paul R. Schratz began his World War II career against German submarines in the North Sea. When the Japanese struck at Pearl Harbor, he entered the submarine service in which he continued to be active throughout the Korean War, where he commanded a submarine of the highly advanced Pickerel class. He has written extensively on both national and international affairs and published a true classic on World War II submarine warfare, <u>Submarine Commander</u>. To the great distress of his collaborators in the current project, Captain Schratz died as the result of an operation for cancer in the very week he completed his assignment.

Dennis Showalter is Professor of History at the Colorado College, Colorado Springs. His principal publications include <u>Tannenberg: Clash of Empires</u>; <u>Railroads and Rifles: Soldiers, Technology and the Unification of Germany</u>; and <u>Voices from the Third Reich: An Oral History</u>, edited with Johannes Steinhoff and Peter Pechel.

Anne Sharp Wells is a member of the administrative faculty of the Virginia Military Institute. Besides co-authoring four books on military history with D. Clayton James, she was newsletter editor of the World War Two Studies Association.

Gerhard L. Weinberg is Professor of History of the University of North Carolina at Chapel Hill. He has also taught at the Universities of Chicago, Kentucky, and Michigan. He gained particular distinction for his activities to promote access to and publication of World War II official documentation. Among his major publications are <u>Hitler's zweites Buch</u>, <u>The Foreign Policy of Hitler's Germany: Diplomatic Revolution in Europe, 1933-1936</u>, and <u>A World at Arms: A Global History of World War II</u>. He holds the degree of Doctor of Humane Letters from the University of Albany and is Vice President for Research of the American Historical Association.

Herman S. Wolk is deputy chief for publications, Office for Air Force History. He is the author of <u>Planning and Organizing the Post War Air Force, 1943-1947</u> and <u>Strategic Bombing: The American Experience</u>. He has contributed to a number of other major studies in Air Force history.